M. F. Howley

Ecclesiastical History of Newfoundland

M. F. Howley

Ecclesiastical History of Newfoundland

ISBN/EAN: 9783741194696

Manufactured in Europe, USA, Canada, Australia, Japa

Cover: Foto ©ninafisch / pixelio.de

Manufactured and distributed by brebook publishing software (www.brebook.com)

M. F. Howley

Ecclesiastical History of Newfoundland

+ Michl. Anthony Fleming
R. C. Bishop

ECCLESIASTICAL HISTORY

OF

NEWFOUNDLAND

BY

THE VERY REVEREND M. F. HOWLEY, D.D.

Prefect Apostolic of St. George's, West Newfoundland

BOSTON
1888

DEDICATION.

Svmmo Pastori
Omnivm Ecclesiarvm Præposito Pontifici

LEONI XIII.

Literarvm Cvjvscvnqve generis Favtori Mvnificentissimo
Jvbilævm Sacerdotale orbe plavdente Cattholico
Hoc Anno MDCCCLXXXVII
Agenti
Inter tot, Disciplinæ, Scientiæ, Religionis
Splendidissima pignora
Ab Omnibvs Mvndi Plagis Oblata Exigvvm hvnc libellvm
Avctor
Avsvs est hvmillime offerre
Operis defectvs
Qvos plane agnoverat.
Cordis Affectv; Animiqve Obseqvio
Occvrrere Discvpiens.

INVOCAZIONE.

A LEONE XIII., P.M.

RISTORATORE INDEFESSO DELLA FILOSOFIA E TEOLOGIA CRISTIANA.

Tu! che sul trono assiso sei, di Piero,
Nobil, rampollo del DE'PECCI stemma
Degno d'ornar il triplo diadema: —
Di cui l'avita strale a raggio Altiero
Brilla ognor nel suo azzur sentiero. —
Che scintillando, qual lucente gemma
Indora 'l cedro Augusto,[1] — atto emblema
Di Lui che al tetro Error sarà guerriero!

"Lume ne'ciel'," dal Santo Irlandese[2]
Ne' tempi or trascorsi, pronunziato
In su tua penna, parsi svolazzare
L'Angelico Dottor, con l'ale estese. —
La voce parsi udir del AQUINATO
Di Nuovo il mondo intiero cattivare!

M. F. H.

---

[1] Lo Stemma dei Pecci.   [2] S. Malachia.

INVOCATION.

TO LEO XIII., P.M.

INDEFATIGABLE RESTORER OF CHRISTIAN PHILOSOPHY AND THEOLOGY.

Hail thou! on Peter's chair enthronèd Pope,
Thou Noble Scion of the Pecci stem!
Worthy to Grace the Triple Diadem. —
Thou whose Ancestral Star, with ray of hope,
Gleams bright within its azure horoscope:
Sparkling with splendor of pellucid gem,
Tints the tall Cedar with a golden hem,[1]
Emblem of him who with dark Sin must cope.

Thou art the very "Light from Heaven" of yore,
By Erin's Sainted Malachy foretold,
For o'er thy haloed brow with wings unfurled
The "Angel of the Schools" is seen to soar
Tipping thy pen with ray of molten gold, —
Once more AQUINAS' voice inthralls the World!

M. F. H.

---

[1] The Arms of the Pecci family.

PREFACE.

ALTHOUGH it is but little over a year since the first "stroke of the pen" was put to the composition of this work, still I may say, with some truth, that it has been in course of compilation for over a quarter of a century. Ever since the happy days of school-boy life I have been always on the alert to gather material. It may be called a "hobby"; it may be called a "craze" or a "crank"; it was certainly an absorbing passion to grasp with avidity everything in any way bearing upon the past history of our country; every anecdote of the olden time; every scrap of manuscript; every inscription or epitaph having the slightest pretension to antiquity; every vestige of the former occupation of Newfoundland, whether civil, military, or ecclesiastical, — in a word, everything with the shadow of a claim to archæological distinction was immediately transferred to the note-book or sketch-book, with a view to being at some future day presented to the public. Hence, it may be imagined that, when at last the momentous step was actually resolved upon to "make a beginning," I was confronted with that serious difficulty so elegantly defined by our French writers as "An embarrassment of wealth." Though knowing that I was deficient in a great deal of documentary lore which I would wish to obtain, yet I was conscious of possessing a considerable amount of information, highly interesting, but of so heterogeneous a nature as to defy any effort at putting it together in a connected form. I was thus bewildered as to what I should reproduce, what reject.

I at first attempted to bring in a great deal of this, what I may call extrinsic information, by way of appendix or notes; but I soon found that the notes would exceed the body of the work. This I knew would be a defiance of all just rules of proportion, so I was obliged to invent some means of incorporating it into the book. That I have not always succeeded in making smooth work I am fully conscious, and can only throw myself on the mercy of the indulgent reader.

Another very great difficulty which confronted me was, that my material naturally divided itself into two classes, of so totally different a character that I at first thought it would be better to make two distinct books. The first class of items contained those concerning the general early history of America, "*quorum magna pars fuit*" Newfoundland, and on which I felt sure I had some facts, theories, documents, maps, etc., never yet published, which would be interesting to the general reader, not only in Newfoundland, but in America and Europe.

The second class consisted of *purely local*, almost household, facts, anecdotes, incidents, descriptions, etc., which could be interesting only to Newfoundlanders, and even to only a section of them, viz., the Roman Catholics.

To separate the work into two books would, I saw, mutilate each, and render them imperfect; to unite them I feared would render the book tedious and unacceptable to many. In this dilemma I was advised by a valued and experienced friend to put them together, and let them sink or swim on their merits. Thus, on this score, again I feel it necessary to crave the reader's forbearance.

When about to commence the work I fortunately came into possession of an unfinished manuscript Ecclesiastical History of Newfoundland, by the Rt. Rev. Dr. Mullock. This history was never published, though the well-known "Lectures on Newfoundland," delivered in St. Bonaventure's College, and published in pamphlet, were compiled from it. I at first intended to use this manuscript as a basis on which to build my superstructure, taking it paragraph by paragraph, and introducing, as I went along, my own notes between brackets. But so much historical information has come to light since Dr. Mullock wrote (now nearly thirty years ago, 1856), that I found it quite impracticable, as it would produce a disjointed and disconnected narrative, and occasion many useless repetitions. I, therefore, determined to draw upon the above manuscript whenever necessary, as a rule making acknowledgment of it.

For the history of Ferryland I am greatly indebted to the work of Henry Kirke, Esq., High Sheriff of Demerara, on the "Conquest of Canada." I regret, therefore, on some occasions being obliged to refute rather warmly some of that gentleman's assertions. Henry Kirke is a descendant of Sir David Kirke, who occupied Ferryland after Lord Baltimore, and died there. Also to Mr. Richardson, of Portland, Me., U.S., for a most interesting article on Ferryland, in the "Magazine of American History."

For the description of Placentia, by Abbé Baudouin, I owe my thanks to J. P. Howley, Esq., F.G.S., Superintendent of the Geological Survey of Newfoundland, and to Mr. Jack, of St. John, N.B., who copied the original French document from the archives of Ottawa.

I must also express my gratitude to T. O'Reilly, Esq., J.P., of Placentia, for many important items concerning the "Ancient Capital."

I acknowledge, with many thanks, the reception of an autograph letter of our first Bishop, Dr. O'Donel, as well as interesting particulars of the last days and final resting-place of that venerable Prelate, from his grand-nephew, the Rev. Mr. O'Donnell, of Harrowgate, England.

To Mr. Justice Joseph I. Little my gratitude is due for a large and most interesting package of letters of the late Rt. Rev. Dr. Fleming; also to the late Mrs. J. Delaney, sister of Father Troy, for letters from Dr. Fleming to that reverend gentleman.

From the Revs. N. Roache and M. O. Driscoll, of Whittles Bay, I received an invaluable collection of notes from the memories of the late Dean Cleary.

It will be observed that the book reaches down only to the year 1850, and closes with the death of the Rt. Rev. Dr. Fleming. My reasons for not including the episcopate of Dr. Mullock are principally the following: —

First. I fear the book will be already rather too bulky to be convenient.

Secondly. Being anxious to bring out the work by the close of the present year, so as to make it a jubilee offering to our Holy Father, Leo XIII., I could not possibly do so were I to include these twenty years of our history.

Thirdly. I think it would be unworthy of the glorious Episcopate of Dr. Mullock to tack it on, as it were, to the end of a book already sufficiently large, even were I in a position to do so, which I am not; and this may be given as —

Fourthly. Though possessing a large number of letters, documents, pastorals, printed addresses, and lectures of Dr. Mullock, I still feel that I am very far from having sufficient material for a biography of that illustrious Prelate. If the present work should prove acceptable, and if the necessary documents can be procured, nothing would give me greater pleasure than to compile a "Life and Times of Dr. Mullock."

With these remarks, which may be taken as an apology from a neophyte in the art of book-making, I send forth this maiden effort upon the ocean of historical literature.

I have nothing to say of the workmanship of Messrs. Doyle and Whittle; it is there to speak for itself. I need only say that in all business relations they have proved themselves most obliging and satisfactory.

M. F. HOWLEY.

SANDY POINT, ST. GEORGE'S BAY,
    WEST NEWFOUNDLAND,
The Feast of St. Michael, September 29, 1887.

CONTENTS.

CHAPTER I.
INTRODUCTORY.

Spirit of Geographical Research Aroused in the Fifteenth Century — The Art of Printing Invented by a German Catholic — Unfair Criticisms of Protestant Writers — The Polyglot Printing Office of Propaganda — The Popes the Encouragers of Science and Discovery — Their Great Political Power — Character of Columbus — His Desire for Gold Explained — Missionary Spirit of the Early Navigators — Champlain — His Religious Sentiment — Père Le Clerq, O.S.F. — Captain Richard Whitbourne — His Enthusiasm for Newfoundland — His Anxiety for the Conversion of the Red Indians — The Institution of the "*Propaganda Fide*" — Contrast between the above-mentioned Voyagers and Sir Humphrey Gilbert 23

CHAPTER II.
PRE-COLUMBIAN VOYAGES. — [800-1497.]

Traditions of a Western Land — Prophecy of Seneca — Seneca and Columbus, a Coincidence — Plato's "Atlantis" — Voyage of St. Brendan — St. Malo — Catholic Missions in Iceland — The Fláto Saga, A.D. 860 — Discovery of Greenland by Gunlbærn, 886 — Rediscovery by Eric Raud, 980 — Discovery of America by Bjarni, 985 — Labrador, Newfoundland, Nova Scotia, Discovered by Lief, 1000 — It Myla, or Great Ireland — Vestiges of an Irish Colony in America — Episcopal Sees in Greenland, 1021 to 1406 — Voyage of Zeno, 1380 — Reliques of John Guy's Colony at Cuper's Cove, or Cupid's 37

CHAPTER III.
COLUMBUS AND HIS FOLLOWERS. — [1497-1534.]

Discovery of Newfoundland by Cabot — Cabot's Map Shown to be Tampered with — The Name *Baccalao* — Relic of Early Missionary — Cortereal — Map of Varrese from the Vatican — St. John's Becomes Important, 1527 — The Aborigines — Their Name, Beothuck — Ruthlessly Shot down — Their Character, Religion, etc. —

CONTENTS.

Early Maps of the Country — Map of Jerome Verazzano, 1528 —
Of Ribero, 1529 — Ancient Map in Borgian Museum, Propaganda
— " Dividing Line " drawn by Pope Alexander VI., 1493 . . 47

CHAPTER IV.

JACQUES CARTIER. — [1534–1611.]

Neglect of Colonies by England — Henry Kirke Refuted — Catholic
Countries Encourage Colonization — Jacques Cartier's Voyages,
1534–35 — Arrives at Catalina — First Mass in Newfoundland —
Catholic Missions in America — Testimony of Bancroft — Cartier
Enters the Straits of Belle Isle and Explores the St. Lawrence —
Old Fort — Anticosti, Bay Chaleur — Saguenay, Quebec, etc. —
Settlement by John Guy in Conception Bay 67

CHAPTER V.

JOHN GUY'S SETTLEMENT. — [1610–1618.]

Failure of John Guy's Colony — Intercourse with Red Indians —
Cruel Treatment of them by English Sailors — Difficulties
between Planters and Fishermen — Whitbourne Arrives as Commissioner, 1615 — John Guy Abandons his Colony and Returns
to England — Whitbourne Sent out by Dr. Vaughan to Found a
Colony at Ferryland, 1618 — Calvert's Views on Colonization . 78

CHAPTER VI.

FERRYLAND. — [1618–1622.]

Sir George Calvert — His Early Career — Bancroft's Bigotry — Calvert's Conversion — His Enthusiasm — " A Baltimore Penny " —
Colony of Maryland — Lord Baltimore's Spirit of Toleration —
Persecution of Popery by the Protestant Parliament, 1654 . 83

CHAPTER VII.

FOUNDATION OF FERRYLAND. — [1622–1628.]

Foundation of Ferryland Colony — Lord Baltimore's Patent — Its
Extent — Edward Wynne, First Governor — Meaning of the Name
" Ferryland " — Description of Settlement from Captain Powell —
Sir Arthur Ashton Arrives, May, 1627 — Lord Baltimore Arrives in
Ferryland, July 23, 1627 — Brings out Jesuit Priests — Catholic
Religion Established — Mass Celebrated Daily — Indignation of
the Anglican Minister, Rev. Mr. Stourton — His Expulsion from
the Colony — Calvert Arrives, Second Time, with his Lady and
Family, 1628 94

CHAPTER VIII.

FERRYLAND, *Continued.* — [1628-1660.]

PAGE

Causes of the Failure of the Ferryland Colony — Lady Baltimore Leaves for Maryland — Lord Baltimore Follows, 1629 — Lady Baltimore Lost at Sea — Baltimore Refuses to Take the Oath of Allegiance as Proposed by Governor Pott of Jamestown — He Returns to England and Dies, 1632 — Sir W. Alexander Founds Nova Scotia, 1627 — French Huguenots — Claude de St. Etienne — Sir David Kirke — He Captures the French Fleet at Gaspé — Quebec Capitulates, 1629 — Kirke is Refused his Prize-money — Kirke and Baltimore Contrasted — Kirke Receives a Grant of Ferryland, and Arrives in Newfoundland, 1638 — Reconstructs the Settlement — The Seven Years' War in England — Kirke is Arrested, 1651 — And Deprived of his Colony — He Returns to Newfoundland, 1653 — And Dies at Ferryland, 1656 — His Character — Cecil, Second Lord Baltimore, Recovers Possession of Ferryland, 1660 — Policy of Britain Detrimental to the Advancement of the Country, 109

CHAPTER IX.

MISSIONARIES IN CANADA. — [1610-1670.]

Placentia — Description of Settlement by Dr. Mullock — Founded by the French long before 1660 — Document Signed by Louis XIV. — Monseigneur de Laval, First Bishop of Quebec — Mgr. de St. Vallier, Second Bishop — Defence of the Jesuits — Settlement of Port Royal, 1611-15 — Arrival of the Franciscans at Quebec, 1615 — Missionary Labors of Père le Caron among the Indians — Henri, Duc de Levis, Introduces the Jesuits to Quebec, 1626 — Jesuits cordially Received by the Franciscans — Henry Kirke's Statement to the Contrary Refuted — Religious Withdrawn on Capture of Quebec by Sir David Kirke, 1629 — Jesuits Return after Treaty of St. Germain-en-Laye, 1632 — Franciscans in 1670, 128

CHAPTER X.

PLACENTIA. — [1660-1696.]

Extent of the Diocese of Quebec — Mgr. de St. Vallier Visits Placentia, 1689, and Founds a Franciscan Convent there — Troubled State of Newfoundland — Encroachments of the French — Obstruction Policy of England — Placentia Attacked unsuccessfully by Commodore Williams — St. John's Attacked by the French, 1694 — The Whole Island, except Carbonnière and Bonavista, Captured by D'Iberville, 1696 — Graphic Account of this Expedition by Sieur Baudouin, Military Chaplain — Capture of Ferryland, Bay Bulls,

16   CONTENTS.

PAGE

Petty Harbor, St. John's, Torbay, Kerividi, Portugal Cove, Harbor Men, Brigue, Carbonnière, Havre de Grace, Havre Content, Bay Ver, Nieu Perlican, etc.— Final Decadence of French Power in the Western World 141

CHAPTER XI.

CATHOLICITY AFTER THE TREATY OF UTRECHT.— [1696-1728.]

Treaty of Utrecht, 1713 — Conditions, French allowed to Depart or become British Subjects — Catholic Religion publicly Practised in Newfoundland — The Fishing Admirals — Opposition of the Merchants to the Appointment of a Governor — Appointment of the First Governor, Captain Henry Osborne, 1728 163

CHAPTER XII.

RELIGIOUS PERSECUTION.— [1728-1762.]

Governor Osborne — Hostile Attitude of the Merchants towards the Progress of the Country — Persecuting Enactments of the Governors — Governor Dorril (1755) Persecutes the Catholics — Confiscations and Fines at Harbor Main — Capture of the Island by the French, 1762 — Final Recapture by the English . . . 170

CHAPTER XIII.

RELIGIOUS PERSECUTION, Continued.— [1763-1784.]

Treaty of Paris, 1763 — Its Disastrous Effect on France — Persecution of the Catholics under Governors Palliser, Shuldham, Duff, and Edwards — First Irish Missionaries — Rev. Fathers Cain, Lonergan, Daily, Bourke. Whelan, Hearn, and A. Cleary . . 177

CHAPTER XIV.

RT. REV. DR. O'DONEL, PREFECT APOSTOLIC.— [1784-1794.]

Appointment of Father O'Donel, First Prefect Apostolic — State of the Country — Biography of Father O'Donel — Foundation of " The Old Chapel " — Persecution not yet Ceased — Bigoted Conduct of Surrogate Captain Pellu — Extraordinary letter of Governor Milbanke — Father O'Donel's Letters to Dr. Troy, Archbishop of Dublin — Friendly Action of Governor Waldegrave and Judge Advocate Reeves — Great Influence Acquired by the Bishop — He Quells a Mutiny among the Military — Beastly Character of Prince William, Duke of Clarence — He Assaults the Bishop . 185

CHAPTER XV.

RT. REV. DR. O'DONEL, FIRST BISHOP.— [1794-1801.]

Memorial of the Clergy to have Father O'Donel made Bishop — He is Appointed Vicar Apostolic, and Consecrated Bishop at Quebec — Letter of Father Yore — Address of the Merchants and Citizens of St. John's to Dr. O'Donel — He Visits Placentia and Administers Confirmation — Diocesan Statutes — Loyalty of the Catholics . 196

CHAPTER XVI.

RT. REV. DR. O'DONEL, *Continued.*— [1801-1806.]

Establishment of Parishes and Districts — State of the Country — "The Old Chapel"— "The Old Palace"— Retirement of Dr. O'Donel — Appointment of Dr. Lambert — Testimony of Respect to Dr. O'Donel on leaving the Country — Magnanimous Conduct of the Merchants and Inhabitants — Churlish Conduct of Governor Gower — Dr. O'Donel Receives a Pension of £50 *per Annum* — His Departure from the Island, Last Days, Death (1811), Epitaph — Review of his Episcopate — Personal Character . 206

CHAPTER XVII.

EDUCATIONAL INSTITUTIONS.

The "Benevolent Irish Society"— The "Orphan Asylum"— State of Education in the Island — Its Various Phases Traced — The Irish Society's Schools — Father Fleming Endeavors to get Control of them, 1829 — Protestant Educational Institutions — First Education Act, 1843 — Foundation of Protestant and Catholic Colleges, 1844 — General Academy of St. John's — Formation of the Roman Catholic, Church of England, and General Protestant Academies, 1850 — Opening of St. Bonaventure's College, 1855 — Establishment of Wesleyan Academy, 1858 — Dr. Mullock's Views on Education — "The Monks"— The Christian Brothers 225

CHAPTER XVIII.

RT. REV. DR. LAMBERT, SECOND BISHOP.— [1806-1817.]

Dr. Lambert — His Visitation of Conception Bay and Ferryland — He Enlarges the "Old Chapel"— Delicate State of Health — He Resigns in Favor of Dr. Scallan 236

CONTENTS.

CHAPTER XIX.

RT. REV. DR. SCALLAN, THIRD BISHOP.— [1817-1830.]

Dr. Thomas Scallan — His Consecration in Wexford — Arrives in Newfoundland, 1816 — Priests in the Island at that Time — His Report of the Mission to Propaganda — Character of Dr. Scallan — Excess of Liberality — Dr. Bourke appointed First Bishop of Nova Scotia — Declining Health of Dr. Scallan — Accounts for his Weakness of Purpose — Seeks a Coadjutor — Father Michael Anthony Fleming is Appointed and Consecrated in the "Old Chapel," 1829 — Death and Burial of Dr. Scallan — His Monument in the Cathedral — Review of his Episcopate 240

CHAPTER XX.

LABRADOR.

Origin of the Name — Population — Moravian Missionaries — Anticosti Annexed to the Diocese of St. John's — Division of Parishes — Increase of Catholicity 249

CHAPTER XXI.

RT. REV. DR. FLEMING, FOURTH BISHOP.— [1829-1833.]

Commencement of Dr. Fleming's Episcopate — State of the Colony — Catholic Emancipation — Its Effect on Irishmen Abroad — Intolerance in St. John's — Degrading Taxes — Funeral and Marriage Fees Imposed on Catholics — Dr. Fleming Refuses to Pay them — Redivision of Parishes — Arrival of Nine New Missionaries, Fathers Troy, Nowlan, Berney, P. Cleary, etc. — Dr. Fleming Presents Memorial in Favor of Emancipation — Forwards Subscription to the O'Connell Fund — His Liberality towards Dissenters — Obtains for them Religious Liberty 552

CHAPTER XXII.

THE PRESENTATION NUNS.— [1833.]

The Presentation Nuns — Mother Magdalen's Narrative — Journey to Dublin — Waterford — Voyage to Newfoundland — Opening of the Schools — The Presentation Convent — "The Fire of '46" — Convent Destroyed — New Convent and Schools Erected — First Religious Reception — Jubilee, 1833-34 — Other Conventual Establishments in America 275

CONTENTS.

CHAPTER XXIII.

DR. FLEMING'S VISITATIONS. — [1834–1836.]

Establishment of a Protestant Bishopric — Dr. Fleming's Visitation Northwards, 1834 — Fogo, Tilting Harbor, Herring Neck, Green Bay, Morton's Harbor, King's Cove — Visitation Southwards, 1835 — Petty Harbor, Ferryland, Fermeuse, Reneuse, Burin — Discomforts of Missionary Life — St. Pierre, Bay d'Espoir, Galtois, Conn River, Indian Settlement — Simplicity and Piety of the Indians — Great Placentia — St. Mary's — Small-pox in St. John's and Petty Harbor 301

CHAPTER XXIV.

THE CATHEDRAL. — [1836–1849.]

Commencement of the Cathedral — Difficulty of Obtaining Ground — Reception of Dr. Fleming on his Return from Rome — Further Difficulties placed in his Way — He Returns to England in Winter, 1838 — Correspondence relating to Cathedral Ground — Assistance Rendered by the Irish Parliamentary Party, O'Connell, Lynch, Moore O'Ferrall — Father Troy Appointed Vicar General — Letter from Dr. Fleming to him — The Ground for Cathedral secured — Enthusiasm of the People — Mullins' Ghost — Mickle's "Crooked Furrough" — Fencing in the Ground — Preparation of Materials for the Cathedral — Laying the Foundation Stone, 1841 — Completion of the Cathedral 337

CHAPTER XXV.

THE MERCY NUNS. [1837–1850.]

Persecution of Dr. Fleming — The "Secret Affidavits" — His Visit to Rome — Honor Conferred on him by the Pope — Appointed Domestic Prelate to His Holiness and Assistant at the Pontifical Throne — Introduction of the Sisters of Mercy, 1842 — Arrival of the Nuns — Enthusiastic Reception — Sister Francis Creedon — Sister Joseph Nugent — Mother Mary Vincent — The "Famine Fever," 1848 — The Cholera, 1856 — The Orphanage — Mother Xavier — The New Orphanage — St. Bride's Academy . . 365

CHAPTER XXVI.

POLITICS. — [1832–1838.]

General Review — State of Politics — Petition for Home Rule — Local Legislature Granted, 1832 — First Elections — Judge Boulton — Affair of Drs. Carson and Kelly — Patrick Morris, Esq., Attacks the Judge in the Assembly — Messrs. Nugent, Kent, and Carson Appointed a Delegation to London on the Boulton Case — Dr. Fleming's Views on the Subject — His Great Influence at Home, and in Local Politics — Judge Boulton Condemned and Removed, 378

CHAPTER XXVII.

AFTER "THE FIRE." — [1847-1850.]

Sufferings of the Citizens — "The Camps" — Generosity of the People in Subscribing to the Relief of the Famine-Stricken in Ireland — Dr. Fleming Applies for a Coadjutor — Father J. T. Mullock, O.S.F., Appointed — Arrives in Newfoundand, May, 1848 — Newfoundland Erected into a Diocese, to be Annexed to the Province of Quebec — Dr. Fleming Objects to this Arrangement, also Dr. Mullock — Arrangement Rescinded by Rome — Project of a Colonial Ecclesiastical Seminary — It is Opposed by Dr. Fleming — He Gives his Reasons — His Prejudice against a Colonial Priesthood — Noble Views of Dr. Mullock on this Subject — Establishment of St. Bonaventure's College — Distinguished Newfoundland Priests Abroad — Revs. T. Brown, S.J., F. Ryan, S.J., L. Kavanagh, S.J., and J. Bennett, C.S.S.R.— The "First Native Priest "— Father P. Meagher, S.J.— Rev. Messrs. Greene, Mulloy, Hogan — Sister M. Baptist, First " Native Nun " — Rev. James Brown, First Actual Missionary Born in the Country — Last Days of Dr. Fleming — He Celebrates the First Mass in the Cathedral — His Death and Funeral 384

APPENDIX 397

LIST OF ILLUSTRATIONS.

	PAGE
RT. REV. DR. FLEMING	*Frontispiece.*
COLORED MAP OF NEWFOUNDLAND	*Facing* 23
ZENO'S MAP, 1400	45
SEBASTIAN CABOT	48
SEBASTIAN CABOT'S MAP, 1494	51
BOX (COVER)	54
BOX (BOTTOM)	55
VATICAN MAP	57
OUTLINE MAP OF VERRAZANO	*Facing* 66
JACQUES CARTIER	69
LORD BALTIMORE	79
CECIL, SECOND LORD BALTIMORE	85
WATERVILLE PENNY	87
HARE'S EARS	100
SITE OF LORD BALTIMORE'S SETTLEMENT AT FERRYLAND	*Facing* 110
SILVER SNUFF-SPOON UNEARTHED AT FERRYLAND	124
TOWN OF PLACENTIA	*Facing* 142
FAC-SIMILES OF OLD TOMBSTONES AT PLACENTIA	145
RUINS OF FRENCH FORT AT CASTLE HILL	*Facing* 150
"THE OLD PALACE"	222
CATHOLIC CATHEDRAL, HARBOR GRACE, CONCEPTION BAY	*Facing* 266
RT. REV. DR. MULLOCK	*Facing* 294
CITY OF ST. JOHN'S	*Facing* 340
CATHEDRAL OF ST. JOHN THE BAPTIST, ST. JOHN'S	*Facing* 352

rint-
s —
s of
s —
am-
ard
on-
ast

ic
y,
th
-
g
ir

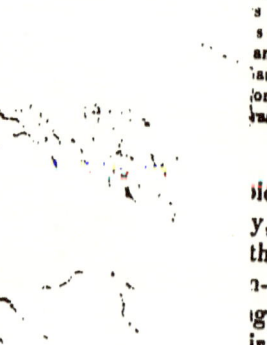

ECCLESIASTICAL HISTORY

OF

NEWFOUNDLAND.

―――・―――

CHAPTER I.

INTRODUCTORY.

Spirit of Geographical Research Aroused in the Fifteenth Century — The Art of Printing Invented by a German Catholic — Unfair Criticisms of Protestant Writers — The Polyglot Printing Office of Propaganda — The Popes the Encouragers of Science and Discovery — Their Great Political Power — Character of Columbus — His Desire for Gold Explained — Missionary Spirit of the Early Navigators — Champlain — His Religious Sentiment — Père Le Clerq, O.S.F. — Captain Richard Whitbourne — His Enthusiasm for Newfoundland — His Anxiety for the Conversion of the Red Indians — The Institution of the " *Propaganda Fide* " — Contrast between the above-mentioned Voyagers and Sir Humphrey Gilbert.

IN reading the accounts of the voyages of those heroic men who, towards the close of the fifteenth century, following in the wake of the great Columbus, sallied forth upon the unknown deep in search of new worlds, we cannot but be struck with the strong religious spirit, amounting almost to enthusiasm, which animated them in all their glorious enterprises.

This particular point of history marks the commencement of what may be called "The Great Transformation Scene" of the world's drama: the transition from the romantic epoch which men are pleased to call "the dark ages," to the utilitarian period, which seems to have reached its culmination in this our nineteenth century.

It was the dawn of a new era, when the lance and the lute of the knight-troubadour began to give place to the pen and the ledger of the accountant. Men were beginning to seek something besides honor and glory as the reward of their labors, and were no longer satisfied with the wave of a silken kerchief from some " fayre ladye " immured in castle-keep.

We behold the first cropping up of the practical view of matters which has become paramount in these modern times, and which immediately considers things from a financial stand-point, asking such pertinent questions as "Will the venture *pay?*" "Are there likely to be any dividends?" "What are the risks and probabilities of success or failure?" etc.

The great development of thought and the spirit of enterprise, which manifested themselves about this time, have been generally attributed to a sudden awakening from darkness to light; from the dim shadows of the superstition and ignorance of the middle ages to the full sunburst of modern enlightenment. It is not our object to dwell diffusely on this subject here. The theme is daily handled by our best Catholic writers. It is enough to say that such is not a correct view of the intellectual and scientific awakening of the fifteenth century. It was, in fact, but another step in the gradual and regular onward march made by mankind through the course of centuries. The human race was ever steadily advancing in the path of progress. One century beheld a particular region of knowledge subdued and taken possession of; the next, another. That century is remarkable for conquests in the domain of astronomy; this, for its creations in the world of art; another, for the spread of colonization.

The period of which we are now writing was signalized by a wondrous spirit of geographical research. Men were desirous of finding out the extent of this, their earthly habitation, and of exploring it to its utmost limits.

The magic art of printing, invented towards the middle of the century, is considered by many as one of the great causes of modern civilization and enlightenment. No doubt this is true; but it ought to be looked upon rather as the effect of the desire, so strongly existing in the world at the time, of communicating knowledge and bringing minds into converse with each other. "This invention" (says Sir Walter Scott, by the mouth of Galeoth, in "Quentin Durward") "may be likened to a young tree, which in succeeding ages shall bear fruit as fatal yet as precious as that of Eden, . . . changing the whole form of social life, establishing and overthrowing religions, erecting and destroying kingdoms!" Flippant writers are accustomed to glory over this invention as "the delivery from monkish superstition and ignorance." The poor monks, who for centuries had spent their lives in copying and preserving and multiplying the manuscripts of preceding ages, are scoffed and jeered at as being now at last deprived of the power of "concealing their knowledge from the world." Even such a brilliant and generally fair-minded writer as Washington Irving cannot do justice to this subject. He says ("Life of Columbus," Book I., Chap. I.): "During a long night of monkish bigotry and false learning, geography, with other sciences, had been lost to European nations. . . . And" (Chap. VI.) "the recent invention of printing . . . drew forth learning from libraries and convents. . . . Volumes of information, . . . carefully treasured up and *kept out of reach of the indigent scholar*, . . . were now in every hand." The taunt is most unjust, besides being unintelligible. If the monks had not "treasured up" this learning, by years of labor and study, it would not have been there "in libraries and convents" for the art of printing to "draw forth." Surely, then, we owe gratitude, not contempt, to the unwearying copyists!

Such writers also forget that the very art itself of printing we owe to a devout Catholic man, Laurentius, *custos*, or *œdituus*, of the Cathedral of Haarlem; and instead of the monks and priests endeavoring to retard science, or check the spirit of enterprise and discovery, it was quite the contrary. When Christopher Columbus had pleaded in vain for eighteen years, at the courts of kings and the castles of

the nobility, for assistance to carry out his great design of
the discovery of a new world, he was treated with contemptuous disdain by those proud and wealthy men; and it
was from a humble friar of the Order of St. Francis, Fra
Juan Perez, and a Dominican monk, Dom Diego de Deza,
that he received encouragement to persevere. And the
Catholic Church, so far from fearing or seeking to suppress
the art of printing, seized with avidity upon it. Editions of
the Bible and other religious and scientific books began at
once to pour forth from Catholic universities and printing-houses in Germany, England, France, and Italy.

In Rome the celebrated polyglot printing-office of Propaganda was established by the Pope, which has since become
the most wonderful institution of the kind in the world. It
publishes works in fifty-five different languages, not only
works of spiritual doctrines, scripture, and theology, but
grammars and dictionaries of the various languages. There
are type fonts for twenty-seven European, twenty-two
Asiatic, three American, and three African languages.
There are two sets of Chinese characters, each of which contains *ten thousand* letters or symbols. In the year 1870 the
"Our Father" was printed in an album in two hundred and
fifty different languages and dialects, and in one hundred
and eighty different sets or fonts of characters. In 1860 to
1870 the celebrated Vatican Bible, called the *Codex Vaticanus*, was reproduced in fac-simile in the beautiful *stichometrical* type of the fifth century.

Pope Innocent VIII., a man of enlightened views and a
fellow-citizen of Columbus, stood also his firm friend, and
gave his pontifical blessing to his expedition.

The Popes were always foremost in every undertaking
which tended to advance science or enlarge the sphere of
man's knowledge. They were, in fact, bound to do so by a
double obligation: First, as the divinely appointed guardians of men's souls. Secondly, as the most powerful and
influential sovereigns in the world. Whenever a new
country was discovered, the right of the Pontiffs to the

spiritual dominion thereof was not for a moment questioned, even by the State or Sovereign to whose kingdom the new lands were annexed and the new peoples subdued. Nay, more, the superior right or power was acknowledged in the Pope to compel civil princes to do justice to their subjects, and to fulfil their duties to God; and to punish them by interdict, and even dethronement, in case of defalcation or contumacy. However much modern writers may fume and chafe over this assumed power and arrogance of the Popes, as they call it, it would be far more philosophical to look the facts straight in the face, and to admit that, whether right or wrong, the deposing power was freely conceded to the Popes by the sovereigns themselves; and they were the first, in case of difficulty, to appeal to the Pope for redress. All were willing that the Pope should exercise his supreme power upon their neighbors, but it was only when they felt its pressure upon themselves that they considered it rather inconvenient. On the discovery of new countries, then, the Popes, mindful of the spiritual charge to teach all nations, sent forth at once their missionaries. Hence we find the envoys of the Cross following hard upon the heels of the conquering legions or in the wake of the adventurous explorer. Thus, no sooner had the illustrious traveller, Marco Polo, returned from the distant lands of India (A.D. 1247) than Pope Innocent IV. despatched two friars, Carpini and Ascelin, as apostolic ambassadors, to procure the conversion of that great nation.

The discovery of foreign countries, and the extension of commerce and diffusion of wealth accruing therefrom, may be looked upon as the remote cause of the spirit of infidelity and indifferentism so sadly prevalent in those times. But this great change did not take place all of a sudden; hence we find in the explorers of the fifteenth and sixteenth centuries what seems sometimes an incongruous mixture of worldly and religious motives.

Columbus himself, though he never ceased to speak of the harvest of souls to be gleaned, still does not neglect, in his pleadings with the Court of Spain, to take full advantage of the prospects of honor, glory, power, and, above all, of wealth, which his New World will bring to strengthen the empire. This was only to be expected, as he wished to use every available argument to ensure assistance. But it would appear that he had himself a strong desire for obtaining wealth by his enterprise. He stipulated with the king that "one-tenth of all pearls, precious stones, gold, silver, spices, and all other merchandise" should be his. Again, when he landed on the shores of the New World, after having first given thanks to God, his first thought was *gold*. He said he would stop nowhere till he had discovered the region of gold; the kingdom of the Grand Khan, the king of kings; of whose wealth Marco Polo, in the preceding century, had told such wondrous tales: Of the beautiful city of Quisnai, with its twelve thousand bridges, its grand market-places and canals, its marble palaces and terraces, groves and gardens; of Cambalew, where the people dressed in cloth of gold, and cambrics of the finest fabric, and furs of ermine and sable; of Cipango, where the palace of the Grand Khan was roofed with tiles of gold, and floored with plates of the same precious metal.

Columbus sailed about among the Bahamas from island to island, all the time seeking this gold-bearing country, but in vain. This trait in his character was altogether unintelligible until light was thrown on it by documents afterwards discovered. The avaricious and inordinate love of gold is universally acknowledged as an index of a low and sordid character, a narrow mind, and ungenerous soul. Such a disposition is the very antithesis of the noble, generous, heroic discoverer. How, then, account for it? The answer is given by Irving (Book II., Chap. VII.): "Anticipating boundless wealth from his discoveries, he suggested that the treasures thus acquired should be consecrated to the pious purpose of rescuing the Holy Sepulchre of Jerusalem from the power of the infidels. In his will he imposes the obligation on his son Diego to expend in this holy object all the moneys collected from his expedition; and to go himself, if necessary, with the king to fight for the liberation of the holy places."

Here we have the key to the lofty and apparently ambitious demands of vice-regal dignity, and a tenth part of all the profits; and of his eager search for gold. He wanted to fit out an expedition of fifty thousand men, on his own account, in case the king refused. Thus, the apparent weakness or defect of character, which would be an obstacle to *heroic* virtue, and consequently to the prospects of his canonization,[1] like all other objections of the "Devil's advocate," is not only dissipated, but becomes a proof of greater sanctity.

The missionary spirit, which was developed in a heroic degree in Christopher Columbus, who was himself a member of the Third Order of St. Francis, we find also very ardently burning in the breasts of those brave voyagers who followed in his track in the succeeding centuries.

In his second voyage, commenced on the 25th of September, 1493, he was accompanied by twelve priests, under the charge of the Benedictine Father Boïl. After the discovery of Florida by Ponce de Leon, in 1512, numerous expeditions succeeded each other, all accompanied by missionaries. The adventurer, the soldier, and the priest always landed together on newly discovered strands; and the cross always accompanied the standard of Catholic nations. In 1534–5 Jacques Cartier brought out priests to Newfoundland and Canada. In 1539 Friar Mark, of Nice, penetrated to the interior of Mexico, and brought the symbol of faith to the savage tribes of the interior. In 1610–11 the Jesuits, and in 1615 the Franciscans, were brought out to Canada by the Sieurs de Poutrincourt and Champlain; all of which events will be more particularly described in the course of this work.

Champlain, who possessed all the zeal and fervor of

---

[1] A petition, signed by a large number of the fathers of the Vatican Council, was presented to Pope Pius IX. in 1870, asking to have the "Cause" of the canonization of Columbus mooted or "promoted."

Columbus, has left ample and graphic accounts of all his voyages in the quaint Old French of the period, which are preserved in the archives of Quebec, and which show, in every page, the sincere religious spirit which animated him. He tells us, with rare simplicity and *naïveté* (Voyage of 1615, p. 9), how, while waiting at Honfleur for a fair wind, he and all his crew prepared themselves, "so that each one of us examined himself and cleansed himself of his sins by a penance and confession of them, in order to say his good-by to God (or to make his salutation, *faire son bon jour*), and to put himself in a state of grace; so as thus being more free, each one in his conscience, to expose himself to the Eyes of God, and to the Mercy of the vast depths of this great and mighty ocean."

His constant thought was the conversion of the poor savages. Thus he concludes the account of the voyage of 1616: . . . "We arrived in good health at Honfleur, thanks to God, on the 10th September, . . . where having arrived, we rendered praise, and Acts of thanks to God; for the so much care He had of us, in the preservation of our lives; and for having, as it were, snatched us, and drawn us from so many dangers to which we were exposed, as also for having led us back in safety and health to our own country; and praying Him also to move the heart of our king, and the Lords of his Council, to contribute the necessary assistance to bring the poor savage nations to the knowledge of God: of which the honor would revert to his Majesty, to the Greatness and the advancement of his Empire: to the utility of his subjects, and the Glory of all his designs; and to God, only author of all perfection, to whom be honor and Glory. Amen."

In the voyage of 1618 he was accompanied by priests of the Order of St. Francis. Père Le Clerq, O.S.F., has given a description of their hardships and trials ("Première Etablissement de la Foi," Tom. I., p. 104), so interesting that I am tempted to transfer the following quotation: "The voyage was long and stormy. . . . Having arrived about

60 leagues from the Grand Bank, they found themselves surrounded by immense ice-fields, which the winds and currents pushed violently against the vessel. In the general consternation, Père Joseph Le Caron, seeing that no human succour could save them from shipwreck, very earnestly besought Heaven by vows and prayers, which he publicly made on board the vessel. He confessed them all, and placed himself in a state to appear before God. It was a sight to touch one with compassion, to see Madam Herbert raise the smallest of her children to receive the blessing of the Good Father. They escaped almost by a miracle after 13 weeks of voyage."

These quotations, though rather lengthy, will not, it is hoped, prove uninteresting. They give us a lively picture of the dangers accompanying the expeditions of the early colonizers of our country some three hundred years ago. They show also of what metal they were made. They teach us that simplicity of faith, and the open practice thereof, are not incompatible with the noblest deeds of courage and scientific enterprise; and as such are a stunning rebuke to the braggart spirit of modern times, which would relegate all expression of religious sentiment to old women and children, as a mark of weakness or superstition.

It is difficult for us to realize the bravery of these men. We can hardly believe what a daring thing it was to face the wide Atlantic in the then imperfect state of nautical knowledge, and in the frail and unsuitable barks which then existed. The largest of Columbus' vessels, the "Santa Maria," was only ten tons register, not much larger than a modern fishing-smack! It may then well be believed that the voyages of these men surpassed in stupendous daring and bravery any of our exploits of later times.

One other writer shall be quoted before entering more particularly on the historical part of this work, namely, that fine old English sailor, Captain Richard Whitbourne.

To no other of the early navigators do the sons of Newfoundland owe more gratitude than to this hardy old West countryman. Throughout all his "Narrative" he breathes the highest religious sentiments, blended with an ardent and enthusiastic love for "The New-found-lande." This worthy old sea-captain, between the years 1579 and 1618, made many voyages to Newfoundland, and entered almost every cove and harbor on her shores. In the preface to his "Voyage," etc., he says, "And for the Newfound lande, it is almost so familiarlie known to me as my owne countrie." He was present in St. John's harbor in 1583, when Sir Humphrey Gilbert took possession of the Island, in the name of Queen Elizabeth, of which event he tells us he was "an eyewitnesse." In 1615 he came out with a commission from the High Court of Admiralty, giving him full jurisdiction over the whole island.

"And," says he, "I did then arrive at the coast of Newfound lande, in the Bay of Trinitie, upon Trinitie Sunday, being the 4 of June; and there in the name of the Holy and Indiuiduall Trinitie, began the use of Your Most Sacred Majestie's power, by vertue of that commission to send forth a precept," etc. (p. 64).

He opened the first court ever held in Newfoundland, and made many useful enactments. He has written an account of his voyages in a book, now very rare, addressed to "The High and Mightie Prince James," etc., with a very long title, commencing "A Discourse and Discoverie," etc. He urges strongly upon His Majesty the conversion of the Indians, in many places, as page 163: . . . "Which people, if they might be reduced to the knowledge of the True Trinitie indeed no doubt but it would be a most sweete, and acceptable Sacrifice to God; an everlasting honour to your Majestie; and the Heavenly Blessing to those poor creatures, who are buried in their own superstitious ignorance. The taske whereof would proove easy, and no doubt but God Himself would set His hand to reare up and advance so noble, so pious, and so Christian a building." Again, page 14: "It is most certain that by a plantation there, and by that means only, the misbelieving inhabitants of that country may be reduced from Barbarisme to the knowledge of God and the light of His Truth, and to a ciuil and regular kind of life and government. This is a thing so apparent that I need not enforce it any further, or labour to stirre up the charity of Christians therein, to give their furtherance towards a worke so pious, every man, knowing that even we ourselves were once as blinde as they in the knowledge and worship of Our Creator, and as rude and savage in our liues and manners. By means of these slender beginnings, which may be made in Newfound lande, all other regions neere adjoining thereunto may in time be fitly converted to the true worship of God. . . . The first thing which is to be hoped for and which hath beene your Majestie's principall care is the propagation of the Christian Faith. . . . And so all the regions adjoining (which betweene this place and the countries actually possessed by King of Spain, and to the North of Newfound Lande are so spacious as all Europe) may be brought to the Kingdom of God."

These are noble sentiments, and worthy of a Columbus or a Champlain, and contrast remarkably with those of that doughty knight of Devon, Sir Humphrey Gilbert, who, on taking possession of Newfoundland (1583), brought no missioners with him, but a royal proclamation, ordering the Book of Common Prayer to be used for the future all over the Island; and decreeing that "Whosoever should violate this command should loose their ears!" Fortunately for Newfoundland, the author of this cruel edict perished. at sea on his homeward voyage, and thus it was not put into practice.

Since those who have up to the present time written what are called "Histories of Newfoundland" unite in one loud pæan in praise of Sir Humphrey Gilbert, as a sample of which I quote the following from the latest work published, the Rev. Moses Harvey's "History": "Thus perished one of the noblest and bravest of those who in that age," etc. . . . "The loss to Newfoundland of Sir Humphrey Gilbert was great and irreparable," etc. (p. 17); and as the outcome of

this sentiment a movement was set on foot in 1883, the third
centenary of his death, to have a monument erected to his
memory, — it may be well, once for all, to remove this false
estimate, and place this hero in his proper niche, as regards
what we Newfoundlanders owe to his memory. This
redoubtable character, then, was one of a band of " Aristo-
cratic freebooters," of English gentry, who received patents
from Queen Elizabeth for the colonization and civilization of
Ireland! " Sir Thos. Smith, the secretary, suggested to the
queen a new method to colonize the forfeited districts with
English settlers, who, having an interest in the soil, would be
willing to oppose the *rebels!* (Irish) without expense to the
Crown! . . . Grants of large territories were made to
them." (Lingard, Vol. VIII.) Among these filibustering
adventurers were Sir Humphrey Gilbert and his half-brother,
Sir Walter Raleigh. "The consequence was," continues Lingard, quoting from Irish authorities, Leland, Camden, etc.,
"the districts which they took possession of were reduced to
the state of a wilderness, by endless destructive wars." Some
small force was organized in Spain by Fitzmaurice, brother
of the Earl of Desmond, for the relief of Ireland. They
landed at Smerwick, in Kerry, but were overwhelmed by
superior numbers. Being attacked by land and sea, they surrendered conditionally, namely, that they should be allowed
to retire in order. But Raleigh, breaking his parole, "entered
the fort, received their arms, and then ordered them to be
massacred in cold blood." (Lingard.) Gilbert overran
Galway and the neighboring counties, striking terror into all
hearts by his indiscriminate slaughter of all who came in his
way, without regard to age or sex. For these services he
was rewarded, in 1570, by knighthood and the governorship
of Munster! Barcia, a Spanish copyist, in his "Ensayo
Cronologico," speaking of his death, says: "He was punished
for his greed."

Bancroft (Vol. I., Chap. III.), though trying to speak in his
favor, yet admits he was "censured for his ignorance of the
principles of religious freedom." He took possession of St.

John's, and a territory extending two hundred leagues in every direction, with "feudal rights." A turf and a rod were presented to him. He framed three laws : " *1st.* Establishing the religion according to the Liturgy of the Book of Common Prayer. *2d.* Declaring it high treason to plot against Her Majesty's Government; and, *3d.* Decreeing that whosoever should utter a word of dishonor against Her Majesty *should have his ears cut off.*" A pillar of wood was erected on the shore, with the Arms of England, engraved in lead, attached thereto, and the land by the seaside parcelled out into separate lots, the proprietors consenting to pay an annual tribute for the same. (Harris' "Travels." Chapell, "Voyage of Rosamund," etc.)

Some fifty years previous, when Jacques Cartier took possession of Bay Chaleur, we read that he erected, not a pillar, but a *cross*, with the Arms of France, thus taking possession, first, in the name of the *Christian* faith, and, secondly, of the earthly monarch of whom he was a subject.

This was the beginning and end of Humphrey Gilbert's connection with Newfoundland. He was lost on his homeward voyage. Impartial readers can judge for themselves how much gratitude we owe him.[1]

It was in the year 1619 that Whitbourne wrote his appeal to King James, urging the sending out of missioners to convert the savages. He seems to have been entirely ignorant of the fact that, some years previously (1611 and 1615), both Jesuit and Franciscan fathers had been brought out from France to the neighboring colonies, as we shall see farther on.

It was just about this time, namely, in the year 1622, when the development of geographical research was daily opening up new countries, that Pope Gregory XV., true to the traditions of the Catholic Church and her divine mission

---

[1] If the question of a monument were to be raised (and I long to see the vacant niche on the Lobby of the Colonial Building at St. John's filled), our first debt of gratitude should doubtless be paid to the Cabots; but after these no man deserves better of the country than good old Sir Richard Whitbourne.

to "go and teach all nations," established the Congregation of the *Propaganda Fide* at Rome. This institution consisted, at first, of a Committee or Congregation of Cardinals, whose express duty it was to take charge of the workings of the foreign missions. The business had become so immense, of the founding of new missions in the distant and uncivilized countries brought to light by the great discoverers, that it was found necessary to establish a particular bureau. A few years afterwards (1627), under Pope Urban VIII., the Missionary College of Propaganda was formed in connection with the Congregation, in which a free education is given to some two hundred and fifty students from all nations. During the past two and a half centuries the work of this Congregation has grown to such an extent that it has its missions in every corner of the globe. It has at present four hundred and fifty provinces in both hemispheres, in which are about fifty thousand churches, and about one hundred thousand priests and Bishops. In America alone some thirty thousand schools, with half a million of children, are conducted by priests and nuns, under the supervision of Propaganda; in Canada four thousand schools, and in India and China two thousand, with nearly one hundred thousand children. There are about fifty-five different languages and dialects spoken by the students within its walls; but, to prevent a Babel, they are restricted during school and study hours to the Italian and Latin.

It is not necessary to remind our readers that the modern Italian Government, under the oft-prostituted name of *Liberty* and *Progress*, has plundered with sacrilegious hand the funded property of this "World's Institution."

CHAPTER II.

PRE-COLUMBIAN VOYAGES. — [A.D. 800-1497.]

Traditions of a Western Land — Prophecy of Seneca — Seneca and Columbus, a Coincidence — Plato's "Atlantis" — Voyage of St. Brendan — St. Malo — Catholic Missions in Iceland — The Flato Saga, A.D. 860 — Discovery of Greenland by Gunbiœrn, 886 — Rediscovery by Eric Raud, 980 — Discovery of America by Bjarni, 985 — Labrador, Newfoundland, Nova Scotia, Discovered by Lief, 1000 — It Myla, or Great Ireland — Vestiges of an Irish Colony in America — Episcopal Sees in Greenland, 1021 to 1406 — Voyage of Zeno, 1380 — Relics of John Guy's Colony at Cuper's Cove, or Cupid's.

THE Catholic Church has always displayed, in a marked manner, as already remarked, the active spirit of missionary enterprise, so that whenever a new land was discovered we find the missionary bearing the cross and preaching the gospel among the aborigines.

There are many vague traditions afloat concerning a pre-Columbian discovery of the New World; but if, as is now almost certain, there were any foundation of truth in these recollections, it is no less certain that all authentic records of them had been lost, so that they do not in any way detract from the glory of Columbus' discovery.

The great navigator, however, had made some voyages to Iceland, where, no doubt, he must have heard the tales of the discovery of western lands, and been fired with the ambition of rediscovering them. But it is certain that Columbus never *knew* that he had discovered a new continent, but died in the belief that he had come, by a short route, upon the eastern shores of Asia.

It is only natural that people living upon the borders of the great ocean, looking out daily across its boundless waste, and seeing its huge billows roll in one after another with ceaseless murmur, should begin to wonder whence they come, and to picture to themselves some far-off land peopled

by a strange race of beings, and that the hope should spring
up in their minds that the day would come when man, by the
triumph of genius and talent, should penetrate this vast,
unknown abyss, and bring to light the New World!
Such were the thoughts which filled the mind of the phil-
osophic Seneca, as he paced the stately *plazas* of the noble
city of Cordova, or roamed pensive along the sands of the
little village of Palos, at the mouth of the Guadalquivir,
looking out upon the wide Atlantic, and which he handed
down to fame in the immortal prophecy of the Medæa,
" *Venient annis sœcula seris*," etc. For, by a remarkable
coincidence, Seneca, who foretold, so many centuries before,
the voyage of Columbus, under the symbolical name of
Typhis, was a native of Cordova, that royal city where
Columbus first exposed his great design to the Court of
Ferdinand and Isabella; and it is not improbable that these
memorable verses were composed upon the very spot where
(some fifteen hundred years after) Columbus walked around,
with his faithful and enthusiastic friend and supporter, Friar
Juan Perez, making preparations for his great expedition, by
which he was to fulfil the prophecy of Seneca by "unloosing
the bonds of things, and giving to the world a *New Orb*,"
and thus depriving "Far Thule" of the honor or fame of
being "the last among the Lands"!

Again, Seneca was learned in all the wisdom of those days,
and Cordova was then a seat of education and civilization and
refinement. It possessed a library of great extent, containing volumes and manuscripts of the rarest value. Here he
may have read the wondrous account of Plato's Atlantic
island, in which is distinctly foreshadowed the Great Western
Continent, "the opposite Continent which surrounds the
Great Ocean." This account Plato wrote 400 B.C. He
received it from his ancestor, Solon, who, 600 B.C., had
learned it from the wise men of the city of Sais in Egypt.
(Plato's "Atlantis." Donnelley.) Thus we see how great is
the antiquity of the tradition concerning the Western World.[*]

Ireland, being the most westerly land of Europe, and

placed, as she is, out upon the bosom of the Atlantic, has naturally retained many of those traditions most vividly. Among them the most constant and wide-spread is that of the voyage of Saint Brendan, in the beginning of the sixth century. Divested of various romantic accessories the story runs thus: Brendan, or Brandon, son of Findloga, was born in 484; went to Wales; lived under Saint Gildas at Shan-Carvan; afterwards founded the Monastery of Clonfert. Beryne, or Barinthus, a holy abbot, and cousin of Brendan, came to visit him, and told him a monk of his monastery "determined to sayle into an ylonde farre into the sea besides the mountaynes of stones, and with XII. monkes, set saile in a vessell vytalled for VII. Yeares. But ere they entered the Shyppe they fasted XL. days and lived devoutly, and eche of them receyved the Sacrament. He badde the Shyppe-men wynde uppe the sayle, and forth they sayled in Goddes name. After XL. days and XL. nights they saw ylonde ferre fro them, but it proved to be only a great fisshe named Iasconye;" but after three days more they found land in earnest. This tradition is supplemented by other nations bordering on the Atlantic, e.g., at St. Malo, in France, so called from Maclovius, or Macluthus, a nephew of Brendan. In the life of this saint by John Bosco, in the "Bibliotheca Florincense," it is stated that he determined to go and visit an island situated in the ocean, and named Iman. He took ninety-five companions with him, and remained seven years away, so that they celebrated seven Easters at sea: "*Septies contigit eis in mari celebrare Sanctum Pascha.*"

It is related in the Acts of St. David of Wales, that, riding one day upon a whale, he met St. Brendan sitting on a sea-horse (*insidens equo mari*). The Bollandists explain these legends by saying that this may only be a romantic or poetic way of describing their ships, which might have had these names, or emblems, or signs, as marks of distinction. Whatever may be thought of it, these stories seem to point to a wide-spread tradition of the existence of a western continent. Add to this the constant belief of the Norsemen

from Iceland, who declared that, on the discovery of
America by them in the ninth century, they found there a
colony of Irish! The historian Colgan mentions, without
the expression of a doubt, the voyage of St. Brendan, A.D.
500. One of the first books printed by Caxton, in England,
was this "Voyage," showing how popular it was at that
time; that is, shortly before Columbus' discovery. The
Society of Northern Antiquaries at Copenhagen also inserted it among their collection of pre-Columbian voyages,
in 1837. Professor Rafn also confirms the tradition, and
Dr. Von T. Schudi, in his work on "Peruvian Antiquities,"
says that it is "most probable" that the country which lay
along the coast from Chesapeake Bay, down into the Caro-
linas and Florida, was peopled by Irishmen. And in a note
he says that "a manuscript has been found since he commenced his work which converted the conjecture into a certainty." Humboldt, in his "Kosmos," confirms the tradition.
In the twelfth century an Arabian geographer, Aboul Ab-
dullah Mohammed Edrisi, mentions "Great Ireland." He
wrote at Palermo in Sicily, a port frequented by the Northmen, from whom, doubtless, he obtained his information.

We have it on undoubted authority that Irish missions
were established in Iceland even in the time of St. Patrick
(fifth century), when St. Aiblems, Bishop of Emly, sent
twenty-two of his disciples to evangelize that country. Eight
Irish missionaries and martyrs were buried there, and a
church was erected, dedicated to St. Columba. These facts,
now admitted by the best archæologists, were found related
in the *Skalhort Saga*, now preserved in the Smithsonian
Institute, Washington. From the *Bullarium Pontificum*, a
collection of the decrees of the Popes, we find that, in the
year 840, the Holy See delegated Ebbon, Archbishop of
Rheims, and St. Anscarius, apostle of Northern Europe, to
preach the faith in Iceland and *North America*.

The Icelandic Sagas, or Legends (*sagan*, to tell or say),
discovered in a monastery at the Island of Fläto, in the
Brede Fiord, on the north-west coast of Iceland, in 1650, give

us all that is known of the history of these northern explorations. The principal saga is the *Flätoyer Annal*, or Codex Flätoyensis. It was purchased from the owner, Jonas Torfesen, for King Frederic III., by Bishop Swendeson, of Skalholt. It is a large folio manuscript, beautifully written on parchment, and contains a collection of sagas copied from older writings. (Kirke, "Conquest of Canada," p. 99.) It was written between 1387 and 1395. It is now preserved in the royal library at Copenhagen. It is divided into two parts, or cantos — the *Eric Raud* and the *Karlsfenè*. From it we learn that Iceland was discovered, about 860, by a Danish navigator, named Naddod. He called it Snæland or Snow land. In 864, another Norseman, Gardar Svaffarson, was driven there by a storm. He called the country Gardar's Holm, or Gardar's Island. Finally Fläko gave it the name of Iceland, which it still retains.

Greenland was discovered, in 886, by Gunbiærn, and was called Gunbjarn's Rocks until about a century later (980). It was rediscovered by Eric Raud, who had fled there on account of some family dispute concerning the succession to the government of Iceland. He determined to found a colony of his own, and, in order to induce settlers to come, he, by a clever piece of diplomacy, gave the country the name of Græn-land, "because," said he, "people will be attracted thither if it has a good name."

About three or four years after the establishment of the colony of Greenland (namely, 985), Bjarni, son of Herjulf, saw for the first time the main-land of America. On a voyage from Iceland to Greenland he was driven westwards by a storm. He saw land three times on his return eastwards, but he did not go ashore or name these lands. But, about the year 1000, his brother Lief made the same voyage and discovered the same lands. The first he called Great Helluland, or Great Stone Land, supposed to be Labrador; next, Little Helluland, which is supposed to be Newfoundland. It is described as "A land without grass. Snow and ice covered it, and from the shore to the mountains it was a plain or flat covered with stones, and he gave it the name of Hellu-land," from Hellu or Hella, a stone. " Then he discovered Mark Land, and called it so from its woods (supposed to be Nova Scotia).

"After this he coasted south and west, and discovered *Vinland* (supposed to be Rhode Island, near Mount Hope Bay, or Narragansett), where wild vines grow abundantly. In the following years voyages were made by several other of these Norsemen along the shores of the American continent, and various strange stories are told of their experiences. In 1004 Thorwald, son of Eric, was killed by the Indians and buried near Massachusetts. A voyage was made by Thorstein in 1005. In 1006 the celebrated Karlsfenè founded a colony in Markland and Hellu-land, bringing with him one hundred and forty men and women; but, owing to the attacks of the Indians, they withdrew in 1010. The Northmen called the land south of Vinland It Myla or Great Ireland, or the White Man's Land. According to Professor Rafn, a great Scandinavian authority, this country extended from the Chesapeake Bay to East Florida. It was said that when first discovered by the Norsemen it was inhabited by a tribe of white men ' who spoke Irish.' . . . And they found on the shore crosses, bells, and sacred vessels of Irish workmanship." (*J. Gilmary Shea's Lecture before the Catholic Institute, New York, 1852.*)

"It is very improbable," writes Dr. Mullock (*Lectures on Newfoundland*, p. 6), "that so many accounts of voyages would be preserved; the names of the discoverers and navigators; the births of some of their children recorded; the wreck of one of their ships on Keeler Ness, Kell Cape or Ship Cove, and the locality marked out now as Keels, in Bonavista Bay, by the certain but rude way of determining the latitude; that is, the length of the longest day in the summer solstice,[1] — if it were all a work of imagination. I have no doubt that these sea-kings, after establishing colonies in

---

[1] On the shortest day in the Scandinavian Calendar the sun rose 7.30 A.M., and set 4.30 P.M. — *Hist. America, William Cullen Bryant.*

Greenland and Iceland, visited this country and made some
settlements here ; but I believe the few people they brought
with them either perished in their wars with the Skroe-
ligers, or the Esquimaux, or that the remnant left the
country, which they could not then have found very inviting.
In the year 980, as mentioned, Eric discovered Greenland.
Christianity was introduced soon after, and it became the See
of a Bishop in 1021. The historians of ancient Greenland
give a list of the Bishops of that country from 1021 to
1406, when all communication between it and the mother-
country ceased, and the imperfect civilization introduced was
finally lost. A few ruins of walls or stone fences now
mark the site of the Norwegian colony." (Dr. Mullock's MS.)
Abbé Garnier mentions a Bull of Pope Nicholas V., of date
about 1447, concerning this church of Greenland. But on
searching the *Bullarium* in the Propaganda Library, Rome,
in 1885, I could not find it. "We are told that one of the
Greenland Bishops, named Eric, visited Vinland in 1121, to
endeavor to bring back his countrymen from the barbarism
into which they had lapsed to a knowledge of Christianity.
The kings of Norway were the founders of the Greenland
bishopric, which extended its jurisdiction over the regions of
the unknown North. If Newfoundland and Vinland be the
same, this is the first account we have of any missioner
putting his foot on the Island ; though, if a Bishop did really
visit it, other priests must have preceded him. We can,
however, through the mist of ages, only collect a few
scattered facts intermingled with much fable." (Dr. Mullock.) These colonies on the west coast of Greenland
survived until 1406, when the seventeenth and last Bishop
of Garda was sent from Norway. Those on the east
flourished till 1540, when they were destroyed by a physical
cataclasm, which accumulated the ice in that zone from the
60th degree of latitude. (DeCourcy, " History of the Church
in America," Chap. I., p. 12.)

A few years ago some ruins were brought to light at
Clarke's Beach, near Brigus, in Conception Bay, N.F.,

among which were found some old European gold coins with German letters, some of copper without inscription, and some mill-stones. They were thought to be the remains of a Scandinavian settlement, though it now seems placed beyond a doubt that these relics must be attributed to the English settlers who came out, in 1610, with John Guy, from Bristol. It had hitherto passed current in the published histories of Newfoundland that this plantation was settled at Mosquito; but the idea has now been exploded by the researches of J. P. Howley, Esq., F.G.S., who has published the charter, and some letters from John Guy to Mr. Slaney, dated from Cuper's Cove, 16th May, 1611: "The name, like most others on our charts, became corrupted, or, rather, in this instance, I should say *improved*, and this must have occurred at an early date. . . . A work published in 1630 by Sir William Alexander . . . has as follows: The first houses . . . were built in *Cupid's* Cove," etc. (J. P. Howley.) It is most probable, then, that the establishment at Clarke's Beach may have been an offshoot of this settlement.

Before coming to the undoubted historical period of the Cabots I shall mention one more of those semimythical traditions, viz., the voyage of the brothers Zeno, Venetians. This expedition is said to have taken place in the year 1380, or more than a century previous to the discovery of America by Columbus. But what throws suspicion upon its authenticity is that the account was not published till 1558, or sixty years after Columbus' voyage. To account for this damaging circumstance Zeno stated that the manuscript had come to him as a family heirloom; that when a child he had torn it up, but afterwards, recognizing its value, he had collected the fragments and gummed them together. The documents relate, after many other voyages, that the Zenos made a voyage northward, and arrived at a land named Frisland, the king of which was called Zichmni. Thence they sailed to Engroniland, where they discovered a monastery of Friar Preachers (*i.e.*, monks of the Order of St. Dominic), and a church dedicated to that saint. It is stated that the monks heated their apartments by water, from a hot spring, which they brought by pipes to all their rooms. They also made use of it for cooking, heating their artificial gardens, etc., so that they had quite a tropical and fruit-bearing conservatory. Mention is made of a land farther west, called Estotiland, and supposed to be Newfoundland; and Drogeo, the mainland of America; and, finally, an imaginary land called Icaria. A map accompanies the document.

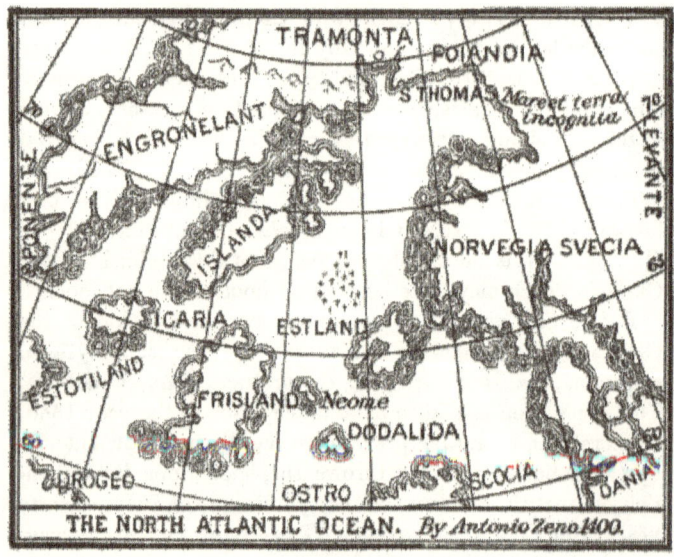

ZENO'S MAP.

The introduction of Grecian mythology, as shown in the name Icaria, from Icarus, son of Dædalus, is very suspicious, and throws an air of forgery over the whole narrative. The above facts and traditions, gathered from various sources, contain nearly all that is yet known of these pre-Columbian voyages; as yet the knowledge is meagre and unsatisfactory enough, but, putting it altogether, it is almost impossible to doubt that the eastern world was at one time cognizant of the existence of a western land, though the tradition had been all but lost. We now come into more certain waters, and shall commence the next chapter with the second discovery of Newfoundland, under the Cabots; though here, too, all is not as clear as we should wish, especially regarding the religious complexion of the times, which is the more immediate object of these pages.

CHAPTER III.

COLUMBUS AND HIS FOLLOWERS. — [1492-1534.]

Discovery of Newfoundland by Cabot — Cabot's Map Shown to be Tampered with — The Name *Baccalao* — Relic of Early Missionary — Cortereal — Map of Varrese from the Vatican — St. John's becomes Important, 1527 — The Aborigines — Their Name Beothuck — Ruthlessly Shot down — Their Character, Religion, etc. — Early Maps of the Country — Map of Jerome Verazzano, 1528 — Of Ribero, 1529 — Ancient Map in Borgian Museum, Propaganda — "Dividing Line" drawn by Pope Alexander VI., 1493.

THE Italian navigator Columbus, sailing under the Spanish flag, discovered America in 1492, and gave a new world to Castile and Leon. This astounding discovery, the most important in its results to mankind of any that ever took place, raised not alone the curiosity and excited the adventurous spirit of Europe, but also the ambition of her rulers. England was then enjoying one of those intervals of internal peace so rare in her history. The Wars of the Roses were at an end; the ancient aristocracy had almost perished in these destructive contests, which is the reason that, with few exceptions, the present aristocracy of England is the most modern in Europe, most of the great houses only dating from the so-called Reformation, and enriched, not like the bold barons of old, by the strong hand, but by the plunder of the Church, and chicanery. The royal power, as invariably happens after revolutions, was strengthened; the people, weary of bloodshed, only wanted repose, and, having lost their liberty, were prepared to submit to the despotism of the Tudor Sultans. Two Venetian navigators, — though some say they were the sons of a Venetian, but born in Bristol, — the brothers Cabota, or, anglicized, Cabot, offered their services to Henry VII. to seek for new lands in the west, or a passage by that course to India. The offer was accepted, and in 1497 Sebastian Cabot left England, and on the 20th of June, the same year, discovered Newfoundland. He gave the name of *Buona Vista*, or *Happy Sight*, to the cape which first met his view, — a name which, together with the great bay of which it forms the southern headland, it retains to the present day." (Dr. Mullock's MS.)

SEBASTIAN CABOT.

There is an impenetrable mist and confusion (emblematic, perhaps, of the fog that hangs over our Great Bank) enveloping the history of the early voyages of the Cabots, — a mist or uncertainty which the contradictory statements of contemporary documents render it useless to endeavor to dissipate, even if such effort were not outside the scope of the present work. The principal points of controversy may be reduced to these two: —

First. To which of the Cabots, John or his son Sebastian, is to be given the honor of the voyage and discovery?

Second. What land did he, or they, really discover?

It will sound strange to the ear of the ordinary reader that there should be a doubt on either of these questions; yet such is really the case, and although, as already stated, it is somewhat outside the scope of the present work, I deem it of sufficient relevance to give, at least, the substance of this historical disquisition.

John Cabot had three sons, Lewis, Sebastian, and Sanctius. That the family was of Italian origin is beyond doubt, but it is not certain whether John was born in Italy or in Bristol, England; if in Italy, whether in Genoa or Venice. He became a citizen of Venice in 1476, and in his patent of discovery, given by Henry VII., he is called " of Venice," or, rather, a citizen of Venice, "*civi Venetiano.*" This would not prove that he was a *native* of Venice. A map of the voyage was drawn by Sebastian Cabot, and cut by Clement Adams, in 1544, which, being in the Privy Gallery of Whitehall, bore the inscription, "*Effigies Sebastiani Caboti Angli filii Joannis Caboti Venetiani.*" This makes Sebastian an Englishman, and his father, John, a Venetian. Peter Martyr, a learned clergyman, and a personal acquaintance, in the "Decades of the Ocean," calls Sebastian "a Venetian born," who in his infancy was carried to England. Richard Edens, also a particular friend of the Cabots, says Sebastian told him his father died soon after the news of Columbus' discovery. Strype says Sebastian was an Italian; Grafton, that his father was a Genoese, but that Sebastian was born in England. John Stowe also says John Cabot was born in Genoa. Campbell ("Lives of the Admirals," p. 373) says Sebastian was born in Bristol in 1477; he would then be but twenty years of age at the time of the voyage. Was he old enough to take charge of the expedition? So much for the first question. Then, —

Secondly. What land did they discover? We must remember the object of Cabot in this voyage: it was to find a north-west passage; hence he kept a course almost west from Bristol, and Edené tells us "that he directed his course by the tract of islande uppon the Cape of Labrador at LVIII. (58°) degrees." In another place (report of conversation with Gelatius, etc.) he says that he sailed *west* from Bristol, and thence (when he had struck land) steered north to 58°. In either case it would be most probable that he would have first made either some part of the north of Newfoundland or Labrador. The tradition that Bonavista was the first land sighted was in undisturbed possession until some few years ago.

In the year 1856 a map, said to be Cabot's, was discovered in Germany, and is now preserved in the Imperial Library of Paris.

It gives the point first discovered as "Prima Vista," from the description given by Campbell, in his "Lives of the Admirals," who says John Cabot so called it because it was the "land first seen." Now, as will be observed, the point on the map thus marked is not Bonavista Cape, Newfoundland, but what is now Cape North, in Cape Breton Island. This destroys the beautiful tradition, held for nearly four centuries, so graphically touched by Dr. Mullock. (Lectures, p. 12.) "The Italian perhaps, often deceived by fog-banks, sees at length the cape well defined, the surges breaking on the 'Spillers,' the dark green of the forest, gives expression to his feelings in his own musical tongue, and cries out, Bona Vista!—O, happy sight!" This newly found map, if authentic, would thus deprive Newfoundland of her time-honored boast of being Britain's oldest colony. I am sorry to see that the Rev. M. Harvey, in his "History" (p. 5), gives up the claim most serenely, and without a struggle. He calls the map "most trustworthy." For my part I think it anything but such, and that there is nothing in the map to shake our long-founded faith in Bonavista, and deem the matter of sufficient interest to state, at some length, my reasons.

Whatever may be thought of the authenticity of the map, as a whole, there can be no doubt that the words PRIMA VISTA are the work of a later hand. They are printed in large, square, and most conspicuous characters, entirely different from anything else on the map. But, not

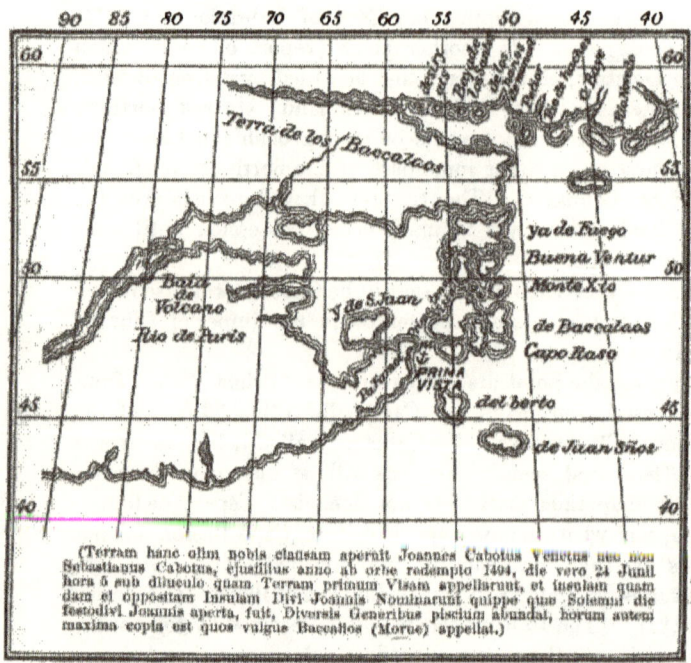

(Terram hanc olim nobis clausam aperuit Joannes Cabotus Venetus nec non Sebastianus Cabotus, ejusfilius anno ab orbe redempto 1494, die vero 24 Junii hora 5 sub diluculo quam Terram primum Visam appellarunt, et insulam quam dam ei oppositam Insulam Divi Joannis Nominarunt quippe quæ Solemni die festodivi Joannis aperta, fuit, Diversis Generibus piscium abundat, horum autem maxima copia est quos vulgus Baccallos (Morue) appellat.)

SEBASTIAN CABOT'S MAP.

content with this, the author (or interpolator) repeats the words in the following manner: "*Prima Terra Vista*," marking the same spot. Here, again, are signs of tampering, for these words are in *Italian*, while all the rest of the map (with two remarkable exceptions) is in Spanish. The map bears the date of 1544. At that time Sebastian Cabot was "pilot major of his Sacred Imperial Majesty Don Carlos the V. of his name;" and, no doubt, if he *had* made this map, he would have written the names in Spanish. The interpolator, however, overlooking this fact, and counting on Cabot's supposed nationality, inserted the words in Italian. "*Prima Vista*" is either Italian or Spanish, but *Terra* is distinctly Italian, the Spanish word being *Tierra*. But this is not all. The first of the remarkable exceptions mentioned above is, that a third effort is made to signalize that spot on the map as the first land seen; and this time it is in English. There is an anchor, with the word or figure "1st," thus, "⚓ 1st," meaning first anchorage. This seems like overdoing the matter. The second exception mentioned is the French word *morue*. This word occurs in the inscription attached to the map. The inscription is in Latin, and was evidently written by a Frenchman; for, after the word *Bacalios*, he explains by the word *morue* in parenthesis, the French name for *cod*. There can be no possible reason given why Cabot should have translated this word into French, supposing he wrote the inscription, and supposing he knew the French word, which is doubtful. We have nothing to induce us to believe that Cabot knew French, and he certainly had no connection with that country. It would, therefore, be most absurd to imagine his inserting that French word into his Latin inscription. It was evidently written by a Frenchman, and we have here also, for the first time, a corrupt form of spelling of the word *Baccalaos*, namely, Bacalios, a form gradually approaching the modern French *Bacalieu*. Again, it would be impossible for a voyager coming from Bristol to sight Cape North in Cape Breton without first passing for *some days* in sight of Newfoundland. Finally, it is stated that Cabot, having made the land sailing west from Bristol, coasted north to the fifty-eighth or sixtieth degree of latitude; he then returned to his starting-point and coasted south and west as far as Florida. All this is inconsistent with the idea of his having made *Cape North*. He could not have gone north from that without sailing through the Straits of Belle Isle, and seeing Newfoundland on the starboard. This we know he did not do. The Straits were only discovered by Cartier in 1534. Again, sailing west and south from Cape North would have brought him into the Gulf of St. Lawrence, or Bay Chaleur, instead of to Florida. Many other reasons might be given.

One of the motives which has induced writers to adopt the "Cape-North Theory" is on account of the words in Campbell's "Lives of the Admirals": "On the 24th of June at 5 o'clock in the morning they discovered the first land. . . . Another island less than the first he styled St. John." In the inscription on Cabot's map this island is thus spoken of: "That Island which lieth out before the land first seen he called St. John." But there is no difficulty whatever in applying these words to the theory of Cabot having first seen Cape Bonavista, then Baccalieu Island; and, crossing the mouth of Conception Bay, he made Cape St. Francis. He thus thought that the peninsula of Avalon was another and "lesser Island." And so it is marked on the map, and so it was believed to be for many years after. Having entered the harbor on the 24th of June he gave it the name of "St. John's." All this applies better to this theory than to the other, for Prince Edward Island, supposed to be the St. John in question, lies rather "behind" than "*before*" Cape North. Again, Cabot says this island was "barren in some places," which applies unfortunately too well to Avalon, but not at all to Prince Edward Island. And, lastly, there is no tradition whatever of Cabot having landed on Prince Edward Island on St. John's day; while our city has an unbroken claim to it right up to the time immediately succeeding Cabot's discovery.

I have dwelt longer than I intended on this point, but have only given an outline of the arguments *pro* and *con*. What more directly touches upon our object is the question, Had Cabot any missionaries with him? It has already been remarked that the missionary went hand-in-hand with the discoverer. And in those pre-Reformation times England was not backward in this respect. At the time of Cabot's first voyage (1497) Columbus had already made his second,

BOX IN POSSESSION OF SAUNDERS FAMILY. (COVER.)

and was preparing for his third, which took place the following year (1498). He was accompanied by priests, and established a regular mission; and though we have no account of Cabot having missionaries with him, yet it is not improbable that he had. The names which he gave to the

BOX IN POSSESSION OF SAUNDERS FAMILY. (BOTTOM.)

first lands discovered are an indication that he was actuated by the same religious spirit as Columbus. The name of *Buona Vista* was rather an involuntary expression of joy

than an actual naming of the place. But all are agreed that
he called his first landing-place St. John's, in honor of the
Baptist, on whose festival day he entered our harbor. It is
probable, also, that to Cabot we owe the beautiful names of
Conception Bay and Cape St. Francis, he, like Columbus,
being a fond disciple of the lowly ascetic of Assisi.

Peter Martyr, a clergyman, contemporary and intimate
friend of Cabot, writing from Spain to Pope Leo X. about
the year 1515, says that Cabot named the new land "Baccalaos, or *Terra Baccalearum*, because he found in the seas
there a multitude of large fish like tunnies, which the inhabitants called Baccalaos." The name *Terra di Baccalao* appears in the maps of those times, and for many years after
for that portion of the land now called *Labrador;* the
name of Baccalà, now gallicized into *Baccalieu*, being restricted to a small island at the mouth of Conception Bay.

We have, as already remarked, no account of the establishment of missions or the performance of religious services
at this period, but some relics have been found which might
possibly indicate the presence of priests in those days;
among the rest, a brass box, now in the possession of Mr.
Saunders, of Greenspond, Bonavista Bay, of curious and
antique workmanship.

There can hardly be a doubt that it forms part of the
equipment of some early missionary. The figure of the Remonstrance shows at once that the box was used as a pyx,
or case, to hold the altar-breads for the Holy Sacrifice of the
Mass. The box is about five inches by four, in form of an
ellipse. The figures are scratched in a not altogether in-
artistic, though not quite professional, style. It has been in
possession of the Saunders family from time immemorial.
On the cover is engraved a ducal crown as crest, with an
escutcheon supported by two heraldic animals. On the field
of the shield are the following letters: P̧V̧ D L C D L G,
which I interpret (until a better explanation be forthcom-
ing), Pura Immacculata ViRginE, "Pure and Immaculate
Virgin," for the monogram; and for the smaller letters, "Deo

Laus Cui Debetur Laus et Gloria;" that is, "Praise to God, to whom is due Praise and Glory."

On the under part of the box is a Remonstrance, or Os-

VATICAN MAP.[1]

tensory, resting on a throne, attended by two angels with trumpets, and accompanied by stars and doves.

In the year 1500 the King of Portugal sent out Gaspar de

---

[1] Copied from the original by the writer in 1885.

Cortereal, who also came the following year with his brother Michael. He sailed round the Island, and named many places; among the rest, Portugal Cove. In a map, painted by Varrese, upon the walls of the Vatican Palace, Rome, in the *Loggie di Rafaelle*, about the year 1556, the southern part of Labrador is called "*Terra di Cortereal.*"

No vestige of the event now remains unless we may consider Cottrel's or Cottel's Island, a small place in Trinity Bay, as a corrupt form of this navigator's name. (J. P. Howley, Esq., F.G.S.)

Although St. John's was not chosen as the *first*, nor even the second, capital of the Island, yet it was very soon a place of importance in the country. Owing to its splendid harbor and naturally safe conformation, surrounded by lofty hills, and secured from the great swell of the Atlantic, while at the same time it is right on the verge of the ocean, so as to be easy of access at all times; its important situation on the most easterly point of the Island, the nearest to the Old World, and in the immediate path of ocean traffic; the splendid adaptability of its shores for the formation of a great city,—from all these natural advantages it is no wonder that, from the very earliest stages of our history, it begins to assume a prominent place as a great port of commerce and fishery operations, and to give clear signs of that future greatness which was to render it finally the capital of the Island.

As early, then, as 1527 we find (Purchass' "Voyages," Vol. III., p. 800) a letter was written to King Henry VIII. by one John Rutt, master of a ship then lying in the haven of St. John's, in which he states that in that port alone there were, at the time, eleven ships from Normandy and one from Brittany, engaged in the cod-fishery.

From this period until the arrival of Sir Humphrey Gilbert, 1583, we do not read of any attempt being made to establish religion in Newfoundland. In fact, while France, Spain, and Portugal were vying with each other in their efforts to explore and colonize new countries, to civilize native tribes and bring them to a knowledge of Christianity, England seemed to take no interest in her territory on the western ocean. The policy of England, or at least of those who floated her flag in the New World, in regard to the savage tribes, and especially in Newfoundland, is one of the greatest blots upon her history's page.

"The natives" (Dr. Mullock writes in his manuscript) "were a fine race of men, called by themselves BEOTHICS, supposed by some to have been partially descended from the Northmen, but now unhappily extinct. Little more than twenty years ago (1842) a remnant of the tribe wandered among the forests and along the shores of the great lakes of the interior; but the fire-arms of the English settlers and of the Micmac Indians cut them off to the last man. Cold-blooded murderers living in our own day used to boast of the numbers of Indians they killed, as if they were so many head of deer. When too late the government was at length aroused, and endeavored to put an end to such barbarity. An expedition was sent to try and save the remnant, but it was unsuccessful. ... The Newfoundland Indian never knew the white man but as a murderer, and when he could he retaliated. Now all are exterminated; the ruins of their huts and deer fences yet remain, but will soon decay. A few barbarous names, imposed on places where the whites attacked them, as Exploits, Bloody Bay, and a tradition of ruthless murders perpetrated, are all that remain to tell that such a race ever existed under three centuries of British rule. I was most happy to find that among all the inquiries I made I never could connect any of our Catholics with the murder of this race. The Micmac Indians, indeed, fought with them, and their semi-civilization and knowledge of the use of fire-arms gave them the advantage over the powerful Beothic, — for these were almost a gigantic race, — but never could I learn that an Irish or a Newfoundland Catholic raised a gun against one of them to rob him of the furs he wore, which was often the only temptation to shoot him."

The name Beothic, or Beothuk, by which the aboriginal Red Indians of Newfoundland became known in history, seems not to have been their original name in their own language, but one given them by the Micmacs. In the Micmac language it means "the fore-foot of a deer," and was probably given them in consequence of their swiftness of foot. This would account for the name of "black foot," by which they were also known; and a harbor on Labrador still bears the name of *Penware*, probably a corruption of *Pied Noir*, evidently having some connection with the extinct race. The name, however, of Beothuc has been differently explained. Robert Gordon Latham ("Comparative Philology") thinks it means "Good-night Indians," from the word *beatha*, to go home, and thus its real meaning is, "I am going home." Mr. A. S. Gatschet, who read a paper on the subject before the American Philosophical Society in 1885, says the name *Beothic* is a generic name for Indian. He also says (p. 413) that he made a research, at the "earnest solicitation of Mr. James P. Howley, surveyor and assistant geologist of Newfoundland, who, through his numerous expeditions, has become familiar with all parts of the Island. With accuracy he (Mr. H.) compared the faulty vocabulary of Loyd, and corrected about twenty-five misspellings, and gathered many words hitherto unknown." The vocabulary spoken of was obtained from Mary March, or Demasduit, by Rev. J. Leigh, and there was another obtained from Shanandithit, by Cormack. These two women were the last of the Red Indians. Demasduit, or Waunathoake, called Mary March from the month in which she was captured, was taken in 1819 by the late John Peyton, who shot her husband at Red Indian Pond, and brought herself to St. John's. She remained during the year, and being sent home in January, 1820, died on the way, of consumption. Shanandithit, or Shawnadithit, afterwards vulgarized into *Nancy*, was, with two of her daughters, brought to St. John's by William Call, in 1823. She remained among the whites till she died (in a hospital in St.

John's), in 1829.[1] The vocabularies obtained from these persons and other sources amount to about three hundred and fifty words. The name given for themselves (the Red Indians) is *Shawatharott*. The language is said not to resemble that of any of the neighboring tribes of Canada or North America. Hence, though nothing satisfactory has yet come to light to determine their true ethnological position, Mr. Howley is fully convinced they are not Algonquins, though hitherto thought to be a branch of that great tribe which inhabited all the north shore of the St. Lawrence, from the Saguenay river to the territory of the Esquimaux.

As to their character Peyton described them as "fierce and savage." But this is entirely contrary to the accounts of the early navigators, and was probably only an excuse to cover his own inhuman cruelty to them. He was one of those who boasted of the number of "head" of them they had killed, and scored it on their gunstocks. From the earliest times we have the most favorable accounts of these Indians. Cabot brought three of them to England with him, who became civilized, and were seen some years afterwards at Westminster Palace, by Kerr, who "could not distinguish them from Englishmen." Frobisher (1574) says they were "altogether harmlesse." Whitbourne says (1622) they were "an ingenious and subtill race," and "tractable when kindly dealtwithall." "Much good," he continues, "might be wrought upon them, for I have apparent proofes of their ingenious and subtill dispositions; and that they are a people full of quicke and lively apprehensions." He does not, however, seem to have discovered any clue to their religious belief. He says they had no knowledge of God, nor any civil government. The discovery of bows and arrows and drinking-cups, in the graves of some of the tribe, on the banks of the Red Indian Lake, in 1828, would seem to indicate a kindred belief with the

---

[1] The mother and one of the daughters died, but the third, whose name was Shanandithit, survived about two years, etc. (Rev. M. Harvey, "History of Newfoundland"); but in his article "Records of an Extinct Race" he gives the facts as in the text.

other tribes of North America in the "happy hunting-grounds of the future."

Peyton informed Mr. Howley that he thought that, if they had any worship at all, it was that of the Sun. They had a superstition concerning a devil, or evil spirit, which haunted the Grand Lake, and which they called Ashmodshim, or Ashmodyim.

Dr. Mullock (manuscript) quotes from an edition of Ptolemy's geography, published in Venice in 1561 by Girolamo Ruscelli, and now preserved in the library of St. Isidore's Franciscan Convent, Rome, a description of the Island of Newfoundland and the aborigines. It contains, also, a map of the Island as then known to the Italians, both of which, he writes, "are so curious and so totally different from the reality that I thought it would be interesting to reproduce them here." Unfortunately I have not found this copy of the map; if ever made it has been lost. Dr. Mullock then goes on to describe the map. "It will be perceived that Newfoundland was then thought to be a collection of small islands, — the appearance it presents at present to those who sail at some distance along its shores and see only the headlands and the open sea between them, on account of the width and depth of the bays. It is remarkable, also, that though the map is an Italian one, and published in Italy, all the names are Spanish; so that it appears to be the copy of a map published by the Spanish navigators." (Probably of Cabot's of 1544, mentioned above.) The description accompanying the map is as follows: "Tierra Nueva de los Bacalaos. Bacalaos, or Baccallaos, is a sort of large fish which the people of Ireland, and also the English, fish for. It is this which gives the name to the Province, which, however, is very small and not well inhabited, as it is a very cold country; hence both men and women are clothed in bear-skins. They are of a bestial nature: eat everything raw and even human flesh; they have neither religion nor law, and they adore, some one thing, some another; as the Sun, Moon, Stars, or anything else. The land of Labrador is said to be the last of all those newly discovered towards those northern parts, and is about fourteen leagues distant from the Island of Iceland, or 'The Lost,' which the ancients called Tile (Thule); and it is the last part of the world towards that side. . . . We pass over a period of eighty-six years, and find another map, published in Florence, in 1647; we may perceive that a very passable knowledge of the form and extent of the country had been acquired." Thus far Dr. Mullock, but we see from the maps of Newfoundland, drawn by Champlain as early as 1618–19, that Newfoundland is represented *as one large island*, and bears a very fair resemblance to its present outline on our latest maps. That it should have been at first supposed to consist of a number of small islands is not indeed to be wondered at, when we find on Verrazano's map (1528) that England and Scotland are represented as separate islands. Indeed, it would appear that particular attention was paid to the exact delineation of our shores at a very early date; and the correctness of the drawing, and naming of places, is truly astonishing, considering the rudeness of the instruments, the remoteness of the localities, etc. There is nothing to confirm the statement made above that the aborigines were cannibals. Kerr, in his " Travels," speaking of those Indians whom he saw at Westminster, says: "They did eat raw flesh." But, then, firstly, he must have spoken from hearsay; secondly, he does not say *human flesh*, but *raw* flesh. In this gastronomical feat they are closely followed by some civilized savages. Again, it is not certain whether these men brought home by Cabot, on his second voyage, were Beothics or not; for, on that occasion, he coasted as far as Florida, and touched at many places. Finally, savages in all climes are more faithful observers of nature's laws than civilized man; and it is a well-known ethnological fact that the consumption of human flesh in northern or cold climates is fatal, nature requiring a more oleaginous substance; hence the seal, the bear, and the walrus are bountifully supplied by an All-seeing Providence.

That the Beothics had a knowledge of the use of fire, and of a rude culinary art, are facts beyond dispute. For the production of the former they ignited the down of the blue jay (*Corvus Canadensis*) by striking together two pieces of iron pyrites or *mundic*. (Howley.) As to their knowledge of cooking, Cormack describes having found various culinary utensils among their wigwams at Red Indian Lake.

The map of Verrazano, before alluded to, is preserved in the Propaganda, or Borgian Museum, at Rome, where also are several other ancient maps which have been brought into great prominence lately by having been used by Pope Leo XIII. in deciding the dispute between Spain and Prussia concerning the dominion of the Caroline Islands. This fact may be looked upon as one of the most extraordinary occurrences of the nineteenth century. The powerful Protestant premier of Prussia, Prince Bismarck, a man whose life was spent in opposition to the Papacy, and who made the vain boast that he "would never go to Canossa," led by an instinct of the profoundest policy, but in which the hand of God is visibly seen, applies to the Pope, kneels before Leo like another Henry IV. before Gregory. Bismarck acknowledges Leo, in the midst of this materialistic nineteenth century, as the Great Arbiter of nations! This is, indeed, a portentous event. And, as if it were to accentuate its significance, Leo, in 1885, makes use of the identical map used some four hundred years before (1493) by Alexander VI. for the same purpose, namely, to settle the differences arising between the kings of Spain and Portugal concerning the dominion of the new found lands of the western world.

Being in Rome in 1885, I was kindly permitted to examine and copy some of these rare specimens of cosmography, as well as a Latin document accompanying and illustrating them. I here give a reduced sketch of part of Verrazano's map.

In 1523, Giovanni Verrazano, a Florentine, was sent out by Francis I., King of France, and discovered the eastern coast of America, which he claimed for France. It would seem that England had let her right go by default, as Cabot had discovered and claimed in her name all this coast some thirty years before. The Latin manuscript of the Borgian Museum, explanatory of the maps, says that Verrazano found the country called *Hucatenet*, and gave it the name of *Nova Gallia*, or New France. The map of the lands discovered by Verrazano was not made till five years after, viz., 1528. It was drawn by Jerome Verrazano, as the inscription states, "*Hieronymus Verrazano faciebat*." It shows the line drawn by order of Alexander VI.; but, of course, it is not the map used actually by that Pope, who died in 1503, twenty-five years before this map was made. All the maps of this period copied the above dividing line of Alexander VI. It is to be seen, also, on another map preserved in the museum, namely, that of Diego Ribero, cosmographist of Spain, whose map was drawn in 1529. The actual original map used by Alexander VI., and probably drawn by Paolo Toscanelli, is also preserved in this library, and is the one lately used by Pope Leo XIII. On examining these maps we find two different lines of demarcation between Spain and Portugal. One is drawn through the Atlantic Ocean about 5° west from the Azores; the other is about $18\frac{1}{2}$° farther west, or 30° west from Cape Verde, and runs through part of the continent of South America. The history of the discrepancy between these two lines is most interesting and instructive. The bold navigators of Portugal had pushed their explorations southward along the coast of Africa many years before the discovery of America by Columbus, till at length, in the year 1497, Vasco da Gama rounded the Cape of Good Hope, and discovered India and the land of the Great Khan, and gave to Portugal undisputed dominion over all the lands of the East. After Columbus' discovery they began to fear the incursions of Spain; and hence, as a matter of ordinary proceeding, recurrence was had to the Pope to lay down a boundary line. In those days the Pope was acknowledged as the divinely appointed guardian of all peoples, and the supreme judge in matters of international disagreement. His action was not, therefore, an *interference* unwarranted, as assumed by many modern writers, but was asked for and expected by kings and princes. Hence the Pope was appealed to, to prevent a collision between Spain and Portugal. The Pope ordered the line of demarcation to be drawn "One hundred leagues (or about 1¾ degrees) west from the Azores and Cape Verde Islands, measured from a point midway between the two groups; all islands, etc., on the west of this line to belong to Spain; those on the east to Lusitania or Portugal." This decision was confirmed by a brief drawn up on the 4th of May, 1493, solemnly signed, and the line drawn on the map. The King of Portugal was not satisfied with the decision, and tried every possible means to make the Pope reverse or revise his sentence; but he would not swerve an inch from his first proposal. King John then brought about a meeting, at Tordesillas, with the weak-minded Ferdinand, and easily persuaded him to move the line farther westward, so as to give his ships more sea-room; arguing that a few leagues, more or less, on a boundless ocean was not of any consequence. The line was therefore removed some three hundred and seventy leagues, or 18½°, farther westward. This accounts for the second line on the map (shown in our reproduction as a heavy black line, while the line of Alexander VI. is shown by us in red as it is drawn on the original). This agreement was made the 17th day of June, 1494, as mentioned on Ribero's map. By this concession King Ferdinand ceded, though unwittingly, to Portugal, the kingdom of Brazil. It is a very extraordinary fact that the line drawn by the Pope, and adhered to with such determination, is the only one that can be drawn on the Atlantic which runs from pole to pole without encountering any land. It is certain that the Popes were far in advance of the rest of the world in knowledge of geography and other branches of science, and that they had gathered around them the most learned and skilled cosmographers of Europe. Yet, even admitting this, it seems an astounding thing that Pope Alexander should have been able, at that early date, to fix with such precision this dividing meridian. (Fr. Knight, S.J., in the "Month," November, 1876.)

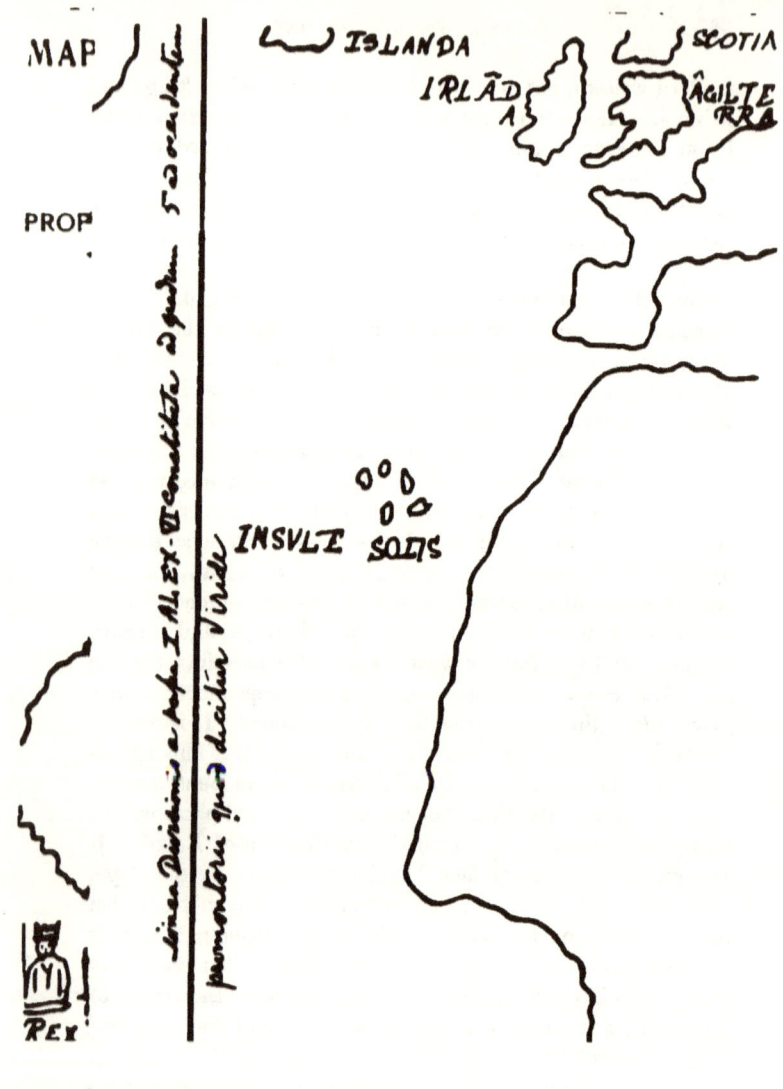

CHAPTER IV.

JACQUES CARTIER. — [1534-1611.]

Neglect of Colonies by England — Henry Kirke Refuted — Catholic Countries Encourage Colonization — Jacques Cartier's Voyages, 1534-35 — Arrives at Catalina — First Mass in Newfoundland — Catholic Missions in America — Testimony of Bancroft — Cartier Enters the Straits of Belle Isle and Explores the St. Lawrence — Old Fort — Anticosti, Bay Chaleur — Saguenay, Quebec, etc. — Settlement by John Guy in Conception Bay.

FOR some quarter of a century after the discovery of Newfoundland by Cabot, England seems to have taken no interest in her Newfoundland acquisition of territory, but to have abandoned it to the use of foreign fishermen, who fully availed themselves of her valuable fisheries. Kirke, in his "Conquest of Canada," p. 22, attributes this lethargy of England to the old *bête noir*, "sacerdotalism and monkery." These he tells us were not dead in England till the reign of Elizabeth, a queen "thrifty and penurious." With her accession dawned a new era, and "England awaked to new life." The dissolution of monasteries conferred wealth on the aristocracy, so that "all example and precept (*sic; qu.* pretext) for idleness had disappeared." So it was "only in the latter half of the sixteenth century, seventy-two years after Cabot's discovery, that any attempt was made to utilize it by England." Yet, strange to say, this same writer, in the very next page, tells us that Spain, where "monkery and sacerdotalism" were in full vigor, — this benighted country (at the very time that England was so busy killing out monkery), — "was reaping a rich harvest from America"! "And yearly vast treasure-ships sailed across the Atlantic to empty into her bosom the spoils of a new continent." And, what is still more strange, it was those very "lazy monks" who were the life and soul of those enterprises! So do men, blinded by early prejudice, fail to read history correctly!

France, too, another country overridden by "monkery and sacerdotalism," while England was revelling at home in the supereffulgent light of the new Reformation, and contenting herself with the treasures wrenched from the dissolved monasteries, was pushing her explorations onward in the western ocean, and winning for herself new glories in the shape of vast colonial possessions.

In the years 1534-35 Jacques Cartier, a great French navigator, explored the coast of Newfoundland, penetrated the Straits of Belle Isle and the great Gulf of St. Lawrence, and gave to France the boundless region of Canada.

Cartier, as stated, made two voyages, the first in 1534, on which occasion he discovered Canada; the second in 1535, on which occasion three fine vessels were fitted out by the French king, Francis I. (the same who twelve years before sent out Verrazano, 1523), for a voyage to Acadia. Each carried a complement of sixty men.[1] Cartier was a bold and skilful pilot of St. Malo, a seaport in the north-west of France, in the Province of Bretagne. This little town had been, like Palos in Spain, intimately connected with the vague pre-Columbian traditions of the unknown country of the West, which, doubtless, inspired its children with the spirit of adventure.

Jacques Cartier set out on his first voyage on the 20th of April, 1534, and, following the example of Cabot, held a due western course. On the 10th of May, after a very quick passage of twenty days, he sighted land, almost at the same point which Cabot had made thirty-seven years before, namely, the beautiful headland of Bonavista. He found this cape so much beset with ice that he was constrained to steer more to the south, and take refuge in a harbor about five leagues to the south-east. This harbor is called, in the narratives of the voyage, St. Catherine's Haven. Dr. Mullock, speaking of this name, attributes it to the Spanish voyagers. "The soft Spanish word for Catherine, *Catalina*, like Kath-

---

[1] It appears that he made a third voyage, in 1541.

leen in Irish." But it is expressly stated by Ferland that it
was so named by Cartier, and on this very occasion of his
being obliged to take refuge there from the ice-floe. It is
evident, from what we have just read, that Cartier was a
man of a thoroughly religious turn of mind, and, like Columbus and Cabot, fond of naming places after the saints. Now,

JACQUES CARTIER.

he left St. Malo on the 20th of April, and would have been
just ten days at sea, and about half-way on his voyage, when
the feast of the great Saint Catherine, of Siena (20th
April), occurred. It is quite possible that, in performing
his devotions and meditation on that day (a practice never
neglected by these early navigators), he made a vow or resolution to name in her honor the first port he should enter.
Again, he may have attributed to her intercession his safety
from a storm; for, although the voyage was a rather quick one,

yet it was rough. De Bourbourg says it was "*longue et pénible*,"— long and difficult; and Ferland gives some particulars (p. 22) : "There were three ships,— the 'Grand' and 'Petit Hermine,' and the 'Ermillon.' Cartier, with several young gentlemen volunteers, was aboard the first. The ships were separated by a succession of violent tempests, and did not reach their rendezvous, Blanc Sablon, on the coast of Labrador, till the 26th of July."

He remained ten days in Catalina, and started northward on the 21st of May. He arrived at an island called the Funk Island, where he filled his boats with birds, which were most numerous there. He came to the Straits of Belle Isle, which he called Golfe des Chateaux. This name, still retained by a cape and harbor on the Labrador coast, was given by Cartier on account of the peculiar and fantastic formation of the cliffs. They are thus described by Chapel, in the "Cruise of the Rosamond," 1813, p. 161 : This bay "is so called from the remarkable resemblance which it bears to an ancient castle; its turrets, arches, loopholes, and keeps are beautifully represented by a series of basaltic columns. The author could only regret his inability to delineate this singular headland, for it certainly presented as fine a subject for the pencil of the artist as the celebrated Cave of Fingal, or the no less noted Giant's Causeway." He thought then that this was the only entrance to the Grand Gulf. A little later he found the southern and wider entrance, between Newfoundland and Cape Breton. He entered Les Islettes, to-day called the Port of Bras d'Or, — a port afterwards called Port of Phelypeaux, — visited the Bay of Brest on the feast of St. Barnabas, Apostle (June 11), where he had Mass celebrated for the first time. He revisited the coast of Newfoundland, and on the 3d of July entered Bay Chaleur; anchored at Isle Bonaventure, Cape Percé, which he called Cap de Prato (Ferland); entered Gaspé 16th July and planted the Cross, and finally, on the feast of St. Ann (July 26), he arrived at the rendezvous Blanc Sablon. On the 15th August he arrived at St. Malo on his return.

In the following year (1535) preparations on a larger scale were made. The departure of the brave mariners on their perilous voyage was made the occasion of a scene of the greatest religious enthusiasm on the part of their fellow-citizens. The Abbé Brasseur du Bourbourg (p. 7) thus describes it: "Religion this time mingled the pomp of its solemnities with the departure of the fleet. All the crews, with their officers at their heads, after having confessed, went to the Cathedral of St. Malo, and received Communion from the hand of the Bishop. After that the Prelate gave them his solemn blessing, and it is to be believed that, according to the pious custom of the times, many chaplains departed with them." Ferland (p. 21) describes it as follows: "On Sunday, the Feast of Pentecost, the 16th of May of the year 1535, by command of the captain, and of the free-will (*bon vouloir*) of all, each one made his confession, and we received all together Our Creator (*Notre Créateur*) in the Cathedral Church of St. Malo, after which we went to present ourselves in the sanctuary (*au chœur*) before our reverend father in God, Monsieur of St. Malo, who, in his episcopal dignity (*état épiscopal*), gave us the benediction."

Two priests, or chaplains (*aumôniers*), accompanied them, namely, Dom Guillaume le Breton and Dom Antoine. From that time till the establishment of the bishopric of Quebec (1658) the Bishops of St. Malo had entire jurisdiction in New France.

Cartier set sail on his second voyage on Wednesday, the 19th May, 1535. His fleet consisted of three vessels: the "Grand Hermine," one hundred and twenty tons, the "Petit Hermine," sixty tons, and the "Ermillon," forty tons. He steered direct for the Straits of Belle Isle. He first made Cape Tiennot, and then entered the harbor of St. Nicholas, on the Labrador coast; thence he was blown by a gale to a harbor on the Newfoundland coast, on the 10th of August, the Feast of St. Lawrence, and he named it in honor of the saint. This place is described as a "very beautiful harbor, full of islands and with many entrances, and good anchorage in all weathers . . . there is an island like a head of land (*cap de terre*), which stands out beyond the others." Charlevoix remarks how the name of St. Lawrence, given to this harbor, afterwards extended to the whole gulf, called before "the River of Canada." Comparing Cartier's description with that of Captain Bayfield (Sailing Directions, Gulf of St. Lawrence), we find it to be the harbor now called St. Genevieve. "The islands of St. Lawrence are nine leagues from Port aux Esquimaux," says Rev. M. Plammodon, missionary priest. "I was struck by the resemblance of the Bay of St. Genevieve with St. Lawrence, described by Cartier; you cannot be mistaken. I recognized the mountain formed like an ear of corn (*tas de blé*) ; to-day it is called Partridge Head. I saw the great isle, like a *cap de terre*, which advances beyond the others," etc. Another account, however, states that he landed on the Island of Cape Breton, and built a fort near Cape North. He named the island "St. Lawrence," though it had been called by the English before that time Cape Britton, as appears in the account of the voyage of the "Dominus Vobiscum" in 1527. In Hore's Voyages, 1536, it is called Cape Breton, and in the time of Champlain, 1603, this name began to prevail. There is still a cape near Cape North called Cape St. Lawrence, which appears on Varrese's map, 1556. "It is established beyond doubt" (*constaté*), says Cheauveau ("Instruction Publique en Canada"), "that in those first two voyages Jacques Cartier had priests with him ; that Mass was said for the first time in New France, at the harbor of Brest, now Old Fort, on the coast of Labrador, on the 11th of June" (the Feast of St. Barnabas, Apostle, 1534) ; "but it does not appear that these priests were able to instruct or evangelize the Indians." Since, then, we know that there were priests with Cartier, and again that he remained ten days at Catalina before visiting Labrador, it is more than probable that Mass was celebrated there, and, if so, it would be the first time and place in which the Holy Sacrifice was offered in Newfoundland, or in all North America, as far as we have any authentic record.

It has already been remarked that we have no record of

any minister of the English Church accompanying the expedition of Sir Humphrey Gilbert. But, since he came with the express intention of establishing the Protestant form of worship, it is more than likely that he brought some minister with him and established him in the country. If so, the mission must have failed, for we hear nothing of it. In the year 1635 an enactment was passed by the Star Chamber, to the effect that in Newfoundland "Divine service should be performed, according to the ceremonial of the Church of England, on Sundays." Whether this necessarily implies the presence in the country of a minister or clergyman of that church, or not, I am not sufficiently initiated to pronounce.

We know, from the colonial papers preserved in the Record Office in London, that there was a minister of the Protestant Church in Newfoundland at the time of Lord Baltimore's settlement (1622), whose name was Stourton. It is probable that he came out with the colony of John Guy, some few years before (1610). He came to trouble with Lord Baltimore, as shall be seen further on.

This was probably the first attempt at the performance of missionary work by the ministers of the Reformed Church in the New World. The Plymouth Fathers did not come out to New England till the year 1620. "The Protestant citizens of the United States," says De Courcy ("History of Church in America," Chap. I.), "boast of the Puritan settlement in New England as the cradle of their race; but long before the Separatists landed at Plymouth in 1620, and while the English settlers hugged the Atlantic shore, too indifferent to instruct in Christianity the Indians whose hunting-grounds they had usurped, other portions of the continent were evangelized from north to south, and from east to west."

Even Bancroft, a Protestant writer, bears testimony to the fecundity of the Catholic missions. After drawing a magnificent picture of the Jesuit missionaries, whose early explorations of the wilderness, even from a scientific and commercial point of view, must win the admiration of all, he adds, "Thus did the religious zeal of the French bear the Cross to the banks of the St. Mary and the confines of Lake Superior, and look wistfully towards the homes of the Sioux in the valley of the Mississippi, five years before the New England Eliot had addressed the tribe of Indians that dwelt within six miles of Boston Harbor."

For several years immediately succeeding the unsuccessful attempt at colonization by Sir Humphrey Gilbert we read of isolated voyages made to Newfoundland, but no organized effort at forming a settlement. In 1593 Richard Strange, of Apham, made a voyage with the intention of prosecuting the seal-fishery. He made his head-quarters at Ramea, on the southern coast. In the following year, 1594, we read of a voyage of Captain Richard Jones. From this time forward numerous ships came out annually, and the coast was harassed by pirates. In 1596 the French pirate Michel de Sanci captured the English fishing-captain Richard Clarke. These pirates infested our coasts for many years. Whitbourne, writing in 1618, speaks of the archpirate Peter Easton, who kept him a prisoner for eleven days. There was also a celebrated French pirate of Rochelle, one Daniel Tibolo, and he (Whitbourne) tells us that there were even pirates from Barbary cruising on our coasts, so valuable were the prizes of fish and "trayne oil." This annoyance from the pirates was also one of the causes of the failure of Lord Baltimore's colony, as we shall see.

In 1597 Charles Leigh and Abraham Van Herwick, two London merchants, came out to Newfoundland. About the beginning of the seventeenth century the fisheries began for the first time to enlist considerable attention in England. French fishermen had already prosecuted the industry to such an extent that, in the year 1578, there were no less than one hundred and fifty vessels on the coast, and before the year 1609 one French fisherman had made more than *forty* voyages to America.

About this time Newfoundland narrowly escaped being

taken possession of by the French. The attempted colony of Quebec by Roberville and De la Roque having disastrously failed, Le Marquis de la Roche, a Breton gentleman, in 1598 was given a patent, with ample rights to found a colony in Newfoundland; but having imprudently chosen for the site of his settlement the miserable sand-bank known as Sable Island, all his followers, after unspeakable hardships, perished. Thus Newfoundland still remained a British colony.

In 1600 the Sieurs de Chauvin and Pontgravé, merchants of St. Malo, received from the French king, by royal patent, the monopoly of the fur trade. They established themselves at Tadousac, at the mouth of the Saguenay. A previous unsuccessful attempt to colonize Sable Island had been made by the Baron de Léry and St. Just in 1518, and again by the Portuguese in 1553. (Ferland, "Hist. du Canada.")

In 1609 John Guy, a merchant and alderman of Bristol, formed the "Newfoundland Company," and prepared to enter on colonization on a larger scale and in a more organized manner. The Company, consisting of Bristol and London merchants, was duly authorized, and, as usual, received a most generous patent from His Majesty King James I. The patent covered all Newfoundland "from the 46° to the 52° of north latitude, together with the seas and islands lying within ten leagues of the coast." Among the members of this company were the Earl of Northampton, Keeper of the Privy Seal, and Sir Francis Bacon. It is a mistake to speak of this nobleman as "Lord Bacon," as is generally done by writers of histories of Newfoundland. (See Harvey and Hatton, p. 21.) There was no such title. At this time he was simply Sir Francis Bacon. He was afterwards raised to the titles of Lord Verulam in 1618, when he was made Lord Chancellor of England, and Viscount St. Albans in 1621. He was a member of the Privy Council of James I., and Keeper of the Great Seal. He was a man of considerable learning and great literary taste. After the fashion of the public men of the day he gave a good deal of attention to colonization. He lent his name to the Bristol Company, but beyond that he does not seem to have taken much interest in the enterprise. In his "Historia Naturalis Experimentalis" he speaks of the rigor of the climate of Newfoundland, and explains it by the Arctic current and fogs.

Mr. John Guy was appointed first governor of the new settlement, and John Slaney, merchant of London, first treasurer. John Guy came out with his family and a company of about forty persons, in three ships, in 1610. It has been stated by all writers on the early history of Newfoundland that Guy established his colony at Mosquito [see Note 1], a small cove between Harbor Grace and Carbonear. Researches, however, lately made by James P. Howley, F.G.S., as already remarked, have brought to light the original letters written from Newfoundland by John Guy to John Slaney, which letters are dated from *Cuper's Cove*. Mr. Howley has no doubt whatever that the site was *not* Mosquito, but the settlement some miles farther south, in Conception Bay, now called *Cupid's*. In fact, the name had, as he shows, taken this corrupted, or rather improved, form at a very early date, for Sir William Alexander, the colonizer of Nova Scotia (1630), says, "The first houses for inhabitants were built at *Cupid's* Cove, Bay of Conception." Mr. Howley thus speaks of Mosquito: "The unlikelihood of selecting so bleak and exposed a situation as Mosquito does not appear to have occurred to any person. With nothing to recommend it either as a harbor for shipping or in the fertility of its soil; . . . neither does it appear that any relics, remains of buildings, etc., were ever discovered there." With regard to Cupid's he says: "Nowhere else was there to be met with a more choice locality. It is probable that it included the entire Bay de Grave. The long line of shingle beach, with the lagoon in the rear, now so well known as Clark's Beach, together with the two beautiful estuaries of Northern and Southern rivers, would offer just such attractions in their then primeval beauty."

Guy immediately set about building a fort and erecting houses, and made an enclosure one hundred and twenty feet by ninety feet, on which he mounted cannon. He remained two years in the country, and in his letters, lately published by Mr. Howley, speaks highly of the climate and natural resources. By his prudence and kindness he conciliated the Red Indians, and opened up a trade with them. His principal object was, no doubt, commercial enterprise; but though we have no account of his bringing any ministers of religion with him, still he seems to have had in view, at least as a secondary object, the conversion of the savages. A special mention of this purpose is made in the patent of James I. to the Bristol Company. "Thinking it a matter and action well beseeming a Christian King to make true use of that which God from the beginning created for mankind, and therefore intending not only to worke and procure the good and benefit of many of our subjects, but principally to increase the knowledge of the Omnipotent God, and the Propagation of our Christian Faith."

Guy sent on Captain Whittington " into the bottom of Trinity Bay, a place always frequented by the natives." (Kirke.) He had some interviews with the Indians, but we find no account at this time of any attempt to evangelize them. Trade and traffic were the paramount idea. Kirke, in the letter quoted from above, says, "Alderman Guy continued with his family in Newfoundland two yeares and amongst other designs especially aymed at a trade with the Indians." In describing a meeting between Whittington and the Indians he says, "And they did eate and drinke together for the space of three or four hours and exchanged furs and deere skins for hatchetts and kniues." He says that for years many French and Biscayans have traded with the natives of the country. He bears the following testimony to their shrewdness: "We can assure you . . . that if you had been amongst them you had beene confuted to the purpose with the hardest bargaine that ever you concluded since you were men of business.

CHAPTER V.

JOHN GUY'S SETTLEMENT.— [1610–1618.]

Failure of John Guy's Colony — Intercourse with Red Indians — Cruel Treatment of them by English Sailors — Difficulties between Planters and Fishermen — Whitbourne Arrives as Commissioner, 1615 — John Guy Abandons his Colony and Returns to England — Whitbourne Sent out by Dr. Vaughan to Found a Colony at Ferryland, 1618 — Calvert's Views on Colonization.

AT the time of the inception of the colony in Conception Bay under John Guy and his Bristol and London company, a young man came to the front in English diplomatic circles who was soon to take a leading place in the colonization movement, and who was to bring forward into a more prominent position the religious element in the British Plantation schemes.

This was George Calvert, afterwards Lord Baltimore. Although it does not appear that Calvert took any active or actual part in the formation of Guy's colony, yet it is certain that even before that time he had turned his mind to the subject of Plantation, and had formed distinctly pronounced views on the matter, — views which he afterwards endeavored to put in practice in his colony of Ferryland, and which he so successfully carried out in his colony of Maryland as to cause it to be held up as a model to all future colonies.

In a passage in the "Bibliographia Britannica" a contrast is made between the views of Chief Justice Popham and those of Calvert on the subject of colonization. "Judge Popham and he agreed in the public design of foreign plantations, but differed in the manner of managing them. The first was for extirpating the original inhabitants, the second for converting them. The former sent the lewdest people to those places; the latter the soberest. The one was for making present profit, the other for a reasonable expectation."

Judge Popham died in 1607. Calvert was then about twenty-eight years of age, and was a clerk in the service of Sir Robert Cecil, in the Treasury Department, so that it may possibly refer to Calvert's views at a later period as at

LORD BALTIMORE.

that time. As far as we know he had not taken any public part in colonial matters, and was not in a position of sufficient importance to have been quoted in opposition to Judge Popham. At the time of Guy's colony, 1610, he had been promoted to the position of clerk of the Privy Council. There can be no doubt, then, that he took a most lively interest in the new colony, as we find him soon after (1620) entering deeply into the project himself at Ferryland. Many causes combined to cause the failure of Guy's colony, among which must first be mentioned the incursions of the Indians, as in the case of Lord Baltimore, subsequently, at Ferryland; but from the account given by Kirke, from which we have quoted, it would appear that the Europeans were generally the first aggressors in those skirmishes with the Indians. On the occasion elsewhere spoken of, the interview between Captain Whittington and the Indians in Trinity Bay, it was agreed that a meeting should be held the next year " by a signe (as is their manner in other parts of America), when the grass should be of such a height, to bring down all their furs and skins for traffique with the English. . . . It soe fell out that the next yeare, at the time appointed for their meetinge . . . instead of Captain Whittington . . . there came a fisherman . . . and seeing a companie of Indians . . . let fly his shott from aboard amongst them . . . and they . . . retyred immediately into the woode and from that day to this have sought all occasion every fishinge season to do all the mischief they can amongst the fishermen." Whitbourne also describes an act of robbery committed upon a party of Indians at the harbor of Heart's Ease, at the north side of Trinity Bay. The mariners of the ship " Tapson," of Devon, " being robbed in the night of their apparell did the next day seeke after them, and happened to come suddenly where they had set up three tents and were feasting. They had three canoes, great store of fowle's egges, skins of Deere, Beavers, Beares, Seales, Otters, and divers other fine skins, which were excellent well dressed; as also great store of seuerall sorts of flesh dryed; and by shooting off a musquet towards them, they all ran away naked . . . all their three canowes, their flesh-skins, yolkes of egges, targets, Bowes and Arrowes and much fine Okar, and divers other things they tooke and brought away, and shared among those that took it." Thus we see the origin of that feud between white man and Indian which terminated in the extinction of the savages. We need not wonder, then, to hear of such speedy and terrible reprisals as those described by Sir David Kirke.

"In the Harbor of Les Ouages," he says, "about eighty Indians assaulted a company of Frenchmen while they were pleyinge upp their fishinge, and slewe seven of them; proceedinge a little further, killed nine more in the same manner, and clothinge sixteen of their Company in the apparell of the slayne French, they went on the next day to the Harbor of Petty-Masters, and not being suspected, by reason of their habit, they surprised them at their works and killed twenty one more. Soe in two days having barbarously maymed thirty seven, they returned home, as is their Manner in great triumph, with the heads of the Slayne Frenchmen."

Add to these causes the troubles which Governor Guy had to contend with among the fishermen. The charter or patent of colonization reserved the rights of fishing on the coasts to all comers, English or others; but many abuses and bad customs crept in, and the governor issued a proclamation in order to repress them. He also laid a tax upon their cargoes, and levied some other exactions. This excited complaints among the fishermen. They ignored and repudiated the proclamation, and sent in a petition and divers complaints to the Privy Council. They complained, *First*, that the "planters" had expelled them from some of the best fishing harbors. *Secondly*, That their provisions had been seized by the "planters." *Thirdly*, That they had been prevented from taking birds for bait for fishing; and that pirates were permitted to harbor on the coast to their great annoyance. (Kirke, "Conquest of Canada," p. 138.) These complaints were forwarded by the Earl of Bath, October, 1618. They were all and singly rebutted and denied by the planters. They complained of the disorders of the fishermen and of pirates, and petitioned for naval protection. To remedy this state of confusion Sir Richard Whitbourne was sent out with a commission from the Admiralty to empanel juries and try disorderly fishermen. We have already given, in

Whitbourne's own language, an account of his arrival on Trinity Sunday, June 4, 1615, at Trinity Harbor, and of his holding the first court of justice in the island. He drew up several statutes to remedy prevalent abuses, such as "Working on Sabbath, stealing salt, boats, hooks, lines, nets, idling about during working time."

All these increasing difficulties caused Governor Guy to lose heart in the settlement, so that, as before stated, he retired with his family after two years' sojourn in the Island, and the settlement gradually sank into insignificance before the newly rising settlement in the South, though, for some years after, a governor was left in charge of the settlement. In the year 1621, John Mason being governor, all the rights of the company were bought out by Sir George Calvert.

We have seen that, in the year 1615, Richard Whitbourne came out commissioner to exercise judicial authority in Newfoundland. It would appear that this commission expired soon after, as we find from his own narrative that he was again in Newfoundland on his own account, the following year, 1616, "with a ship of 100 ton," and that on her return voyage she was rifled by "a French Pyrate of Rochell one Daniel Tibolo."

About the following year, 1617, Dr. Vaughan purchased from the patentees of the Newfoundland Company a tract of land in the southern part of the country, of which he appointed Whitbourne governor. This plantation was intended to be set up at Ferryland. Whether any actual settlement was made on the spot is not quite certain. Whitbourne states that he came out in the year 1618 to found this plantation, and that one of his ships was "intercepted by an English erring Captaine who went forth with Sir Walter Rawleigh. He took the master, boatswain and two of the best men, and all the victuals," and thus hindered the plantation.

CHAPTER VI.

FERRYLAND. — [1618–1622.]

Sir George Calvert — His Early Career — Bancroft's Bigotry — Calvert's Conversion — His Enthusiasm — " A Baltimore Penny " — Colony of Maryland — Lord Baltimore's Spirit of Toleration — Persecution of Popery by the Protestant Parliament, 1654.

SUCH was the state of affairs in the colony when Sir George Calvert began to turn his mind more earnestly towards the work of colonization. At the time of the foundation of the Newfoundland Company (1609) Calvert was, as we stated, about twenty-nine years of age. He was born about the year 1578, of a respectable family of Ripling, in the chapelry of Bolton, Yorkshire, and was at that time employed as secretary to Sir Robert Cecil, who the year previous (1608) had been appointed Lord High Treasurer, so that he was in a position to be well informed upon all matters concerning the new plantations.

In the year 1617 he was knighted. He had been educated at Oxford, and had passed with high honors, having published a Latin ode while an undergraduate which displayed great scholarly taste. (Richardson.) In 1618, the same year in which Dr. Vaughan made his attempt to colonize Ferryland, Sir George was made Secretary of State to the King, who settled £1,000 per annum upon him. (Kirke.) He had married in 1604, and his eldest son, Cecil (named after his quondam patron, and afterwards founder of Maryland), was then (1618) just fourteen years old. Sir George was chosen by an immense majority to represent in Parliament his native county of Yorkshire. His capacity for business, his industry, and his fidelity are acknowledged by all historians. (Bancroft.)

Dr. Mullock, in his lecture, speaks of Calvert as a "zealous

Catholic and most enlightened philanthropist." He was,
however, a convert from Protestantism. Bancroft gives the
following generous account of his religious convictions: "In
an age when religious controversy still continued to be
active, and when the increasing divisions among Protestants were spreading a general alarm, his mind sought
relief from controversy in the bosom of the Roman Catholic
Church; and, preferring the avowal of his opinions to the
emoluments of office, he resigned his place and openly professed his conversion." (Vol. I., Chap. VII.) It is to be
regretted that Bancroft, in the last revised and centenary
editions of his work (1875 and 1883), should have been
so influenced by a wave of bigotry that passed over the
American continent as to change, or entirely omit, all the
several passages in which, in fifteen former editions, he had
done honor to the noble liberality of Calvert and to his true
catholic spirit. In the last edition he states, on the mere *ipse
dixit* of one Rev. Mr. Neil, a Presbyterian minister, that most
of the men brought over by Calvert were Protestants; that
the colony was, in effect, a Protestant colony; and that
Lord Baltimore was influenced, not by religious motives,
or the desire of founding a colony where religious persecution should not be tolerated, but solely by a desire to
aggrandize his family. For a full and triumphant refuta-
tion of these unfair and ungenerous statements see a
series of articles in the "Catholic World," October and
November, 1883, and April and May, 1884, by Rev. H.
Clarke, LL.D. Nearly all the authors whom I have read
state that Calvert was a convert. Richardson, however, in
the article "A Baltimore Penny" ("Magazine of American
History"), from which I have been drawing largely, says
it is not certain that he was not a Catholic all his lifetime,
and that the fact was only made publicly known on his
refusing to take the oath of allegiance. It is well known
that the taking of the oath was frequently evaded, and that
many who were privately known to be Catholics, or at least
suspected of Popish leanings, were allowed to go unmo-

lested. The immediate occasion of Calvert's public declaration of his faith arose out of the following circumstances: A treaty of marriage had been entered into between the kings of Spain and England on behalf of the Prince Charles and the Infanta. The prince, with the Duke of Bucking-

CECIL, SECOND LORD BALTIMORE.

ham, went to the court of Spain to urge his own suit; but the result was that the match was broken off. This was received with joy by the people, who did not wish a Catholic alliance; but it was a source of deep regret to Calvert, for he knew that it meant the continuance of the penal laws against the Catholics, which, in the event of the marriage, King James had promised to relax. Buckingham resented

Calvert's disapproval, and a coolness arose between them. Calvert resigned his office of secretary, but was retained in the Privy Council. "After the coronation of King Charles (1625) the oath of allegiance was tendered to the Privy Councillors, but Lord Baltimore declined to repeat the formula. . . . The oath then in use was devised after the discovery of the Gunpowder Plot in 1605, and contained the following passage: 'I do further swear, that I do from my heart abhor, detest and abjure as impious and heretical, this damnable doctrine and position, that princes which be excommunicated or deprived by the Pope may be deposed or murthered by their subjects or any other whatsoever.' These words implied, and were meant to imply, that a suspicion of disloyalty and treason might justly rest upon every Catholic subject. Lord Baltimore refused to countenance this suspicion, but he retained the king's esteem and friendship unabated. "It was not by Catholics that King Charles was afterwards deposed and murdered, but by a Puritan Parliament. On the contrary, when Charles raised the Royal Standard, in 1641, against the rebels, and invited all his faithful subjects to come forward in defence of the Crown, the Roman Catholics, though fettered with penal laws, and branded with the repute of disaffection towards a Protestant sovereign, hastened among the foremost to testify their loyalty. They levied troops at their own expense; they marched against the rebels; they sacrificed their property, their ease, their health and lives, for the king and constitution; and this at a time when many of their clergy were iniquitously dragged like malefactors to prison, and from prison to the gallows." (Reeves, "History of the Church," p. 593.) It is generally thought that the refusal to take the oath by Lord Baltimore indicated a change of religion; but it is quite possible that he had never before been confronted with the oath, and thus his Catholicity was not publicly known. This does not show any weakness of faith on his part, for, whenever seriously called upon, he was always ready to profess it at any cost. Thus, when a few years later (1629), on leaving his colony of Ferryland and arriving in Virginia for the first time, the Puritan Governor Pott tendered him the oath of allegiance and supremacy which had been administered to all the colonists, he again refused to take it. (Richardson, p. 209.)

Kirke, who was by no means favorably disposed towards Calvert, attributes his desire of settlement in the New World to the necessity in which he found himself, on account of "his changed religious views, of escaping from unpleasantness in England," after his conversion.

This is, however, doing but scanty justice to the noble

THE WATERVILLE PENNY.

sentiments which really actuated Calvert in the establishment of his new colony. That his religious convictions were strong cannot be doubted, from the fact of his resigning, on account of them, his position of honor and emolument at court. But the after-events of his career show that they must have reached the enthusiastic, if they did not actually verge upon the heroic. His calling his new colony by the name of Avalon shows a mind of a high religious and romantic turn. Even Kirke, in a note (page 144), says: "It was so called by Lord Baltimore with the idea that this province was the place in America where Christianity was first introduced; Avalon being the name of an ancient place in Somersetshire, on which Glastonbury now stands, and which is said to be the place where Christianity was first preached in Britain." He seems to have been so thoroughly imbued with this idea of establishing Christianity in the New World, that it lends a tinge to each incident of his enterprise. Thus we find that he gave the name of "The Ark of Avalon" to his principal ship, and that of "The Dove" to her pinnace. "And on a coin which he had stamped is seen a thorn with the motto '*Spinâ Sanctus*' (sanctified by the thorn), in allusion to the original Avalon, where there is a miraculous thorn which blossoms at Christmas-tide, and is believed to be the veritable staff of St. Joseph of Arimathea, . . . thus picturing himself at one time as a new Joseph of Arimathea, inspired to plant the Christian religion in a heathen land; and again, as a modern Noah, sailing in the ark over the waste seas to found a better community than that which for him was doomed and lost beyond the watery horizon."

The coin above mentioned is minutely described by Richardson in his very learned article already quoted from. The subject is so interesting that, at the risk of being tedious, I here give an outline of this curious relic. It was discovered while making some excavations in the village of Waterville, Me., in June, 1880. It bears no date; it is copper, and of excellent workmanship. It shows on obverse side a harp or lyre, surrounded by a wreath of bay-leaves, and bearing the inscriptions, beneath the lyre, "*Orpheus*"; above, the Greek legend, *APIΣTON MHN AHP* (Ariston Men Aer), "*The air is the best.*" On the reverse is a shield with a cross in field, surmounted by a mitre with crosier and processional cross; beneath the shield, a thorn and an oak branch. The legends are, below, "*Spinâ Sanctus*"; above, "*Pro patria et Avalonia.*" Calvert had undoubtedly the right to coin money. He was Lord Palatine of Avalon, and he was also invested with absolute ecclesiastical as well as civil authority; hence the mitre and crosier. The cross and the lyre or harp were adopted from the money struck about this time by King James, and later (1649) by Cromwell. The cross was the Cross of St. George. The harp is supposed to have first appeared on copper coins, "with the purpose, it is believed, of sending them to Ireland if the English people refused them." The word *Orpheus* indicates the introduction of civilization and the fine arts. *Spind Sanctus* has been already explained. *Pro patria et Avalonia*, "For fatherland and Avalon," explains itself. The legend about the good quality of the air seemed to puzzle Mr. Richardson. "Conjecture," he says, "fails to define the significance of the phrase"; but I think I have found the solution, for the first governor of the new colony of Ferryland, Edward Wynne, writing to Lord Baltimore, in 1622, speaks in glowing terms of the climate, and uses the identical words, "The ayre is very healthful." Mr. Richardson, however, has since informed me that he is strongly inclined to believe that the coin belongs to the British Avalon; but it seems not at all likely that such a coin would be made for England, or, if so, that it could find its way to the village of Waterville.

"The strong religious spirit which actuated Lord Baltimore is again apparent in the foundation (a few years later) of the colony of Maryland; for, no way daunted by the failure and disappointments and heavy financial losses met with in Newfoundland, he entered with the same enthusiastic spirit upon his second venture. No sooner had he obtained his charter for the Province of Maryland than he immediately applied to Father Blount, the first provincial of the newly-created English province of the Jesuits, and also to Father Mutius Vitelleschi, the sixth general of the Society, for some of the English subjects to accompany the expedition, and to attend to the Catholic planters, and instruct and convert the native Indians. The design was approved of, and Father Andrew White was selected and ordered to prepare for that mission."[1] The apostolic labors of Father White are matters of history. He is said to have taken a leading, though unobtrusive, part in framing the constitution of the

---

[1] Bro. Foley, S.J., Records of the English Jesuits. Vol. VII., p. 335.

new colony; and the bill by which religious freedom is
granted to all persons in the State is said to have been drawn
up, or at least inspired, by him. This is stated on the unsuspected authority of Mr. Kenedy, a Presbyterian member of
the Assembly of Maryland. Father White was assisted by
Fathers Altham, Knowles, and Copley. "They were summoned to sit in the first Assembly of 'freemen' in the Province; but, earnestly desiring to be excused from taking
part in the secular concerns of the colony, their request
was granted."[1] On the first occasion on which they were
summoned (January 25, 1637) they are excused on the
ground of sickness. The entry in the "Archives of Maryland" is as follows: "M^r. Thomas Copley Esq. of S^t.
Maries hundred Gent. M^r. Andrew White, M^r. John Altham of the same hundred. Robert Clerke gent appeared
for them, and excused their Absence by reason of sickness."
And on the second occasion (January 26) Robert Clerke
"made answere for them that they desired to be excused
from giving voices in this Assembly, and was admitted."

It may not be without interest to quote here some portion
of the "Act concerning Religion," passed in the "Gen'āl
Session held at S^t. Maries on the One and Twentieth day
of Aprill Anno Dñi. 1649," and supposed to have been inspired, if not composed, by Father Andrew White, S.J.:—

"Fforasmuch as in a well governed Xpian Comōn Wealth
Matters Concerning Religion and the honor of God ought
in the first place to be taken into serious consideracion
. . . Whatsoever p'son or p'sons shall . . . blaspheme God . . . that is curse Him or Deny Our Saviour Jesus Christ to bee the Sonne of God . . . or shall
deny the Holy Trinity . . . or shall utter any reproachfull Speeches concerning . . . Said Trinity . . .
shall be punished with death . . . or shall utter any
reproachfull words Concerning the Blessed Virgin Mary

---

[1] Bro. Foley, p. 337.

... the Holy Apostles or Evangelists ... the sume of *ffive* pounds."

"Whatsoever p'son ... shall ... call or denominate any p'son ... an heretick, Schismatick, Idolator, Puritan, Independent, Calvinist, Anabaptist, Brownist, Antinomian, Barrowist, Roundhead, Sep'atist, or any other name or terme in a reproachfull manner shall forfeit ten shillings sterling."

"Be it therefore enacted ... that no person ... professing to believe in Jesus Christ shall ... bee any waies troubled molested, or discountenanced for or in respect of his or her Religion, nor in the free exercise thereof ... nor any way compelled to the beliefe or exercise of Any other Religion against his or her Consent."

How very different from this liberal and enlightened piece of legislation is that of the acts passed a few years later (1654) by the same Assembly, under the guidance of its Puritan masters, who, owing to the change of affairs in England, had become lords of the new colony! England had gone through the throes of a civil war (1641); had arrested and executed a king (1649); the monarchy had given place to a republic. "Englishmen were no longer lieges of a Sovereign, but members of a Commonwealth." Murmurs began to arise among the colonists against the quasi monarchical power of Baltimore. Visions of liberty arose. "The overthrow of the monarchy in England" (says Bancroft) "seemed about to confer unlimited power upon the embittered enemies of the Romish Church." "The dissolution of the Long Parliament threatened a change in the political condition of Maryland" (p. 197). An ordinance was issued by the Commonwealth for the reduction of the rebellious colonies, *i.e.*, the colonies that had remained faithful to the dethroned monarch, Charles II. Acting on this ordinance, Clayborne, governor of the neighboring colony of Virginia, who had always been the jealous enemy of the colony of Maryland, took possession of the settlement, deprived Stone, Lord Baltimore's deputy, of his commission, and immediately proceeded to the enactment of a law proscribing the Catholic religion (Oct. 20, 1654), of which the following is an extract: —

SECTION 4. "It is enacted . . . that none who profess and exercise the Popish Religion, Commonly known by the Name of the Roman Catholick Religion, can be protected in this Province, . . . but are to be restrained from the exercise thereof. . . . Such as profess faith in God . . . shall be protected . . . in the profession of the faith, Provided this liberty *be not extended to Popery or prelacy*."

So great was the zeal of the Jesuit fathers, and the number of their conversions so large, that after a few years the anger of the Puritans, who had taken possession of the neighboring colony of Virginia, was aroused, and several complaints were made to Lord Baltimore against them by his secretary, Mr. Sewgar, in whose charge he had left the infant colony. This gave occasion to Father Henry Moore, then (1640) Vice-Provincial of the Jesuits in England, to write a lengthy appeal to the Cardinal Prefect of Propaganda, from which we obtain another testimony to the religious motives of Lord Baltimore. "The said Baron (Lord Baltimore) immediately (on obtaining his patent) treated with Father Richard Blount, at that time provincial, at the same time writing to the Father General, earnestly begging that he would elect certain fathers, as well for confirming the Catholics in the faith, and converting the heretics who were destined to colonize that country, as also for propagating the faith amongst the infidels and savages."[1] But the religious zeal of Lord Baltimore was not of the fiery, persecuting character; it was, on the contrary, of the mildest and gentlest tone, so that the constitution of his new colony

---

[1] Bro. Foley, *loc. cit.*, p. 364-5.

had for its fundamental principle freedom of religious belief, commanding only as a *sinè qua non* the belief in the Godhead, of the Trinity, and the divinity of Jesus Christ. So bright an example, and so exceptional was this new colony, of moderation and liberty, that it has called forth unbounded encomiums, especially from Protestant writers. Bancroft (Vol. I., p. 187) says, "Religious liberty obtained a home, its only home, in the wide world, at the humble village which bore the name of St. Mary's. . . . Every other country in the world had persecuting laws. . . . The Roman Catholics, who were oppressed by the laws of England, were sure to find a peaceful asylum in the quiet harbors of the Chesapeake, and there, too, Protestants were sheltered against Protestant intolerance. . . . Ever intent on advancing the interests of his colony Lord Baltimore invited the Puritans of Massachusetts to emigrate to Maryland, offering them lands and privileges and *free liberty of religion*" (p. 191). . . . "The disfranchised friends of Prelacy from Massachusetts, and the Puritans from Virginia, were welcomed to equal liberty of conscience and political rights in the Roman Catholic province of Maryland" (p. 191).

This lengthy digression concerning the foundation of the colony of Maryland will be pardoned, first, as, though not immediately connected with the history of Newfoundland, it throws great light on the character and designs of the man who made so strenuous and expensive an effort to colonize Newfoundland, and whose name, notwithstanding the failure of his attempt, deserves undying gratitude from every son of our Island home. Second, because the documents concerning the foundation in Newfoundland are but meagre and scarce, and the more ample archives of Maryland help to fill up the blanks, and to show us what Lord Baltimore would have done for Newfoundland had his first settlement been a success.

CHAPTER VII.

FOUNDATION OF FERRYLAND.—[1622-1628.]

Foundation of Ferryland Colony — Lord Baltimore's Patent — Its Extent — Edward Wynne, First Governor — Meaning of the Name Ferryland — Description of Settlement from Captain Powell — Sir Arthur Ashton Arrives, May, 1627 — Lord Baltimore Arrives in Ferryland, July 23, 1627 — Brings out Jesuit Priests — Catholic Religion Established — Mass Celebrated Daily — Indignation of the Anglican Minister, Rev. Mr. Stourton — His Expulsion from the Colony — Calvert Arrives, Second Time, with his Lady and Family, 1628.

IN the manuscript history of Dr. Mullock a spirited outline is drawn of the foundation of Lord Baltimore's colony; but since that was written (1860) more than a quarter of a century has passed, and many documents have been brought to light, not only among the colonial archives, but also among family papers and domestic chronicles, which enable us to fill in the accessories of the picture in all its details.

Whitbourne's "Discourse and Discovery," etc., in which he wrote so glowingly of the soil, climate, and products of the Island; of the gentleness of the natives; even of the meekness of the wolves; of the great advantages of a settlement, etc., was printed by order of King James, and distributed largely throughout the kingdom, and awakened a very lively interest in the Island. On the title-page of the book we read, "Imprinted by Authority at London by Felix Kingston, 1622. A Discourse and Discovery of Newfoundland with many reasons to prove how worthy and beneficiall a Plantation may there be made after a far better manner than now is."

After the dedication comes an address,—"To His Majesties good subjects." He continues: "The island of Newfound Land is large, temperate and fruitful. . . . The Natives are ingenious and apt by discreet and moderate governments to be brought to obedience." He points out the "Overpopulousnesse of England"; the advance of the "Lowe Countries" by their colonies; the glory of enlarging dominion; "and that which will crowne the worke will be the advancement of the Honour of God in bringing poor Infidels to His worship and their own salvation." After seventy-two pages full of information and encouragement follows a "Second motive and Inducement, as a louing inuitation . . . showing the particular charge for Victualling forth a Ship of 100 tons burthen with 40 men, for the advancing of His Majestie's Most hopefull Plantation in Newfound Land." Then follows "A conclusion," showing forth some things omitted. It may be imagined that such an enthusiastic and glowing account excited great interest among all classes in England, and Sir George Calvert, who had already conceived the idea of founding a colony, was induced by it to choose Newfoundland as the site of his settlement. Accordingly he applied to the king for a patent, which he obtained on the last day of the year 1622, the very same on which Whitbourne's "Discourse" was published. In March, 1623, the grant was confirmed under the king's sign-manual, with additional privileges.

It is generally stated by historians that the patent of Lord Baltimore included only that portion of Newfoundland known as the Eastern Peninsula, or the Peninsula of Avalon, and not merely, as Dr. Mullock states, "all that portion of the coast extending from Bay Bulls to Cape St. Mary's." Bancroft (Vol. I., p. 181) speaks of it erroneously as "the southern promontory of Newfoundland." Kirke ("Conquest of Canada," p. 144), says, "He obtained a grant of Newfoundland, or rather of the south or smaller part of the Island"; and in a note he says, "Lord Baltimore's province, which forms the south-east part of Newfoundland, is a peninsula of twenty-six marine leagues in length, and from five to twenty in breadth. It is separated from the main island by two extensive bays, the heads of which are divided by a narrow isthmus or beach not exceeding four miles in width."

This applies to the whole peninsula of Avalon, and is
the common opinion of nearly all historians. Richardson,
however, contends strongly that Calvert obtained the whole
island, having bought the rights of the former grantees,
that is, the Newfoundland Company, founded by John Guy,
and *they* undoubtedly possessed all the island, as we have
already seen. In support of this view, Richardson quotes a
portion of the words of the patent, as follows: "All that entire
portion of land situate within our country of Newfoundland,
and all the islands within ten leagues of the eastern
shore thereof." But these words do not seem conclusive on
the point. They are evidently incomplete, and may be interpreted
as a *part* of the Island, if they do not actually imply
such a meaning. The words quoted are taken from Gainsbury's
"Calendar of State Papers, Colonial Series," p. 42.
In the same document we find: "1622 Decr 31 Grant to Sir
George Calvert and his heirs of the whole country of Newfound
Land." Again, when, some years after, Sir David
Kirke received a patent for the colony abandoned by Calvert,
it is distinctly declared to cover "all that whole Island,
Continent or Region knowne by the Name of Newfound
Land."

Whatever may have been the extent of the territory conceded
to Calvert, — and it must be confessed the sovereigns
of those days were extremely *generous*, and rather vague in
their notions of New-World geography, — it is certain that
jurisdiction of the highest form was conferred on Calvert.
His patent was couched in the same terms as those granted
to Sir William Alexander in Nova Scotia, to Sir Ferdinando
Gorges in New England, and his son, Cecil, afterwards for
Maryland. He was made Lord Palatine, with power to coin
money, to grant titles, to appoint clergymen, as well as civil
and military officers. In fact, he was invested with absolute
civil and ecclesiastical authority. The scheme of colonization
was modelled on that of the mediæval palatinate, of
which, at that time, the only one remaining in England was
the county of Durham. The Bishop was Lord Palatine, and

combined civil and religious jurisdiction. Hence, on the coin of Lord Baltimore, as before mentioned, is seen the mitre and crosier, in token of spiritual dominion. (Richardson, *loc. cit.*)

Sir George Calvert sent out, as first governor and general agent of his new colony, one Capt. Edward Wynne, with a small body of men. There is a discrepancy between the dates given by historians and the letters of Governor Wynne published at the end of Whitbourne's "Discourse." Kirke states that Calvert obtained his patent "on the 31st day of December, 1622." Richardson (quoting from the Colonial Papers, pp. 25, 26) gives the following account: "In March, 1621, his (Calvert's) attention had been officially called to the plantation in Newfoundland by a petition from the Company of Adventurers" (namely, John Guy's Company in Cupids). We have already seen the grievances complained of by the settlers at various times between the years 1610 and 1620, the colonists asking for naval protection against the encroachments of the fishermen, the attacks of the Indians by land and the pirates by sea. They requested that John Mason, governor of the colony, should be appointed king's lieutenant with two ships to correct these irregularities. The petition was referred to Secretary Calvert.

It was not until the last day of the year 1622 that Calvert acquired possession of his territory, and his patent is dated March, 1623 (April 7, according to Gainsbury's "Calendar of State Papers.") Calvert, however, must have sent over the first instalment of colonists previous to this time; for the first letter to Lord Baltimore from Governor Wynne is dated "Ferryland, July, 1622," and is entitled "A letter from Captaine Edward Wynne Governor of the Colony at Ferryland within the prouince of Aualon in Newfound Land unto the Right Honorable Sir George Calvert Knight, His Majestie's Principall Secretary: July 1622." With regard to the origin of the name of the colony so beautifully conceived by Dr. Mullock, the above-quoted letter forces us reluctantly to reject his opinion that the name is a corruption of Verulam. Dr. Mullock writes as follows in his manuscript history: "A zealous Catholic and enlightened philanthropist he (Calvert) determined that his territory should be blessed with the faith of Christ, and the names he imposed on the Province he acquired and the town which he founded, are a proof of his Catholic feelings. At Glastonbury, in Somersetshire, was an ancient and venerable abbey dedicated to St. Joseph of Arimathea, who took down from the Cross and interred in his own tomb the body of Our Saviour. The ancient name of this abbey was Avalon. It was a tradition equally cherished by Britons, Saxons, and Normans that St. Joseph was banished from Judea, after the death of Christ; that he went to Britain, and finally settled in Avalon; introduced the gospel, and there founded the first Christian establishment in the Island. Though this pious tradition rests on no historical foundation, still the abbey, which covered sixty acres of land, and whose magnificent ruins still remain . . . flourished amidst the veneration of the people till suppressed by Henry VIII., who put the last abbot to death for refusing to surrender his sacred trust to the hateful tyrant. Calvert then wished to revive the name of Avalon, the cradle of Christianity in Britain, on this side of the Atlantic. And now the whole Eastern Peninsula of Newfoundland bears the sacred name, and is called the Province of Avalon. On a beautiful promontory on the Southern Shore he erected his own residence, and with true Catholic and British feeling he called the settlement VERULAM, the Roman name of the present town of St. Alban's. This saint was the protomartyr of Britain. When the land became Christian, a magnificent abbey was erected there, one of whose abbots, Breakspear, became Pope, under the title of Adrian IV., and the town itself lost its Roman appellation, and was called after its patron. Calvert, therefore, called his province Avalon, in honor of St. Joseph of Arimathea, and his town VERULAM, in honor of St. Alban. The name was at first corrupted into *Ferulam*, and finally settled down into the vulgar and trivial name of Ferryland." Thus Doctor Mullock; but we cannot accept the very beautiful theory, at least so far as the name of Ferryland is concerned; for, in all the letters written by the governor of the place at the first founding of the colony, those of Captain Powell, of a gentleman signing himself " N. H.," and also of Lord Baltimore himself, addressed from the colony to King Charles, of date Aug. 19, 1629, the name is distinctly spelt FERRYLAND, and there is no vestige of a corruption from *Verulam*. No doubt this idea was suggested to Dr. Mullock from the fact that Sir Francis Bacon, Lord Verulam, was a member of the first Newfoundland Company established at Cupids; but he had no connection with Lord Baltimore's colony. Moreover, the ancient name of Verulam was not known in England in the time of Calvert, it having been superseded by that of St. Alban's, which would more probably have been the name chosen by Calvert for his new town had he thought of it.

The place was called Ferryland before Calvert settled there. Captain Richard Whitbourne, writing in 1619, previous to Calvert's establishment, calls it *Foriland*. On a map published in Taverner's " British Pilot," 1747, it is spelt Foriland and Foreland. This writer probably thought it might have been named after the points so well known in the British Channel as the North and South Forelands. But it is *certainly* a corruption of the French word *Forillon*. This old French word signifies *separated* or *standing out from*, as it were a piece of rock *bored* or dug out from the rest of the land by the action of the waves; from the Latin *forare*, to dig or bore; French, *forer*. In a note in Champlain's "Voyages," 1603, p. 4, we read: "*Gaspé ou Gachpè suivant M. L'Abbé J. A. Mourault ce nom serait une contraction du mot Abenaquis Katespi qui est ' Separément' qui est separé de l'autre terre on sait en effet que le Forillon aujourdhui miné par la violence des vagues était une rocher remarquable separé du cap de Gaspé.*" Gaspé or Gachpí, according to Father J. A. Mourault, is a contraction of the Abenaquis

(Indian tribe) word *Katespi*, which means *separately*, or that which is separated from the mainland; and, in fact, it is well known that the *Forillon*, to-day dug out by the violence of the waves, is a remarkable rock separated from the Cape of Gaspé. This rock, which was known as "The Old Man and Woman," has been so undermined by the action of the water that it crumbled away and disappeared some few years ago. Now, there can be no doubt that Ferryland is an English corruption of this French word

THE HAZURES, OR HARE'S EARS, AT FERRYLAND, CALLED BY THE FRENCH "FORILLON."

Forillon. The well-known rock at Ferryland head, called the *Hazures* (itself a corruption of hare's ears), corresponds exactly with the description given above of Gaspé. This name was of general use by the French to designate such rocks. There is one of the same sort near St. Lawrence, Placentia Bay, called by the same name, and by the fishermen of Newfoundland it is corrupted to *Ferryland*. The settlement continued to be called *Forillon* by the French up to the date of 1696, when it was captured by the Sieur D'Iberville. An account of the capture (from which we shall afterwards quote) was written by the chaplain of the army, M. l'Abbé Baudouin, in which he speaks of it all through as *Forillon*.

In the letter above alluded to as written from Ferryland by Governor Wynne, in July, 1622, he speaks of a former letter written by him the previous year, "the last letter of the previous year dated September 5, 1621," which implies that he must have written other letters during that year of 1621. It is, therefore, certain that the colony was founded about that time. It was certainly then in its infancy. He acknowledges the receipt, on the 17th of May, 1622, of a letter written by Calvert on the 19th of February, brought by one Robert Stoning. There were only twelve men all that winter in the colony, until the spring. On May 26, 1622, Captain Daniel Powell arrived with an additional reënforcement of twenty men, making in all thirty-two. Powell brought letters from Calvert, dated March 14. Powell, however, did not take shipping from Plymouth till the "18th of Aprill," making a voyage of less than five weeks, which was very fair for the season of the year. Governor Wynne gives a minute description of the buildings erected and in course of construction. The first range of buildings erected about All-hallowtide was "forty-four foot of length and fifteen foot of breadth," containing a hall, entry, cellar, four chambers, kitchen, staircase, passages, etc. He "raised up a face of defence to the water side-ward, 'sowed some wheat for a triall' and many other businesses besides." After Christmas he built "a parlour fourtene foote and twelve foote broad, and a lodging chamber, a forge, salt works, a well sixteene foote deep, a brew house, a wharfe, and a fortification so that the whole may be made a prettie street." He speaks in most favorable terms of the soil and climate. A second letter from Governor Wynne to Lord Baltimore is dated the 17th of August 1622. Here again he speaks enthusiastically of the climate and products of the soil, "wheat, barley, oates, beanes, pease, radishes, cale cabbidge, lettice, turneps, carrets, 'and all the rest of like goodnesse.'" He sends home "a barrell of the best salt that ever my eyes beheld." Also a list of articles required, and, at the end, gives the names of the thirty-two men and boys staying with him.

There is a letter from Captain Powell to "Master Secretary Calvert," dated July 28, 1622. He describes the voyage from Plymouth, with several incidents, such as the death of "three ewe goats, by reason of their extreme leannesse." They have now "but only one ewe goat and a buck goat left;" on the 16th of May the "furnace took fire." They arrived in Capeling Bay on the 26th of May. They found the governor and all his company in good health, "as we all continue in the same, praised be God for it." He then describes the situation of the colony, which was on the margin of what is known as "The Pool." "The house is strong and well contrived, standeth very warme at the foot of an easie ascending Hill on the South East and defended with a Hill standing on the further side of the Hauen on the north west. The beach on the North and South side of the land locke it and the seas on both sides are so neare and indifferent to it that one may shoote a Bird bolte into either sea. . . . The land behind it being near one thousand acres of good ground for hay, feeding of cattell, and plenty of wood almost an island, safe to keepe anything from ravenous beasts." He then describes Aquafort, about six miles to the southward, and asks leave to take thirteen men there to form a settlement. Calvert sent £2,500 sterling with Wynne, as an earnest of what he intended to do for the colony. According to a memorial afterward presented to Charles II., in 1637, by the younger Lord Baltimore, touching his father's claim on Newfoundland, Lord Cecil says that his father spent £20,000 on the fort, mansion, and public works. In a petition to Charles II., immediately after the Restoration, 1660, he states the expenditure to have been £30,000. The accounts furnished by Governor Wynne and Captain Powell were no doubt highly colored and exaggerated, so that Lord Baltimore was induced, after a few years, to come out himself to see his new colony.

He had spent very large sums of money on his enterprise; and, though he constantly received the most glowing accounts from his agent, yet it appears that he began to entertain doubts that all was not going as well as was represented. And he feared that, unless he should go in person to visit this colony, it might become a total failure. Thus he writes from London, on the 21st May, 1627, to Sir Thomas Wentworth, afterwards Earl of Strafford: "I am heartily sorry that I am further from my hopes of seeing you before leaving this town . . . for a long journey. . . . It is Newfoundland I mean, which it imports me more than curiosity only to see. For I must either go and settle it in better order or else give it over and lose all the charges I have been at hitherto for other men to build their fortunes upon." However, that was not the only reason, for he speaks of Newfoundland as "a place which I have long had a desire to visit and have now the opportunity and leave to do it." It will thus be seen, then, that it was not, as before observed, on account of his conversion that he turned his thoughts to colonization, yet it must be admitted that his religious convictions, coupled with the peculiar turn of Imperial politics at the time, if they were not the cause, gave him at least the opportunity of giving his mind more entirely to the project. He had, as before stated, strongly urged the marriage of Prince Charles with the Infanta of Spain, hoping thereby to obtain a suspension of the penal laws against the Catholics. The failure of that project was as great a disappointment to him as it was a triumph to the Duke of Buckingham, his opponent. The latter, suspecting or knowing Calvert's Catholicity, urged strongly the enforcement of the penal laws with the utmost vigor, as also the tendering of the oath of allegiance to all suspected persons, particularly the members of the Privy Council, of whom Calvert was one. Calvert resigned his office, but he did not lose the king's favor, and a few days before the death of the latter he was appointed Baron of Baltimore, in the Irish peerage, in 1625. From that time he seems to have laid aside all connection with the affairs of state, and given himself up more exclusively to the subject of religion and of his new colony. In this same year, 1625, he made a journey to the north of England with the Rev. Sir Tobias Matthew, S.J. Sir Toby Matthew was a noted convert, who died October 13, 1655, at Ghent, in the English House of Tertians of the Jesuit Order. He was son of Dr. Toby Matthews, Protestant Bishop of Durham. He was a friend of Calvert, and it is probable that at that time arrangements were made for the sending out of Jesuit missionaries to Newfoundland. Sir Toby took a great interest in the project, and it was probably he who selected the Fathers Smith, Longville, and Hacket, whom Lord Baltimore brought out with him a couple of years subsequently. It would appear that after this date Lord Baltimore retired to his Irish estate in the county of Longford, where, remote from the cares of state, he seriously set about making preparations for his long-wished-for visit to his rising colony of Avalon.

In the month of April, 1627, he sent out two ships, viz., the "Ark of Avalon," of 160 tons, and the "George," of Plymouth, 140 tons. These ships were sent out under charge of Sir Arthur Ashton, who afterwards was governor of Avalon. "Early in the summer Lord Baltimore himself followed, and arrived at Ferryland about the 23d July, 1627. He brought with him two seminary priests, Fathers Anthony Smith and Longville." (Richardson, from the "Colonial Papers," pp. 86-92.[1])

Although the colony established by John Guy, of Cuper's, had been abandoned some ten or twelve years previous

---

[1] Mr. Richardson furnishes me with the following items as being all that he could glean concerning these priests. That they were probably selected for the mission "by Sir Tobias Matthew, S.J.; that Smith returned to England with Lord Baltimore in the fall of 1627, and that Hacket appears to have come out the next year to take Smith's place." In Brother Foley's (S.J.) exhaustive work I find no mention of these fathers; and, having written to him on the subject, he replies (30th Oct., 1884), "I can trace no English Jesuits of the names of A. Smith, Hackett, and Longville." Considering the immense extent and depth of Brother Foley's researches, it seems unaccountable that he did not come upon these fathers. At the same time it must be remembered that, owing to the persecuting spirit of the times, the Jesuits were obliged to adopt various disguises, and frequently to change their names. Hence it is quite possible that the above names may have been merely *aliases*.

to Lord Baltimore's settlement at Ferryland, still there is no doubt that some settlements yet remained in that bay. Governor Wynne, at the close of his letter to Lord Baltimore, of July 28, 1622, after giving the names and occupations of the thirty-two inhabitants of his settlement, says: "I look for a mason and one more out of the Bay of Conception." Thus we are not surprised to find that there was also a minister of the Church of England, named Erasmus Stourton, already established in the country. The religious animosity which raged so strongly against the Jesuits in England was in no wise cooled by its contact with the icebergs on the coast of Newfoundland; hence we find the Rev. Mr. Stourton waxed exceedingly wrathy when he heard of the arrival of the priests. But his indignation seems to have passed all bounds when he heard that a third priest and forty more papists had come out, and that Mass was celebrated daily in the big house at Ferryland. Governor Wynne, in his letters to Lord Baltimore, though he describes most minutely all the buildings erected, and in course of construction, makes no mention of a chapel. So that it is probable the Mass was celebrated in the parlor of the great house, a room described by Wynne as of "fourteene foote besides the chimney and twelve foote broad, of convenient height"; or in the hall, which is described as "18 feet long, the whole building being 44 foot of length and 15 foot of breadth." This was the first building erected, and no doubt there was sufficient room for the small congregation at that time existing in the settlement. What particular act of opposition the Rev. Mr. Stourton was guilty of does not appear, but it must have been of a very grave and aggressive character to have forced a man of such tolerant disposition as we know Lord Baltimore was to exercise his supreme power by banishing from the colony "the audacious man," as he calls him, "for his misdeeds." Our readers may judge, from what we have already shown concerning Lord Baltimore's generosity and toleration of religious differences in Maryland, that the conduct of this man must have been altogether unbearable, and most likely seditious.

His conduct, after his return to England, will help us to form an opinion upon this matter. Richardson says: "He busied himself in ineffectual efforts to stir up the Privy Council against the Popish Colony." Dr. Clarke ("Catholic World," October, 1883) says: "The Rev. Erasmus Stourton, resident Protestant minister at Ferryland, made formal complaint against his lordship to the authorities in England, that, in violation of the law, Mass was publicly celebrated in Newfoundland." "He had no sooner landed in Plymouth," says Kirke, quoting from the "Colonial Papers," Vol. IV., No. 59. "than he hastened to present himself before Nicholas Sherwill, Mayor, and Thomas Sherwill, Merchant, both Justices of the Peace, and into their horrified ears he poured his astounding tale of Lord Baltimore's misdeeds. How the said lord arrived in Newfoundland the 23d of July, 1627, and brought with him two seminary priests, one of them called Longville, and the other Anthony Smith; but Longville returned to England with the said Lord Baltimore, who brought out, the same year, another priest named Hacket, and with him about 40 papists: and how the said Hacket and Smith said Mass every Sunday and used all other ceremonies of the Church of Rome in the ample manner, as 'tis used in Spain: and how the child of one William Poole, a Protestant, was baptized into the Romish Church by order of Lord Baltimore and contrary to the wish of his father! The brothers Sherwill, amazed at these enormities, sent Rev. Mr. Stourton post-haste to the Privy Council with a copy of his deposition in his pocket." This extract from a certainly unsuspected source shows us how Lord Baltimore had fully established the Catholic religion in his colony, thus verifying the supposition of Dr. Mullock, who, not being aware of the existence of the above records, wrote as follows in his "History," p. 14: "We have no records of the state of Catholicity during Lord Baltimore's residence in Newfoundland; but it is to be supposed that

such an ardent Catholic, who stamped forever the mark of
Catholicity on the very soil by the names of 'Avalon' and
'Verulam,' did not leave those who followed him to the
wilderness without making sufficient provision for their
spiritual wants." Although Lord Baltimore no doubt heard
the futile calumnies of Rev. Mr. Stourton, it does not
appear that any formal notice was taken of his complaints.
Certain it is that Lord Baltimore did not lose the King's
favor, for, on August 19, 1629, he writes the King, thanking
His Majesty for the loan of a ship sent out. It is in this
letter that he alludes to Stourton as "an audacious man,
banished from the colony for his misdeeds." The King replied
in November; told him he was not fit for such rugged
work as founding a new colony; advised him to return,
where he might be assured of such respect as his former
services and late endeavors justly deserved.

Dr. Clarke, it will be seen, alludes to Mr. Stourton as the
resident minister at Ferryland. It is, however, almost certain
that there was no resident minister there at that time.
As we have seen, a settlement was attempted at Ferryland
by Dr. Vaughan in 1617, but it did not come to anything.
Anspach, in his "History of Newfoundland" (p. 86), states,
I know not on what authority, that "a considerable colony,
composed chiefly of Puritans, accompanied to Newfoundland
Captain Edward Wynne, whom Sir George Calvert had sent
with the commission of Governor." That Lord Baltimore
did not *exclude* Puritans and other Protestants we may
readily believe, as was the case also in the Maryland plantation;
but it is evident that, while tolerating other forms
of religion, he established the Catholic worship in his colony,
and we may thank Mr. Stourton for being the means of
placing on record such a full account of the religious state of
the colony.

In April, 1628, Lord Baltimore came out a second time to
Newfoundland, bringing with him his lady and children.
This was his second wife; his eldest son, Cecil, afterwards
founder of Maryland, was then twenty-three years of age;

and the second, Leonard, who afterwards, as lieutenant, conducted the colony to Maryland, in the same old ship, "The Ark," was then twenty-two years old. His daughter, and Mr. William Peasley, afterwards his son-in-law, and Rev. Father Hacket, S.J., accompanied him.

CHAPTER VIII.

FERRYLAND, *Continued.* — [1628-1660.]

Causes of the Failure of the Ferryland Colony — Lady Baltimore Leaves for Maryland — Lord Baltimore Follows, 1629 — Lady Baltimore Lost at Sea — Baltimore Refuses to take the Oath of Allegiance as Proposed by Governor Pott of Jamestown — He Returns to England, and Dies, 1632 — Sir W. Alexander Founds Nova Scotia, 1627 — French Huguenots — Claude de St. Etienne — Sir David Kirke — He Captures the French Fleet at Gaspé — Quebec Capitulates, 1629 — Kirke is Refused his Prize-money — Kirke and Baltimore Contrasted — Kirke Receives a Grant of Ferryland, and Arrives in Newfoundland, 1638 — Reconstructs the Settlement — The Ten Years' War in England — Kirke is Arrested, 1651, and Deprived of his Colony — He Returns to Newfoundland, 1653, and Dies at Ferryland, 1656 — His Character — Cecil, Second Lord Baltimore, Recovers Possession of Ferryland, 1660 — Policy of Britain Detrimental to the Advancement of the Country.

THE arrival of Lord Baltimore and his colonists on the shores of Newfoundland seemed to presage the dawn of a bright and glorious era in the history of our Island home. If that noble effort had succeeded, who can picture what would to-day have been the result? Ferryland, instead of remaining as it is, a lone and straggling fishing-village, would be the modern Baltimore, — the great mart of commerce, manufacture, and science! But, alas! it was not destined to be so.

Many were the causes which combined to bring about the failure of the new colony; but they were all accidental or extrinsic. There was no inherent obstacle, either in the country or climate, as some authors say, and many believe; even Lord Baltimore himself thought so. If Baltimore had had the good fortune to settle in St. John's, Trepassey, or some of the fertile regions of St. Mary's Bay, and had spent there the twenty or thirty thousand pounds so fruitlessly squandered on the sterile rocks of Ferryland, or more probably misappropriated by dishonest agents, what a wonderful difference would it have caused in the future prosperity of Newfoundland!

Among the causes of failure of the colony of Ferryland may be stated as the primary one the fact already alluded to, viz., the sterile nature of the land. The harbor is by no means fitted for a port of trade to any great extent, being greatly exposed on the northern side to the fury of the Atlantic waves, which are but very imperfectly kept out by a low-lying reef. There is no level site for a town, the spot upon which the settlement stood, now called "the Downs," not being at all well adapted for an extensive city; and, above all, there is no belt of fertile country in the rear capable of cultivation to make a feeding-ground, so necessary an adjunct to a large commercial centre of population. Among the other causes of failure, Dr. Mullock, in his "Lectures," mentions "the incursions of the Indians and the attacks of the French." Lord Baltimore, in his letters from Newfoundland, makes no mention of the incursions of the Indians; and with regard to the attacks of the French, neither does he attribute his failure to that source. It is true that no sooner was he well settled down in his new colony than a hostile French fleet appeared in the waters of Ferryland; but Lord Baltimore, by his skill and courage, soon drove them away. The following letters, reproduced by Kirke from the "Colonial Papers," give, in his own words, a graphic account of these adventures. Both letters are dated Ferryland, August 25, 1628. One is addressed to the King, the other to the Duke of Buckingham:—

"MOST GRACIOUS AND DREAD SOVEREIGN:—

"In this remote wilde part of the worlde, where I have planted myselfe, and shall endeavor by God's Assistance to enlarge your Majesty's Dominions, and in whatsoever else to serve your Majesty loyallie and faithfullie with all the powers both of my mynde and bodye, I meete with great difficulties and incumbrances at the beginninge (as enterprises of this nature commonly have) and cannot bee easilie

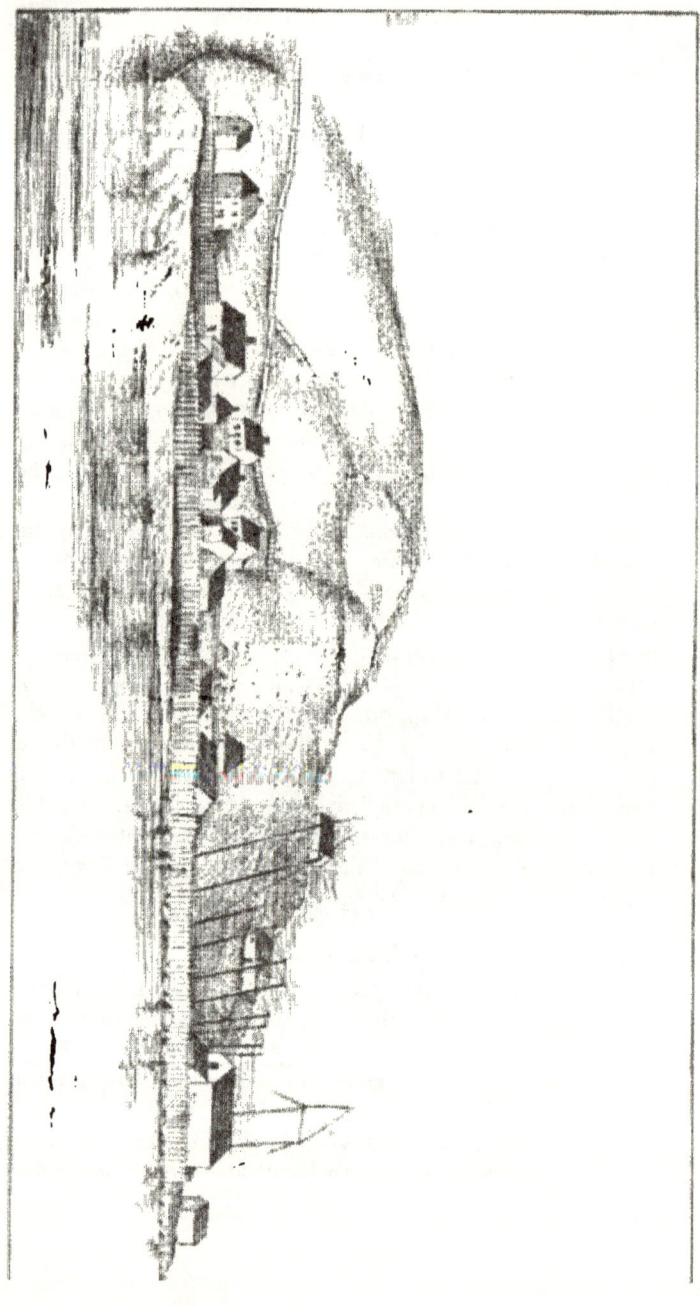

SITE OF LORD BALTIMORE'S SETTLEMENT AT FERRYLAND NFLD. AS IT APPEARED 1890

overcome by such weake bands as myne without your Majesties special protection, for which cause I must still renew my addresses to your Majestie, as your most humble subject and vassall for the continuance of your Princely favor to mee and this work which I have taken in hand. Your Majestie's Subjects fishing this year in the harbours of this land have been much disquieted by a Frenchman of Warre, one Monsieur de la Rade of Deepe, who with three ships and 400 men well armed and appointed came first into a harbor belonging to me called Capebroile, where he surprised divers of the fishermen, took two of their shipps in the harbor and kept the possession of them till I sent two ships of mine with some hundred men being all the force we could make upon the suddayne in this place where I am planted: uppon the approach of which shipps near to the Harbor's mouth of Capebroile one of them being 300 tons with 24 pieces of ordnance, the Ffrench let slip their cables, and made to sea as fast as they could, leaving behind them both the English shipps, whereof they had formerly possession, 67 of their own countrymen on shore, whom I have had since here with me prisoners. We followed the chase so long as we saw any possibility of coming upp with them, but they were much better of saile and we were forced to give it over. The said de la Rade hath since donne more spoils uppon other of your Majestie's subjects in the N. parts of this land, as I was given to understand which caused me to pursue them a second tyme, but they were driven out of the country by a shipp of London before mine could get thither. Hereuppon being still vexed with these men, and both myselfe and my poor fisherie heere, and many other of your Majestie's subjects much injured this year by them I directed my ship in consort with Captain Fearne's Man-of-Warre then in this Country to seek out some of that Nation at Trepasse, a harbor to the south of where they used to fish. There they found 6 shipps 5 of Bayonne and one of St. Jean de Luz, whom they took with their lading, being Fish and trayne, and have sent them to England. I do humblie beseech your Majestie's service, and to give me leave upon this occasion to be an humble suitor unto your Majestie both for myne owne safetie, and for many thousands of your subjects that use this land and come hither every yeare, for the most parte weakely provided of defences, that by your Majestie's supreame Authority for the preservation of your people, being Seamen and Mariners and their shipps, from the spoile of the enemye (the loss whereof much imports your Majestie's service) two men-of-warre, at leaste may be appointed to guard this coast, and to be here betymes in the yeare: the fishermen to contribute to the defraying of the charge which amongst so many will be but a small matter, and easily borne. I have humbly entreated My Lord Duke to recommend and mediate it unto your Princely wisdome, beseeching your Majestie to pardon this unmannerly length wherewith I have presumed to trouble your patience.

"God Almightie preserve your Majestie with a long Raygne and much happiness.

"Your Majestie's most loyal subject and
"Humble servant,
"GEO. BALTIMORE.

"FERRYLAND, 25 August, 1628."

To the Duke of Buckingham, on the same date, he writes:—

"I remember that his Majestie once told me that I write a fairer hand to look upon a farre as any man in England, but that when any man came neare it they were not able to read a word! Whereupon I got a dispensation both from His Majestie and your Grace to use another man's pen when I write to either of you, and I humbly thank you for it, for writing is a great pain to mee nowe.

"I owe your Grace an account of my actions and proceedings in this plantation, since under your patronage, and by your honorable mediation to his Majesty, I have transplanted myself hither. I came to build, to sett, to sowe, but I am faln to fighting with Frenchmen. . . . I have desired this bearer M^r. Peasley some time a servant of our late Sovereigne, who for company, I have had heere this summer to attend your Grace on my behalf, and I humbly beseeche you to vouchsafe me accesse to your person, as there shall be occasion, with favour, and I shall always rest the same, now and forever,

"Your Grace's most faithfull and
"Humble servant,
"GEO. BALTIMORE.

"FERRYLAND, Aug. 25, 1628."

William Peasley, afterwards Lord Baltimore's son-in-law, was the bearer of these despatches.

His request was granted, and two of the ships which he had taken as prizes in Trepassey, the "Esperance" and the "S. Claude," were sent out to Newfoundland under command of Leonard Calvert, his lordship's second son, a youth of twenty-two years of age. From this it would appear that it was not fear of the French which drove Lord Baltimore from Ferryland. He had proved himself well able to defend himself against them · and the remains of numerous pieces of heavy ordnance still to be seen, half buried in the sand, upon the Downs and the opposite island, called "Isle o' Boys" (*Isle aux Bois*), show that he had made ample preparations to repel their attacks. The fact is that a series of unpropitious circumstances culminated in causing the failure of the colony. That winter happened to be a most unusually severe one. Sickness broke out among the colonists, and Lady Baltimore soon found that the trials and privations of colonial life were more than she could bear. She remained but one winter in Newfoundland, and left some time in the spring of 1629, conducted by her son, Cecil, for Virginia. No doubt the departure of this lady tended much to render Lord Baltimore discontent with his new colony; so, wearied out at length by so many trials, he wrote to the King on the 19th August, 1629, asking for a grant of land in Virginia. In this letter he explains some of his motives for leaving

Ferryland. "I have," he writes, "met with grave difficulties and encumbrances here, which in this place are no longer to be resisted, but enforce me to presently quit my residence, and to shift to some other warmer climate of this New World, where the winters be shorter and less rigorous.

"For here your Majesty may please to understand that I have found by too dear bought experience, which other men for their private interests always concealed from me: that from the middlest of October to the middlest of May there is a sad face of winter upon all this land both sea and land so frozen, for the greater part of the time, as they are not penetrable, no plant or vegetable thing appearing out of the earth until about the beginning of May, nor fish in the sea, besides the air is so intolerable cold as it is hardly to be endured, by means whereof, and of much salt meet my house hath been an hospital all this winter; of one hundred persons fifty sick, myself being one, and nine or ten of them died.

"Hereupon I had strong temptations to leave all proceedings in plantations, and being much decayed in my strength to retire myself to my former quiet, but my inclination carrying me naturally to these kind of works; and not knowing how better to employ the poor remainder of my days, than with other good subjects to further, the best I may, the enlarging of Your Majesty's domain, Virginia where, if Your Majesty will please to grant me a precinct of land, with such privileges as the King your father was pleased to grant me here I shall endeavor to the utmost to deserve it." (Richardson, from Neil's "Founders of Maryland.")

The King, though urging him to return to England, yet granted his request. He left Newfoundland for good about the month of September, 1629, a little over two years from the date of his first arrival, in July, 1627. "Thus," says Dr. Mullock (p. 15), "Newfoundland sustained an irreparable loss, which retarded her progress for two centuries." It would, perhaps, have fared better for him, and for Lady Baltimore, too, had they remained on the shores of Newfoundland, which, if bleak, were at least free from persecution. No sooner did he arrive at Virginia than Governor Pott, of Jamestown, tendered him the Oath of Allegiance, or rather Supremacy, an oath which, we have already seen, he refused in conscience to take previously in England. This device was resorted to designedly by his enemies in order to exclude him from that country, and to afford the pretext of accusing him of disloyalty. He of course refused to take the oath in the form in which it was presented, and was compelled to return to England, leaving his wife and family and valuable plate and property behind him. In the following year, 1630, he sent out a vessel to bring them home, but the unfortunate lady was lost at sea. In the year 1631 Lord Baltimore renewed his application for a patent in Virginia; and, notwithstanding the strong opposition and misrepresentations of his enemies, the grant was made to him by the King, whose favor he retained all through. The charter was drawn up by Lord Baltimore himself, and was mainly modelled on the Avalon patent. Before it had passed the seals he died, April 9, 1632, in the fifty-third year of his age, and the charter was issued in June to his son. We have already seen how Lord Baltimore, on receiving his patent, immediately applied to Father Blount, provincial of the Jesuits, for some of the fathers of the Society to accompany his colony. At that time Father More, who afterwards became provincial (in 1640), and defended Lord Baltimore in a letter to the Cardinal Prefect of Propaganda, was in high authority and esteem in the Society. He was great-grandson of the blessed Sir Thomas More, the celebrated chancellor, who suffered death for his faith under Henry VIII. Now, it is most probable that this Father More assisted Lord Baltimore in the drawing up of the magnificent and noble constitution of the new colony of Maryland, and that they modelled it as near as possible upon that most perfect of commonwealths imagined, or perhaps foreseen, by Sir Thomas More, and described by him under the name of *Utopia*. Major-General Johnston, a Protestant writer, in his "Foundation of Maryland" says:

"The religious institutions of the ideal state, Eutopia, were exactly such as Baltimore founded in Maryland." And a comparison of the two documents shows a most striking and instructive resemblance.

To return to Ferryland. In order to account for the appearance of the French fleet in a hostile attitude in the waters of Newfoundland, as well as for the subsequent history of this ill-fated colony, it will be necessary to take a retrospective glance at the contemporary history of the neighboring colonies. It is difficult, indeed, to unravel the confused web of contradictory events and conflicting accounts which present themselves to the student of this portion of colonial history. The cool and magnanimous nonchalance with which the sovereigns of Europe gave out vast and unlimited grants of unknown territories in the New World could not but be productive of strife and contention, a relic of which prevails even to the present day on what is called the "French Shore" of Newfoundland. Rights mutually incompatible were serenely conceded by their majesties, Britannic and Most Christian, at the Treaty of Utrecht, which have been an endless source of bickering and discontent between the fishermen of France and the inhabitants of the Island of Newfoundland, and a heavy clog upon the progress of the colony.

Since the foundation of Quebec, by Champlain, in 1608, France had retained possession of all Canada and Acadia, under the title of "Nouvelle France"; but, in 1621, Sir William Alexander obtained a grant of a portion of Acadia, which he called "Nova Scotia." Nothing was done in the way of colonization at the time, as the French were in full possession, and a party of emigrants sent out returned again to England. King James I. died in 1625, and Sir W. Alexander had the grant confirmed by Charles I., July 12, 1627. At that time France presented a pitiful aspect. Intestine war between the Catholics and Huguenots prevailed; and the Duke of Buckingham (Villiers) unwarrantably drew England into the contest by offering himself, with an English fleet, for the relief of the Protestant stronghold of La Rochelle.

This ill-managed attempt was an ignominious failure. From this time we behold the contemptible spectacle of men who, having first renounced their national faith, completed their degradation by renouncing their national allegiance and fighting under a foreign banner against their own countrymen. Such were Claude de la Tour, *alias* Claude de St. Etienne, David Kirke, and Captain Mitchel. Speaking of the former, de la Tour, Henry Kirke, M.A., etc., in his work on the "Conquest of Canada," says (page 59) he was "a French adventurer, equally devoid of religion and honesty; a Huguenot and a Protestant under the British monarch; a Catholic under Louis XIV. At all times an active, enterprising, treacherous, and unscrupulous man, who made religion a stalking-horse to gain the object of his ambition." "This enterprising man" (says Garneau, "History of Canada," Chap. III., p. 106), "a French Protestant, who had lately taken service in the English navy, had been taken prisoner . . . and carried to London, where he was well received at court. . . . He married one of the maids of honor, and was created a baronet of Nova Scotia. . . . The ungrateful duty devolved upon him of attempting to bring his own son under submission; the latter, true to his country's cause, being in command of a French fort at Cape Sable." Now, it may not be very pleasant for Mr. Henry Kirke to hear his ancestor, Sir David, in whom he takes such a pride, spoken of in unfavorable terms; yet he is treated by French historians pretty much in the same trenchant style as Mr. Kirke himself deals with the renegade de la Tour. David (afterwards Sir David) Kirke was "a master mariner of Dieppe," that is to say, a Frenchman by birth. His father, indeed, was an Englishman, Gervase Kirke, a London merchant, who, in order to increase the wealth and mercantile influence of his family, married Elizabeth, daughter of M. Gondon, of Dieppe. David, the eldest son, was born in 1597. In 1627, David being then about thirty years of age, a company was formed in London by Sir William Alexander, on the renewal of his grant by King Charles.

Gervase Kirke was a member of this company. A small fleet of three ships was fitted out and placed under the command of David Kirke. "They had obtained letters of marque from the King under the broad seal, giving them authority to capture and destroy any French ships they might encounter" (Kirke, p. 61). The following is the manner in which French authors speak of this expedition: L. Abbé Brasseur de Bourbourg ("Histoire du Canada," Chap. II., p. 35) says: "Sir David Kirck, a Frenchman, native of Dieppe, but a Huguenot, who had passed over to the English, whose treason was rewarded by titles and honors, received a special commission for Canada." M. Ferland ("Cours d'Histoire du Canada," Chap. VII.) says: "Some Frenchmen, Huguenots, undertook to destroy the French establishments in Canada. David Kertk, born at Dieppe, had passed over, with his brothers Louis and Thomas, into the English service, as did in those days many other Calvinists who preferred England to their own country. The three brothers had contracted a taste for dangerous enterprises, and were reputed as very good navigators by the Dieppians, at that time the most skilful and hardy sailors of France. Thanks to their talents and energy the Kertks advanced rapidly in England. The head of the family, Sir David Kertk, with the assistance of his brothers and some wealthy relations in England, fitted out, at great expense, several ships. Having received a commission from the King of England he sent . . . three ships . . . to drive the French out of Quebec."

Kirke exercised his privileges to the fullest extent. He captured and plundered French vessels wherever he met them. He waylaid a convoy of twenty ships at Gaspé laden with provisions and general supplies for Quebec, under Roquemont, and returned to England with the prizes. The capture of this fleet reduced Champlain and his people in Quebec to the verge of starvation, so that they were obliged to subsist on roots and herbs. The Kirkes were declared in France traitors and public enemies, and burnt in effigy in Paris.

(Henry Kirke, p. 66.) In the spring of 1629 a more powerful armament of five ships and three pinnaces, well armed and manned, was fitted out by the London Company and placed in charge of the Kirkes, David, Louis, and Thomas. They carried all before them. Quebec, reduced to the utmost extremity by the want of every article of food, clothing, implements, and ammunition, fell an easy victim, and capitulated on the 9th of August, 1629. Kirke returned home flushed with triumph, and laden with booty, peltry, etc. But what was his consternation to find that peace had been proclaimed between France and England on the 24th of April previous, just one month after he had sailed from Gravesend (25th March), and that the English king had pledged his word that all forts captured by the English after that date should be restored, as well as all furs and other merchandise brought by the Kirkes from Canada. In vain Kirke petitioned, showed how he had supplied provisions, etc., to the French at Quebec. He was summoned before the Mayor, ordered to deliver up the key of the warehouse where the goods were kept; and all their property was taken. However, a commission was formed to estimate the losses of the Company, and an award adjudged, to be paid by the French government, of £20,000. Finally, the French government repudiated the claim, and the money was never paid. (Henry Kirke, p. 89.)

I have gone into this digression in order that my readers may have a complete acquaintance with the character and antecedents of the man into whose hands the abandoned colony of Lord Baltimore afterwards fell. That he was a skilful mariner and a bold and brave commander cannot be denied; but, looked upon from a higher stand-point, it is evident that, for breadth of view, for nobleness of conception, for statesman-like ability, for philanthropic sentiments, and all that goes to make up the character of a "great" man, Sir David Kirke cannot at all compare with Lord Baltimore. At the same time it must be admitted that his rough, seaman-like training, his indomitable courage and practical turn of mind, made him a fitter man for the founding of a colony in a wild, new country,—a work for which Lord Baltimore's court training and rather Utopian ideas to a great extent unfitted him.

Henry Kirke, so often quoted, and from whom I shall be obliged, mainly, to draw for the remaining portion of the history of Ferryland, and whose work, "The Conquest of Canada," may be considered as a panegyric of his illustrious ancestor, says, at page 165, "Sir David had an equal dislike to both Catholics and Puritans." Now, from what we have seen of Baltimore's character, it is plain that he rose above such feelings altogether.

Sir David Kirke, having found all efforts unavailable to obtain the money stipulated for him, and which no doubt was his due, asked permission of the King to take up the colony deserted by Lord Baltimore in 1629, nearly eight years previously.

On the 13th of November, 1637, Kirke received a patent of "all that whole Continent Island or region, commonly called or known by the name of New found Lande bordering upon the Continente of America." Kirke came out to Ferryland with one hundred men in the spring of 1638. He formed a company to carry on the trade, giving a new impetus to the colony. "He was accompanied by a faithful and devoted wife. Children had been born to him, and his house at Ferryland was filled with stalwart sons and fair daughters." (Kirke, p. 183.) He was not dismayed by the difficulties which had driven away Lord Baltimore. He wrote a highly interesting account of the country. He pronounces the climate healthy, though rather severe. "He was," says Henry Kirke, "a good Churchman and an admirer of Archbishop Laud, with whom he kept up a regular correspondence." He acknowledged the great source of wealth in Newfoundland to consist in her fisheries, and strove to develop them. He encouraged all fishermen frequenting the coast, erecting sheds, etc., for them. This aroused the jealousy of the British fishermen, whose policy from the beginning was to prevent all permanent settlement in the country. A petition was sent to the Privy Council against him in 1640. He was accused of seizing their property and selling or disposing of it to aliens; setting up taverns "whereby the fishermen waste their estates and grow disorderly." He writes from "Ffereland 12th of September 1640" to the Privy Council protesting before God "that all that they have alledged ag^t me is most false." "Many of the Fishermen themselves," he says, "upon what grounds I know not, have this yeare driviue their stages and Cooke-roomes in, so much that ye most sevill and wisest men amongst them did themselves complaine to me of these outrages. . . . I confesse he that would interrupt the ffishinge of Newfoundland which is one of the most considerable Business ffor the Kingdoms of His Matie and benefit of his subjects and navigation, is worthy the name of traitour, the least thought and imagination whereof I do abhorre."

We now enter upon the memorable period of the ten years' civil war in England, between the King and the Covenanters, the Royalists and Roundheads, which culminated in the capture and execution of the unfortunate monarch, Charles I., on the 30th of January, 1649. During these internecine struggles the brothers Kirke remained loyal to the King, and Louis distinguished himself at the siege of Gloucester and the battle of Newbury, and was knighted by the King at Oxford, 1643.

"Sir David remained in undisturbed possession of Newfoundland, and kept the Royal Standard continually hoisted in front of his house and fort at Ferryland" (p. 171). He even offered the King an asylum there when England became unsafe for His Majesty. He procured, by offers of high pay, four hundred seamen to man his ships, which he armed with heavy guns, to maintain his position. On the death of the King and the triumph of the Cromwellians he still determined to hold out, and wrote to Prince Rupert, who was cruising in the English channel with a fleet, to make sail for Newfoundland; but, the rumor of his intention having been brought to London, a fleet, under Sir George Ayscue, was

sent against him, and he changed his course for Barbadoes.
After the conquest by the insurgents, the victors, as is to be
supposed, set to work to divide the spoils. All who had
espoused the cause of the King were declared rebels to the
Commonwealth, and delinquents, and their property seques-
trated. The Kirkes, who were known to be zealous Royalists, did not, of course, escape; yet the position of Sir David
was something exceptional, and not an ordinary one. He had
not actually borne arms in the Royal cause. By his grant
he exercised palatinate jurisdiction in Newfoundland of the
highest sort. The Government, therefore, fell back on the
charges which had been made against him before the war
broke out; and, consequently, on the 8th of April, 1651, a
warrant was issued against him, and Thomas Thoroughgood
was ordered to sail in the "Crescent" to Newfoundland and
bring Kirke to England to answer the charges. An order
was issued at the same time to John Treworgie and Walter
Sykes to proceed in the "Crescent" and sequestrate all ordnance, houses, boats, etc., belonging to Kirke; and to collect
taxes from the fishermen.

They arrived in England in September, 1651; but the
cause was delayed from time to time, and was not heard
till the 11th of June, 1652, when the committee decided
that "Sir David Kirke had no authority in Newfoundland under the grant of Charles Stuart; that all forts, houses, stages,
and other appurtenances relating to the fishing trade and
established on the Island . . . should be forfeited to
the Government; . . . that he is at liberty to send
over his wife and servants to take care of his estate;" at the
same time instructions were given to Walter Sykes and
others "to repair thither immediately and take possession of
ordnance, etc., to collect impositions, until Parliament declare
their further pleasure." Permission was granted to Kirke to
go out to Newfoundland provided he would give security to
return when required, and to pay such sums as should appear
due from him to the Commonwealth. He came out to Newfoundland in 1652, and returned to England in 1653. He

was ordered to appear before the Council on the 1st of April of that year. There is no doubt but he was harassed in a very ungenerous manner during this time. He made a friend of Col. Claypole, Cromwell's son-in-law, and the matter was finally settled by his obtaining the removal of the sentence of sequestration of all the property with the exception of the ordnance and forts; and he was allowed to return to Newfoundland upon entering into a bond of double the value of his estate to answer any charges which might be brought against him. He arrived in the autumn of 1653. "And," writes his descendant, Henry Kirke, in the book from which we have condensed all the foregoing particulars, "at this time his troubles seemed to be over, and he might with reason look forward to a life of happiness and usefulness in the wild but interesting country in which he had established himself. . . . But all these hopes and expectations were blighted by his death, which took place in the winter of 1655-6, in the fifty-sixth year of his age." In his death the prospects of Newfoundland received another irreparable blow; for, though he appears to have been not so lenient in religious matters as Lord Baltimore, and to have completely eradicated the foundations of Catholicism planted by Calvert, yet it cannot be denied that he was a man of great energy and perseverance, and one who would have done much for the material advancement of the country had Providence so willed it. We have no reluctance in indorsing every word of the encomium passed on him by Henry Kirke (pp. 184-5):—

"He was of a robust constitution; but trouble and anxiety and the exposure for many years to the rigor of an extremely cold climate must have made him prematurely old, and laid the seeds of the disease which eventually carried him off at a comparatively early age. . . . If we may judge by his actions, he was certainly an extraordinary person. He was essentially a practical man. His theories were never stultified by his actions. His success in most cases, certainly in those 'which depended on his own exertions, far exceeded his expectations. But throughout his life he was most unfortunate in all his undertakings. Never were the achievements of an English officer more unrequited. The capture of Canada and Nova Scotia, the destruction of a French fleet of eighteen sail, and the expenditure of £40,000, was ill-rewarded by an honorary addition to his arms. But, instead of being discouraged by his ill-success, he was only spurred on to new exertions. He was the only man of his time who fully appreciated the value of the Newfoundland fisheries; and, undeterred by the failure which attended Lord Baltimore, Lord Vaughan, and others, who had attempted to colonize Newfoundland, he determined to risk his life and estate in a similar attempt."

SILVER SNUFF-SPOON UNEARTHED AT FERRYLAND.

His three sons, George, David, and Philip were with him in Newfoundland at the time of his death. They probably remained there until the time of the Restoration (1660). He was buried at Ferryland, but no vestige of his resting-place can now be found. The oldest tombstones in the graveyards do not reach beyond 1770. It is most likely that he was buried on the peninsula, and that the grave has since disappeared. Unfortunately, the nature of the ground is a loose gravel, and it is constantly falling away year after year, so that very little now remains of the original establishment. The foundations of Lord Baltimore's house are, however, still quite recognizable. In the year 1880 some excavations were made and a few relics unearthed; among the rest a silver snuff-spoon. It bears the letters G. K. pricked upon it,—evidently the initials of George Kirke. It is now in possession of Mr. Carter, revenue officer at Ferryland. I have been permitted to copy it, and give here an engraving, full size.

These snuff-spoons, now out of fashion, except in some parts of the Highlands of Scotland, were much in vogue after the introduction of snuff and tobacco from Virginia. They were used in connection with the large pouch, or snuff-horn, called in Scotland "*the spleuchan*." Sir Walter Scott alludes to it in "Guy Mannering" (Chap. L.), where Dandy Dinmont offers the "siller in the spleuchan."

Kirke's family remained, as stated, in Newfoundland until the Restoration (1660). Upon the Restoration their uncle Louis put in a petition in their favor to Charles II.; but Cecil, Lord Baltimore, then governor of the Maryland colony, also laid claim to Newfoundland under the grant given to his father by James I. Henry Kirke strongly maintains that the Baltimores had totally abandoned the colony of Newfoundland, "having left the plantation in no sort provided for." The grant was given to Sir David Kirke in 1637, and no complaint or remonstrance was made at the time by the Baltimores. In the grant to Sir David it is especially stated: —

"But the sayd Lord Baltimore deserting the sayd Plantation in his life tyme, and leavinge the same in noe sorte provided for, accordinge to the sayd undertakinge, and yet leavinge divers of our poore subjects in the sayde province livinge without Government, the sayd Lord Baltimore shortly after dyed, and Cecile his sonne and heire apparent hath alsoe deserted the sayd province and plantation: and also Sir Francis Bacon Knighte deceased, afterwards Lord Albans, and late Lord Chauncellor of England our citye of London, and divers others to whom severall graunts of divers parcells of Newfoundlande aforesayd were alsoe by severall letters patent formerly graunted have alsoe deserted the province and plantation."

It must, however, be remembered that the Baltimores left a governor in Ferryland, and that, after Lord George's death, Cecil appointed William Hill governor. "But," says Richardson, " in 1637, while England was on the brink of a civil war, Sir David Kirke surreptitiously obtained a patent, and the next year went over and took possession of the Island. Lord Baltimore waited patiently until after the restoration of the Stuarts, in 1660, and then recovered from Sir David's heirs the houses and lands which had belonged to his father." Whatever may be the rights of this controversy, certain it is that King Charles II. issued a warrant to Sir Louis Kirke, Elizabeth, widow of Sir David, and his sons, Philip, George, and David, to deliver up possession of all their property in Newfoundland, as it belonged to Lord Baltimore by the grant of James I. to his father (Henry Kirke, p. 189).

From this period till about thirty-six years subsequently (1696), when Ferryland was taken by the French (which shall be described by and by), we have but very meagre accounts of the history of Newfoundland. There is an account of Lord Falkland, Lord-Lieutenant of Ireland, having at this time sent out a colony of Irish emigrants; but the policy of non-colonization on the part of the British merchants was all-powerful, and bore down all before it. To this fatal cause, primarily, we owe the backward state of Newfoundland, and the failure of so many attempts to colonize her shores. This policy of repression and discouragement began in 1683, its source being the notorious Star Chamber (Harvey, p. 30). The English fishermen believed that it would be ruinous to their business if the Island became settled with a fixed and resident population; hence severe and stringent laws were enacted to prevent such a catastrophe. Shippers were bound under heavy penalties to bring back in the fall all the hands whom they employed during the summer. "No master or owner of any ship should transport any persons to Newfoundland who were not of the ship's company, or such as were to plant or settle there" (Enactment of 1660). A little later (1696), at the instance of most urgent petitions, "some settlers were allowed to remain during winter for the preservation of boats, . . . and the preparation of stages for the fishery; but they should not *exceed one thousand*" (Harvey, p. 31).

A certain governor of the Island, Lieutenant Elford, some years later, endeavored to carry out the principles of St. Senanus by preventing *any women from being landed on the Island.* His motives, however, were not exactly the same as those which actuated the saintly ascetic of Scattery Island. Every means was adopted to prevent the colonization of the country, and to preserve the monopoly of these West-country fishing-masters. They represented the country as a barren, uninhabitable rock; the climate, as an alternation of fogs, storms, and intense, unbearable frosts. The country was declared to be only useful as a nursery for sailors for the British navy, and to be, as it were, a gigantic training-ship. It is easy to imagine that this baneful influence clung like a leaden clog around the neck of the young colony, strangling all its rising aspirations, and giving it a downward tendency which it has scarcely been able to shake off up to this day, after nearly two centuries and a half. Nevertheless, in spite of all this opposition, the colony made certain steps in advancement. In the year 1650 there were more than three hundred and fifty families permanently settled on the coast in different places. About this time the French began to settle on the shores of the great southern bay of the Island, to which, from the name of their capital, they gave the name of "Baie de Plaisance," hispaniolized afterwards into "Placentia," the history of which we shall trace in the following chapter.

CHAPTER IX.

MISSIONARIES IN CANADA. — [1610-1670.]

Placentia — Description of Settlement by Dr. Mullock — Founded by the French long before 1660 — Document Signed by Louis XIV. — Monseigneur de Laval, First Bishop of Quebec — Mgr. de St. Valier, Second Bishop — Defence of the Jesuits — Settlement of Port Royal, 1611-15 — Arrival of the Franciscans at Quebec, 1615 — Missionary Labors of Père le Caron among the Indians — Henri, Duc de Levis, Introduces the Jesuits to Quebec, 1626 — Jesuits cordially Received by the Franciscans — Henry Kirke's Statement to the Contrary Refuted — Religious Withdrawn on Capture of Quebec by Sir David Kirke, 1629 — Jesuits Return after Treaty of St. Germaine en Laye, 1632 — Franciscans in 1670.

ABOUT the same time that the English settlement on the eastern shore of the Island was undergoing the vicissitudes mentioned in the last chapter, and was being claimed and reclaimed by different masters, a large and important settlement was being founded by the French on the more western portion of the southern coast.

It is impossible to say exactly when the French first organized this settlement, but it was prior to 1660, as stated by Monseigneur Turgeon, Archbishop of Quebec, in a letter to Dr. Mullock, 1858. "Previous to 1660," writes Dr. Mullock (MS., page 16), "the French fishermen who frequented Newfoundland began to establish the town of Placentia. Situated on a magnificent bay, 90 miles deep and 60 wide at the mouth; studded with hundreds of islands and teeming with fish; enjoying the advantage of a fine port easily fortified, and a beach capable of drying the fish of a thousand ships; a climate exempt from fog, while the rest of the bay and the southern shore are frequently enveloped in it; beautiful scenery, and two arms of the sea which remind the traveller of the arrowy Rhône, — it united in itself everything necessary for the capital of a fishing island, and its natural beauties, fine climate, and picturesque scenery justly entitled it to the name given it by the French, — Plaisance, or Placentin. The great ruins of forts and castles, which still survive the wreck of time and the more destructive rapacity of the modern inhabitants, who use the remains of the buildings as a quarry, prove how well the French, in the palmy days of the monarchy, before the whole nation was corrupted by the example of the Regent of Louis XV., and by the writings of the infidels Voltaire, Rousseau, & Co., appreciated this beautiful possession. It is remarkable that many of the old farms and fishing-sites in the neighborhood are still held under the old French titles, the parchments bearing the bold signature of Louis le Grand, and countersigned by his minister, Phelypeaux.[1]

When the French first took possession of Canada, or New France, as all the northern portion of the continent and islands was then called, the *Recollets*, or Franciscans, of the strict observance, accompanied them as chaplains and missioners to the aborigines. Established since 1502 in the Spanish possessions, they commenced their labors in Canada in 1615. On the 25th June of that year the first Mass was celebrated in Quebec, and the same year a Franciscan convent was established there, which flourished till the surrender of the city to the English (1629).

It was not till thirteen years after the foundation of this convent — the mother of all the religious establishments in North America — that any attempt at civilization was made by the French in Canada, the riches of the forest appearing to them then the only valuable productions of the country; but by degrees the country was explored, and its resources were better appreciated. Among the first apostles of the land, Père Caron, in Quebec, and Père Huet, at Tadousac (Sag-

---

[1] In the Appendix we give a *verbatim et literatim* copy of one of these curious and interesting documents. It is engrossed on parchment, in a peculiar hand, and abounds in difficult signs and abbreviations. It is in the possession of a family named Green, and was in a very soiled and damaged state when I rescued it and had it framed between two sheets of glass, in 1878. I know not its fate since, but would recommend that, if existing, and purchasable, it should be secured by our Government or Historical Society, for the Museum.

uenay), where he celebrated the first Mass, in 1615, deserve
particular mention. The Church of Canada, or New France,
soon became too extensive, and it was too remote from the
mother-country to be left without direct episcopal superintendence. Up to this period the territory known as New
France was under the spiritual jurisdiction of the Bishop of
Rouen, in Normandy, though the Bishop of St. Malo also
claimed jurisdiction over it.

Quebec, though founded in 1608, was still little more than
a fort, surrounded by a few cabins and about twenty acres
of cultivated land, when it was taken by the English in 1629,
and the Franciscans were sent home to France. It was not till
1632, on its restoration to the French crown, that its population began to increase, and the spiritual jurisdiction was
separated from that of the mother-country. It was first constituted into a Vicariate Apostolic by Alexander VII., by a
brief expedited the 5th July, 1657, and it was erected into a
diocese in 1674 by Clement X. The first Bishop appointed to
govern these northern regions was Francis de Laval de Montmorency. He was one of the high nobility of France, and at
the time of his appointment he was Archdeacon of Evreux
and chaplain to the King. He was consecrated Bishop of
Petrea *in partibus* on the 8th December, the feast of the
Immaculate Conception of the Blessed Virgin, 1658, by the
Pope's nuncio, in the Church of St. Germain des Près, Paris,
and landed in Canada on the 16th of May, 1659, — the first
Bishop of whom we have any authentic account who visited
these northern provinces. In 1674 he was appointed Titular
Bishop of the newly erected See of Quebec; and he conferred
many and most important benefits on his See. He spent
50,000 of his own private fortune — an enormous sum in
those days — in the foundation of the Grand Seminary of
Quebec, now the University Laval Montmorency.

Newfoundland was included in the new diocese, which
comprised all the French possessions in North America;
indeed, the whole continent and islands to the north of the
Spanish possessions. This island, the remotest eastern por-

tion of the diocese, though the nearest to France, very early attracted the attention of the Bishop and missionaries. In the archiepiscopal archives of Quebec we have some curious documents relative to the early state of religion in Newfoundland, the visit of Monseigneur de St. Vallier, and the establishment of Franciscan missionaries in the Island.

The venerable Bishop Laval, after an episcopacy of twenty-six years of the most noble and apostolic labors, among which may be counted the evangelization of the Iroquois and several other Indian tribes; travelling through forests on snow-shoes, carrying on his back his portable altar; the establishment of an episcopal seminary (1663); the consecration of the cathedral (1666); the abolition of the liquor trade among the Indians; the recall of the Franciscans, or Recollets (1669) after an absence of nearly forty years; the establishment of the same in the missions of Three Rivers, Isle Percé, River St. John, and Frontenac; the encouragement of the missions of the Jesuits, particularly of the wondrous voyage of Father Marquette down the whole length of the Mississippi (1673), which gave to France the possession of all western and interior America, and Louisiana; the canonical erection of the diocese and chapter of Quebec (1670); the reconstruction of the ancient chapel of La Bonne Ste. Anne de Beau Pré, and the authentic collection of the miracles of that world-renowned shrine,—after all these, and many other noble works, the venerable Bishop, then past his sixtieth year, began to feel his strength failing, and set out for France in 1684 for the purpose of procuring a coadjutor and successor. His choice fell upon the Abbé Jean Baptiste St. Vallier, a noble of Dauphiné, chaplain to the King, Louis XIV., a man of great piety and rare good example, and distinguished at court for his modesty and regularity of life. St. Vallier was sent out at first to Quebec as their Vicar-General in 1685, Monseigneur de Laval remaining in France. He (St. Vallier) stayed two years in Canada, regulating the affairs of the diocese, and returned to France in 1687, where he was consecrated in the Church of St. Sulpice, Paris, on the 25th of January, 1688. He came back to Canada the same year, Monseigneur de Laval having gone some months before, notwithstanding the earnest and urgent persuasions of his friends and relatives to remain at home. Like a good shepherd, he wished to spend his last days among his faithful flock, and lay down his life in the midst of them. He died, full of years and merits, and in the odor of sanctity, at the seminary of the Jesuits, at Quebec, in the year 1708.[1]

Allusion has been made more than once to the dismissal of the Franciscan friars from Quebec on the capture of the place by the English, and their recall again on its restoration to the French crown. Although these events cannot be said to have actually a place in the history of the Catholic religion of Newfoundland, yet I think it will not be considered too great a digression to give here a brief account of these early missionary efforts. It will help the reader to form a correct estimate of contemporary history, and to comprehend more clearly our own early ecclesiastical state. The first French mission in Newfoundland, as already mentioned, was founded by these Canadian Franciscans, and there has always existed a cordial feeling and a kind of spiritual affinity between the Church of St. John's and Quebec. From the time of the discovery of the St. Lawrence by Cartier (1535) France claimed full dominion over Canada and all countries north of 40° of latitude. Several companies were formed, and fortified with ample patents from the King, giving them the right of the fur trade with the Indians. In 1578 the Marquis de la Roche received his patent; in 1588 two nephews of Cartier. In 1600 Le Sieur de Pontgravé, a great navigator and merchant of St. Malo, with Captain Chauvin, formed a company, and received rights and privileges. After the death of Chauvin, Champlain became captain of the Company. He made his first voyage to Canada in 1603. After this the Company fell to the

---

[1] The "process" for the canonization of this great and holy Bishop has been commenced at Rome, and is now under investigation by the S. Congregation.

charge of Le Sieur de Monts, a Calvinist, and a man of great ability. In 1606 James I., of England, had granted to the Virginia Company the country as far north as 45°, thus encroaching on the French claim, a source of future difficulties and warfare between the two nations. In 1604 the colony of Port Royal, now Annapolis, on the Baie Française, now Bay of Fundy, was founded by De Monts, Champlain, Lescarbot, Poutrincourt, and other distinguished Frenchmen, Catholics and Huguenots; and we are also informed that they were accompanied by "clergy of the best character," sent by order of the King. (Garneau, p. 74.) The Baron de Poutrincourt was governor. The colony, harassed by Dutch marauders and opposed by a clique of merchants of St. Malo, was abandoned after three years (1607). Poutrincourt, however, had not given up all hope of maintaining the colony. He determined to return, after securing substantial aid and assistance, and, in reality, succeeded in his efforts after two years' endeavors. Having concluded an arrangement with some merchants of Dieppe, he came out again to Port Royal in 1610, bringing with him a body of colonists, with skilled artisans. He brought also a secular priest of the diocese of Langres, Le Sieur Jessé Fléché, a learned and virtuous man, who was sent out by order of Robert Ubaldini, Papal Nuncio. This was the first evangelist of New France, for we have no record of any work done by the fathers who came out with De Monts in 1604. Père Fléché was much beloved by the Micmacs, and was called by the French *Le Patriarche*, — a word which the Indians softened into *Padlias*, and by which name they designate a priest at the present day.

On the feast of St. John (June 24), 1610, Père Fléché had the happiness of baptizing the sagamo, or Chief of the Indians, Mambertou, with some twenty-three or twenty-four of his tribe. Poutrincourt had refused to take out with him to Port Royal the Jesuit fathers, offered to him at the desire of the King. On this point Kirke (p. 45) says: "Poutrincourt, though a Roman Catholic, had a great aversion to the

Jesuits, . . . and being at length forced to take them,
plainly told them they must not meddle with the affairs of
the colony." The fact is, however, thus stated by Garneau
(p. 78), a very impartial writer: "His partners were either
Huguenots or men who had prejudices against the Jesuits,
whom they regarded as the authors of the League and the
murder of Henry IV., and preferred to retire from the Canadian
Association rather than to admit them into the colony."
They declared that they would admit the Capucins, Cordeliers
(cord-bearers, a reformed branch of the Capucins), the Recollets,
or Franciscans, but not the Jesuits (Ferland, p. 80).
"But," says L'Abbé Brasseur de Bourbourg (p. 25), "the
fact is that the Huguenots, who had obtained for themselves
liberty of conscience in the countries of New France, thought
to monopolize that liberty for themselves, and to exclude
Catholicism altogether from a country where they were
admitted to the profession of their religion by grace or favor
of that liberty which they attempted to deprive others of.
Sworn enemies of the Jesuits, they took every means to
exclude them."

Charlevoix, himself a Jesuit, seems to think, however, that
Poutrincourt was, though "a very honest man, and strongly
attached to the Catholic religion, impressed by the calumnies
of the pretended reformers against the Jesuits, and he
was firmly resolved not to admit them to Port Royal."
"Champlain also," says Garneau, "distrusted the Jesuits, and
preferred the Franciscans, as having less political ambition;"
yet he admits that to the Jesuits, afterwards, he owed chiefly
his success in the colony of Quebec, "for more than once the
French kings were about to renounce the colony, and each time
they abstained therefrom chiefly through religious motives.
In these crises the Jesuits directly interested in Canada
powerfully seconded the founder of it." And Champlain, in
acknowledgment of these services received from the Jesuit
fathers, left in his will a portion of his estate to them.
Bancroft, a Protestant writer, says (Vol. III.): "Every tradition
bears testimony to their (the Jesuits') worth. If they

had the fault of a superstitious asceticism, they knew how to
resist with an unconquerable constancy and a deep calmness
of soul the horrors of a life passed entirely in the wilderness
of Canada. Far from all that lends a charm to life, far from
every occasion of vainglory, they were totally dead to the
world, and found in their inmost conscience a peace that
nothing could disturb."

In the " Relations des Jesuites " for the year 1611, written
by Père Baiard, it is stated that Poutrincourt had no objection
on his own part to bring out the Jesuits. On the contrary,
M. Robin, merchant of Dieppe, and manager of the Company,
said, " *Qu'il sçauait assez que le Sieur de Potrincourt Se
sentiroit fort honoré de les auoir auprès de soy* " (that he knew
well that Monsieur Poutrincourt would feel himself highly
honored by having them (the Jesuits) with him). All
the delay and obstruction is attributed to the merchants of
Dieppe, who swore their highest oath (*leur plus haut juron*)
that if the Jesuits entered the ships they would put nothing
into them.

Madame the Marchioness de Guercheville, a lady of great
wealth, high in the favor of Queen Mary de Medicis, and
zealous for the spread of the gospel in savage countries, became
indignant at these delays, and declared herself the protectress
of the Jesuits. She bought out the claims of the Huguenot
merchants, and raised among the nobles at court the sum of
twenty thousand francs, besides sacrificing a large portion
of her own fortune.

She equipped the expedition, and sent out Poutrincourt,
having on board the Fathers Pierre Baiard and Enmond
Massé. They left Dieppe the 26th of January, 1611, and
after a long voyage arrived at Port Royal on Pentecost Sunday, 22d of June. On their voyage out they encountered
vast fields of ice and countless icebergs. "These ice fields
were monstrous, for in some places the sea was all covered
with them as far as the eye could reach; and in order to
pass through them it was necessary to break them with bars
and prizes (*auec barres et leuiers*) placed against the beak or

stem (*aux escobilles*) of the ship. In some places high and prodigious mountains of ice appeared 30 to 40 fathoms wide and big as if you were to join many castles together (*chateux*), and as you would say if the Church of Notre Dame of Paris with a part of its Isle and houses and Palaces went floating on the water." — *Relations des Jesuites.*

For nearly three years the new colony thrived wonderfully. Numerous conversions were made among the Algonquins and the Abenaquis. But in 1613 it was attacked and captured by Argall, an English captain from Virginia. A Jesuit lay brother (Du Thet) was shot; Father Baiard was taken prisoner and sent home to France, where he died in 1622. This was the end of the first Jesuit mission in Acadia.

In 1615 Champlain found himself in a position to put into execution his long-cherished desire of bringing out the Franciscans. He applied to Le Sieur Houel, secretary of the King, a man of great piety, who immediately interested himself in the project, and communicated with Père Garnier, the Provincial of St. Denis' convent of Recollets — for so the Franciscans are called in France. On hearing of the request all the fathers consented to go on the mission. The following were chosen: Frs. Denis Jamay, John D'Olbeaut, Joseph le Caron, and Brother Pacifique de Plessis. They left Honfleur on the 24th April, 1615, at 5 P.M., in the good ship "Etienne," 350 tons, Captain Pontgravé, and arrived at Tadoussac, mouth of the Saguenay, on the 25th of May. There they remained two days, repaired ship, took in water, and started for Quebec, where they arrived on the 2d of June. The first Mass was celebrated on the 24th of June, in the presence of all the Indians. In the year 1618 their ranks were recruited by the arrival of Père Paul Huet.

The mission was now well established, and made great progress, until unfortunately it was again broken up by the capture of Quebec by Sir David Kirke in 1629. During these fourteen years great work was done by the Franciscans. They founded a chapel on the spot now occupied by the Cathedral of Quebec. Father le Caron penetrated the lands

of the Mohawks and the Wyandots. He made immense
journeys in canoes and on foot, and finally reached as far as
Lake Huron and Niagara. In the year 1624, Henri de Levis,
Duc de Ventador, became Viceroy of Canada. He was an
ardent protector of the Jesuits, and took Holy Orders himself, and introduced the fathers in the year 1626.

The introduction of the Jesuits into Canada was, as might
be expected, the signal for a new onslaught on that much-abused Society, and another series of false statements. These
may be summed up in the following extract from Kirke (p.
49): "He" (Duc de Ventador) "sent Jesuits to Canada.
This was a great mortification to the Recollets, so that incessant bickerings and quarrels arose between them and the
Roman Catholics." This statement is contrary to fact, as testified to by all historians of Canada. Dr. Mullock (p. 18) says:
"The Jesuits came under the protection of the Duke of Lèvi,
and were hospitably received by the Recollets, in their
newly-established convent of St. Mary of the Angels, at
Quebec. The field was vast enough for all, and laborers of
every Institute were welcome."

Abbé Brasseur de Bourbourg (page 32) says:—

"With that sure penetration which has more than once
enabled the sons of Ignatius to see into the future, they
understood at a glance the importance which Canada was
destined to be for France. . . . The Recollets of the
little monastery of Notre Dame des Anges offered to them
on their arrival the most cordial welcome, and continued, as
long as the Jesuits required it, to give them a hospitality
the most generous and fraternal."

Not only were the Jesuits welcomed by the Franciscans,
but we learn from Abbé Ferland (p. 214), who quotes
from official documents, that the Franciscans actually asked
for the assistance of the Jesuits in their vastly growing
missions. "In the meantime the Recollets saw that it would
be necessary for them to secure new laborers. . . . They
concluded to apply to some religious community which
possessed more means than they (*qui jouissaient de secours*

plus abondants). They therefore determined to send to France to make the proposal to the Jesuits," whom they thought the best suited (*les plus propres*) for the rude missions of Canada. They sent one of their fathers (Père Piat) to France on this mission. "The Recollets and the Jesuits worked together in many missions in the most perfect harmony (*avec une entente toute cordiale*)."

The bickering and quarrels referred to by Kirke were not between the Jesuits and Franciscans, but between the merchants and the latter; and are thus explained by Garneau (p. 95): "Father Irenæus le Piat, O.S.F., gave an invitation thither to a few Jesuits. The 'associated merchants' at first would not sanction the proceeding. They set out for Canada notwithstanding; but when they reached Quebec they were not permitted to land till the Recollets should find them a permanent asylum in the infant city." "The greater part of these merchants," says Ferland, "were Huguenots, and they had no great love for religious Orders. They tolerated, indeed, the poor Recollets, but they looked with a sinister eye (*mauvais œuil*) on the coming of the Jesuits, who had powerful friends at court."

For two years they lived under one roof with the Franciscans in perfect accord (*dans la meilleure intelligence*), till in March, 1620, they received a plot of ground near the river St. Charles. They immediately commenced their missionary work, and also to teach the Indians to cultivate the land. Their apostolic labors among the Indian tribes of Upper Canada for three years form a beautiful and touching chapter in the history of that country, but are outside of our present scope. We have seen that in 1629 Quebec was captured by Sir David Kirke, the religious all sent home, and Canada possessed by the English till the treaty of St. Germain-en-Laye in 1632. On the return of the French to Canada it was decided by the minister, Cardinal Richelieu, with the consent of the General of the Capucins, that the Jesuits only should return to Quebec, as the country was not yet able to support a mendicant Order. The Recollets,

however, were permitted to return to their mission of Holy
Cross, in Acadia. The Capucins established themselves on
the banks of the Kennebec and the Pantagonet or Penobscot
river. They had expected to be able to take possession of
their mission in Quebec, and, indeed, had obtained permission of Cardinal Richelieu to return, but objections were
made by the "Company of the Hundred Associates," on the
grounds that the introduction of two Orders in a country
where there was as yet no Bishop might cause some jealousies
or difficulties. The ecclesiastical authorities therefore withdrew the permission from the Recollets. They were greatly
grieved not to be allowed to continue their apostolic labors,
and to leave their bones in the country where they had first
planted the Cross, and which they had moistened with their
sweat. Such chagrin was felt by the noble Father le Caron,
the first apostle of the Hurons, that he fell sick, and died
March 29, 1632.

The desire to return to their mission was always cherished
by these good fathers; but it was not until after a patient
expectation of nearly forty years that their wishes were
realized. In the year 1670 M. Talon, Intendant of Quebec,
by his influence obtained an order from the King, Louis XIV.,
for their restoration. He brought out with him Père Allard
and three others, and they were reëstablished in all their
former rights and possessions, their houses and lands, on the
banks of the river St. Charles. They were received with
the most cordial welcome by the Jesuits. Père le Mercier,
S.J., thus speaks of their arrival ("*Relations des Jesuites*,"
An. 1670) : —

"Les Reverend Pères Recollets qu'il (Talon) a amenez de
France, comme un nouveau secours de Missionnaires pour
cultiver cette Eglise nous ont donné un surcroy de joye et
de Consolation ; nous les avons receus comme les premiers
Apostres de ce païs, et tous les habitans de Quebec pour
reconnoistre l'obligation que leur a la colonie Françoise que
ils ont accompagnée dans son premier établissement ; ont

êsté ravis de revoir ces bons religieux éstablis au mesme lieu où ils demeuraient il y a plus de quarante Ans."

"The Reverend Franciscan Fathers whom he (Talon) has brought out from France, as a new help to the missionaries to cultivate this church, have given to us an increase of joy and consolation. We have received them as the first apostles of this country, and all the inhabitants of Quebec, in order to acknowledge the obligation which the French colony owes to them, whom they accompanied on their first establishment, have been rejoiced to see again those good religious settled down in the same place where they had dwelt some forty years before."

After this ingenuous and cordial welcome it can scarcely be maintained by Protestant writers that any jealousies intervened between these two religious orders.

CHAPTER X.

PLACENTIA. — [1660-1696.]

Extent of the Diocese of Quebec — Mgr. de St. Vallier Visits Placentia, 1689, and Founds a Franciscan Convent there — Troubled State of Newfoundland — Encroachments of the French — Obstruction Policy of England — Placentia Attacked unsuccessfully by Commodore Williams — St. John's Attacked by the French, 1694 — The Whole Island, except Carbineers' and Bonavista, Captured by D'Iberville, 1696 — Graphic Account of this Expedition by Sieur Baudouin, Military Chaplain — Capture of Ferryland, Bay Bulls, Petty Harbor, St. John's, Torbay, Kenvidi [Quidividi], Portugal Cove, Harbor Men [Maine], Brigue [Brigus], Carbonnière, Havre de Grace, Havre Content, Bay Ver, Nieu Perlican, etc. — Final Decadence of French Power in the Western World.

AT the time that the management of ecclesiastical affairs in Canada was assumed by the energetic and zealous Monseigneur de St. Vallier, France was the greatest European power in the New World. Her dominion extended in the north and east over all Acadia, Newfoundland (except a small portion of the eastern seaboard), Labrador, as far as Hudson's Bay. Towards the south-east her banner waved over half of the States of Maine, Vermont, and New York, and in the West over all the vast valley of the Mississippi, Texas, and Rio Grande. In the north-west she had pushed her settlements as far as Niagara and the shores of the great lakes; from Port Nelson, in Hudson's Bay, to the Gulf of Mexico. Such was the vast territory then claimed by the French king, and such also the extent of the diocese over which Monseigneur de St. Vallier exercised his spiritual jurisdiction. When he beheld the vast field of his future labors he was anxious to seek out coöperators, and accordingly the year after his arrival in his diocese he determined to visit Newfoundland and establish a Franciscan convent at Placentia, the then capital of the Island. Accordingly he published a *mandement*, directed to the guardian of the Franciscans in Quebec, calling on the brethren of that convent to assist him in his apostolic labors. It appears by this document that a Catholic church was already built in 1689 in Placentia, and that a priest, though never regularly inducted as curé, officiated there. The *mandement* is as follows:—

John, etc.

"To Our beloved brethren Seraphin Georgien, guardian of the Convent of Recollets, of Our Lady of the Angels at Quebec and to the Bretheren of the Community destined as Missionaries to the Island of Newfound Land Health and Benediction in the Lord.

"Whereas being about in a few days to visit in person, as befits our pastoral solicitude the most remote portion of Our Diocese, especially the Island called Newfound Land consulting for the salvation and spiritual profit as well of the inhabitants there of, as of those who come there every year. We have proposed to take you also with us as the companions of our travels and our labors with the Intention that in the town commonly called Placentia you may have a hospice or even a convent the better to facilitate your labors for the salvation of the inhabitants of that place, and whereas for the establishment of a hospice or convent the license of the Bishop and the King are required and you have humbly postulated for both, we therefore wishing to favor your prayers and desires, as far as the Episcopal license is required, most fully and as far as in Us lies, irrevocably grant the same to you willingly by these present letters: so that on receipt of them We allow you to erect in the said town a hospice or even a Convent with whatever means are furnished by pious persons: there to exercise the usual duties of your Order. The Chapel also which has been consecrated to God in the said town: the sacred vessels destined for Divine Worship, and the Ecclesiastical Vestments which shall be in the said Chapel at the time of our Visitation shall belong to you there being and residing, as far as the statutes of your Order allow and We can Grant them. It is Our Will also that you discharge the duties of the Mission to the faithful and towards

the unbelievers in the said town, and other places adjacent, having first however received, as is proper, the Approbation of Us, or of our Vicar General. It is Our desire likewise that this Our license should be available to you in Order to Obtain the Royal License which we hope will be easily obtained from His Most Christian Majesty. We grant the aforesaid license to you with the agreement and condition, that you will be always ready to discharge the duties of the Mission in the aforesaid places, either by your selves or by other Religious of your Order, to be deputed by the guardian or other superior of the Convent of Our Lady of Angels at Quebec, who shall first of all be obliged to obtain Our Approbation or that of Our Vicar General. Besides, since it is Our intention to assist you in the Work so Conducive to the Salvation of Souls, We have desired That the Parish either already erected in the said town, or to be erected by Us, since the Care of it has hitherto been entrusted to some pastor not fixed, as not being installed by Us, or by Our Illustrious Predecessor, be united and attributed to Your Order as far as in Us lies, and by these present letters We unite it in fact and for ever decree it to be united, on condition that the Supreme Pontiff Authorise it, and on condition also that the Care of it be deputed to one individual selected from among the Religious who dwell in said Hospice or Convent, approved of by Us or by Our Vicar General presented or recommended by the Father Guardian, or other Superior of the Convent of Our Lady of Angels of Quebec without lesion however to the Authority of the said Guardian over his subjects. Desiring also that the Royal Bounties, and other Charitable donations be conferred on you, and granting to you also all dues tithes, and offerings. In faith whereof these present Letters, signed by Our hand, sealed with Our Seal and Countersigned by Our Secretary We have given to you.

"JOHN, *Bishop of Quebec.*

" Quebec one thousand six hundred and eighty-nine the 22 day of the Month of April."

The royal license alluded to in the foregoing document was not obtained until some three years after (1692), owing probably to difficulty of communication, though it is most probable that the mission was established at once on presumption of the King's acquiescence. From this document we also find that a church or a chapel already existed in Placentia previous to 1689, and was furnished with requisites for divine worship, though there was not a fixed pastor; but probably one of the naval or military chaplains officiated there. Dr. Mullock (Lectures, p. 15) says "the convent and church of the Franciscans were established on the site now occupied by the Protestant church and burial-ground. . . . Most of the French tombstones were taken by the English settlers after the surrender of the place by France in 1713 and applied to the ignominious purpose of hearthstones and door-steps." Two or three of these old monuments have escaped the ruthless hands of the destroyer, and have been lately carefully placed in the church. The oldest dates we find are 1694 and 1676. They are very much mutilated, and can with difficulty be deciphered. The language is distinctly Latin and French, though one or two words on one stone are unintelligible. They have lately been pronounced by an expert of the British Museum to be in the Basque language. It may be so, or it may be that they form but broken parts of Latin words. I give facsimiles of some of the most ancient stones, taken from the originals with great care.

In a letter of Monseigneur Turgeon, Archbishop of Quebec, written to Dr. Mullock in 1858, his Grace says: "These fathers (the Franciscans) will probably have been the first resident missionaries, although the French establishments were much more ancient, and extend far beyond 1660; but at the time of the siege (1696) Charlevoix confesses that the French were not less deprived of spiritual than of temporal succor (Vol. II., p. 186), which leads us to believe with reason that the foundation of the mission was not much anterior to that epoch. However, we cannot find anything in our rec-

FAC-SIMILES OF OLD TOMBSTONES AT PLACENTIA.

ords more ancient than these letters ; " *i.e.*, that of Bishop de St. Vallier, previously given, and that of the King, Louis XIV., giving the royal sanction and license for the foundation, which is dated 1692, and is as follows : —

"1692. Louis, by the grace of God, King of France and Navarre, to all present and to come. Health:

"Our beloved and faithful Counsellor the Lord Bishop of Quebec has made known to us that a Convent of Religious Recollets of the Order of Francis being in existence at Quebec, he would dispose a number of said Religious in various localities of New France, the Island of Newfoundland and other parts of North America. And particularly in Montreal, Placentia and the Island of St. Peter, and the inhabitants of those places might have from the said Religious, all the spiritual succours which might be expected from their zeal and piety, and he is desirous of giving a fixity to their establishments in the said places that they may be more and more attached to the Missions, and other functions to which they apply themselves. For this reason we have permitted and permit the said Recollets to continue their Establishments, as well in the said City of Quebec as in Ville Marie, Montreal, the Island of Placentia, St. Peters and all other places where they shall be judged necessary, on condition nevertheless, that this be done with consent of the Governor or Lieutenant Governor of the said countries and of the inhabitants of the places where they wish to establish themselves; and in the said places they shall discharge the functions of chaplains to our troops, and shall exercise also the parochial functions wherever the Bishop shall judge necessary, and shall empower them to do so. And for which they shall receive as alms the allowances appointed by Our Estates to be furnished to the Chaplains of our said troops. And we have also enfeoffed, And by these letters signed by Our hand we do give in fee their Churches lodgings and Cloisters of the Convents established or to be established, without their being obliged to pay to us, or to the Kings our Successors on this account any fines or indemnities of all which by these presents We make them a grant and remittance. We command our faithful and well beloved Counsellors of the Council of Quebec and declare to all others whose duty it is to cause them to be registered and to give the enjoyment of the rights contained in them to the said Religious fully and peaceably and in perpetuity ceasing and causing to cease, any trouble or hindrance, for such is Our pleasure. And that this may be a matter for ever fixed and stable, We have caused our seal to be affixed to these presents.

"Given at Versailles in the Month of March the year of Grace one thousand six hundred and ninety-two, and of Our reign the fifty-ninth.

"(Signed) LOUIS.

"By the King, PHELYPEAUX."

On the outside the document is labelled as follows:—

"Letters for the Establishment of the Recollet Fathers in Canada, Island of St. Pierre, and Newfound Land, signed Phelypeaux, and with the Great Seal of Green Wax pendant by a silk string, green and red, compared with the original extant on Parchment, by Louis Guillon de Fonteny, Our Garde de Notes of the King at St. Germain-en-Laye, undersigned 17th April 1692."

From this document it appears that the Franciscans were established also this same year in St. Pierre and Miquelon.

We have seen that though the English claimed dominion over Newfoundland, yet the possession was not considered of much account, and a policy of repression prevailed all through the seventeenth century. Every effort was made to prevent the permanent settlement of the country. Bonnycastle (Vol. I., p. 83), writing of this period of Newfoundland history, says: "We have a long, uninteresting space filled with quarrel and complaint from . . . 1663 down to 1692. . . . The Island underwent many convulsions; . . . for nearly ninety years misrule reared its head, and society was in a wretched condition, owing to the constant animosity between the merchant adventurers and the settlers. . . . The struggle was not so much of a political as of a personal nature, and it arose from the unlimited discretionary license of the illiterate masters of vessels . . . and the absurd policy of the parent state in discountenancing settlement by every means in its power." In 1670, owing to a pamphlet of Sir Josiah Child, the Lords of Trade and Plantation obtained an order that the whole colony should be rooted out, and the land reduced to a desert. Sir John Berry, a humane naval officer, was deputed to burn the houses and drive out the settlers. He remonstrated against the cruelty, and in 1676 Mr. John Downing, a resident, procured an order from the King to annul it. Still it was expressly declared that no fishing-vessel was to be permitted to take out emigrants, and all persons were forbidden to settle. In spite of these obstacles a resident population sprang up, and it became necessary at last to recognize the fact. A regulation was then passed by the Board of Trade in 1697 in which it was declared that "the resident population should not be allowed to increase beyond *one thousand*." The policy of the French, however, was quite the reverse. Appreciating the value and importance of Newfoundland, they endeavored, step by step, to advance to the possession of the whole island. In the year 1635 the French obtained permission to dry fish on the shores of the Island. This was the first step towards forming a permanent settlement. Insensibly they encroached until, as we have seen, by the year 1660 they were well settled and strengthened in position at Placentia, and probably in other places. In 1675 the English king (Charles II.) remitted the tax hitherto paid on imports by the French as a token of sovereignty. Within a few years they had established their dominion over a territory of two hundred miles in extent. On the accession of William III. to the throne of England, 1688, owing to European combinations, war was declared against France, and, as usual, spread to the colonies.

It was just about this time that the French were establishing themselves in all security in Placentia, and preparing to found a regular ecclesiastical mission there. The eyes of the English began to be at last opened to these rapid and firm encroachments; but it was almost too late. In the year 1692 an English squadron, under Commodore Williams, appeared before Placentia; but the French fortifications were impregnable, and the attack was unsuccessful. The ruins of the forts still existing give us some idea of the strength of the fortress. "The environing hill," says Dr. Mullock (Lecture I., p. 15), "the two arms of the sea with a rapid tidal current reminding the French of the arrowy Rhône in their own land, and the almost total exemption from fog in a bay remarkable for it, induced them to call it Plaisance, — a pleasant place, — now Placentia. They early saw the importance of the acquisition, and provided for its security by strong fortifications. These are now in ruins, — they have served as a quarry for the few buildings requiring stone or brick. The great demilune which guarded the entrance of the port (and was called Fort Louis) is now a shapeless heap of rubbish, its vaulted brick casements have been all destroyed, and the remains of a castle on Creveceur Hill are slowly perishing."

The history of Newfoundland from this time, 1090, until the Treaty of Utrecht, 1713, at which time the French abandoned it for good, is but a continuance of skirmishes, attacks, and reprisals on the part of the two rival nations. "We see," says Dr. Mullock (Lectures, p. 16), "two great and powerful nations established on the shores of Newfoundland, opposed in politics, in interest, in religion, and it is easy to imagine that the progress of the country must have been not only retarded, but absolutely impossible."

In the year 1694 a French fleet of ten sail, under Chevalier Nesmond, was ordered to join the Rocheford squadron and proceed to Newfoundland and drive out the English. They attacked St. John's, but were repulsed.

In the year 1696-7 a more formidable attack was made

overland from Placentia, under the command of Pierre le
Moine D'Iberville, on which occasion the whole Island, with
the exception of Carbineers' Harbor and Bonavista, was captured by the French, and remained in their possession for
several years, till the Treaty of Utrecht, 1713.

An interesting account of this expedition, written by M.
Baudouin, chaplain to the French army, has lately been discovered in the Ottawa Library. It was kindly copied in the
original French by Mr. Jack, of New Brunswick, for J. P.
Howley, Esq., F.G.S., to whom I am indebted for permission to give some extracts from it. It has never yet been,
as far as I am aware, published or translated into English.
It is the intention of Mr. Howley to do so soon. Though
not immediately connected with the ecclesiastical history of
Newfoundland, yet it may be deemed sufficiently relevant as
showing in a graphic manner the state of the country at the
period of which we are writing. It is addressed to some
Bishop, as appears from the title of *Monseigneur*. The good
abbé, though full of zeal for his spiritual mission and for the
conversion of savages, yet seems to be of a thoroughly mar-
tial spirit, and describes with evident *goût* and vivacity the
several naval and military engagements which he witnessed
at Baye des Espagnols (Sydney), where they arrived on the
26th June, and he baptized and married several Indians.
Thence they proceeded to St. John, N.B., where they engaged two English ships and captured them. He then describes the taking of Pemkuit and several other exploits.

ACADIE. — 1696–1697.

JOURNAL OF SIEUR BAUDOUIN, MISSIONER.

"JOURNAL OF THE VOYAGE WHICH I HAVE MADE WITH M.
D'IBERVILLE, CAPTAIN OF A FRIGATE OF FRANCE, IN ACADIE,
AND FROM ACADIE TO THE ISLAND OF NEWFOUNDLAND."

On the 3d of September they set sail for Placentia, and
arrived there on the 12th in the morning. A boat came

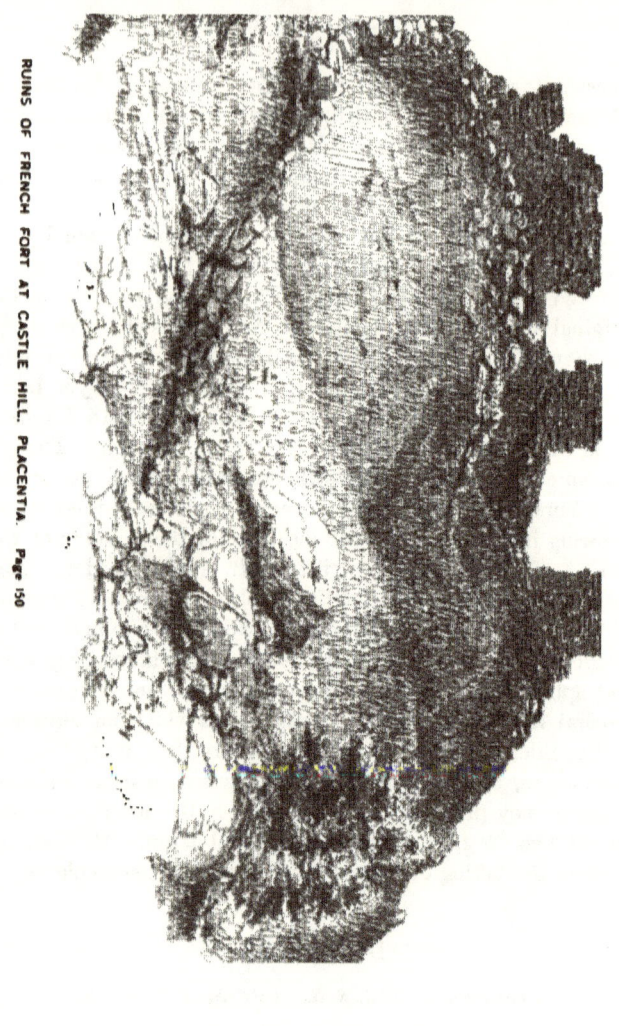

RUINS OF FRENCH FORT AT CASTLE HILL, PLACENTIA. Page 150

from the shore and brought a letter from the Lieutenant of
the King to say that M. de Brouillon, the governor, had left
with the Malovians (men of St. Malo). Messieurs D'Iberville
and Bonaventure (his lieutenant), casting anchor, went to ask
for provisions of the lieutenant-governor. The *Envieux*,
M. D'Iberville's vessel, had been obliged, for some time past,
to supply with provisions the *Profond*, M. de Bonaventure's
vessel. The lieutenant-governor informed them that there
was nothing to spare in the settlement. They then entered
the port (that is, inside the gut) and awaited the arrival of
the *Postillon* or the *Wasp*, with provisions. These were,
doubtless, prizes taken from the English. They did not arrive,
however (probably from France), until the 10th of October.
M. de Brouillon, the Governor of Placentia, arrived
on the 17th. He had been on an expedition with some Malovian
soldiers or sailors, to attack St. John's, but failed.
Guyon arrived from Boston with his men, and M. D'Iberville
prepared to go in a bark canoe to take Carbonniere and
St. John's,—a feat which, as the sequence will show, was not
so easy, at least as regards the former place. He proposed
to relegate to the spring-time the capture of Bonavista, and
the gutting of the merchant ships there. In this little game
he also reckoned without his host. On the 18th some
prisoners arrived from St. John's, and informed them that
there were eight ships at Carbonniere, laden with fish. A
dispute then arose between Srs. de Brouillon and D'Iberville.
The former wished to march at once upon St. John's, leaving
Carbonniere for after-work. D'Iberville refused, and said he
would return to France. The soldiers, Canadians, probably
Micmacs or half-breeds, refused to go with De Brouillon, and
would return to Canada, unless D'Iberville should command
in person. After some time they came to an understanding.
De Brouillon left in the *Profond* for Rognouze, and D'Iberville,
with 120 men, started for Forillon (Ferryland), on All
Saints Day (November 1st).

Next day (All Souls) they took the land, having walked
on the ice up the S.E. Arm, for about a league and a half from

the settlement. The travelling was very bad, the men sinking on the wet moss to the knees (*jusqu'a mi-jambe*), and in passing the lakes and rivers, up to the waist in water. After ten days' route they arrived at Forillon (on the 10th). They were coming short of provisions for the last two days, and found about a dozen horses at this place, which came in very *apropos*. It seems they took Forillon without any difficulty.

On the 11th Sr. de Rancogne arrived from St. John's with three men, who were almost famished. The people of Forillon, to the number of one hundred and ten, had fled to Bay Boulle, which they were fortifying. Another disagreement arose between Messieurs D'Iberville and De Brouillon concerning the booty.

On the 21st they set out for Bay Boulle in boats, where they captured a merchant ship of 100 tons, the crew of which, as well as the inhabitants of the place, fled into the woods.

On the 26th D'Iberville, with seven men, started in advance of the main body, and took Petty Harbor, which made a pretty strong resistance; thirty-six of the English were killed. There were sixty men in Petty Harbor, — all very comfortable. They marched thence on to St. John's. At about seven and a half miles from Petty Harbor, on the 28th, they encountered a body of English, numbering eighty-eight, who were posted in a burnt wood, full of rocks, behind which they lay in ambush. After about half an hour's fighting they dislodged them, and drove them back on St. John's. M. D'Iberville seized the first two forts of St. John's, which the enemy had abandoned, and made thirty-three prisoners. The rest of the inhabitants took refuge in the grand fort, and in a ketch (*quaische*) in the harbor. There were about two hundred men in St. John's. The fort, as described, was probably on the site of Fort William.

It was besieged. On the 30th a man came out from the fort with a white flag, to treat of a capitulation. The fort was given up the same day, and the French took possession. The governor of the place was only a simple citizen, elected by the captains of the vessels for the year. On the 2d of December the French took Portugal Cove, which contained three families; also Torbay, which had likewise three families, and Kerividi (Quidi Vidi), which had nine families. They burnt every house in St. John's, and the boats in the harbor. On the 14th January, 1697, they started for Portugal Cove, and arrived there on the 19th. Thence they travelled along the shore of Conception Bay to the bottom, where they found some men sawing wood, who had come from Carbonniere. On the 20th they took Harbor Men (Maine), where there was one house. On the 23d they left in three boats for Carbonniere. They passed by Brigue, where there were about sixty men, and arrived at Port Grave, which they took. There were one hundred and ten men and seventeen houses there, well armed. On the 24th they set out for Carbonniere; Le Sr. de Montigny was sent with a detachment to take Musquito. In passing from Harbor Grace to Carbonniere in boats they discovered that the inhabitants of this latter place had entrenched themselves on the Island, and they fired some cannon shots at the French. There were about two hundred on the Island, having fled there from Harbor Grace, Musquito, and even St. John's. They had erected barracks and strong forts. Having arrived at Carbonniere, the French sent to summon the people on the Island, but were met with defiance. They found it impossible to attack it, as it was steep on all sides, with the exception of two places of landing, which were well guarded. On the 29th they received prisoners from Brigue, among whom were eight Irishmen, "whom," says M. Baudouin, "the English treat as slaves."

Several attempts were made by M. D'Iberville to land on the Island, but in vain. On the night of the 1st they went all round the Island in boats.

On the 3d they took Bay Ver, where there were some fourteen houses and about ninety men. From there they went to Old Perlican; there were there nineteen houses, several stores, more than thirty head of horned cattle, and

a number of sheep and pigs. On the 7th they went to Ance
Havre (Hants Harbor). There were four houses, but the
people had all fled. On the morning of the 8th they started
for Celicove (Silly Cove), where there were four houses and a
great quantity of fish and cattle. Thence they came to New
Perlican; there were there nine houses and stores. They left
immediately for Harbor Content (Havre Content), where
there was a sort of fort or barricade, made of boards, with
portholes above and below. This temporary fortress was
commanded by an Irishman. They surrendered on being
summoned. There were thirty men, besides women and
children. Having left the place in charge of M. Deschau-
fours with ten men, they started the following day for Carbonniere. When arrived there they found that the English
had taken prisoners one Frenchmen and three Irishmen, who
had taken part with the French. A detatchment under Boisbriand was sent to burn Brigue, Port Grave, etc. Harbor
Grace had fourteen houses, Carbonniere, twenty-two, — the
best built in all Newfoundland. Some of the merchants were
men of £100,000 worth of property. On the 17th they entered
into negotiations with the people on the Island for an exchange of prisoners. The English demanded one Englishman in lieu of their French prisoner, and three for each
Irishman. The place of exchange was agreed upon, namely,
out of gunshot of the Island, about half-way between it and
the shore. The English came without their prisoners, and
some words ensued. The French accused them of breaking
their word, and casting ridicule upon the orders of the King.
The French seized the English officers, and took them prisoners. On the 28th they burned Carbonniere, and left again
for Havre Content. On the 1st of March M. D'Iberville
sent MM. de Montigny and de la Peiriere to go with all
the prisoners (about 200) to Bay Boulle (Bay Bulls Arm,
in the bottom of Trinity Bay). He left M. de Boisbriand
with a detachment at Havre Content, with orders to keep a
strict watch on Carbonniere, and he himself, with nine men,
set out across the woods for Plaisance. "The road," says

M. Baudouin, dryly, "is not as good as from Paris to Versailles."

On the 19th of March M. D'Iberville left Placentia in a boat for the Bay of Cromwell (Oliver's Cove). Here they met with M. Peiriere, who came from Bay Bulls Arm to meet them. He had come from Havre Content with nine boats, and sixty men prisoners. On the 20th Sr. de Montigny arrived with twenty Irishmen, who had taken part with the French. On the 28th they went to the Bay of the Sound (Random), and to Trinity, where they burned two houses. M. D'Iberville went to Placentia to gather all the forces possible for the attack on Bonavista, "which," says Baudouin, "is the last which remains entire in the hands of the British." It contains three hundred men, and about forty houses. M. D'Iberville awaited at Placentia the arrival from France of the fleet, under the Sr. de Serigny, which event did not occur until the 18th of May. In the meantime M. de Montigny and de la Peiriere went to New Perlican and captured a vessel; thence to Bay Ver and to Havre Content, where they found M. de Boisbriand. An Irishman, who had escaped from the Island by swimming ashore at night-time, found his way across the country from Carbonniere to Havre Content. He had been three days in the woods without food or firing, and was very much frost-bitten. He told them there were 300 men on the Island, and others arriving daily from all parts, even from Placentia. M. Baudouin says nothing more about Bonavista, except simply that M. D'Iberville did not go there. He then gives an account of the English and the country generally, which, though no doubt very much exaggerated, yet is so graphic, and contains so much evident truth, that I fain to quote more fully from it: "The French, and I say it with shame for our nation, deem the country impassable. . . . Not so the English, they know it perfectly, even that part which belongs to France, for they guided us everywhere, through the woods and along the coasts, where, for more than one hundred and ninety leagues, they have roads beaten, fit to ride upon horseback. More than two hundred of them spend the winter hunting in the depths of the forest, where they kill beavers, otters, deer, bears," &c.

He says these English hunters are good shots, but great cowards, so that one hundred of them would fly before one Frenchman. He then describes, in most deplorable terms, the abominable lives led by these men. "They have not," he says, "a single minister of religion in these establishments, though more than twenty of them are larger settlements than Placentia. They do not know what religion they belong to. The greater part of them, born in this country, have never received any instruction, and never make any act of religion, no more than mere savages. Drunkenness and impurity are common and public among them, even among the women." In fine, he gives a tabular statement of the places taken by the French (36), the number of houses (149), number of men (1,753).

The Hon. Judge Prowse, in his lecture on "Episodes in our Early History," says: "The French and English accounts of this attack are very contradictory;" and so they indeed are, if Judge Prowse is to be relied on for the summary given by him from the English point of view. For instance, the learned Judge writes: "The French account says that they (the French) entered the fort with the English." This is not quite correct, as will be seen from M. Baudouin's diary. The skirmish on the old Petty Harbor road took place on November 28th. On that day the French captured two smaller forts in St. John's; but not the "grand fort" (Fort William), into which the English had retired. "Seeing they were about to defend themselves," says M. Baudouin, "we sent to Bay Boulle for the mortars and bumbs and powder. On the night of the 29th and 30th MM. de Mins and de Montigny went with sixty Canadians to burn the houses near the fort;" and, according to him, the fort did not yield till "the 30th, day of St. Andrew." So, on this point, it will be seen that the French gave credit to the English for three days' resistance. Judge Prowse continues to describe the most revolting barbarism practised by the French. "The French took one William Drew, an inhabitant, a prisoner, cut all around his scalp, then by strength of hand stripped his skin from his forehead to his crown, and then sent him back into the fort, assuring the inhabitants they would be all served the same way if they did not surrender." This statement is altogether too horrible to be believed, and the Abbé Baudouin says not a word about it, but describes the surrender in quite a different manner. "The 30th," he says, "the day of St. Andrew, a man came from the fort with a white flag, to speak of surrender. . . . The Governor with four of the principal citizens came for an interview. They would not allow us to enter the fort, lest we should see the miserable plight to which they were reduced. It was agreed they should surrender on condition of being allowed to depart for England. The capitulation was brought in writing to the fort, and approved of by the principal citizens (*bourgeois*) and signed by the Governor and M. de Brouillon."

All this certainly looks like the most approved style of civilized and orthodox warfare. And, again, M. Baudouin tells us that a thoroughly religious spirit pervaded the French forces. Before going into fight they all received absolution, and during the campaign they frequently approached the Sacraments, and that the greater part of them had the fear of God, to which he attributes their wonderful success. "I have never before," he says, "seen so clearly accomplished that which God says regarding those who serve him." On the other hand, he draws a most lamentable picture of the state of the English inhabitants. "It is impossible," he says, "to imagine anything more abominable than the life led by the English of these coasts." They are left altogether without the succor of religion, and are degenerated into a race almost worse than savages. Crime of the most loathsome nature is quite public among them; not only that, but, as the Abbé Baudouin states, "they endeavored even to entice our men to evil." Now, even making full allowance for the patriotism and prejudice of this zealous chaplain, we can scarcely doubt that the state of these poor people at that time must have been very low in the moral scale. As to the French, it is amazing to think that they could have brought an army through those trackless woods, — a thing which now, after the improvements and changes of over two hundred and seventy years, could scarcely be attempted. That they were courageous, enthusiastic, perhaps severe even to the verge of cruelty, we can easily believe. Warfare at best is not a mollifier of human passions; but I think we must decline to give credence to the barbarous story of the scalping. It is true that there was a contingent of Canadian Indians and half-breeds with the French troops who might possibly have been guilty of such an outrage; but instead of being acknowledged or countenanced by the French officers, it is most probable that if discovered it would be punished with the utmost severity.

Speaking of this period of our history, Bonnycastle (Vol. I., pp. 82 and 86) says: "For nearly ninety years misrule reared its head, and society was in a wretched condition. There was no English clergyman in the country until about nine years after the events recorded by Abbé Baudouin. This year (1705) was remarkable for that in which the first resident clergyman or missionary of the Church of England arrived in Newfoundland. . . . His name was Jackson."

It was not till about sixty years afterwards (1765) that the first Methodist minister arrived in Newfoundland. This was the Rev. Mr. Coughlan. He was established in Harbor Grace; but, according to Rev. Mr. Bond, in the St. John's "Daily Evening Telegram," Christmas, 1885, quoting from Wilson's "Wesleyanism in Newfoundland," he was not a recognized Methodist minister, having been "ordained by the Bishop of London" as an Anglican clergyman, and sent out at the expense of the "Society for the Propagation of the Gospel." Nevertheless, he

seems to have reconciled it to his conscience to act in a
dual capacity. "Though a clergyman," says Mr. Bond,
"he was still a Methodist preacher." Whether this is
compatible with the principles of Wesleyanism or not I
am not sufficiently initiated to pass an opinion; but, certainly, viewed from the stand-point of honesty, it has, to
say the least, a doubtful appearance.

For the next fifteen or sixteen years the history of Newfoundland consists of a series of alternating conquests and
defeats between the French and English. "The Island was
torn and harassed by petty warfare and depredation, being
sometimes in possession of one power, sometimes of the other"
(Bonycastle, p. 87.) In 1698 Admiral Neville and Sir John
Gibson appeared off the coast. In 1703 Admiral Graydon
came; but the French still held possession, though it seems
they were ousted from some places for, in 1704 we find
some of the Abenaquis Indians had established themselves in
Newfoundland, and were attacked by the English. They
applied to the Governor of Placentia, M. Vaudreuil, for
assistance. M. Montigny was sent to their aid with about
fifty Canadians. In 1705 M. Subercase, having succeeded
M. de Brouillon in the government of Placentia, endeavored to
make thorough work with the English. The French were
this time assisted by the Abenaquis, under their celebrated
leader, Nescambouit. They set out from Placentia with an
army of some four or five hundred, and travelled on snow-shoes,
as did D'Iberville's men a few years before. They started
about the 15th of January, and did not meet up with the
English till the 26th, having suffered much from the cold.
The place of encounter is called in Anspach (p. 133) *Rebou*,
which may be a corruption of Renouse, or more likely a
typographical mistake for *Bebou*, which would be a French
way of writing *Baybulls*. They next took Petty Harbor.
They then pursued in the track of D'Iberville towards
St. John's, which was again in possession of the English.
After some time, they were obliged to raise the siege on
account of want of powder. They retraced their steps to

Forillon, which they captured and burnt on the 5th of March; "after which," says Charlevoix ("Nouvelle France," Vol. II., p. 300), " Montigny, with his faithful Nescambouit, went and destroyed all the coast, including Carboniere and *Booneviste*." In 1706 the British again expelled them. In 1708 St. Ovide, French admiral, took St. John's and all the Island, excepting Carbonear, which, as usual, was gallantly defended by the fishermen. The French then held it until the Treaty of Utrecht, 1713. By this treaty, as is well known, the sovereignty of the whole Island was ceded to Great Britain; but unfortunately for the future prosperity of the Island, the French were allowed certain fishing rights, which have been the source of all our troubles. The Island was then placed under the nominal administration of the Governor of Nova Scotia. In 1729 the first governor of Newfoundland was appointed in the person of Sir Henry Osborne. Although the governor was nominated as commander-in-chief, still the fishing admirals, who had been established since 1700, were retained. The commission also included Placentia, which, since the Treaty of 1713, had been a separate command, as a deputy governorship under the Governor of Nova Scotia.

The signing of the Treaty of Utrecht gave the death-blow to French power and prestige in the New World. " Had her ministers," writes Dr. Mullock (MS., p. 22), " either ordinary foresight or patriotism, and had a few millions of the wealth squandered at Versailles, or worse, in vice and infamy, during the regency and the reign of Louis XV., been expended on the French settlements in America, not alone Canada, but the whole of the western portion of the continent, the Southern States bordering on Mexico, the lower provinces of New Brunswick, Nova Scotia, Newfoundland, and Prince Edward Island, would now be French in blood, language, and religion. What religion did for Spain, in the days of her glory, when her 'Golden Banner,' surmounted by the Cross, waved over half the world; when the Spanish soldier and the Spanish friar penetrated together to the remotest ends of the earth; when the fortress and the convent rose side by side, — she would have done as effectually for France; but infidelity was then eating into the vitals of the nation. . . . The opposition of Louis XIV. to the Pope; the so-called 'liberties' of the Gallican Church, which favored and nurtured Jansenism, and, subsequently, developed during the regency and the reign of Louis XV.; the frightful infidelity of Voltaire and his associates, — lost to France the New World. In her madness she rose against God and against His Church, and her glory departed forever. It is only once in the cycle of ages that a nation has the power of establishing her religion, her language, her laws, and her character over a large section of the human race; and no nation ever threw away such a splendid opportunity of doing this as France. Her forts, beginning at New Orleans, encircled the contracted territory of the thirteen original States, and to the north, to the shores of Baffin's Bay, the land was all her own. Her log forts are now great cities, — the Sees of Bishops and the marts of commerce; the deserts and forests where her flag then waved are now the homes of great nations; but her sun is set forever; her language is there no longer spoken. A few sugar islands,[1] and the islets of St. Pierre and Miquelon, now comprise her whole transatlantic territory. About a million of Canadians, among thirty-six millions of North Americans, speak her language, and these will, in the course of time, be absorbed in the Anglo-Celtic race. . . . Such is the state in which her parliaments, her kings, and her encyclopædists have left her. Her glory in the Western Hemisphere is departed. Forty millions may hereafter use her language as their vernacular throughout the world, while English will be the mother-tongue of at least two hundred millions of the human race. Voltaire and his satellites satisfied the last generation, and made them believe that infidelity was the panacea for the social evils for their country. Now no Frenchman can

---

[1] Cayenne.

tread the soil of America, where his language and nationality, except in a small part of Canada, have perished, without feeling the blush of shame mantling his cheek. . . . Without doubt the great Revolution was sent by God to chasten and reinvigorate the mocking and frivolous generation which then encumbered the soil of France."

CHAPTER XI.

CATHOLICITY AFTER THE TREATY OF UTRECHT.— [1696–1728.]

Treaty of Utrecht, 1713 — Conditions, French allowed to Depart or become British Subjects — Catholic Religion publicly Practised in Newfoundland — The Fishing Admirals — Opposition of the Merchants to the Appointment of a Governor — Appointment of the First Governor, Captain Henry Osborne, 1728.

THE political history of Newfoundland during the latter part of the seventeenth century is but a record of obscure skirmishes between small detachments of English and French; the only remarkable transaction was the taking of St. John's, in 1708, by the French. They retained possession of the town till 1713, the date of the Treaty of Utrecht. During that occupation the Catholic religion was publicly professed and practised. By the above-mentioned treaty France abandoned all claim to the Island of Newfoundland, retaining only the small islands of St. Pierre, Langlade, and Miquelon, and the right of fishing on the shores from Cape Bonavista to Point Riche. The dominion of the soil was nominally secured to England, but the French secured such rights as have ever since clashed with the maintenance of British rule on that coast. The French were guaranteed the right to fish, while for British subjects it was only by the toleration of the French that they could exercise such a right. The French were allowed to dry and cure their fish on shore, and to cut such wood or boughs as might be necessary for their flakes and stages. It is easy to see how such rights, conflicting with those of British subjects settling on the shore, were soon the source of insurmountable and ever-increasing difficulties and contests.

According to the treaty, France, though obtaining full dominion of St. Peter's, was prohibited from fortifying it, or keeping a garrison of more than one hundred men upon it.

One of the articles of the treaty was that the Catholic religion was allowed (but with the sinister proviso, "as far as the laws of Great Britain will allow"!) in all places ceded by the French, — to French subjects who might wish to remain and become British subjects.

In Hannay's "History of Nova Scotia," p. 308, we read as follows: "On the 23d June, 1713, nearly three months after the Treaty of Utrecht was signed, Queen Anne wrote to Nicholson, Governor of Nova Scotia, as follows: 'Whereas our Good Brother, the most Christian King, hath at our desire released from imprisonment on board his galleys such of his subjects as were detained there on account of their professing the Protestant religion, We being willing to show by some mark of our favor towards his subjects how kind we take his compliance therein, have therefore thought fit hereby to signify Our will and pleasure to you; that you permit such of them as have any lands or tenements, in places under your Government in Acadia and Newfound Land, that have been or are to be yielded to Us by Virtue of the late Treaty of Peace; and are willing to continue our subjects; to retain and enjoy their said lands and tenements, without molestation as fully and freely as other of our subjects do: or may possess their lands or estates or to sell the same, if they shall rather choose to remove elsewhere. And for so doing this shall be your warrant.'"

Anspach says ("History of Newfoundland"), speaking of this period: "The priests publickly practised their sacerdotal functions as if popery were the established religion of the country. Richards, the English Commander-in-Chief, judiciously endeavoured to abridge their impolitick indulgences, . . . but was not supported in those measures. The influence thus obtained by the Church of Rome was the more pernicious as it was in the hands of the Jesuits, who, equally regardless of the laws and interests of their government considered their Mission in these parts of the world as intended merely to propagate their tenets and extend the power and wealth of their order."

"This ignorant piece of Protestant declamation," writes Dr. Mullock, "is valuable as a historical record of the public exercise of the Catholic religion in Newfoundland; and the bigoted attempt of the governor to violate the treaty by which he got the power to govern the Catholics of the Island. . . . The attack on the Jesuits is only another proof of the lamentable ignorance of such writers when treating of Catholic affairs. Even the grave debates of Parliament display such ignorance of Catholic matters (as, for instance, the *Bulla Cœnæ*, in a great measure identical with the common law of England) that they provoke the contempt and disgust of foreigners. We have no records of any Jesuits being settled in Newfoundland, and if any came to the country, they preached no peculiar tenets; nothing but the doctrines of the Catholic Apostolic Church."

From what has already been written concerning Ferryland, it appears that documents and records recently brought to light show us that Jesuits had actually been in Newfoundland in the time of Lord Baltimore (1623); but it is not likely that there were any here at the time of the Treaty of Utrecht, nearly a century later (1713).

Protestant writers frequently confound all missioners of the Catholic Church with the Jesuits, whereas the illustrious Order of St. Ignatius forms but a small, though active, part of the Church's army. Newfoundland was not a likely place for them to pretend to spread their power and influence, especially after its surrender to the English.

In all probability the priests who gave such umbrage to Governor Richards by legally performing their religious functions were the curés of St. John's and Placentia and other settlements; in all probability "king's priests," as the Recollets (Franciscans) were called, because they served as chaplains in all the forts, ships, and galleys of the French monarch. By a royal ordinance the Franciscans were obliged to furnish and provide one of their own Order as chaplain for every fort containing a garrison of forty men, and for every ship of war of his Most Christian Majesty. The friar, while acting as naval or military chaplain, received the appointment and rank of a captain of the line and two hundred livres per annum, one-half of which went to his convent. As their occupation interfered with the strict observance of the rule of St. Francis, Innocent XI., in the year 1685, granted them the necessary dispensations. On account of the scarcity of clergy in the vast diocese of Quebec, they were also obliged to send a priest from one of their convents to take charge of any convent becoming vacant till a curé was appointed.

The French population had no great inducement to remain in Newfoundland, — looked upon with an evil eye by the English Government; and having no great faith in the treaty by which their religion was guaranteed, they in most cases disposed of their properties in St. John's, Placentia, and Trepassey, then their principal settlements, and left the country. Thus the Island was once again delivered to Protestantism, and Catholicity, after the final departure of the French, seemed forever extinguished. But the ways of God are inscrutable. It was once more established on a more firm basis by Irish immigration.

The English laws and English sentiment opposed all attempts at colonization. The Island was regarded as a great ship moored in mid-ocean, to be yearly manned and put in commission by the fishermen of England and the Channel Islands. Acts were passed by the British Parliament (10 and 11 Will. III., 1698) to discourage settlement and cultivation. This act was the most extraordinary law ever passed for the ruin and confusion of a country. By it the masters of the *first three vessels* arriving in the Island to prosecute the fishery were invested with the titles of admiral, vice and rear admiral for the year. Thus men without education, legal knowledge, or any other qualification, immediately became possessed of magisterial powers of a high order, having uncontrolled right to decide all matters regarding the fishery, as well as all public rights of a civil nature. We may easily imagine how these men, bigoted, uneducated, and cruel, used the uncontrolled power — a barbarous enactment — put into their hands in a most tyrannical manner. Flogging an Irishman (which name was a synonyme for a Catholic) was a common occurrence. But this brutality did not cease with the fishing admirals. As late as 1821 two men were flogged in Conception Bay by order of a surrogate who was at the same time a Church of England parson. Their crime was that they fell into debt to a mercantile house. This was, however, the last time such barbarity was practised in the Island. A delegation was sent to London. The affair was brought before the colonial authorities, and the surrogate jurisdiction was abolished forever.

The state of religion and morality in the Island under the English rule during the remainder of the eighteenth century must have been at a very low ebb, even judging from the statements of Protestant authors themselves. Reeves (p. 68 and *seq.*) quotes the report sent home from time to time by the commodores to the Board of Trade, from which I clip the following (A.D. 1728): "Another of them says the admirals prove generally the greatest knaves. . . . It would be requisite to have a civil government to administer justice, that they may be governed like Britons, and not like banditti, . . . without laws or Gospel, having no means of religion, there being but one clergyman in all the country." Again, the Board of Trade represented to His Majesty that the Bishop of London, as Ordinary of the Plantations, should send a clergyman, whose salary might be put on the establishment of the garrison of Placentia. In 1699 a petition was made for a governor. The matter was referred to the Lords of Trade and Plantations. Their Lordships did not think fit to recommend the petition; but for keeping the people living there in Christianity they proposed that His Majesty should send a chaplain in the convoy ships. Meantime, while these efforts were being made to establish and support the Protestant religion in the Island, a gradual influx of Irish Roman Catholic population was imperceptibly pouring into the country and taking deep root in the various bays and harbors. It would be an interesting study to trace the origin and progress of this silent but ever onflowing stream of immigration ; but as yet no records have been found to throw light upon it. We have already learned from the diary of Père Baudouin that as far back as 1696 there was a considerable colony of Irish established in the country, especially in Conception Bay.

In 1670 we find the Lords of the Committee for Trade and Plantations complaining that many owners of ships carried out passengers *contrary to the laws and constitutions* of the fishery to the great detriment of the fishing trade. That many owners also victualled their ships from *Ireland* instead of England. Here we have a faint glimpse of the origin of Irish immigration, which was to take such deep root and to play so prominent a part in the future history of Newfoundland.

The page we are now opening in the annals of our country is one which we would fain see blotted out by the tears of the genius of Terra Nova, for it is blotted with

"Whole pages of sorrow and shame."

For nearly a hundred years we see nothing but the meanest and most cruel efforts on the part of the fish lords to crush out the rising life of the hardy little colony, alternated by weak and despotic acts on the part of the British Government to carry into execution those narrow-minded and selfish views.

We have already alluded to the arbitrary power placed in the hands of the fishing admirals. The most stringent enactments were passed to prevent by all possible means the colonization of the Island. On the 4th December, 1663, the Lords of the Privy Council wrote a letter enforcing the law "that no master or owner of any ship should transport any persons to Newfound Land who were not of the ship's company, or such as were to plant and settle there."

In 1667 the people made an agitation for the purpose of obtaining a governor. The merchants of Totness, Plymouth,

Dartmouth, etc., strenuously opposed the movement. They wrote to the Lords of the Privy Council to say that "several persons upon specious purposes, and for *sinister ends*, were endeavouring to establish a governor, which had *always been pernicious to the fishery*."

In 1674 the question of appointing a governor was again mooted, and again met with the most determined opposition from the merchants. They used every argument and influence in their power to frustrate the object. They urged the rigors of the climate; the infertility of the land; that the inhabitants traded with New England rather than the Old Country; that they received their wines and brandies from France, and so forth, — arguments which, after a lapse of two hundred years, when the resident population has increased from seven thousand to two hundred thousand, we find reëchoed to-day with marvellous exactitude by the inveterate opponents of the country's progress.

Notwithstanding all these desperate efforts to frustrate the aspirations of the young colony, we find her steadily progressing. In 1751 the population was 4,588; in 1761 it amounted to 11,457; and in 1763 to 13,112, of whom 4,795, or about one-third, were Roman Catholics. The *fixed* population, however, was about 7,500; so that considerably more than one-half were Roman Catholics. At length, in 1718, a governor was appointed (Henry Osborne), and a new phase of our country's history inaugurated.

CHAPTER XII.

RELIGIOUS PERSECUTION. — [1728-1762.]

Governor Osborne — Hostile Attitude of the Merchants towards the Progress of the Country — Persecuting Enactments of the Governors — Governor Dorril (1755) Persecutes the Catholics — Confiscations and Fines at Harbor Maine — Capture of the Island by the French, 1762 — Final Recapture by the English.

IT was natural to suppose that, under such a system as that of the fishing admirals, tyrannizing over a floating population, crime and disorders of every sort would prevail, and that without a permanent government society could not exist nor social order be established in the country. In 1728 Lord Vere Beauclerk, the commodore on the station, made a report to the home Government showing the necessity for the appointment of a governor for the security of life and property; and, after considerable delay and investigation, at length the first governor was appointed in the person of Captain Henry Osborne, of H.M. ship "Squirrel."

"The merchants, however," writes Dr. Mullock, "coalesced with the fishing admirals to render nugatory the regulations made by the established authority. It is remarkable that in every movement for the amelioration of the country we invariably find the merchants obstructing and opposing the improvement. In 1729 they upheld the rule of the fishing admirals, and opposed the establishment of a Crown governor; when it was necessary to establish law courts, and appoint a Chief Justice and assistant judges, again they are in opposition. The establishment of a colonial Legislature found the majority of them opponents, and, latterly, the principal opposition to Responsible Government and Free Trade came from the mercantile body. Their interests and those of the people were never identical. They were but transitory residents, adventurers struggling to make fortunes, and then

leave the country; and among the hundreds who left the
Island with millions of money, not even one was found to
leave any permanent mark of his residence in endowed schools,
hospitals, or other benevolent institutions." These words
were written by the enlightened pen of Dr. Mullock some
thirty-one years ago (1856). They contain a terribly severe
indictment, but not too much so. They are the deductions
of a clear historical mind from the study of our past history.
The pages of Chief Justice Reeves, an impartial authority,
tell the tale in terms not less terrible from being couched in
the authentic records of the period; and at the present day,
after a lapse of over thirty years of modern development and
enlightenment, have we anything to mollify and erase in
the strictures of Dr. Mullock? Alas, no! On the contrary,
many other counts must be added to the indictment. The
merchants were opposed to the construction of our dry dock,
to the undertaking of railway work, to the opening up of
mines, topographical and geological surveys, and such public
enterprises; in fact, to all that could raise Newfoundland
from the condition of a fishing-station. On the great question of Confederation, it may be said that the mind of the
country is not fully formed, and it is believed that we may
at any moment be brought again face to face with this momentous question. It is not my intention, nor does it come
within my scope, to express an opinion on the subject in these
pages. It is sufficient to remark that the merchants, as a
body, are strenuously opposed to this movement. This fact
should be of great weight, in connection with the study of
the attitude of the merchants to our country's progress, in
helping our people to form their opinions on the vital subject
of Confederation.

"The merchants, then, of that day" (1728), continues Dr.
Mullock, "banded themselves together in opposition to the
appointment of an Imperial governor as an infringement on
their rights." One point alone of union existed among all
parties, — a hatred of Catholicity and of permanent settlement
in the country. We hear but little of Catholics in those days;

in fact, their existence is only manifested by the continuous series of persecuting enactments and proclamations levelled against them. When there was such tenacity in persecuting them they must have been numerous, for the growing power of Catholicity can always be ascertained by the virulence of the persecution. Each governor in succession considered it his duty to signalize his tenure of office by a bigoted proclamation against Catholics, and the memory of the many acts of tyranny thus perpetrated has not as yet faded from the minds of the old inhabitants.

In 1755, Hugh Dorril being governor, we find among the records of his rule that an order was forwarded to Mr. George Garland, of Harbor Grace, to apprehend a priest said to have been in that town, and to send him to St. John's. It does not appear, however, that the priest was captured; probably he got notice, and concealed himself. About this time, also, a house was burned in Harbor Grace because Mass was said in it. A proclamation was also published by Dorril against bringing Roman Catholic servants into the country, and a strict order is given that those brought in during the summer shall be sent home again before the winter. About the same time a person of the name of George Tobin, in Harbor Grace, was fined "£10 for inflaming Catholics against Protestants;" and a ship's captain, of the same port, was fined likewise "£10 for hoisting the Irish colours"! Still the faithful clergy, whose names, we hope, are written in the Book of Life, though we have no record of them, did not desert the people. At the head of Conception Bay lies the town of Harbor Maine, now totally Catholic. It possesses a commodious church, dedicated to Sts. Peter and Paul; a convent of nuns of the Presentation Order, presbytery and schools; in a word, everything requisite for a Catholic town. In those dark days it was otherwise. A priest was known to have offered up the Holy Sacrifice of the Mass in the fishing-room of a man named Keating. The surrogate, or floating judge, heard of it, and Keating was condemned to pay a fine of fifty pounds. But even this enormous penalty was not enough to satisfy the bigotry of the colonial authorities. A ship of war lay in Holyrood. She was ordered round to Harbor Maine, and on her arrival there fastened her hawsers to Keating's fishing-stage, hauled it into the middle of the stream, and set it on fire. Nay, more, Keating was ordered to leave the country in the fall, and several other Catholics convicted of being present at the worship of their fathers. The first discoverers and colonizers of Newfoundland were banished from the country likewise. We find subsequently that a number of Catholics were fined, to make compensation to Keating for the burning of his stage, by which it would appear, either that Keating became reconciled to the Government, or, perhaps, the local authorities saw that this Turkish system of arson could not be justified at home. The punishment, however, in all cases fell on Catholics, who were obliged, first, to suffer the most grievous insult and persecution, and then fined to make compensation for the villany of their persecutors. The Harbor Maine Catholics had not, however, as yet expiated their offence. All the Catholic servants in this harbor were fined, and the amount levied on them, after deducting charges, fees, etc., produced £100 18s., with which a jail was built. Now the jail exists no longer; a church, convent, and schools supply its place, and the people are, without a single exception, Catholics. Such are the fruits of persecution. The ashes of the burnt fishing-stage appeared to have prepared the ground for Catholicity. Another registry, about the same date, informs us that one Kennedy and his wife, having confessed that they were married by a priest, a penalty of ten pounds was imposed on the husband, his house was burned, and he himself ordered to quit the country.

Carbineers' also witnessed the persecuting spirit of Dorril. Two Catholic tenants occupied the house of a man named Pike; it was proved that Mass had been said there, and so rabid was Dorril's bigotry, that, not satisfied with fining the occupiers £40, and banishing them from the country, he ordered the house itself to be burned, though belonging to a

Protestant, and £30 out of the fine to be paid to him for compensation; the remaining £10 was absorbed in court charges.

Again, Daniel Crowley's house, at Mosquito, is ordered to be burned because Mass was said in it. By this refinement of persecution it was thought to suppress all private as well as public worship among Catholics. Little, however, did they know either the priests or the people they had to deal with.

Governor Dorril next directs an order to Michael Gill, J.P., not to suffer any Catholic, nor any person employing Catholic servants, to sell strong liquors; also to cause all houses built by Catholics to be demolished, their land to be taken from them, as many as possible to be sent out of the country, and those who were permitted to remain to be deprived of the use of fire-arms. Obnoxious oaths were also introduced, debarring Catholics from all the offices of distinction. The following is the form of an oath which should necessarily be taken by all who wished to obtain any position whatsoever in the colony: "We, . . . , do declare that we do believe that there is not any *Transubstantiation* in the Sacrament of the Lord's Supper, at or after the consecration thereof by any person whatever."

These extracts from the public records show us the lamentable state of the country at this time. It is not to be wondered at, then, that on the breaking out of war between England and France the whole Island should have fallen an easy prey to the French. The people took but a very slight interest in making a defence, and the Irish Catholics, as might have been expected, either remained neutral or sided with the French, — naturally preferring the dominion of the latter to the brutal sway of an authority wielded by such a petty tyrant as Dorril.

In 1756 a war broke out, as mentioned above, between the two nations, which, from its duration, is known to history as the Seven Years' War. As was usual at this period, the war soon spread to the colonial possessions of these two kingdoms in America. In fact, the disturbed relations of these colonies conduced in no small measure to the actual breaking out of the war. The boundaries of the French and British possessions in North America, though forming special subjects of stipulation, both in the Treaty of Utrecht (1713) and again in that of Aix-la-Chapelle (1748), had not been yet settled with sufficient definiteness, so that very soon there arose complaints of mutual encroachments.

On the 24th June, 1762 (a memorable date in Newfoundland history), four French men-of-war captured Bay Bulls, and landing some troops, they marched on St. John's, which again, for the last time, became a French possession. From the detailed statement of the arms and munitions of war captured by the French, it would appear that the fortification of St. John's at this period was upon a scale very much larger than when some forty years previously it had been taken by D'Iberville. Among the rest we find six pieces of iron cannon, four cast mortars, twenty-five sea carriages or guns mounted, two field pieces mounted, 162 barrels powder, 1,604 cannon balls, 1,530 grape-shot, 9,431 lbs. musket-shot, 660 grenades, etc. In the city of St. John's there were 802 persons and 220 houses.

On September 12 the English fleet, under Lieut.-Colonel Amherst, arrived at Torbay, " whence a path leads to St. John's. A party of the enemy fired some shots at the boats as they rowed in. The fire was returned, and the enemy retreated. The path for four miles was narrow and rough, and through a thick wood. . . . "The country opened afterwards, and we marched to the left of Kitty Vitty." This extract is from a letter of Colonel Amherst to the Earl of Egremont. From the description it will be seen that the army kept to the east over the White Hills. The French were lying in waiting on the rising ground to the south of Kitty Vitty, and here the first skirmish took place. The French retreated to St. John's and the English ascended towards Signal Hill, where they encamped for the night. Next morning the English cleared the Kitty Vitty gut, which had been entirely stopped by the French sinking shallops in the passage. "The enemy had possession of two very high and steep hills, which commanded the whole ground from Kitty Vitty to St. John's — one in front of our advanced posts and the other near to St. John's — namely, Signal Hill and Gallows Hill." On the 15th, Captain McDonell, with a corps of light infantry, dislodged the French from Signal Hill. On the 16th the French abandoned Gallows Hill, and the French fleet quitted the harbor during the night in a fog. On the 17th the English erected a battery about five hundred yards from the fort (Fort William), which completely commanded the latter. On the 18th a letter from the French commander (the Count D'Haussonville) was received by Colonel Amherst, offering terms of capitulation, which were accepted. About eight hundred prisoners were taken, among whom we find the name of Michel Chaplain, thus showing that the French never lost sight of the religious element amid all their warlike undertakings. This was, as we have said, the last capture of Newfoundland. Since that time it has remained a British colony, though the French still retain the rights conferred on them by the Treaty of Utrecht, and confirmed by the Treaty of Paris, which shall be alluded to in the next chapter.

CHAPTER XIII.

RELIGIOUS PERSECUTION, *Continued.* — [1763-1784.]

Treaty of Paris, 1763 — Its Disastrous Effect on France — Persecution of the Catholics under Governors Palliser, Shuldham, Duff, and Edwards — First Irish Missionaries — Rev. Fathers Cain, Lonergan, Daily, Bourke, Whelan, Hearn, and A. Cleary.

IN the year 1763 the Seven Years' War was brought to a close, and a treaty most disastrous to France was signed at Paris. The struggle between the two nations for Western dominion was finally disposed of. The infamous French Government of the day, debauching the people at home and disgracing them abroad, yielded forever the territories acquired by Cartier, Champlain, and the other great men who planted the lilies of France from Newfoundland to the borders of Mexico. By this treaty France gave up Canada, Acadia (or Nova Scotia), New Brunswick, Prince Edward Island, and all other dependencies in the St. Lawrence, and resigned all her title to the territorial possession of Newfoundland; retaining only the islets of St. Pierre and Miquelon, and the rights of fishing within the limits prescribed by the Treaty of Utrecht. These rights were subsequently (1783) confirmed by the Treaty of Versailles, with the exception of the following changes : " The King of France renounces the right of fishing between Cape Bonavista and Cape St. John, on the north-east, in lieu of which concession his rights are extended on the south-west from Point Riche to Cape Ray."

The free exercise of the Catholic religion was guaranteed for Canada, and though persecution of a petty sort was often resorted to, still the Canadians were always able to maintain their rights, their proximity to the United States giving them a great moral strength ; but it was not so in Newfoundland. Governor Graves ruled the country during the French war, and he appears to have had his hands too full to occupy himself in any very violent measures against the Catholics. We only find an ordinance of his calling for the tax imposed by Governor Webb on Catholic and Irish traders, which appears not to have been regularly collected during the troubles.

In 1762 Hugh Palliser was appointed governor, and, difficult as it may seem, surpassed all his predecessors in bigotry. He issued proclamations to the following effect:—

1. Popish servants are not to be permitted to remain in any place but where they served the previous summer.
2. No more than *two* Papists are allowed to live in one house, unless in the house of a Protestant.
3. No Papist to be allowed to keep a public house, or sell liquors by retail.

Finally, as these laws seem not to have been sufficiently stringent to repress Popery, an order is given "to pull down all huts inhabited by Catholics who induced people to stay in the Island, when the intention is that they shall go home in the fall." A permission is granted some time after to license from eight to fifteen houses in St. John's for the sale of spirituous liquors, but with the proviso that no Catholic be allowed to sell any.

Again, another order, even more stringent, is published, "that neither man nor woman, being Papist, who did not serve in St. John's in the summer be allowed to remain in the winter; nor more than two Roman Catholics be allowed in the same house, unless the master be a Protestant." This we should suppose to be sufficiently tyrannical; but it was reserved for Palliser to go beyond even the penal laws of England, and to improve on Turkish barbarity. We find an order published proclaiming that "all children born in the country be baptized according to law." The Turks required a tithe of the children born of Christian parents as recruits for the Janissaries, it was reserved for a British colonial governor to surpass that barbarity, by obliging the parents, not conquered slaves, but *free-born* Britons, as they were absurdly called, to give up *all* their children to the ministers of the Anglican sect.

During the years 1772–4 Governor Shuldham ruled the Island. We find during his time that a Mr. Keen, of Bonavista, complained that an Irish Papist was building a fishing-room in that place. This audacious attempt of Popish enterprise arouses the governor's ire. Keen is immediately ordered to prevent him or any other Papist from building fishing-rooms, such proceeding being contrary to the Acts 10 and 11 of William III.

Governor Duff was appointed in 1775. The only record we have of him is that "he renewed all the regulations against the Papists."

In 1779 Edwards was appointed governor. The persecution against Catholics appears now to have slackened. We no longer see the public records stained with orders for the burning of houses where Mass was said, and the banishing of the faithful for assisting at the worship of their fathers. Among the old people, however, till lately, traditionary tales of persecution lingered, of floggings and house-burnings by the petty local tyrants; for in those dark days Catholics were almost outlaws, and every petty magistrate, when not restrained by terror, considered them fit subjects for persecution.

It is a notable fact of past as well as recent history that every relaxation of the penal laws of England followed hard upon some military reverses. The American war was then raging, and the victories of the Continentals loosened the grasp upon the sword of persecution in the hands of colonial tyrants. It was dangerous to exasperate men who could not be expected to retain their allegiance to the British Crown, and who, incited by the example of their American neighbors, might be driven into rebellion. Accordingly open and legal persecution was abolished, and gave way to a kind of niggardly toleration, accompanied by a contemptuous social exclusiveness.

On the 24th of October, 1784, pursuant to the instructions of His Majesty George III., directed to the governor, justices of the peace, and magistrates of the several districts of the Island, "liberty of conscience" was allowed to all persons in Newfoundland, and the "free exercise of all modes of religious worship as are *not prohibited* by law, provided people be content with a quiet and peaceable enjoyment of the same without giving scandal or offence to the Government."

This toleration, so tardily granted, was forced from the British Government by circumstances as we have seen, and shows a marked contrast to the method of procedure adopted a few years later (1815) by the Crown authorities in relation to the despatch of the first Catholic missionary to Australia, the Rev. Father Flinn. So far from being allowed to afford the consolations of religion to the poor Catholics in that distant land, he was arrested, sent to England a prisoner, and not discharged till he arrived in London. But, of course, Australia had not such a dangerous and audacious neighbor close at hand as the young republic of America.

Speaking of the period immediately preceding the arrival of Dr. O'Donel (1784), Dr. Mullock writes: "I cannot find the names of priests in Newfoundland at this time (though we know that several resided here for a short period), except Father Cain, of the County of Wexford, who came to Placentia in 1770, and remained there six years. I suppose a priest must have resided at St. John's at the same time; but no registry has been preserved. An Augustinian friar from New Ross, Father Kean, or Cain, spent some time in St. John's before the arrival of Dr. O'Donel, and it is most probable that he was the same person who previously lived at Placentia. The Rev. Father Londregan, who subsequently died at Fogo, was also officially in the Island at this time, for a complaint was lodged against him to Governor

Edwards for marrying a couple who were married before, — in all probability two Catholics who were married by a parson. The governor then published an order that no person should be married unless by his permission, and after the publication of banns, which was tantamount to an obligation on Catholics to be married only in the Protestant Church, for it was there alone the banns could be published in those days."

It is impossible to believe that the Catholics could have had any sort of a place of worship in those days, seeing that they were scarcely allowed the privilege of private dwelling-houses; yet it is strange that a foundation-stone discovered on the demolition of the "Old Chapel" in St. John's, and which will be again alluded to, bears the date of 1754.

The records or traditions of the lives and hardships of these early priests are but meagre; indeed, of some we know only the dates of their arrival in, and departure from, the Island; sometimes only the mere fact that they were here; of others, we learn just enough to let us conjecture how they strove to keep alight the flickering lamp of faith amidst the most overwhelming difficulties. They came and went periodically. We hear of their being aboard the fishing craft in the disguise of fishermen, and thus escaping the fury of their persecutors. In Witless Bay a priest made his escape in this way, though the boat on which he was sitting was actually boarded and searched by the authorities. In Todd's Cove a priest had to fly and take refuge in a cellar, and even there the poor owner was afraid to harbor him. As we have seen, there was no mercy for those who protected a priest, or connived at the celebration of Mass in their houses. Hence the priests were obliged to omit the celebration of the Most Holy Sacrifice, and be content to recite for the people the rosary amid the rocks and woods, as was the case with their forefathers in Ireland.[1]

---

[1] A large rock is still shown in Renews, called the "Midnight Rock," beneath which tradition tells us Father Fitzsimmon used to assemble the people to rosary and prayer.

It is doubtful whether these priests had received any jurisdiction, and from whom. It is not likely they would come without having been in some manner sent; and the fact of their being obliged to omit the celebration of Mass may easily account for the tradition handed down as to their being "silenced."

Of the priests who came to the Island before Dr. O'Donel's arrival the names of but five survive, namely, —

Father Cain, or Kean, already alluded to. He was a native of New Ross, County of Wexford, Ireland. He came to Newfoundland in 1770; was at Placentia for six years; afterwards, probably at St. John's. He went home to Ireland, and died in Wexford. He was a friar of the Augustinian Order.

Father Londregan, also an Augustinian. He officiated in St. John's for some time. He also was at Placentia, where he remained three years. He then went to the north of the Island; and died at Fogo, in a cook-room, in a state of great misery.

Father Daily, a native of Cork, also came out with Father Londregan. I find among the names given by the late Dean Cleary those of Fathers Power and Mahony, Augustinians, who returned to Ireland, and died there; but I have no certainty as to the date of their arrival in Newfoundland, nor the scenes of their missions.

There may have been many other such migratory missionaries, who took their parts in this prehistoric period of our Island Church; but though their names are not written in the pages of this world's history, let us hope that their good deeds have been all well recorded by the Angel who guards the Great Book, and that their faults, if any, may be blotted out by their tears and sufferings, aided by our suffrages, which never cease to be poured forth annually for them at our altars.

We have a more extensive sketch of the lives and work of several priests who arrived at the same time as Dr. O'Donel, or very soon after; and this may be judged a fitting place to

OF NEWFOUNDLAND. 183

record whatever is known of them, as received from the most trustworthy traditions.

Father Edmund Bourke, a native of Tipperary, came in 1786, two years after the arrival of Dr. O'Donel. He built the old presbytery and chapel at Placentia. He was the first regularly authorized missionary. He left for Halifax in 1798, the year of the Irish rebellion, through fear of English vengeance, as he was in some way implicated in that historical event. He was a nephew of Father Sheehan, who was beheaded in Clonmel for croppyism. He was one of the three priests who, in 1794, signed the petition to have Dr. O'Donel (who was then only Prefect Apostolic) elevated to the episcopal dignity. He was a Dominican friar. It is thought that he was brother to Dr. Bourke, the first Bishop of Halifax. He remained twelve years on the mission, and worked hard. His district included all Placentia Bay, as far westward as Burin.

The next priest whose name I find mention of is the Rev. Patrick Whelan. The exact year of his arrival is not known, but he was here in 1794, as he signed the above-mentioned petition, from which also we gather that he was a Franciscan or Friar Minor, and was stationed in the Mission of Harbor Grace. He was drowned in 1799, and I am indebted to the Hon. J. L. Prendergast, of Harbor Grace, for the following graphic and interesting account of that melancholy event:—

"Father Whelan was a most exemplary and zealous priest, whose name is embalmed in the memory of the people. Twice every year, spring and fall, he made a visitation of his parish. It was when returning, in September, 1799, that he lost his life during a storm. His boat reached Grates Cove, and in attempting to land, the boat was swamped, and all on board perished. The body of Father Whelan was the only one recovered from the waves. He was found erect in the water, his Breviary under his arm, a cane in one hand, and a small bag containing his vestments (probably the pyx) in the other. The body was taken to Harbor Grace, and his sorrowing people laid him to rest in the old Catholic graveyard. A monument is erected over his remains, on which is engraved a long and panegyrical epitaph of some twenty-five lines, extolling his many virtues and noble deeds, and testifying the affection and esteem of the flock for the memory of their faithful pastor."

There was another Father Whelan, also a Franciscan, who came out in 1808. He was stationed on the mission in Placentia. He went home to Ireland in 1810, and reëntered his monastery.

In 1810 arrived the Rev. Andrew V. Cleary. He was on the mission in Placentia, where he died, and was buried in 1829. He was uncle of the late venerable Dean Cleary. He had as curate the Rev. Father Devereux, who was the first priest stationed in Burin. He built the house and old chapel there, and is buried in the graveyard of that place.

The Rev. A. Hearn was also a curate of his, and succeeded him (Rev. A. V. Cleary) in the mission of Placentia. The Rev. Michael O'Donel, nephew of the Bishop, came out with him in 1784, and remained in the country till 1806, when he left for Ireland.

It appears that there was also a priest on the southern shore at this time, whose name was Fitzpatrick. The life and labors of other early missioners shall be briefly outlined in a future chapter. We now approach what may be considered the birth of the Church in Newfoundland; its final establishment by the arrival of the first authorized Prelate, Dr. O'Donel, with full power and jurisdiction from Rome to place her upon a sure foundation, and set her forth upon that career, advancement, and progress which has developed into the glorious plenitude of hierarchical life which we enjoy at the present day.

CHAPTER XIV.

RT. REV. DR. O'DONEL, PREFECT APOSTOLIC. — [1763-1784.]

Appointment of Father O'Donel, First Prefect Apostolic — State of the Country — Biography of Father O'Donel — Foundation of " The Old Chapel " — Persecution not yet Ceased — Bigoted Conduct of Surrogate Captain Pellu — Extraordinary Conduct of Governor Milbanke — Father O'Donel's Letters to Dr. Troy, Archbishop of Dublin — Friendly Action of Governor Waldegrave and Judge-Advocate Reeves — Great Influence Acquired by the Bishop — He Quells a Mutiny among the Military — Beastly Character of Prince William, Duke of Clarence — He Assaults the Bishop.

WE have now arrived at what may be called the modern period of the Ecclesiastical History of Newfoundland. We have seen, to all appearances, Catholicity firmly established in the Island by the French, protected by the great monarch, Louis XIV. But all these bright prospects failed; yet the ways of God are inscrutable. The persecution of the faithful in Ireland, bringing, as usual, poverty in its train, forces every year numbers of the hardy children of that Catholic land to seek abroad that reward for their labor denied to them at home. The rude and dangerous occupation of the Newfoundland fisheries tempted them, by the prospect of good wages, to brave the dangers of the ocean and the tyranny of the petty colonial officials and fishing admirals. Religious persecution was for ages their portion at home, and faithful priests were found from time to time to cross the Atlantic, and by stealth afford the consolations of religion to their expatriated countrymen. Obliged at home to offer up the Adorable Sacrifice in the lonely mountain glen, or in the obscure cellar or garret of the town, they were prepared in Newfoundland to say Mass under a flake or in a cook-room. Many tales are still current among the people of the escape of the priest, when some cruiser was on the coast, and the captain was desirous of showing his zeal for the House of Brunswick by the daring exploit of capturing a priest; and it is gratifying to have to remark that in very many instances the old English Protestant settlers were the first to give notice of the danger, and assist in providing a place of concealment for the persecuted priest. Catholicity was now tolerated; open persecution had ceased, and was followed by a system of exclusiveness from all public situations of honor or profit.

The population of the Island at this time, in spite of opposing laws, had increased to somewhere about 25,000, of whom about three-fourths were Roman Catholics. Among the enactments passed with the intention of preventing the Island being peopled was the celebrated Palliser Act of 1775, by which it was decreed, in order to insure the return of the fishermen each winter, that masters should be authorized to detain forty shillings out of the men's wages, for paying their passages home. Another most effective clause was the prohibition to take females to the Island, so that at this time there was only about one-seventh of the population female, or about 3,500; and about one-fifth of the population (from four to five thousand) migrated annually. The men who remained were employed only for the half-year, at a rate of about £30.

The attention of the Holy Father was now called to the spiritual interests of the Island. Up to this period it was, properly speaking, a portion of the vast diocese of Quebec; but being so remote, and the communication so rare, the priests who, from time to time, visited the colony acted like naval chaplains, considering the people here as if having their domiciles in the dioceses of Waterford, Ferns, or Cork, and affording them in Newfoundland aid on the strength of the faculties they exercised in the dioceses they had left in Ireland; and the transitory state of the population, and the necessities of the case, would appear in some measure to justify the irregularity. Thus it continued till the year 1784, when Dr. O'Donel, the first Prefect Vicar Apostolic and Bishop, arrived in the country; and from that time the Newfoundland Church was organized, and took its place among the provinces of Christianity.

This great and good man, James Louis O'Donel, was born in 1737, at Knocklofty, on the banks of the Suir, about four miles west from Clonmel, in the county of Tipperary, in Ireland. His father, a most respectable farmer, was a very pious man, and having given him the best elementary education to be obtained in the neighborhood, under a domestic tuitor, sent him to Limerick to be instructed in the classics, together with a younger brother, Michael. Both having soon displayed a vocation for the priesthood, and also for the religious Order of St. Francis, they were accordingly received into a convent of the Order in that city, and in due time ordained priests. This Father Michael O'Donel never came to Newfoundland, but died in Ireland, on the 26th of June, 1790, just four years before Dr. James O'Donel's appointment to the bishopric. The Father Michael O'Donel already mentioned, who accompanied Dr. James to Newfoundland, was his nephew. He left the Island with his uncle, in 1806.

The Irish Franciscans at that time possessed four National establishments on the continent of Europe: Louvain, in Belgium; Bonlay, in France; Prague, in Bohemia; and Rome. Dr. O'Donel was appointed by the Irish Provincial a member of the Prague Community, and accordingly received the habit of St. Francis in the College of the Immaculate Conception in that city. He performed his novitiate, and made his religious profession; went through his studies with honor, and was ordained priest. He lived as chaplain for the next few years, with several distinguished families, on the Continent, and did not return to Ireland till 1775. For the next eight years he applied himself with zeal to the discharge of the missionary duties of an Irish friar, and as a proof of the esteem in which he was held by his brethren, we find that at a Provincial Chapter, held on the 19th of July, 1799, he was elected Provincial, or Superior of the whole body of Franciscans in Ireland; having been previously Prior at Waterford. He held the important office of Provincial till the next Chapter, held on the 22d July, 1781. Three years afterwards he was elected by the Holy See to organize the

Church in Newfoundland, and was appointed Prefect Apostolic, with power to administer the Sacrament of Confirmation.[1]

In 1784 he landed in St. John's, and immediately commenced his labors in the districts of St. John's, Ferryland, and Placentia. The people were then almost destitute of all practical religion. The absence of all fixed spiritual guidance, though occasionally they had a priest among them; the prevalence of drunkenness; the lawless character of many who came to the country, and the abundance of money in the hands of persons who knew not how to use it, unless as a means of low, sensual gratification, — induced a deplorable laxity of morals, and even weakened the faith of many. French infidelity, then so fashionable, was the boast of those who pretended to enlightenment, and indifference to all religious observances was common to all classes. Such was the howling moral wilderness in which Dr. O'Donel commenced his labors. The English Government, always wisely availing themselves of every available means to preserve and consolidate their power, not only sanctioned the residence of Dr. O'Donel in the country, but, subsequently, gave him an allowance of £75 a year. Yet never were services so cheaply purchased; but his loyalty rested on more solid motives than mere temporal reward. French infidelity and revolutionary doctrines, as remarked above, were making rapid advances among the people, and England, though not bearing any warm love for Popery, felt that it was safer to preserve the people in Catholicity, as a safeguard against anarchical atheism. It was better to have the Newfoundlanders loyal Catholics than Gallican rebels; and Dr. O'Donel's influence was cheaper and more serviceable than an armed force.

In those days no house, nor even a chimney, could be erected without permission of the Governor; nor could

---

[1] The late Venerable Dean Cleary stated that Dr. O'Donel first came out to Newfoundland as a simple priest, and was soon after elevated to the dignity of Prefect. Dr. Mullock, however, is more likely to be correct, as he had access to the Franciscan annals.

leases be granted, unless under the same authority. Dr. O'Donel, therefore, sought permission to take out a lease of the ground where the "Old Chapel" afterwards stood. A lease of a house and garden was accordingly taken for ninety-nine years, at a rent of £28 per annum, and the first Catholic chapel was erected in the Island since its cession by the French, one hundred and seventy years previously.

Three years after his arrival in St. John's, Dr. O'Donel writes to Dr. Troy, recently promoted to the archiepiscopal See of Dublin, a letter, from which the following extract is taken, and which throws a light upon the state of the Church in Newfoundland at that period [1] : —

"I want two clergyman more, one to the southward and one to the northward of this place. . . . I send for Father John Phelan, of Waterford, and a Father McCormack, of St. Isidore's, who, I am informed, is a man of morals and powerful abilities. He wrote to me, and offered himself for this Mission. He has made three *Public Acts* in the *Sapientia Romana*. In default of him a Father Yore, who likewise offered himself, of your Grace's diocese, if a man who can be recommended for irreproachable conduct and ability, will be to me very acceptable.
"BROTHER JAMES O'DONEL."

This letter shows us the anxiety of the good Prefect for the sanctity and intelligence of his priesthood. It does not appear that the Father McCormack mentioned above ever came to the Island, and as to Father Yore, his long and glorious career fully verified the possession of the qualities desired by Dr. O'Donel.

In 1788 a letter of accusation against Dr. O'Donel was presented to the surrogate-magistrate.

---

[1] The late Most Rev. Dr. Conroy, Bishop of Ardagh, and Delegate Apostolic to Canada, while occupying the position of Secretary to His Eminence Cardinal Cullen, compiled from the archives of the archdiocese the letters of Dr. O'Donel, which were published in the "Irish Ecclesiastical Record" of August, 1866, to which I am indebted for the extracts above cited.

"This letter," writes Dr. O'Donel, Nov. 16th, "was not only read in the court-house, where the surrogate publicly denounced Pope and Popery, priests and priestcraft, and, in an ecstasy, blessed this happy Constitution, that it was cleanly purged from such knavery; but also carried about this town by him and his officers, to the great satisfaction of those who envied our large congregation, stately chapel, and the esteem I have been heretofore held in by the Governor. This surrogate, by name Pellu, of French extraction, closed his surrogation to the admiral with the modest request that the priests should be turned out of the country; that circular letters should be sent to the magistrates, that if any more priests arrived to ship them off immediately; and that no priests should be left but where there was a garrison to keep them in awe. When I heard this, I waited on the secretary, who told me that the admiral had made up his mind and adopted the measures of his favorite, Captain Pellu. . . . I drew up my defence in writing, waited on the Governor, who most politely received me, entirely changed his opinion, and assured me that he came to this country with a great esteem and regard for me, as his friend, Admiral Campbell, often spoke respectfully of me to him, and that, from what he could personally observe in my conduct, he quitted the Island with the same good opinion of me. I am truly a son of persecution, and a child of persecution, since I came to this country. However, I could not suffer in a better cause.

"BROTHER JAS. O'DONEL."

Although the Catholic religion was supposed to be tolerated, and liberty of worship had been granted some eight years before (1782) by Governor Campbell, and although, to some extent, the policy of the English Government towards the Roman Catholics of Newfoundland was changed, and a sort of protection was accorded to them, we are not to suppose that persecution and insult had totally ceased. The following extraordinary letter will prove that the old spirit still in a great measure prevailed.

Father O'Donel applied for permission to erect a few chapels for the growing population, for without this license not a stick could be laid; and so determined was England to prevent the improvement and colonization of the country, that every merchant was empowered by law to stop forty shillings out of every servant's wages to pay his passage home in the fall; the money was retained, but many of the servants forfeited their right of passage, and remained in the country. Hence, in spite of all opposition, the resident population increased, and Dr. O'Donel made to Governor Milbanke the application above mentioned, and the following is the characteristic reply:—

"The Governor acquaints Mr. O'Donel that, so far from being disposed to allow of an increase of places of religious worship for the Roman Catholics of this Island, he very seriously intends next year to lay those established already under particular restrictions. Mr. O'Donel must be aware that it is not the interest of Great Britain to encourage people to winter in Newfoundland, and he cannot be ignorant that many of the lower order who now stay would, if it were not for the *convenience* with which they *obtain absolution here*, go home for it at least once in two or three years (!); and the Governor has been misinformed if Mr. O'Donel, instead of advising their return to Ireland, does not rather encourage them to winter in this colony."—"On board the 'Salisbury,' St. John's, 2d November, 1790."

In a letter to Dr. Troy, dated December 6th, 1790, Dr. O'Donel alludes to the above event:—

"MY LORD,— Our very numerous and increasing congregations have brought the eye of the enemies of our faith upon us, as you will find by the enclosed answer to a memorial drawn up by the people of Ferryland for leave to build a chapel in that district. . . . I wrote to Father Callenan, of Cork, requesting him to use his influence on Mr. O'Leary to apply to some member of the Privy Council to prevent those prejudicial restrictions. . . . Criminals of all kinds are allowed the unreserved privilege of a clergyman, and why not an industrious set of men, who are inured to the hardships of the sea, and ready upon any emergency to serve His Majesty? The toleration hitherto granted is rather an encouragement to them to emigrate than a discouragement, as the generous monitor supposes; for many of those hardy fellows would never obtain their parents' consent to cross the seas if they had not the consoling prospect of the presence of a clergyman in case of sickness or death. Moreover, the ingredients which make up the Sacrament of Penance, and the prerequisites of *Absolution*, are not of such easy digestion to a set of fishermen as to induce them *to go home for it at least once in two or three years!* I really look upon these intended restrictions as a breach of public faith. . . . Admiral Campbell sent a circular letter to all the justices of peace in this Island in those very terms: 'You are to allow all people inhabiting this Island a free exercise of all such modes of religious worship as are not prohibited by law; pursuant to the King's instructions to me."

In the same letter Dr. O'Donel alludes to some person as C. P. — doubtless Captain Pellu, above mentioned:—

" 'Tis true," he says, "that he can act as he pleases in this place, as he is king, priest, and prophet in the Island. The reason of this prerogative is that the country is not supposed by law to be inhabited, except in summer. In case of war I believe none of us can subsist, as the servants upon whom alone we depend will be all pressed, and obliged to become either sailors or soldiers. This is a far more miserable year with the wretched inhabitants than last."

On the 8th December, 1791, he writes:—

"The Governor most faithfully adhered to his promise of representing the Catholic clergy of this Island as encouragers of the people remaining during the winter in this country, contrary to the interest and intention of the Government; but in this even he has not succeeded according to his mistaken zeal, as Providence guided the steps of a Mr. Reeves to this country, who has been appointed Judge-Advocate. This truly good and benevolent man would not suffer me even to expostulate with the Governor on his foul misrepresentation, as he assured me the state of the Catholic Church should remain unmolested here; and it so happened."

The clouds of persecution seemed now being dispelled and the sun of peace bursting forth. For three successive years the admirals had not interfered, and Dr. O'Donel has great hopes for the future. He asks for another missioner of the Franciscan Order for the district of St. Mary's and Trepassey. "It is absolutely necessary that he should speak Irish." He writes again on December 8, 1792. After speaking of the horrors of the French Revolution and the barbarities of the Jacobin Club, then at their height, all of which he learns from papers received from Europe of date as late as the 26th September, he says:—

"Our present Governor (W. Waldegrave, Esq.) and Judge-Advocate made very solemn professions of friendship to me. The former returned me public thanks at his own table for the unremitting pains I have taken these eight years in keeping the people amenable to law; and on being told he overstated my slender endeavours, he said he was too well informed to think so. . . . We are now at perfect ease, and restored to the same degree of respect that we enjoyed for the first three years of our residence here.

"BRO. JAS. O'DONEL."

On December 27, 1793, he again writes to Dr. Troy, congratulating him on his pastoral letter, just received through a Mr. Bolan. He says:—

"Our affairs in this Mission wear a most pleasing aspect. The Governor continues his friendship to me with great warmth. I was the only landsman who dined with him, on the eve of his departure, aboard his elegant ship, where I had the pleasure to hear him declare, in the presence of five captains of frigates, that the Catholics were the best subjects His Majesty had. I am sorry we have no longer lease than one year more of him. . . . We had 300 French prisoners here during the summer. Their officers were at liberty, and I must own I did not like to see them coming every Sunday to my chapel with large emblems of infidelity and rebellion plastered on their hats. It was much more pleasing to see three companies of our volunteers, headed by their Protestant officers, with fifes and drums, coming to the chapel to be instructed in the duties of religion and loyalty."

After ten years of missionary life, working and organizing ecclesiastical matters, we find Dr. O'Donel also ingratiating himself into the favor of the civil authorities, and gradually acquiring that influence and weight, even in secular affairs of the colony, which has ever since been exercised by his successors, the Roman Catholic Bishops, placing them in a recognized position of the highest importance, second only to the representative of majesty himself, and indeed on many occasions causing the latter to look to them as the only power in the country capable of saving it from ruin in grave and serious crises. As an instance of this we may here mention an event which occurred just a few years after Dr. O'Donel's consecration.

In 1799 a mutiny of the military stationed in St. John's occurred which threatened the most serious consequences. If the soldiers had been joined by the excited people, the whole Island might have been lost to Britain; but Dr. O'Donel threw all his influence on the side of authority, and by private and public admonitions calmed down the exasperated feelings of the populace, and peace was restored. He received a reward for these services, which shall be noticed by and by.

Another circumstance worthy of note occurred also about this time; it was near being the cause of a change in the succession to the British Crown.

Prince William Henry, Duke of Clarence, afterwards William IV., was at that time a midshipman in the British navy, and was attached to the Newfoundland station. He was remarkable only for beastly sensuality and cowardly tyranny. He caused a carpenter at Ferryland to be dismissed from Government employment for no other reason than that he was a Papist. And he was known to spit in the face of Irish Catholics, and use even more beastly conduct towards them (he spat down a man's throat in Placentia), when he could do so with impunity.

This promising scion of royalty was one day in a billiard-room in St. John's when he saw the Bishop passing along the street. Without any regard to the venerable Prelate's age or character, he threw a weapon at him, which fortunately only inflicted a slight wound, but which if better directed would have ended the Bishop's days. When this outrage became known, the whole Catholic population was aroused, and it was for awhile doubtful whether a fourth William would ever occupy the British throne. The Bishop used every exertion to calm the excited people's feelings. Meantime a guard of marines was landed, and the Prince arrested and conveyed on board, and his commander most prudently at once sailed out of the harbor.

Many other stories of quite a discreditable character are still told of the disorderly conduct of this young prince, some of which also nearly cost him his life. On one occasion, being out upon some midnight raid with some companions, either removing gates, robbing gardens, or making some attempt to enter a private dwelling through a window, he was fired upon by the indignant master of the house, but escaped unhurt.

CHAPTER XV.

RT. REV. DR. O'DONEL, FIRST BISHOP. — [1794-1801.]

Memorial of the Clergy to have Father O'Donel made Bishop— He is Appointed Vicar Apostolic, and Consecrated Bishop at Quebec — Letter of Father Yore — Address of the Merchants and Citizens of St. John's to Dr. O'Donel — He Visits Placentia and Administers Confirmation — Diocesan Statutes—Loyalty of the Catholics.

THE Catholics were now sufficiently numerous and the population so permanently established that the Holy See considered the time had arrived when episcopal supervision was needed.

The priests of the Mission also, though few in number, felt that they were on the eve of a new and progressive era, and that the elevation of their noble and saintly Prefect to the episcopal dignity would greatly enhance his power of advancing the interests of the Church in the Island. Accordingly they sent an urgent appeal to the Holy Father, the great Pontiff, Pius VI., Confessor and Doctor of the Faith, who then filled the throne of Peter. The document was couched in Latin of some elegance of style. I consider it of sufficient importance to be reproduced here in the original, with a translation : —

"BEATISSIME PATER : —

"Cum inter multa, eaque preclara facinora, quæ felicissimum Sanctitatis Vestræ Pontificium illustrant atque exornant, haud minimum sit quod fideles Orthodoxos Americæ Septentrionalis incolas, paucis ab hinc annis, mirum in modum consolatus sit; fidemque simul Catholicam amplius dilataverit, valdeque consolidaverit per providam institutionem primi illius regionis Epī, Rmī, nimirum Dñi Joannis Carroll Epī Baltimorensis ; — nos infrascripti, tali exemplo tantaque benignitate animati, nomine nostro, omniumque Catholici nominis incolarum Insulæ Terræ Novæ nuncupatæ, provoluti ad pedes

Sanctitatis Vestræ humilime deprecamur, quatenus Clementer dignetur in Epūm instituere cum titulo in partibus, et in Vicarium Apostolicum præclarum et dignissimum Prefectum Missionis Nostræ R. P. Jacobum Ludovicum O'Donel, Ordinis Fratrum Minorum de Observantia. Hoc siquidem facto illud proculdubro consequetur, ut et maximum ipsi Religioni emolumentum; ingens nobis solatium, atque perenne Sanctitatis Vestræ decus sit accessurum. Supervacaneum porro fore arbitramur Sanctitati Vestræ recensere quam utile nobis foret in tanta locorum distantia, Pastorem apud nos habere Epāli charactere insignitum, qui munia Epālia pro fidelium consolatione possit obire sicut et consulto omittimus eulogium meritorum, præclarissimi Viri a nobis commendati, quippe cum ejus eximiæ, et Singulares Virtutes, compertissimæ jampridem evaserunt Sacræ Congregationi de Propaganda Fide, quare de summa Clementia, ac pastorali Solicitudine Sanctitatis Vestræ confisi in osculo pedum Beatorum prosternimur, Apl̄cam Benedictionem implorantes.

"Datum ex insula Terræ Novæ, Die Vigesimo, Novembris, A.D. 1794.

"Fr. Edmundus Bourke, Ord. Pred., Missionarius Districtûs Placentiæ; Fr. Thos. Ewer, Ord. Min. Strictioris Observantiæ, Mis. Dist. Ferryland; Fr. Patritius Phelan, Ord. Min. Str. Obs., Mis. Dist. de Harbour Grace; Gulielmus Coman, generosus incola S. Joannis; Dav. Duggan, idem; Henricus Shea, idem; Lucas Maddoc, idem; Joannes Wall, id.; Timotheus Ryan, id.; Joannes Bulger, id.; Michael Mara, id.; Jacobus Power, id.; Martinus Delaney, id.; Patricius Power, id.; Gulielmus Mullowney, generosus incola Districtus de Harbour Grace; Joannes Quarry, idem; Demetrius Hartery, id.; Jacob. Shortall, id. Ferryland; Joannes Coady, id.; Joannes Power, id. de Magna Placentia; Joannes Kearney, id. de Parva Placentia."

"MOST HOLY FATHER:—

"Since, among the many and remarkable events which illustrate and adorn the glorious Pontificate of Your Holiness, that is not the least that in a wonderful manner you have consoled the faithful people of North America, and have at the same time spread abroad more fully the Catholic Faith, and greatly strengthened the same by the thoughtful establishment of the first Bishop of that region, namely, the Most Rev. John Carroll, Bishop of Baltimore.

"We, the undersigned, animated by such an example and such benignity, in our own names, and the names of all the Catholics of Newfoundland, prostrate at the feet of Your Holiness, most humbly pray that you would graciously deign to appoint, as Bishop, with a title *in partibus*, and as Vicar Apostolic, the illustrious and most worthy Prefect of our Mission, the Rev. Father James Louis O'Donel, of the Order of Friars Minor of the Observance. The result of such an act would be without doubt a great advantage to religion, an immense consolation to us, and an eternal glory to Your Holiness.

"It is altogether unnecessary for us to state how useful it would be to us at such a distant place to have among us a Pastor endowed with the Episcopal character, who could exercise Episcopal functions for the consolation of the faithful. So, also, we purposely omit any praise of the merits of this most noble man commended by us, inasmuch as his bright and singular virtues are already well known to the Sacred Congregation of Propaganda Fide. Hence, confiding in the supreme clemency and pastoral solicitude of Your Holiness, we again prostrate ourselves in spirit, and kiss the feet of Your Holiness, begging your Apostolic blessing.

"Given at Newfoundland, the 20th day of November, A.D. 1794.

"Brother Edmund Bourke, Dominican Friar, Missionary of Placentia; Brother Thomas Ewer, Franciscan Missionary of Ferryland; Brother Patrick Phelan, Franciscan, Harbor Grace; William Coman, gentleman inhabitant of St. John's; David Duggan, do.; Henry Shea, do.; Luke Maddoc, do.; John Wall, do.; Timothy Ryan, do.; John Bulger, do.;

Michael Mara, do.; James Power, do.; Martin Delaney, do.; Patrick Power, do.; William Mullowney, gentleman inhabitant of the District of Harbour Grace; John Quarry, do.; Demetrius Hartery, do.; James Shortall, do., of Ferryland; John Cody, do.; John Power, do., of Great Placentia; John Kearney, do., of Little Placentia."

Though the memorial bears the signatures of but three priests, — Fathers Bourke, Placentia; Yore, Ferryland; and Patrick Phelan, Harbor Grace, — yet we know beyond a possible doubt that there were others in the Island at that time, namely, Dr. O'Donel's nephew, Father Michael O'Donel, who, perhaps through a sense of delicacy, did not sign it; also Father Fitzpatrick and Father John Whelan. It may be that these fathers were in some distant missions at the time, and could not be reached. The names of many of the laymen who signed the petition are still flourishing among us in their descendants. Among the rest may be noticed the father of Sir Ambrose Shea, lately honored by the Home Government by being appointed the first native Governor of Newfoundland.[1]

The urgent appeal was responded to with cordiality by the Holy Pontiff, and the customary Bulls were expedited for the consecration of James Louis O'Donel as Bishop, with the title of *Thyatira in partibus infidelium*, and at the same time he was appointed Vicar Apostolic of Newfoundland. The Bull is dated 5th of January, 1796, which, owing to the difficulties of communication, and the necessary preliminaries to be gone through, cannot be considered a very long interval from the date of the memorial of the clergy and people. It is quite probable the memorial did not reach Rome till late in the summer of 1795.

The nearest place where he could obtain episcopal conse-

---

[1] Although, owing to circumstances not necessary to be explained here, this appointment was cancelled, yet the merits of the worthy gentleman were acknowledged by his being appointed Governor of the Bahamas. So he is really the first Newfoundlander honored with a colonial governorship.

cration in those days was Quebec; and accordingly he was consecrated in the cathedral of that city by the diocesan Bishop, the Rt. Rev. Francis Hubert, two priests, the Revs. Messieurs Gravé and Desjardins, assisting by dispensation, in lieu of two Bishops, as prescribed by the Rubric. This ceremony, so important to the Church of Newfoundland, took place on the feast of St. Matthew, 21st September, 1796.

The following is a copy of the certificate of the consecration of Dr. O'Donel, taken from the original, which is preserved in the archives of Quebec, together with the signature of the Secretary and Chancellor, of the Archbishop, and also the authentification of Very Rev. Canon Langevin, in sending the document to Dr. Mullock: —

"JOANNES FRANCISCUS HUBERT, MISERATIONE DIVINA ET SCTÆ SEDIS APLCÆ GRATIA.
"EPISCOPUS QUEBECENSIS.

"Notum facimus universis quod Die Vigesima primâ Mensis Septembris in Natalitio S. Matthæi Apostoli et Evangelistæ, in Ecclesiâ Nostrâ Cathedrali accitis et in hoc nobis assistentibus loco Episcoporum, duobus Presbyteris Sæcularibus, Magistris Videlicet Henrico Francisco Gravé et Philippo Joanne Ludovico Desjardins, Vicariis Nostris Generalibus juxta specialem licentiam à Sta Sede Apostolicâ concessam, Nos, Illustrissimo et Reverendissimo D. D. Jacobo Ludovico O'Donell, Presbytero Regulari Ordinis Minorum S. Francisci Observantium Nuncupati, Electo et Confirmato Thyatirensi, munus Consecrationis Episcopalis secundum Bullas Apostolicas ipsi datas Romæ apud Sanctum Petrum die Quinta Januarii præsentis Anni 1796, Pontificatûs, S.S.D.N. Pii Papæ VI., Anno 21°; — ritu consueto et præstitis juramentis assuetis, impendimus; eumque in Episcopum Thyatirensem Consecravimus die et anno qubis supra, presensque instrumentum Signo Nostro Sigilloque

Diæcesis, ac Secretarii Nostri subscriptioni communivimus.

"L.+S.   "+ JOANNES FRANC⁹,
                  Epūs Quebecensis.

" De mandato Illmi ac Revūi D. D. Quebecensis Episcopi.
" J. O. PLESSIS, P*tre*,
                  " *Secretarius.*

" Ego Infra scriptus testificor presentem transcriptum concordare cum originali, Quebeci die 20ª februarii, 1854.
"(Signatum)   EDMONDUS LANGEVIN, P.—D.D.,
                  "*Quebec Archiepī. Secrius.*"

The following is an extract from the Bull of Nomination of Dr. O'Donel giving the title of his See *in partibus:*—

" Excerptum ex Bullis datis Die 5 Januarii, 1796. . . . Ecclesia Episcopalis Thyatirensis in Lydia sub-Archiepō Sardiano quæ in partibus consistit infidelium, per translationem Veñbis Fratris Francisci Zaverii, ultimi illius Episcopi ad Ecclesiam Culmensem."

Immediately after his appointment, Dr. O'Donel wrote a letter of thanks to the Propaganda. He also wrote to Dr. Troy, from St. John's, November 25, 1794 (which seems to be a mistake for 1796). The following extract will give an idea of the state of the country at that time:—

" My Lord, — The vessel that brought out the Holy Oils from Ireland had been captured by a French frigate, but afterwards they arrived safe, being re-taken." He is now in his fifty-sixth year. "I went to Ferryland, only fourteen leagues from this place, last June; was blown out to sea for three days. During the nights we could not distinguish the froth of the sea, which ran mountains high, from the broken ice by which we were entirely surrounded."

During the absence of Dr. O'Donel, on his voyage to Quebec, to be consecrated, the Very Rev. Father Yore, who had been appointed Vicar-General, writes to Dr. Troy, under date September 20, 1796, a very interesting letter, from which we take the following extracts: —

" In the absence of Dr. O'Donel, who has honored me with his care, I feel it a duty to mention the general satisfaction at his promotion, and to acquaint you with the happy change in the sentiments of the people, who not long since burned the houses where Mass was said or priests were sheltered. Religion has made great progress in the country, especially in my own district (Ferryland). I have completed an elegant chapel, with a convenient dwelling, all at my own expense, except £10, which the poor people subscribed last year. The many fruitless attempts of the Methodist preachers have been successfully baffled, and there is now but one of that sect in the districts of Ferryland and Trepassey, and even his family became Catholic this year.

" The Protestants likewise lose ground, and their minister was obliged to decamp, notwithstanding his £70 a year from the 'Society.' Their feelings at such an event are easily conceived; but as he was a generous and well-bred man, we always lived in friendship and parted in peace.

"The place is exceedingly poor from a failure in the fishery, containing nearly 2,500 souls, unequally divided in ten different harbors in the space of about 70 miles. . . . The 8th instant nine French men-of-war hove in sight: one 80-gun ship, six 74-gun ships, and two frigates. The 10th, they bore down on the harbour to attack. The wind not answering them to enter, and discovering our strong and well-manned fortifications, they thought it proper to steer off, and sailed for Bay Bulls, which they attacked and burnt. . . . A vessel which arrived here last Sunday left Quebec on the 5th instant. Mr. O'Donel was not yet arrived. They sailed from this about six weeks since. They went north-about to avoid the enemy. It is generally a long passage, and those who are used to it are not afraid of danger."

This letter shows from the context that it was written at Ferryland; and as the date is September 20th, and he states that Dr. O'Donel left about six weeks before, that would be about the first week in August. Although Father Yore had not up to that date received an account of his arrival, as a matter of fact, at the very moment he was writing, Dr. O'Donel was in preparation and vigil for his consecration, which took place, as we have seen, on the following day (21st September). The circuitous route, around by the north and through the Straits of Belle Isle, could not be made in shorter time, even in our own day. Before his departure from St. John's he received a warm and sincere address, signed by the merchants and Protestant inhabitants generally, by the colonel, then commander-in-chief of the forces, and by the officers, military and naval. It shows what an extraordinary change had come over public feeling since Dr. O'Donel's first appearance in Newfoundland. It is as follows : —

"REV. SIR, — As we understand that you shortly intend to make a voyage to the continent of America, permit us to take this opportunity of assuring you of our good and sincere wishes for your safety and happy return; and how sensible we are of the many obligations we lie under for your very steady and indefatigable perseverance in attending to, and regulating with such address, the morals of much of the greater part of this community, the salutary effects of which have been sufficiently obvious. We are no strangers to the many difficulties which you have from time to time been obliged to encounter, even at the risk of your life, in regularly visiting the different outposts within your reach, and in performing, with cheerfulness and alacrity, those functions from whence have arisen so many advantages to the inhabitants of this Island. That you may long be able to fulfil, with your wonted zeal and attention, the many duties of the honorable office you now hold, is the unfeigned wish of

"Rev. Sir, your most obedient Servants," etc.

As soon as possible after his consecration Dr. O'Donel returned to Newfoundland, and after a most dangerous passage arrived at Placentia, then a place of greater importance than now. It had a lieutenant-governor and a garrison. The Bishop made a pastoral visitation of the district, and administered the Sacrament of Confirmation. This was not the first time Placentia had been honored by the presence of a Bishop. We have before noticed that the Bishop of Quebec paid a visit here some hundred and seven years previously (1689). But it was the first Episcopal visitation since the English obtained entire possession of the Island, and must have been a source of great consolation to the good people.

The pastor of the mission at the time was the Rev. Edmund Bourke, already alluded to.

The Bishop returned as soon as possible to St. John's to resume his arduous labors. He had but two priests to attend to the spiritual wants of St. John's, Torbay, Portugal Cove, and the South Shore of Conception Bay, Bay Bulls, the Southern Shore, and other localities, now all provided with resident clergymen.

In 1801 he published a body of Diocesan Statutes, for the guidance of the priests under his jurisdiction, and particularly adapted to the state of the Church in this country. Among other injunctions, the missionaries are exhorted to visit each other as frequently as possible; all are bound to come to St. John's at least once a year, and the priests of Harbor Grace and Ferryland twice a year. It appears that at the time those statutes were published there were no secular priests in the Island, for in his exhortation to mutual charity he says: "Missionarii omnes sive Seculares (licet adhuc non ad sint), sive Regulares Cujuscunque Ordinis." He concludes the statutes by ordering (we give the words in an English translation) "that public prayers be offered up every Sunday and holiday (though but few of the latter can be observed in this Mission, and the Superior will hereafter, by a private notice, designate such as can be observed) for our Most Sovereign King George III. and his Royal family; that the priests should use every means to turn aside their flocks from the vortex of modern anarchy; that they should inculcate a willing obedience to the salutary laws of England, and to the commands of the governor and magistrates of this Island. . . . We most earnestly entreat, and by all the spiritual authority we hold, ordain that all missioners oppose with all the means in their power all plotters, conspirators, and favorers of the infidel French, and use every endeavour to withdraw their people from the plausible cajolery of French deceit; for the aim of this conspiracy is to dissolve all bonds, all laws, by which society is held together, and more especially the laws of England, which are to be preferred to those of any other country in Europe."

These instructions show that the danger to be dreaded by the spread of revolutionary principles in Newfoundland was not exaggerated; and such being the statements of Dr. O'Donel, it is no wonder that the British Government would not only tolerate, but, in a certain manner, protect Catholicity in the country. Indeed, the loyalty of the Roman Catholics to the English Crown has been frequently tested in the North American colonies. After the successful revolution which elevated the United States from a colonial dependency to a great and powerful nation, Congress, at the instance of Franklin, sent a deputation to Canada, of which he himself formed one, and of which the Rev. John Carrol, Jesuit, and, subsequently, as mentioned before, the first Bishop of Baltimore, was also a member. The object of the mission was to induce the Canadians to raise the standard of independence. But the Canadian Catholics, enjoying perfect liberty of conscience under British rule, and beholding how, even under the glorious eagle of American independence, the narrow-minded and gloomy policy of the descendants of the fanatical Pilgrims of Massachusetts held full sway, refused to swerve from their allegiance. To the extreme bigotry and insolence of these puritanical neighbors England chiefly owes the preservation of her great Canadian empire. The continued aggression, coupled with insult, offered both to their religion and to their nationality, caused the Canadians to shrink from all desire of political association with such a people, and thereby strengthened their loyalty to England.

CHAPTER XVI.

RT. REV. DR. O'DONEL, *Continued.* — [1801-1806.]

Establishment of Parishes and Districts — State of the Country — "The Old Chapel" — "The Old Palace" — Retirement of Dr. O'Donel — Appointment of Dr. Lambert — Testimony of Respect to Dr. O'Donel on Leaving the Country — Magnanimous Conduct of the Merchants and Inhabitants — Churlish Conduct of Governor Gower — Dr. O'Donel Receives a Pension of £50 *per Annum* — His Departure from the Island, Last Days, Death (1811), Epitaph — Review of his Episcopate — Personal Character.

AFTER his consecration the Bishop continued to exercise his missionary duties as before. He divided the whole diocese into missions or districts, of which there were at first four.

First. St. John's, including from La Manche to Holyrood, which was attended by the Bishop and his nephew, Father Michael O'Donel.

Second. Harbor Grace, including from Holyrood to Grates Cove; north from there was visited annually by a priest from St. John's, who also visited Labrador. This district was attended by Father Whelan, who would seem to have been its first missioner. After his death (by drowning), Fr. Yore came from Ferryland, but stayed only a short time; then Fr. Fitzpatrick took charge of this mission, and Fr. Yore went for good there in 1806.

Third. Ferryland, including from Lamanche to Cape St. Mary's. This mission was first attended by Fr. Fitzpatrick until the arrival of Fr. Yore in 1789.

Fourth. Placentia included from Cape St. Mary's to Fortune Bay, and all beyond. It was, as we have seen, first attended by Fr. Bourke till 1798, when he was succeeded by Fr. Whelan.

It has been mentioned that Fr. Yore arrived in 1789. This venerable clergyman played a conspicuous part in the early ecclesiastical history of the country for nearly half a century, and has left his name indelibly printed on our annals. He was a man of imposing presence and indomitable will. Dean Cleary describes him as "a domineering man . . . carrying all before him. He used to go single-handed in a skiff from Ferryland to St. John's." He arrived first on our shores at Ferryland in 1789. His *Exeat*, or credential letter, from the Provincial of the Franciscan Order in Ireland is an antiquated document, bearing the large seal of the Order, the cross, with cross-arms and cross-bones, with the legend, "*Fratrum Minor Strictioris Obs. Provinciæ Hiberniæ.*" I think it sufficiently interesting to reproduce in full: —

"Fr. Jacobus O Reilly, F. F. Minor Strict⁸ Observantiæ, Provinciæ Hiberniæ, Minister Provincialis et Missionarius Emeritus, R. P. Thomæ Yore ejusdem Provinciæ Alumno, Predicatori et Confessario, Salutem et Benedictionem in Domino. Cum ad missionem Americanam anheles, Nobisq. pium hoc tuum desiderium suppliciter exposueris, favore Omnimodo te prosequi volentes justis tuis votis annuimus, proin tenore præsentium facultatem tibi (quantum in nobis est) impertimur ut ad prefatam Missionem quancius accedere valeas. Interim te ceu vitæ exemplaris Religiosum altofatæ Missionis Prefectibus charius in Domino Commendamus. Vale! Nostri in precibus et Sacrificiis Memor.

                " Datum in loco Nostræ Residentiæ Pontanensens hac die 6ᵗᵃ Martii Anno reparatæ
"[L.S.]   Salutis 1789. Sub Nostro Chirographo Provinciæque Sigillo Majori.
"(Signed)   FR. JACOBUS Ō REILLY,
                          "*Minisʳ Prōalis.*"

A man of such physical and mental energy was not one to remain long inactive. Immediately after his arrival he commenced to lay the foundations, temporal and spiritual, of the future Mission of Ferryland. He bought the farm known by the not very euphonious name of "Scroggins," and built a house and chapel not far from the ruins of the establishment abandoned by Lord Baltimore over one hundred and sixty years before. No vestige remains of either house or chapel now, though the site is shown to the eastward of the main road, near "the Pool." He labored assiduously in this Mission for about seventeen years. In the year 1805 or 1806 he went to Harbor Grace, where he continued his labors till his death, in 1833, at the age of eighty-four years. He had been appointed Vicar-General by Dr. O'Donel, after his consecration in 1796. He was one of the three who petitioned the Holy Father for the consecration of Dr. O'Donel. His first act on going to Harbor Grace was to pay off a debt of three hundred and fifty pounds left on the chapel there, for which purpose he travelled throughout every settlement of the Bay. He was succeeded in Ferryland by Father Fitzpatrick, who built the old chapel at Renews (outside of the "Look-out"). On account of some money difficulties he left the country in 1816, and went to Ireland, where he died.

The total population of the Island at this time was about thirty-five thousand, of whom three-fourths were Catholics, and only about one-seventh were females. The ordinary wages of a fisherman was thirty pounds for the half year. They were "shipped for the voyage," so that in winter no wages were given, nor was there any work, except rinding or boat-building. There was no cultivation of the soil; not even potatoes were planted. In the winter men lived in "cook-rooms" attached to the stages, and boarded themselves, or "ate themselves," as they said. Money was plentiful. There was no paper money, except bills of exchange on England; no coppers, but dollars (Mexican) were the current medium; and tradition reports that they were so plentiful that men played "pitch-and-toss" with them. Up to the present day many a good "*cul baitha*" is in existence, in the shape of a stocking crammed with these broad pieces.[1] Every necessary was imported. Bread sold at £9 a bag; pork at £10 a barrel; tea, etc., in proportion; but, then, fish was worth 45s. a quintal.

There was no postal communication with the outer world, but vessels leaving every fall and spring brought letters. There were no roads. People travelled in winter from Placentia to St. John's *via* St. Mary's and Trepassey, Renouze, etc., and from Long Harbor, *via* Heart's Content, to Harbor Grace.

It has already been stated that Dr. O'Donel built the "Old Chapel" at St. John's, though it is most probable a chapel of some sort existed before his arrival here in 1784. According to a statement of the late Dean Cleary, it must have been erected at least ten years before that date, viz., 1774; for when the late venerable Dean was stationed at Bonavista, in 1830, he met with an old man named Harry Black, then eighty years of age (consequently he had been born in 1750). He informed the Dean that the "Old Chapel" was built when he was a young man of twenty-four or twenty-five years of age (viz., in 1774), and that he himself "brought the first stick of wood that ever was placed in it. It was laid under the altar in the north-west corner." Again we have seen that the foundation-stone of the "Old Chapel" bears a still earlier date, viz., 1754.

An old house still (1885) exists, belonging to Mr. Corbett, in the neighborhood of the Star of the Sea Hall, in which Mass was celebrated before the erection of the "Old Chapel."[2] At first the chapel consisted of merely the transepts and part of the nave. It was enlarged in 1825, and the bell [3] erected.

---

[1] This is no imaginary or rhetorical figure. A few years ago a treasure-trove of this sort came into the hands of the present writer, in the shape of a bag containing forty pounds (one hundred and sixty dollars). They had been concealed under a hearth-stone for over forty years.

[2] This house has since been pulled down to make room for the widening of the street, and Mr. Corbett, one of the few who could speak from personal recollection of Dr. O'Donel, has been gathered to his forefathers. He declared that while he lived no sacrilegious hand should be laid upon the old "*shanty*," for it was not much better, and every day till he died he spent an hour in it.

[3] This historic bell, which first sounded the tocsin of the faith over the hills of Newfoundland, bears the inscription, "John Redhall, fecit 1825." It was removed, on

The "Old Palace" was built about 1807 by Dr. Lambert, successor to Dr. O'Donel, though previously to that time there was a small house on the spot, with one chimney (a daring Papal aggression in those days) and one parlor. Before the erection of this primitive dwelling, "the Bishop" (so a very venerable lady informed me) "lived in Tom Williams' house, at the foot of Lime Kiln Hill."[1]

In 1814 the "Old Palace" was enlarged, and was made one of the finest and most imposing looking houses in the town. For a period of nearly seventy years it was the home of the bishops and clergy of the early Church in Newfoundland. Around it hung many sacred and soothing traditions; and many of the anecdotes of its former history, recited by the elder clergy, are full of interest, often most amusing.[2] It

---

the taking down of the "Old Chapel" in 1872, to St. Peter's Chapel, Queen Street, where it continued its holy song of "*Congrego Clerum, Populum Voco*" till that chapel became converted into a school, in 1884, when it was procured by the energetic pastor of Salmonier, Rev. J. St. John, and erected in the bell-chamber of the central tower of the beautiful Church of St. Joseph, which rises gracefully among the fir-trees on that charming estuary of the Bay of St. Mary's. There for many a long year to come the sweet tones of this noble old harbinger of the faith will gladden the ears of the hardy fishermen with the sweet sounds of the "Angelus," or cheer them as they return in their little boats with the gladsome chime of the Vesper peal.

[1] The venerable lady alluded to is Mrs. Kenney, a respectable and pious woman, who died in 1880, having attained beyond her eightieth year. She remembered Dr. O'Donel quite well. She was born in the old house, still existing, in the Duke of York Street, alias Kenney's Lane, which had formerly been the "first Government House." This house, though not of any very elaborate architectural or gubernatorial pretensions, was, nevertheless, something of a more durable and expensive character than the ordinary wooden dwellings of the time, as the oaken beams, still visible, can testify. It is of very remote antiquity. I have not been able to discover the date of its erection, but from the lease and receipts in possession of the Kenney family it appears that in the year 1795 it was rented by "Father O'Donel" (he was not consecrated Bishop till the following year, 1796) "and Dr. Ogden, M.D., for Mr. Brine, father of Mrs. Kenney." The property is called "Mary Stripling's Plantation," and consists of "a house and garden." It belongs to "Mary Stripling, of Ashburton, in County of Devon, Kingdom of Great Britain, spinster"; the rent was £5 15s. for twelve months.

[2] There was one portion, a sort of back linhay, or attic, exposed to the north-east, which was extremely cold in the winter season. It was significantly named "The Labrador," and to it were relegated the junior clergy, on their first arrival in the country, as a place of probation and noviceship. It was probably supposed that the fervor of their young hearts would enable them to bear more heroically the nipping atmosphere of this "remote" attic. The only line of demarcation defining the portion of *territory* allotted to each incumbent of "Labrador," for dressing and washing room, bed, etc., was a chalk line drawn across the floor.

went through many vicissitudes. In the year 1854, on the completion of the superb new palace, on the Cathedral grounds, by Dr. Mullock, the "Old Palace" was abandoned, and Bishop and clergy went to live in the new residence. For some time after this, however, the Saturday evening confessions were heard in the "Old Chapel," and the priests continued partially to occupy the "Old Palace."

In the year 1855, on the dismemberment of the Roman Catholic Academy and the commencement of the new College of St. Bonaventure, the "Old Palace" was fitted up as a temporary school, under the New Education Act, and was placed under the charge of the Very Rev. Fr. (now Archdeacon) Forristal, the first President of St. Bonaventure's. The following year it was found incommodious and unfitted for the large number of boarders which soon began to flock to the college. The establishment was removed to "The Monastery" at Belvidere, the new building not being yet completed. The "Old Palace" was thus again abandoned, and remained untenanted, except by the faithful sacristan, "Tommy Woods," until the arrival of the Most Rev. Dr. Power, in 1870. At this time, it having been reported that the "Old Chapel" was in a dangerous condition, it was examined by competent mechanics, who declared it their opinion that it was unsafe, and it was ordered to be taken down. The site, however, hallowed by so many sacred memories, and sanctified by being made the cradle of Catholicity in Newfoundland, was not permitted to be handed over to any purely secular use. It was secured by the newly instituted Star of the Sea Association, a Catholic society of fishermen, established with religious and mutual beneficial objects, who built upon it their very fine public hall. The "Old Palace," which formed part of the property transferred, did not long survive its alienation from its ecclesiastical owners. It was burnt to the ground in 1874. Thus passed away one of the old landmarks of our Church history. I thought it not unworthy of this brief memoir.

The severe labors of the mission now began to undermine

the constitution of the venerable Prelate; nor is it to be
wondered at, for, besides the cares of the bishopric, he had
to discharge, as was stated, the duties of a missionary priest,
on account of the paucity of clergymen in the vicariate.
He represented the state of his failing health to the Holy
See, offered his resignation, and begged for a successor
to be appointed. Deeply impressed with the responsibili-
ties of the pastoral office, he would not continue to hold
a dignity the duties of which he was unable to discharge,
and the resources of the vicariate were then too limited to
support a coadjutor. Accordingly, he procured the appointment of Dr. Lambert as his successor, and in the year
1807 he left the field of his apostolic labors for his native
soil.

When Dr. O'Donel was leaving the country, all classes
united to show their appreciation of his character. The deep
regret of his own flock at losing their beloved pastor and
father was reciprocated by the Protestant portion of the
community, who lost a friend, and in many cases a protector.
A public meeting was called, and a large silver urn presented
to him as a token of esteem. A letter was also sent to the
governor (Gower) requesting him to forward to the English
Government their request for a pension to Dr. O'Donel. The
governor complied with their request, but in a very un-
graceful manner, as will appear from his letter. The
occasion was one on which it was not necessary to make
a display of his feelings by using the insulting and un-
English word "Romish." The result of the petition was
a beggarly pension of £50 per annum to him whose services
were more useful to the Government of England than a
garrison: the man, in fact, who more than once saved the
colony to the Crown. "While the profligate favorites of
royalty," writes Dr. Mullock, "and the cadets of a beggarly
aristocracy were drawing their thousands annually from the
pension list, *fifty pounds* was considered a sufficient reward
for the acknowledged and invaluable services of a Catholic
Bishop!"

The following is the letter of the merchants and inhabitants generally : —

"ST. JOHN'S, NEWFOUNDLAND,
"9th August, 1804.

"SIR, — We, the magistrates, merchants, and other inhabitants of St. John's, Newfoundland, beg leave to state to your Excellency, that the Right Rev. James O'Donel, chief Roman Catholic clergyman of this Island, has resided among us for twenty years, during which time he has strenuously and successfully laboured to improve the morals and regulate the conduct of the planters, servants, and lower classes of the inhabitants of this and the neighbouring districts, whereby he has effectually prevented the quarrels and animosities which were before frequent, and rendered our persons and properties unsafe, particularly in the spring of the year 1799, when, next to General Skerritt, he was the person who saved this valuable Island from becoming a scene of anarchy and confusion by making the most unwearied exertions and using the extensive influence he had acquired over the lower classes, by which means they were prevented from joining the mutineers of the Newfoundland regiment at a time when General Skerritt had not sufficient force to oppose such a dangerous combination. This the General with candour often acknowledged, and regretted that he had not sufficient interest at Home to procure Dr. O'Donel a pension from Government for the many essential services he has rendered this country ; but to obtain which the General applied to Lord Radstock, Sir Charles Morice Pole, and Admiral Gambier, for their assistance ; who all most readily agreed in promising their support to so just a claim, and testimonies and documents, which would in all probality have obtained this favour were sent from hence, but were lost from on board the " Camilla." These were renewed by General Skerritt the following year, and by him addressed to His Royal Highness the Duke of Kent ; but His Royal Highness being for a considerable time abroad at Gibraltar, the matter seems to have been forgot. This we regret ; yet we now hope that this truly good work, by the guidance of Providence, has been reserved to be accomplished by Your Excellency; and we earnestly request you will use your benevolent influence with His Majesty's ministers to reward this very respectable gentleman with some little independence during the short remainder of a long life spent in the service of his king, country, and neighbours.

"We have the honor to be, etc.,
"(Signed)"

{ Then follow the signatures of the principal inhabitants of St. John's.

The following is the Governor's reply :—

"FORT TOWNSHEND, 10 August, 1804.

"GENTLEMEN, — I have received your letter of yesterday's date stating the important benefits Government has received in this Island from the useful and patriotic services of the Reverend Dr. O'Donel, the Romish Bishop in St. John's, and requesting me to interfere with His Majesty's ministers to obtain him some compensation, in reply to which I have to assure you that I shall with great pleasure lay your representation before His Majesty's Government, and use my utmost endeavours to get his merit rewarded.

"I am, etc.,
"E. GOWER.

"The merchants and principal inhabitants of St. John's."

From a letter of Dr. O'Donel to his nephew, Father Michael O'Donel, P.P., of Clashmore, kindly sent me by the Bishop's grand-nephew, the Rev. Michael O'Donnell, of Harrowgate, England (which letter shall be produced farther on), we can learn to within a day or two the date of Dr. O'Donel's departure from our shores. The letter is dated "Bristol, September the 17th, 1807." He writes : "My dear Michael, — I have to acquaint you of my arrival in Europe after a pleasant passage of 26 days." He arrived first at Portsmouth, where he remained two days, thence it may have taken him two or three days to get to Bristol. He was in Bristol some time before the 29th August. Hence we may conclude he left St. John's about the 26th July.

In a brief account of the life and labors of this "Apostle of Newfoundland," in the "Irish Penny Magazine" of November, 1834, contributed by a writer signing himself "J. E.," there is given, "from various manuscripts in his possession," an "Elegy on the Right Rev. James O'Donel," which I deem worthy to reproduce here, not, perhaps, altogether on account of any very extraordinary literary merit, but as an interesting curiosity, and as also serving to illustrate one or two historical facts concerning the life of our "first Bishop." (See Note 3.)

The letters "J. E.," I am informed by the Rev. Michael O'Donnell, are the initials of James Eaid, grandson of Mrs. Phelan (Dr. O'Donel's sister). "He died many years since in Waterford," writes F. O. D.; "and I, who knew him well, don't believe that a book or a manuscript belonging to him can now be found."

After the line of the "Elegy" referring to "Britain's grateful mite," there is a note stating that "for his (Dr. O'Donel's) meritorious conduct, Government entitled him to accept a free grant of a portion of land in St. John's, now called the 'Bishop's Farm.'" The Right Rev. Dr. Fleming was not aware of this fact, for in his letter (VII.) to Dr. Spratt, September 2d, 1836, he says: "I began to make arrangements, . . . previous to my departure for Newfoundland, to solicit at Downing Street a grant of ground for the erection of a church and public school, in St. John's. *Not a single favor of the kind, not a grant of ground for any public purpose*, having ever been given by the Government to the Catholics of Newfoundland." But this grant to Dr. O'Donel was a private or personal one. There is, however, a small piece of ground near "Palks," at River Head, St. John's, which belonged to Dr. O'Donel, the rent of which is received by Father O'Donnell, of Harrowgate.

"The farm," he says, "has been rented for ninety-nine years, at a rental of £9 or £10. It has been paid, . . . first to my uncle, then to Mrs. Phelan (Dr. O'Donel's sister) and for the last forty years to myself."

A note is added to the second last stanza of the Elegy stating that "the ceremony on the day of his sailing from St. John's was most solemn. All business was suspended, guns were kept firing at regular intervals, and all the vessels in the harbor displayed their colors at half-mast high!"

In the letter mentioned as having been written by Dr. O'Donel, from Bristol, to his nephew, Father O'Donel, of Clashmore, he gives a more detailed account of the proceedings accompanying his departure: —

"The merchants of St. John's behaved with uncommon friendship and singular attention to me. They gave me a farewell dinner at the *London Tavern;* 47 people at table; among whom were the heads of all departments; my nephew, Sullivan, with his friend from Montreal. The President made an appropriate speech upon the occasion, and then drank my health with 3 times 3 cheers. The feast was, as usual, uncommonly expensive and splendid. The General, magistrates, merchants, and principal inhabitants of the town addressed me in very flattering terms on the morning of my departure. All the Protestant merchants waited on me in my own house, and escorted me in procession to Bell's Wharf, where they had another man-of-war boat with 8 oars, and accompanied me in it aboard. All the merchants and inhabitants displayed their colours, both afloat and on shore, to the best advantage. So far the shore business."

The "splendid gift" mentioned in the Elegy is the large silver urn alluded to by Dr. Mullock, which was presented to Dr. O'Donel by the people of St. John's. It was at the time of J. E.'s communication (1834) in possession of Father Michael O'Donel, of Clashmore, from whom it passed to Father

O'Donnell, of Harrowgate, in whose possession it now is. "The urn," he writes, "is safe in my keeping. It bears, without date, the following inscription: 'Presented to the Rt. Rev. James O'Donel, D.D., by the inhabitants of St. John's, New-found-land, in testimony of his pious, patriotic, and meritorious conduct during a residence among them of 23 years.' This urn," continues Father O'Donnell, "his pectoral cross, ring, gloves, false teeth, and stole, are the only articles belonging to him now remaining, as far as I know." The urn or cup did not actually arrive in Newfoundland, but was received by Dr. O'Donel in Bristol. In his letter to his nephew he speaks of it as follows:—

"Messr. Elmes, Rennie, and McBraire waited on me a little before my departure, and said they intended to present me a silver cup at St. John's; but as it did not arrive, requested to know where it should be addressed to me. It is now in my possession, and one of the finest pieces of plate that has ever been seen at Bristol. The devices, raised work, and other ornaments are finished with exquisite taste and elegance. It cost 150 guineas, so that you see my friends were not paying me empty compliments."

This letter, so often alluded to, describes, in pleasant and easy style, the incidents of the voyage. It is written upon very rough paper of large size, unruled, in a good hand of antique style, containing some old-fashioned abbreviations. It is folded, of course, without envelope, and is fast crumbling to pieces. The seal in red wax is almost entirely gone, and the Bristol post-mark nearly obliterated. The address on the outside is rather quaint:—

"Revd Michael O'Donel to be forwarded by
"Mr Daniel Murphy, Shopkeeper
"Broad street
"Stradbally
"Waterford
"Ireland."

Having thus graphically described the embarkation, Dr. O'Donel continues : —

"At sea Lieutenant-General Despard, Governor of Cape Briton, and his Lady were my messmates, and agreeable companions they were; but were highly astonished at the honor done me by the Leading men of the place. She told me the King's Son could expect no more! McBraire said, '*Nor even so much.*'[1] I put in a sea stock that would render all of us comfortable to China, as I was loaded with presents of all kinds by the Ryans, Elmes, and country farmers, who sent me at least 40 pounds of fresh butter; in short, I had so many superfluous articles that I sent most of them to Mrs Agassiz, who remained at McCarthy's Plantation till his return." This was the Captain's lady. The ship was named the "Rattler." "We had a very good soup and four dishes of fresh meat every day at Dinner. Port, Madeira, and Sherry in plenty, of which we left 15 dozen of bottles unconsumed aboard, together with a large stock of poultry, beef, fatt sheep, &c. The Captain can well go and come upon our leavings; we likewyse had every day a *disert*, consisting of preserv^d Plumbs, Strawberries, Cheries, fresh orāges, shadocks, &c. If an Epicure like Maddock had been among us he'd wish for 2 months' passage. Mr Bollard and Betsy McCurdy were Passengers in the gun-room. The latter is married to the Pursar of the 'R^{tler},' by birth an Irishman, and by profession a nominal Catholick of the tepid kind. I remained only 2 days at Portsmouth to take a view of the wonderful machinery in the Dock yard all moved by the steam of one fire. They are well worth the Traveller's notice, and can't fail of exciting his astonishment. I came thence to my old friends M^r and Mrs Butler, where I am very comfortable, and perfectly at home, and where I met Joseph Ryan who was my guide and companion thro' the streets at Bristol. He is temperate in his

---

[1] James McBraire, Esq., founder of the Irish Society, of whom more shall be said farther on.

living, clear in his understanding, and sound in his judgement. He parted me on the 29th of August for Liverpool to proceed thence to St. John's. My Furniture sold well except what I gave Dr Lambert, which would sell much higher had they been disposed of at public vendue. I'll remain here until October, and probably then go to London for some days. I dine nowhere out of this house but at the Revd Mr Ploughdon's, Lady Doager fingal's, and one Sibby's a Banker from London, there are many more at Clifden who wish to see me, O Shea, Mr Brown, but I feel more comfort by dining at home than by attending such gentry as those. I am going tomorrow to see the Bishop of Bath, who has been a Benedictin Monk, and is in a bad state of health. He has got a condjutor of the Order of St. Francis to succeed him, whose Bulls are arrived and whose consecration is soon to take place to which I am asked." [Then follows "Domestick Intelligence," concerning certain parties of St. John's who have died or been married, etc., and it thus concludes] : "I am now tired, and expect you'll write to me by return of Poste. Present my affectionate compliments to all friends at Clonmell and elsewhere, and believe me to be

"Your loving Uncle,
"JAMES O'DONEL.

"Bristol, September the 7th, 1807."

There is a long postscript on business and money matters. He complains of a young lad, "a mulish junk of a boy, who'll never do any good for himself or anybody else." His name is Phelan. No doubt a nephew or son of Mrs. Phelan, mentioned before. He has cost him over £40, but he has gone to Boston, where he intends to earn his bread, "as he says by his *mental operations*. . . . He could get £30 for 2 years from Quarry at Porte-de-Grave, and have nothing to do but attend shop, but he would not serve any man on earth for so long a time." Of his other nephew, Sullivan, he speaks in high terms of praise.

"Sullivan is a tall, handsome, accomplished young man,
fit to keep company with those of the first rank anywhere."
He complains also of some of the servants having stolen "6
guineas and a half," and either stolen or burnt " Bills firsts
and 2^{nds} £32, which are a very great loss ; " but he winds up
philosophically with the aphorism, " No help for Misfortunes !"

The Father Michael O'Donel whom he addresses is the
priest who was out in Newfoundland with him, and who only
returned to Ireland the previous year, 1806. He was for
seventeen years P.P. of Clashmore, where he died, in March,
1832.

I am indebted again to Father Michael O'Donnell, of
Harrowgate, for the following additional information concerning the last years of Dr. O'Donel: "The Bishop, on
his return from Newfoundland, visited the graves of his
ancestors, in the grounds of the old monastic ruins at Kilronan, Co. Waterford, three and one-half miles from Clonmel, — and had erected there a monument" which sets forth
that the Rt. Rev. Dr. O'Donel had placed it there to the
memory of his father, Michael O'Donel, who died at the age
of 68 on the 20th of November, 1767 ; and of his mother,
Ann (Crosby), who died on the 10th of November, 1785,
aged 66 ; and of his brother, Rev. Michael O'Donel, O.S.F.,
who died on the 26th of June, 1790, aged 66.

Dr. O'Donel spent the remainder of his days in Waterford. The long life was now drawing to a close. He died
the death of the just, in the year 1811, in the seventy-fourth
year of his age. His remains were transferred to Clonmel,
and buried in the old chapel of St. Mary's, Irishtown. "A
tombstone, still to be seen," writes Dr. Mullock, 1856, " was
placed over him, and on it was engraved this epitaph, written,
it is said, by himself : —

"'HERE LIE THE MORTAL REMAINS OF THE RIGHT REV
JAMES ODONEL BISHOP OF THYATIRA, THE FIRST QUALIFIED
MISSIONARY WHO EVER WENT TO NEWFOUNDLAND, WHERE HE

SPENT 23 YEARS, AS PREFECT AND VICAR APOSTOLIC OF THE SAID MISSION. HE DEPARTED THIS LIFE ON THE 15TH OF APRIL 1811 IN THE 74TH YEAR OF HIS AGE. MAY HE REST IN PEACE. AMEN."

Being in Ireland in 1869, I made a pilgrimage to the shrine of the first apostle and Bishop of our Island, but, alas! no vestige could I find of his last resting-place; not a relic of the monument or inscription to be seen! Extensive alterations have been made in the church, and everything in the shape of antiquity has been swept away!

"When I was a school-boy at Cahir," writes Father O'Donnell, of Harrowgate, "in the year 1837, I sometimes visited my native town, Clonmel, and often stopped to read the inscription on the tomb of the Bishop in the chapel yard of Irishtown. It stood then where a confessional stands now, in the new and enlarged church, and its *disjecta membra* are hidden away in an obscure passage behind the church where Dr. Baldwin, the parish priest, pointed them out to me shortly after their removal from their original site." Is it too late to hope that these precious *débris* may be gathered together and reset, or at least placed in a monument worthy of this noble man, to whom Newfoundland owes so much, and of whom no memorial of any kind exists among us?

"It is difficult," writes Dr. Mullock, "now even to conceive the obstacles a Bishop had to encounter during the period of Dr. O'Donel's prelacy in Newfoundland. The sullen and unwilling protection offered him by the Government, availing itself of his influence and still hating and insulting its benefactor; the tyrannical conduct of the petty officials to Catholics, which he was frequently obliged to overlook in silence; the rampant bigotry of many uneducated Protestants, who knew nothing of Catholicity but what they learnt from 5th-of-November sermons; the difficulties of communication, for the whole Island was then an impassable wilderness, without a single mile of road; the ignorance of the so-called 'better class,' so that a man like the Bishop, used

"THE OLD PALACE."

to the refined society of the nobility of Catholic Germany, was completely isolated among them; the paucity of missioners, and the impossibility of that close surveillance which a Bishop is bound to exercise over his clergy and people, — such were a few of the difficulties the pioneer of Catholicity had to encounter in this country. Well and nobly was the duty performed by Dr. O'Donel; no difficulties daunted him, no slight or rebuff discouraged him, no dangers appalled him. He put his hand to the plough, and never looked back till the good seed was sown, now, thank God! so abundantly fructifying, and which has made Newfoundland one of the most flourishing portions of God's vineyard.

"The impulse given to Catholicity by the appointment of Dr. O'Donel as Vicar Apostolic and Bishop had a great effect, even on the material prosperity of the Island. It was a recognition, if we may so term it, of the fixity of tenure of the population. The rude answer of Governor Milbanke to the Bishop's petition for leave to augment the number of chapels proves that England still hoped to keep the Island a desert, — 'It was not the interest of England that people should winter in the Island'! And he blames the Bishop and Catholic clergy for inducing them to make it their home. In truth, whatever improvement has been made in the country is almost altogether due to the Catholic clergy. Unconnected with Government, and independent of mercantile interest, they looked to the advantage of the people alone. In every struggle for popular amelioration they always took the lead, and thereby earned the undying hatred of those who desired to keep Newfoundland a mere fishing-station for the advantage of English interests and mercantile monopoly.

"As soon as they were permitted, and in many cases even before permission was obtained, they studded the Island with chapels and parochial residences. They encouraged the people in every settlement to clear land and cultivate gardens, and in most cases were the only shield between the people and mercantile rapacity; for in those days, though the Newfoundland merchants were in many cases men of wealth, still they frequently left nothing after them but the memory of their harshness and a few rotten wooden erections. No churches, schools, hospitals, or asylums for decayed fishermen exist to hand down the grateful remembrance of even one Newfoundland merchant to posterity; and still these were the persons who invariably opposed every improvement, and who, to use the words of the Attorney-General to Sir Thomas Cochrane, 'would as soon think of making a ship at sea their permanent residence as Newfoundland.'" Such is the graphic

and forcible picture drawn by Dr. Mullock of the state of
Newfoundland at this period. In some points it may be
thought to be a little overdrawn; yet the strong indictment
against the whilom merchants is confirmed by all contemporary writers and by facts. It may perhaps be urged that
a change of circumstances, and the march of events have
brought about a new state of things; that many of our principal merchants are now residents of the country, with their
town-houses and country villas; yet recent events show that
it is hard to eradicate the old prejudices.

A census of the population was taken in 1806, and it was
estimated at 26,505. In all probability the Catholics were
more than half. There were about six clergymen permanently established in the Island, — two in St. John's, one in
Placentia, two in Conception Bay, and one at Ferryland.
The northern portion of the Island and Labrador were visited from St. John's, and the baptisms and marriages performed there registered in the St. John's books. Chapels
also were built before Dr. O'Donel's departure in St. John's,
Harbor Grace, Placentia, Carbineers', and Ferryland.

Such are all the data which can be gleaned of the life and
labors of this good and saintly Bishop. He may truly be
called the "Apostle of Newfoundland;" and though some of
the details may appear trifling to outsiders, they are dearly
interesting to us, his spiritual children. They let in a few
side-lights upon the historic picture of the times, and give us
a glimpse at the social state of Newfoundland at this period.

As to his great qualities of courage and zeal, we must let
his works speak for him. His letter shows him a man of
plain and simple tastes, though of wide worldly experience,
full of sound sense and playful amiability; a true pastor, who
"knew his flock" individually, and was not above taking a
lively interest in the smallest domestic affairs, even of the
humblest among them. Such was Dr. O'Donel, whose memory is forever embalmed in the hearts of the faithful of Newfoundland.

CHAPTER XVII.

EDUCATIONAL INSTITUTIONS.

The "Benevolent Irish Society"—The "Orphan Asylum"—State of Education in the Island—Its Various Phases Traced—The Irish Society's Schools—Father Fleming Endeavors to get Control of them, 1829—Protestant Educational Institutions—First Education Act, 1843—Foundation of Protestant and Catholic Colleges, 1844—General Academy of St. John's—Formation of the Roman Catholic, Church of England, and General Protestant Academies, 1850—Opening of St. Bonaventure's College, 1855—Establishment of Wesleyan Academy, 1858—Dr. Mullock's Views on Education—"The Monks"—The Christian Brothers.

THE social gathering so *naïvely* sketched by Dr. O'Donel gives us a peep at the state of society in St. John's at the beginning of the present century; and it must be confessed that the picture on which he draws aside the curtain is a very pleasant one indeed. From it we can judge that St. John's at that time had made no pigmy strides in the path of advancement and social development, and that Dr. O'Donel's position was not altogether so isolated as Dr. Mullock would have us believe. A city in which some forty odd persons could sit down in a public room to such a sumptuous and elegant repast as that described must have possessed all the amenities and soothing influences of civilized life; and society must have achieved a considerable degree of culture. And, indeed, such was the case. One of the surest signs of the advancement of social comfort and the elevation of public taste is the organization of clubs or institutes for intellectual, educational, or benevolent objects,—associations in which men meet together to exchange mutual converse, to assist each other, both temporally, morally, and intellectually, and thus attain the highest degree of human culture. Such has been the natural course of civic and national progress from the times of the ancient Greeks and Romans, with their

academies, their lyceums, their forums, down to our own
times, with their clubs, and institutes, and *cercles*.

So, then, as a natural consequence of the march of events,
we find the people of St. John's at this date putting forth the
first blossoms of her literary and charitable harvest. Those
two other indispensable helpmates of civilization — the post-
office and the newspaper — also sprung into existence in this
year of 1806.

The spirit of religious persecution had ceased. Peace and
harmony reigned among all classes, owing, no doubt, in a
great measure to the prudence, good sense, and kindly heart
of the Rt. Rev. Dr. O'Donel. Men began to think of
drawing together more closely by the bonds of friendship
and fellow-citizenship. To this period, then, we owe the institution of "The Benevolent Irish Society," an institute
which to-day, after its eighty years of existence, is in a
flourishing and ever-advancing condition, numbering among
its associates nearly all of our citizens who either come
directly from the shores of the Old Land, or who glory in
the remembrance that their ancestors claim as the land of
their birth the "green fields of Erin."

The society was founded by one of those mentioned with
so much feeling by Dr. O'Donel in the letter elsewhere quoted ;
a man of large and charitable soul, warm and generous heart,
and who evidently was a sincere friend of the Bishop's, —
namely, James McBraire, Esq., merchant, of St. John's. He
was a true Irishman, though not a Roman Catholic. "He
was a man," says Dr. Fleming, writing to Dr. Spratt,
"always remarkable for the munificence of his donations to
the poor and his kindness to the Catholic clergy." He was
President of the Irish Society for eleven consecutive years,
from 1809 to 1821. Though the most prominent person
in the establishment of the society, he did not accept the
presidency at first, being preceded in that office by two
others, — Captain Winckworth Tonge (1806 to 1808) and
Lieut.-Colonel John Murray (1808 to 1809).

As stated above, Mr. McBraire was not a Catholic ; hence

the society, in its origin, was not a *religious* or *denominational* society. No mention of religious profession is made in its constitution. At the outset the patronage of the society was under the governor for the time being. The outgoing presidents became vice-patrons during their lives. Hence, in 1822, when Patrick Morris, Esq., was elected as the first Catholic president, we find registered as vice-presidents and founders of the society, "His Excellency Major-General Murray, Governor of Demerara," and "James McBraire, Esq., late Major-Commandant of the St. John's Volunteer Rangers, now of Tweed Hill, Berwick." Still, as a matter of course, the Roman Catholic Bishop, as a leading Catholic gentleman in the Island, was given a prominent place in the organization of the society. The preliminary meeting "of a number of Irish gentlemen, desirous of relieving the wants and distresses of their countrymen and fellow-creatures at large, was held at the London Tavern, in St. John's, on Wednesday, the 5th February, 1806. It was unanimously agreed 'That a society, formed upon true principles of benevolence and philanthropy, would be the most effectual mode of establishing a permanent relief to the wretched and distressed.' Under this conviction, it was proposed to elect a committee from the gentlemen present to form a code of rules and regulations for the government of the society, the extension and regulations of the charity, and to consult with the Rt. Rev. Doctor O'Donel and others, whose local knowledge of this country could best inform them as to the most effectual and beneficial mode of establishing a CHARITABLE IRISH SOCIETY upon firm principles of loyalty, true benevolence, and philanthropy, when the following gentlemen were nominated and unanimously chosen: Lieut.-Col. John Murray, James McBraire, Esq., John McKellop, Esq., Mr. Joseph Church, Captain Winckworth Tonge."

From this it will be seen that the society was purely unsectarian in its origin, and all denominations of Christians were admissible to its ranks, the only qualifications required being that one should be either an Irishman or a descendant

of an Irishman. And although, in the course of time, the
society became practically an exclusively Catholic society, as
the lines of denominational demarcation became more distinctly defined in the country, yet the rules and constitutions
on this head were never altered; and, absolutely speaking, a
member of any sect might to-day be presented for admission,
though such is not likely ever to occur.

The object of the society was twofold, — benevolent or
charitable, and intellectual or educational. To carry out
these views, an annual fee of four dollars was demanded
from each member. This was the nucleus of a fund which,
as we shall see, grew to mighty proportions, and produced
noble works; a yearly allocation was made of money, clothes,
fuel, and provisions, for the poor. Only the Recording
Angel knows the thousands of cases of poverty relieved by
this society during the past eighty years. It was not many
years in existence when it was deemed necessary, for the
carrying out of the twofold object of the society, to erect a
building which should contain both a public hall for social
and intellectual gatherings, and a suite of schools for poor
children. Accordingly, in the year 1826, a plot of ground
was secured in the rear of the town, and the building so long
and familiarly known as "The Orphan Asylum" was erected.
It was opened on the 27th May, 1827. It had some pretensions to architecture, having a fanciful central tower
and portico, called "The Observatory." It was, at the time
of its erection, considered one of the neatest buildings in
the city, and was much admired by the typical "Out-harborman," on his annual visit to the capital. The upper portion
of the building contained the grand banqueting hall, where
for over half-a-century sons of St. Patrick held their yearly
dinners, balls, and reunions. Many a lively song and soulstirring speech have made those old walls resound; many a
hearty cheer or ringing laugh has made the chandeliers
rattle; and many are the happy — and not few the sad —
memories which circle around the old spot, recalling those
who are gone, who once filled the highest places in the land.

The lower portion of the building was devoted to the teaching of poor children. It was placed under the charge of a master, and between four and five hundred children of both sexes were instructed therein. It would appear that by this time the society had become practically a *Catholic* society, yet they still strictly adhered to their rules as a *non-denominational* body. The Rt. Rev. Dr. Fleming, in his letters to Dr. Spratt, 1834, and also in a "*Relazione*" of the state of religion in Newfoundland, addressed to the Cardinal Prefect of Propaganda in 1837, complains of this state of affairs. "The schools," he says, "of the Benevolent Irish Society continued to enjoy public confidence because they were based on [non-denominational] principles. And, indeed, so jealous were this body of the character they had acquired, that, although for some years a single Protestant child had not been sent to the school, yet not only would the committee of that exclusively Catholic body not permit the Catholic Catechism to be taught, merely as a task, in school by the master, but they stood up in opposition to 'the priests who attempted to give the children religious instruction *even after school* hours." In his "*Relazione*" he goes more particularly into this matter. He says he went to the school himself to teach the religious instruction, but was refused admittance by what he calls "*questi Cattolici liberali*." He says, however, that those who strongly opposed him were only six in number. As soon as he was appointed coadjutor to Dr. Scallan (1829) he again turned his attention to the school, and, fortified by his new authority, he succeeded in preparing some four hundred children for First Communion, and determined to make a public display on the occasion. His opponents went to the Bishop (Dr. Scallan) and represented that the spectacle of so many children adorned in festive robes might cause some displeasure to the Protestants. Dr. Fleming, however, carried his point, and gave the children Communion in the public church. A few days after, a large number of Catholics called on Dr. Fleming and congratulated him, and the "Council of *Liberals* was disbanded," and "from that time forward the school has been placed under my immediate supervision."

Here we have the history of the commencement of the great fight for Catholic education. What a contrast these words reveal with the state of things to-day, when not four hundred, but *four thousand*, children march annually with "festive robes," with bands and banners, through the principal streets of the town; and when our Protestant friends of all denominations not only do not take umbrage, but vie with their Catholic neighbors in doing honor to the procession, and in catering to the comforts of the youngsters!

The state of education at this period (1826–9) is described by Dr. Fleming, as follows:—

"We had three public schools for the education of the poor generally; one of long standing,[1] 'The St. John's Charity School,' maintained partly by Government and partly by subscriptions of all classes of the community, without distinction of class or creed. To this institution the Protestant minister subscribed as well as the Catholic priest; and the Catholic merchant as well as the Governor. To this I myself have contributed very largely in proportion to my means." The second school was that of the Irish Society.

"The third establishment was erected by one of the numerous British Bible Societies, 'The North American School Society.' But as the British Government have withdrawn their support from this and the St. John's Charity School, an amalgamation of the two has latterly occurred, suggested by that gentleman [Judge Boulton], and thereby the last *apparent* rallying-point of liberality — that focus where all the rays of benevolence of whatever creed *could* converge for the advantage of the poor — was torn down by the most powerful influential interest in the Island."

---

[1] "The 'Colonial and Continental Church Society,' originally the 'Newfoundland School Society,' . . . commenced its operations in 1823" (Harvey, Newfoundland).

Shortly after this time (1832–3) the country received the great boon of Representative Government, with the long-looked-for privilege of making her own laws; and very early attention was given to the promotion of education. At first, liberal grants of money were bestowed, and the sentiment of the people seemed strongly in favor of non-denominational education. In 1843 an act was introduced into the Assembly for the formation of "two colleges, one for Protestant education and one for Roman Catholic." Dr. Fleming sent a petition against it, on the following grounds, namely: 1. While Protestants are secured in their rights, there is no provision to secure the appointment of Roman Catholics as directors for the Catholic college. 2. That according to the tenets of the Catholic religion the Bishop or ordinary is *de jure* and *de facto* Superior of every Roman Catholic college; yet no mention is made of such fact, nor is he by the *act* supposed to have any power or control over it. 3. That the only causes assigned in the act for the vacancy of the position of director are "death, resignation, or absence from the country;" whereas he declares it is necessary that these directors should be recognized members of the Catholic communion, appointed and approved by the said Bishop, and that he should have the power of suspending or dismissing a director for such cause as gross misconduct or departure from the Catholic religion, confession of the tenets of which constituted his original title to appointment. 4. That in the said directors is vested the power of electing the professors and principal of the colleges, who (the principal) "shall be a graduate of either Oxford, Cambridge, or Trinity College, Dublin." This privilege also, Dr. Fleming contends, should be subject to the approval of the Roman Catholic Bishop, and to the condition that such principal and teachers should be Roman Catholics; and, indeed, once the principle of denominationalism is conceded the objections of the Bishop seem most reasonable.

That Dr. Fleming's anxiety to preserve from contamination the little ones of his flock was not at all without sufficient reason is shown from the tone of a set of rules and by-laws which were drawn up in pursuance of this act "for the Government of the Catholic Board of Education." Rule IX. reads as follows: "While it shall be the object of this Board to promote the moral and religious education of Catholic children of the district, they will esteem it their duty — as all schools shall be open to children of every *denomination* — *to forbid that the slightest interference be used with the* religious *principles* of the children." It would seem that this act did not come into operation, and that in the following year, the seventh year of the reign of her present Majesty (1844), an act was passed "to provide for the establishment of an Academy in St. John's." This academy was *non-denominational*, and was held at "Castle Rennie," Signal Hill Road, John V. Nugent being principal, and Messrs. Newman, M.A., Ox., and T. Talbot, professors. This academy lasted till 1850, when the denominational principle again triumphed, and an act was passed to amend the former act. In this one of 1850 it was enacted that "from and after the passing of this act the functions of the present Board of Directors of the said Academy shall cease, . . . and it shall be lawful . . . to nominate three Boards of Directors for the said Academy, viz., a Roman Catholic, a Church of England, and a General Protestant Board." Thus we see the denominational tendency ever slowly but surely advancing. The former act of 1843 gave but two divisions, now we have three. As the salaries of the professors were based on population, the act gives us a criterion from which to judge of the strength of the various denominations. Thus, in Section 4 we read: "There shall be granted . . . £250 towards defraying the salary of the Roman Catholic master, £200 . . . the Church of England master," and £150 for "the salaries of one or more masters of other Protestant denominations." By Section 5 the Masters were "at their own expense to provide rooms," etc. Mr. Nugent still remained master of the Catholic academy, which was thenceforth held at Monkstown Road, till the opening of St. Bonaventure's College, in 1855, and his appointment to the office of High Sheriff.

In the year 1858 the current of denominationalism had made another rush onward, and we find the Protestant branch dividing and throwing out another stream, namely, the "Wesleyan Methodist." By this time that important and rapidly increasing denomination had so far advanced as to demand a separate academy, which was accordingly granted by an act passed on May 10, 1858, by which it is enacted that "there shall be established in St. John's a Wesleyan academy." By this act the salaries range as follows: Roman Catholic, £600; Church of England, £400; the Wesleyan Academy, £200; and the General Protestant Academy, £150. The figures of the latest census of 1884 would seem to indicate that we are not likely to have any other subdivision, at least for some years.

The Rt. Rev. Dr. Mullock, in a lecture on Education, places in strong and eloquent words the unchanging sentiment of the Catholic Church on the all-important question of denominational education: "The Government has made, on the whole, considering the resources of the country, a fair provision for education; and we enjoy, besides, the great blessing, *perfect religious freedom*. As education consists not in learning to read and write, or in the acquisition of science or languages, but comprises the whole training — moral, social, and religious — of the child, and moulds his character for life, it must be evident that the only way to prevent bickering and disunion in the community, and to give justice to all, is the mode adopted by Government of dividing the education grant, *pro rata*, between all denominations. Hence one great source of disunion, so distracting in other countries, does not exist here. All denominations being equally favored, there is no jealousy, no cause of complaint. In all countries of mixed populations where the experiment had been tried of either forcing on the minority the religious education of the majority, or of excluding any definite religious teaching, and endeavor-

ing to substitute for it a system of ethics, under the name of
'Common Christianity,' it has resulted in absolute failure.
Religious dissensions, instead of being eliminated, have become chronic and embittered; and infidelity and indifferentism, the great curses of modern society, have not only undermined all governments, monarchical or democratic, but have corrupted and endangered the fundamental principles of society itself by nullifying parental authority, the indissolubility of marriage, the rights of property, the dignity of man, and the honor of woman, — frightful evils, which we only know, thank God! by hearing. Notwithstanding the imperfect state of our education, naturally to be expected in a new and poor country, with a scattered population and imperfect communications, still our criminals are fewer in number in proportion to our population, and the crimes of a lighter character, than in many parts of either Europe or America, as criminal statistics will prove.[1] So far the moral training of the people of all denominations has not been a failure, and the basis of a solid Christian education has been laid. . . .
It is for the advantage of Catholics that the Protestant community should be well educated, as it is for the Protestants that the Catholics should be equally so. The interests of the two great sections of the community are identical, and the intelligence and morality of each is a guaranty of peace and unity to the other. Indeed, mixed up as they are, it is impossible that any improvement in the education or circumstances of one party should not excite an honorable rivalry in the other equally advantageous to both."

The importance of this lengthy extract must be my apology for its insertion here in a rather digressive position. To return to the subject of the Irish Society's schools. It appears from

---

[1] The convictions for what would be transportable crimes at Home, or punished by long imprisonment, show the following comparison between Newfoundland and the neighboring colonies: —

Newfoundland. — Population in 1845,	96,506;	convictions,	4.
New Brunswick.	"	1840, 153,162;	"	62.
P. E. Island.	"	1841, 47,034;	"	38.

the time that Dr. Fleming got control of them they became exclusively Catholic in their tone and management. In the year 1847 Dr. Fleming procured a branch of the Brothers of the Order of St. Francis from Galway. They had charge of the schools for some years, with great success. They were familiarly known as "the Monks." Owing to a variety of causes they were obliged, in 1853, to give up the schools, which again reverted to secular teachers, with more or less success, until the erection of the grand new St. Patrick's Hall, and the introduction of the Christian Brothers in the year 1876. This was the dawn of a new and glorious era in the history of education in Newfoundland; but it shall be taken up in its proper place by and by.

CHAPTER XVIII.

RT. REV. DR. LAMBERT, SECOND BISHOP.— [1806-1817.]

Dr. Lambert — His Visitation of Conception Bay and Ferryland — He Enlarges the "Old Chapel " — Delicate State of Health — He Resigns in Favor of Dr. Scallan.

HAVING thus traced the history of education up to modern times, we shall now revert to the narrative of events in due order from the year 1806.

We have seen that Dr. O'Donel, worn out more by the fatigue and labor of the Mission, than by old age, had applied for a coadjutor. A member of the same Order, and one whom he had known in Ireland, was chosen, in the person of Father Patrick Lambert. This Prelate was born in Wexford. On his return from Rome, where, in the College of St. Isidore's, he completed his studies, and was ordained priest, he was appointed a member of the Community of Wexford, and was principally engaged as professor of a seminary established in the convent. On the death of the Provincial, Father Stewart, in 1803, he was appointed Vicar Provincial of the Irish Franciscans. While thus engaged in his collegiate duties he learned that he was appointed Vicar Apostolic of Newfoundland, by Pius VII., and successor to Dr. O'Donel, whose resignation had been accepted by the Holy See. He was accordingly consecrated in the Franciscan chapel of Wexford in April, 1806, with the title of Bishop of Chitra *in partibus*,[1] and soon after left his home for the scene of his future labors. Never of a robust constitution, and being rather too old for a laborious Mission like that of Newfoundland, we do not find that he made any extensive visitation.

---

[1] Dr. Lambert thus mentions the title of his See in a letter to Dr. Troy, June 9, 1807: "The name of the diocese *in partibus* is called in my Bull *Ecclesia Chytrensis*, situated in the Island of Cyprus, and suffragan to the Archdiocese of Salamina."

He made, however, a visitation of Harbor Grace (Conception Bay) and Ferryland, in the summer of 1807. He writes to the Archbishop of Dublin (Dr. Troy) as follows: "At the time your Grace's letter arrived here I was in Conception Bay, visiting Father Ewer's district, which I had the happiness of finding in as good order as could possibly be expected in so large a range of coast. I cruised about twenty-one leagues of the coast of it and confirmed almost four hundred children." He also speaks in this letter of having just received the Holy Oils from Ireland, and says: "As your Grace is of opinion that I need not scruple to consecrate them with *one* priest, when no other can be had, I shall do so in future." [1]

In the same letter he mentions another circumstance of some importance, as showing the antiquity of the diocese of St. John's, and its prestige above those of the neighboring colonies. He received a letter from Dr. Plessis, Bishop of Quebec, in which "he complains much of the labor of his diocese, which he says it would take him six entire years to visit. He has lately consecrated a coadjutor, who resides at Montreal, and has petitioned Rome lately for another, who he intends should reside on the coast of the Gulf of St. Lawrence. He presses me very seriously to accept another part of it, that is, New Brunswick and Nova Scotia. But I assure your Grace I think I have too much sailing around the coasts of Newfoundland without going across to the continent. However, before I give a definite answer, I would be glad to have your Grace's opinion on the business."

Writing to Dr. Troy again, in 1810, he says:—

"If I can regulate and arrange matters here to my satisfaction, I intend to take a trip across the Atlantic next

---

[1] According to the prescriptions of canon law, in order to carry out, with all due solemnity, the ceremonial of the consecration of the Oils, it is necessary to have twelve priests, twelve deacons, and seven subdeacons. This rite, however, is not essential to the validity of the act, and is dispensed with in missionary countries, Bishops being allowed to consecrate the Oils with whatever number of priests they can conveniently bring together, but there must be, at least, five,—"*cum sacerdotibus quos potuerint habere dummodo ad minus sint quinque.*"

summer to try if I can prevail on some of those young missionaries that your Grace tells me are now on their way home, to come out with me here to this *land of milk and honey* to enjoy the sweets of it. . . . My health is but middling. . . . Last September I got a fall off a tree that lay across the path as I was returning from Ferryland, by which I broke some of my ribs. They are now, I hope, healed, at least are not very troublesome to me.

"Sir John T. Duckworth, our Governor, showed me much civility and politeness during his stay here. I dined three or four times with him, and he did me the honor of dining once at my table, and seemed happy and pleased.

"I am happy to find that Dr. Plessis has at length received your Grace's letters. He is a most worthy and zealous Prelate, and warmly attached to the Irish prelacy. He prays me to forward your Grace this packet. In imitation of him I have issued nearly similar orders with regard to his Holiness.

"PATRICK LAMBERT."

Dr. Lambert was fifty-five years of age at the time of his consecration. He was accompanied on coming to Newfoundland by two priests, viz., the Rev. A. Cleary (uncle of the late Dean Cleary, of Whittles Bay) and Rev. Denis Kelly, and also Mr. James Sinnott. Father Cleary remained four years as curate in St. John's; thence he went to Placentia, where he died in 1829. Rev. D. Kelly did not remain on the mission, but returned to Ireland, where he died, at Barony Fort, in 1824. He was unfitted for the rough work of the Mission. "He was," the late Dean Cleary used jocosely to say, "*too holy*. He was always praying. He would not hear confessions nor *take any money*." This latter failing was undoubtedly a serious one, and quite a disqualifier.

Mr. Sinnott was sent to Quebec to study theology. He was ordained in 1810, and served on the Mission in Newfoundland for twenty-one years, when he retired to Ireland, and died only a few years since. It would appear, however, from his *Exeat*, that he was only seventeen years on the Mission as priest, but twenty-one years from home; and also that he had at first only permission to retire for a time, which arrangement was afterwards changed. The *Exeat* is in Dr. Scallan's handwriting, and is dated 18th of October, 1827. In it we read:—

"Quoniam post absentiam 21 annorum a patria tua; amicos et natale solum revisitare vehementer desideras . . . tenore presentium hanc veniam impertimur. Precipientes ut quam primum proxima *æstate, ad curam animarum, tibi commissarum redeas.*"

Under Dr. Lambert's reign an episcopal residence, a comfortable wooden building ("The Old Palace"), was erected, and the "Old Chapel" enlarged by the addition of the transepts, to meet the growing wants of the congregation. In 1811 he visited Ireland, and induced the Rev. Thomas Scallan, a member of the same Order and convent as himself, and associated with him in the Wexford seminary, to come to Newfoundland and assist him in the mission. Father Scallan, after serving the vicariate for a few years, returned to Ireland, and was some time afterwards appointed Dr. Lambert's successor. Dr. Lambert continued till 1817, though struggling with ill-health, to discharge the duties of the episcopate. He then resigned, and returned to his native country. He resided in Wexford for a few years, but was subject to frequent epileptic attacks, which soon brought him to the grave. He was buried in the Franciscan convent of Wexford. He is said, by those who remember him, to have been a man of much refinement of manner, but not adapted to the situation of Vicar Apostolic in a young country like Newfoundland. He was better qualified to preside over a college than over a new Mission; but during the few years he spent in this country he conciliated the respect of all classes. A few chapels were built during his episcopacy, and he left seven priests in the Mission on his departure.

CHAPTER XIX.

RT. REV. DR. SCALLAN, THIRD BISHOP. — [1817-1830.]

Rt. Rev. Thomas Scallan, Third Bishop — His Consecration in Wexford — Arrives in Newfoundland, 1816 — Priests in the Island at that Time — His Report of the Mission to Propaganda — Character of Dr. Scallan — Excess of Liberality — Dr. Bourke Appointed First Bishop of Nova Scotia — Declining Health of Dr. Scallan — Accounts for his Weakness of Purpose — Seeks a Coadjutor — Father Michael Anthony Fleming is Appointed and Consecrated in the "Old Chapel," 1829 — Death and Burial of Dr. Scallan — His Monument in the Cathedral — Review of his Episcopate.

DR. LAMBERT, as we have seen, resigned in favor of Father Thomas Scallan, also a Franciscan. The Abbé Brasseur de Bourbourg, in his "History of Canada," inserts here the name of Bishop Gillis as successor of Dr. Lambert. But this is a mistake, as no such person was ever on this Mission. It is intended, doubtless, for Bishop Gillis, of Scotland, who, I think, was sometime in some part of Nova Scotia.

Father Thomas Scallan, O.S.F., was born in Wexford. He went through his studies, and received the Franciscan habit at St. Isidore's convent in Rome. He passed his curriculum with credit. At the conclusion of his collegiate course he was appointed professor of philosphy, and, after a residence of eighteen years in Italy, he returned to Ireland in 1794, and was appointed a member of the convent of Wexford. He was now occupied, not only in the missionary duties of an Irish Franciscan, but also as teacher in a seminary established in the convent. In 1812, as we have stated, he came to Newfoundland with Dr. Lambert, and remained a few years laboring in the Mission, and acquiring that experience which he was afterwards to put into practice as Bishop. Dr. Mullock states that he retired to Ireland previous to Dr. Lambert's departure, and resumed his conventual duties; but Dean Cleary states that Dr. Lambert and he left together in 1815. "He was," says the Dean, "a shrewd man of the world, acute and cautious." He afterwards, however, as we shall see, suffered from a malady of the brain, on account of which he perpetrated some imprudent acts.

He was appointed by a brief of Pius VII., dated 4th of April, 1815, Bishop of Drago *in partibus*, and by another, dated January 26, 1816, was nominated coadjutor to Dr. Lambert. He was consecrated on the 1st of May, 1816, in the parochial church of Wexford, by the Most Rev. Dr. Troy, Archbishop of Dublin, assisted by the Rt. Rev. Dr. Patrick Ryan, Bishop of Ferns, and Rt. Rev. Kieran Marum, Bishop of Ossory; Dr. Lambert, Bishop of Chytra, Vicar Apostolic of Newfoundland, and Dr. Daniel Murray, Ep. Hierapolensis, were also present. Immediately after his consecration he wrote (from Dublin, May 19) a Latin letter to the Cardinal Prefect of Propaganda, saying, that as Dr. Lambert was detained in Ireland, "*infirmitate quæ illum ad officia pastoralia inhabilem reddit*," he would set out for Newfoundland as soon as possible.[1] He arrived in the summer of that year, 1816. "Upon the accession of Dr. Scallan, my predecessor," says Dr. Fleming ("Letters to Dr. Spratt," p. 4) "to the See, though the number of churches had been increased, the number of priests was only seven." "In two years after his arrival in the Island (Dr. Mullock, MS., p. 55) he had ten priests under his jurisdiction."

This History would be imperfect should it allow the names of these old priests, the apostles of our Church, to remain in oblivion. The following meagre items concerning them have been gleaned from tradition, principally from the late venerable Dean Cleary, who for over fifty years bore himself the heat and the burden, and was a sort of living compendium of

---

[1] He continues as follows: "Onus humeris meis impositum cum timore subiens, jacto super Dominum curam meam sperans quod Ille Deus qui me ad hunc statum vocavit me enutriet, et debito officio sancte et cum fructu fungi mihi dabit."

our Church history. The seven priests in the Island on the arrival of Dr. Scallan were: —

1. Fr. Yore or Ewer, of whom full mention has been made before. He came in 1789 to Ferryland, where he remained till 1806, when he was removed to Harbor Grace. There he remained till his death, in 1833. He left some money, about $2,300, which was placed in the funds of the Irish College, Rome, for the purpose of founding a bourse for a student for the Mission of Newfoundland.

2. Fr. V. A. Cleary, who came in 1806, with Dr. Lambert, as before mentioned.

3. Fr. Sinnott, also mentioned above.

4. Fr. Brown was a native of Ross, and a member of the Order of St. Augustin. He spent twenty-eight years on the Mission, principally in Ferryland. He came in 1812, and retired to Ireland in 1840. A Fr. Larrissy, of Callan, and a member of the same Order, came out with him; but he remained only two years, and returned to Ireland in 1814, before Dr. Scallan's appointment.

5. Fr. William Hearn came out before his ordination, in 1814, and, like Fr. Sinnott, was sent to Quebec to finish his studies. He was stationed at Placentia, and had charge, as we have seen, of all Fortune Bay and the West. It is related that on one occasion he pushed his missionary visitation as far west as St. George's Bay, where he was inhospitably received by the English settlers. Fr. Hearn died in Placentia in 1829. About the same year of his arrival (1814) there came out a priest named Cronan; but he only remained a year or so, and left before Dr. Scallan's arrival.

6. Fr. Fitzgerald, a Franciscan, was an elderly man. He came out the year of Dr. Scallan's appointment, 1816. He left for Prince Edward Island or Nova Scotia about 1822. About the year 1812 there came also a Fr. Fitzsimmonds. He was stationed on the Southern Shore. He was a little eccentric in his piety. He raised a flagstaff with

a cross upon it above a large rock at Renews, where he used to celebrate Mass. The rock is still to be seen. He only remained three years.

7. There was also a Fr. Power, who came in 1810; but he was suspended from duty, and lived privately at Twenty-Mile Pond, where he died in 1818.

These, then, were the seven holy missioners who had the care of the seven churches on the arrival of Dr. Scallan.

The year of his arrival was remarkable for a great event in our Church history, — the first ordination of a priest in the Island. This was Fr. Nicholas Devereux, a young man whom the Bishop had brought out with him. He was stationed at the northward, and died at King's Cove in 1845. He was also at Burin and at Harbor Grace. Dr. Scallan, in his report to Propaganda, 1822, says he was a "good, moral, and studious young man."

In 1817 arrived Fr. William Whitty. He died in 1822, and is buried in the "Old Church-yard" at St. John's, near where stood the Scotch Free Kirk. He was uncle of the venerable Fr. Whilty, S.J., master of the Jesuit Noviciate, Manresa, London.

In 1818 came Fr. Denis Mackin, afterwards Dean. He was placed in Harbor Grace, and remained there till 1832, when he was appointed to Brigus, which at that time was separated from Harbor Grace and erected into a separate charge. A man of great taste, he soon had a very beautiful establishment. He called his farm by the sweet, melodious name of "*Ballynamona*," in memory of the place of his birth. And the hospitality with which he welcomed all visitors has become a proverb long to be remembered by those who enjoyed it. He died in March, 1857.

In the year 1822 Dr. Scallan addressed a report in Latin to the Cardinal Prefect, in which he describes the state of the Mission and the character of the different priests. Of Fr. Yore he says he was "Doctus et Venerabilis senex qui optima valetudine functus et jam triginta quatuor annos in

hac Missione laboriosa, et regione inclementi consumpsit.
Ipsi coadjutores sunt. Nicholaus Devereux et Dionisius
Mackin, presbyteres Sæculares ambo probi moralesque,
sed prior majus studiosus." Of Fr. Hearn he says he was
"indefatigabilis ac zelo excellens Missionarius." In King's
Cove, "Rev. Jacobus Sinnott sæcularis quoquo dignus, et
utilis sacerdos." In Bay Bulls, "Rev. Timotheus Browne,
Augustinianus bonæ indolis, predicator Optimus, sed nuper
indolens, ac in refamiliari male œconomus, ita ut ære alieno
gravatus sit ; Mihi sunt duo assistentes in hac civitate unus
Gulielmus Whitty, Sæcularis, probi moratus, et utilis Auxili-
ator. Alter Alexander Fitzgerald, Dominicanus ætate pro-
vectus zelo fervens, et in predicando indefessus, sed indiget
doctrina et prudentia, ipsius rogatu licentium . . . trans-
migrandi in insulam S. Joannis [now Prince Edward] proxima ætate . . . et expecto quod ille factus fuerit Fran-
ciscanus." He then describes at length the case of Father
Power, and gives his reasons for suspending him. He next
gives a description of his diocese. The climate he describes
as follows: "Aeris temperies est valde variabilis scilicet, a
nonagesimo quinto gradu Thermometri Farhenheiti usque ad
vigesimum infra zerum ejusdem." The interior of the country he thus describes: "Pars interior, quæ ut plurimum
montibus, lacubus et paludibus constat, est omnino deserta
et inhabitata. Si excipiuntur perpauci indigenæ, qui tam in-
domiti et feroces sunt ut nullo modo appropinquari possint."
This description scarcely does justice to the character of our
poor Beothics. It was fear of the murderous white man, not
savagery, which made the poor Indians flee the allurements
of civilization. He mentions Anticosti as part of his diocese, but it was uninhabited, except by two families stationed
there by Government to assist the shipwrecked. He concludes by asking for a renewal of his faculties for dispensations in marriages. He speaks of the schools of the "Bible
Society" as being condemned by the Propaganda, but adds
"there are none in this Island." As we have seen, however,
they were established the following year, 1823.

Dr. Scallan, by the suavity of his manners, endeared himself not only to Catholics, but also to Protestants, and with them and with the mercantile classes and Government people he was an especial favorite. He was very hospitable, and we need not wonder that a governor (Prescott), during the episcopacy of his successor, Dr. Fleming, in one of his despatches to the Home Government, praises Dr. Scallan, while he speaks of his successor in the language of coarse vulgarity. Indeed, Dr. Scallan has been censured, and apparently with some reason, for being too yielding in his endeavors to please and propitiate his Protestant friends. "We may hope, however," writes Dr. Mullock, "circumstances at that time excused conduct which at present would be most injudicious."

In 1818 Dr. Bourke was appointed the first Bishop of Nova Scotia, and though the appointment had no immediate influence on Newfoundland, still it was in some sort a strengthening to the Church to have a neighboring province raised to the dignity of a Vicariate Apostolic. It was proof that Catholics were increasing, and that the days of persecution were passing away.

In his later years, Dr. Scallan was affected with a paralytic attack, which slightly affected the brain, and which will account for any weakness which may have occurred in his ecclesiastical rule.

"No one," says Dr. Fleming, in his "*Relazione*" to Propaganda, "could surpass Dr. Scallan in his anxiety for the advancement of the Mission; but, unfortunately, when he had formed his designs to carry out his intended object, he was assailed by a sickness which obliged him to remain for the greater part of a year in a more salubrious climate, and which, after a few years, deprived the Church of a most zealous and estimable prelate."

The fault, or injudicious conduct, hinted at by Dr. Mullock, of which Dr. Scallan was accused, was one which sprung out of his mild and gentle disposition. He was of a most gracious and tolerant spirit, and it would appear that he allowed his yielding temperament to carry him a little too far in his desire to conciliate all religious denominations. No doubt it was with the desire of bringing back the lost sheep to the fold. In his report to the Cardinal Prefect of Propaganda (1822) he says: "The Faith is now slowly but surely increasing, and daily some are coming over to us. No obstacle is placed in our way by those in authority, and the Governor is most friendly to me, and most faithful. I have had him occasionally to dine at my house." In order to carry out those views, however, he slightly outstepped the bonds of prudence. He allowed his clergy to attend Protestant funerals, and to enter the churches and remain present at their funeral services; and also attended himself at some sort of thanksgiving service, on which occasion the prayers were read "by the Protestant Bishop of Nova Scotia." No matter how laudable the motive may be, there are certain limits, beyond which the tenets of the Catholic Church allow not her children to step. We may, and indeed are bound to, assist our neighbors in *all works of mercy and charity*, spiritual and corporal. We may assist as friends or mourners at funeral processions; we may help to bury the dead, and to perform every other act to alleviate the sorrow of our afflicted Protestant fellow-men; but we are not allowed to attend at the *religious ceremony*. This alone is forbidden us, and most reasonably, — for it is the belief of the Church that such service is *heretical*, and it would be a sin to countenance it in any way. It is, therefore, unfair to accuse Catholics of bigotry on this account. They only act up to their religious convictions, and not from any uncharitable spirit. With regard to Dr. Scallan, it is certain that he was a most holy and zealous Bishop, and, as Dr. Mullock writes, "we may hope that the circumstances of the time excused his conduct." We must also remember that he was suffering from a malady which greatly impaired his reason. Nevertheless, he was censured by Rome for this weakness; but as he was on his death-bed when the censure arrived, it was not made known to him.

In 1827 Dr. Scallan visited Rome, and was very well received by the Pope and his superiors in Propaganda. He also made a visitation of Placentia Bay, and administered Confirmation in Burin and Placentia, and several other places. His health now began to give way altogether. He visited Europe more than once. In the year 1828, finding he could no longer discharge his duties, he sought for a coadjutor. He accordingly wrote to Cardinal Caprara, Prefect of the Propaganda, explaining the difficult circumstances of the Mission, the want of priests, and the labors to be undergone by a Prelate who would conscientiously discharge his duty, recommending at the same time as his coadjutor and successor Father Michael Anthony Fleming, for many years the principal missioner in St. John's. He had himself done as much as he could perform; visited the Southern, Northern, and Western shores as far as Burin and Harbor Grace; but the remote north and west, not to speak of Labrador, were entirely beyond his reach. All these reasons being laid before the Sacred Congregation of Propaganda, his prayer was granted, and Father Fleming was appointed coadjutor, Vicar-Apostolic, and Bishop of Carpasia *in partibus*. On the 28th October, 1829, he consecrated his successor in the "Old Chapel," — the first time that an episcopal consecration was ever performed in Newfoundland.

He survived but a short time. Repeated attacks of paralysis undermined his constitution. Day after day he got weaker and weaker, and on the 29th of May following, the feast of SS. Simon and Jude, he resigned his soul into the hands of his Creator. He left the property he possessed to his successor, to establish schools and a seminary. It was not found possible to establish the seminary at the time, and the funds were devoted to the founding of a convent, and partly for providing priests for the Mission.

He was interred in the yard of the "Old Chapel;" but it was intended merely as a temporary resting-place, for his remains, immediately after Dr. Fleming's death, were transferred to the cathedral, and buried in the choir, behind the high altar. Dr. Fleming left some money to have a monument erected for him, and it has been executed by Hogan, and is placed at the gospel side of the great nave of the cathedral. It is in *alto rilievo*, and of Saravezza marble. The dying Bishop is represented on a couch receiving the last Sacraments from his successor. It is a beautiful work, in the most perfect style of art, and will be for ages an ornament to the cathedral.

During Dr. Scallan's episcopacy many improvements took place in the country. The population became more settled, and the people began to look on the Island as their home. Education began to be encouraged; the barbarous laws against colonization were no longer attempted to be enforced; the idea of keeping the country merely as a fishing-station — "a big ship moored near the Banks "— was given up; and the inhabitants might build or repair a chimney without the special leave of the governor, and not dread that (as a few years previously) it would be pulled down by the "English authorities." It was, in fact, becoming a rich and settled country; and though mismanagement, tyranny, and misrule had left their marks of degradation on the people, still some signs of improvement were manifested on every side, and a more warm religious feeling was excited among the Catholic population.

CHAPTER XX.

LABRADOR.

Origin of the Name — Population — Moravian Missionaries — Anticosti Annexed to St. John's — Division of Parishes — Increase of Catholicity.

A NEW and better prospect was now opening for Newfoundland. For three centuries we have seen her, socially and politically, excommunicated; settlement prohibited; cultivation forbidden; roads never thought of; education disregarded; the only religion capable of civilizing and enlightening the people first openly persecuted, and latterly only sullenly tolerated.

A great change, however, was now about to take place. A census taken in 1825 gives the population of the whole Island as 60,088, among whom were 24,882 Catholics; thus giving Protestants, at that time, a majority in round numbers of 5,000, or a twelfth of the whole. The very few inhabitants then on the French Shore and Labrador are not enumerated.

The northern portion of the American continent extending from the River St. Lawrence to Hudson's Bay is called "Labrador." It is generally supposed that this name was given to it by the Portugese navigator, Gaspar de Cortereal, the explorer, if not the discoverer, of this region. "He," writes Dr. Mullock, "imposed this curious name on it, either because he considered it adapted to the labors of the husbandman, or, perhaps, he thought that the robust Esquimaux, the aboriginal inhabitants, might be converted into '*laboradores*,' working slaves, like the African negroes."

Cotterel's Island, in Trinity Bay, is supposed to be called from Cortereal,[1] who discovered this part of the country in 1501. He was the next explorer after

---

[1] J. P. Howley.

Cabot. This is the only remnant of that expedition, unless we also add Portugal Cove, as so called by him in honor of his native land. He is supposed also to have given the name of "Conception Bay." The map painted in fresco on the walls of the *Loggie* of the Vatican Palace, Rome, by A. Varrese, and reproduced in part at page 57 of this work, of date 1556, gives the southern portion of this land as the "Terra de Corte Real," while the central portion is called "Terra de Baccalaos," and the more northerly part is designated as "Terra de Labrador"; while a cape corresponding to the position of the entrance to the Straits of Belle Isle is called "C. del Laborado."

On a map of still older date, namely the "Globus Martini Behaim, Narimbergensis, 1492," this same country, *i.e.*, the southern part of Labrador, is called "Cambia." Sir Richard Whitbourne, writing in 1616 (p. 16) calls it "Cambalew," and it is called, as late as 1747, in the "British Pilot" of Taverner, by the name of "Cambalou." This name owes its origin to the description of Marco Polo, who travelled in the East in the thirteenth century. He spoke of the kingdoms of Cipango, Mango, Cathay, and Cambalou. This latter country he placed "to the north-east of Cathay," that is, China. Now, the navigators who followed Columbus were under the impression that they had discovered the same lands as Marco Polo. Columbus, indeed, never knew till the day of his death that he had discovered the New World. Hence these post-Columbian navigators gave to the countries discovered the same names as those given by Polo, as nearly as they could judge them. Thus, in Behaim's map the land which occupies the position where Newfoundland is situated is called "Cathai"; and as a consequence the land to the north of it is called "Cambalou." On Cabot's map the whole of Labrador is called "Terra de Baccalaos." It received its name of "Labrador," as Dr. Mullock rightly suggests, from Cortereal. Richard Edens, writing as early as 1555, speaks of it as the coast of the land of "Laboradores." The inhabitants are men of good corpora-ture, although tawny like Indians, and *laborious*. He says it had this name before Cortereal, and that he called it after his own name. It is called on Champlain's maps (1603) "Nouvelle France;" but he gives that name to all Canada, in fact to all America. Pietro Pasquaglio, Venetian ambassador in Portugal, 1501, says Cortereal brought home thirty-seven of the inhabitants of the new country, who are pronounced "admirably adapted for *labor*"; hence he calls the land " Terra de los Laboradores " — land of the laborers. If the name had reference to the agricultural capabilities of the region itself it was most inappropriate, for the coast is bleak and barren, and the summer season too short for vegetation. It was not more appropriate as applied to the people. The Esquimaux are neither numerous nor willing to apply themselves to continuous labor, being, like all the North American Indians, chiefly fishers and hunters. The wealth of Labrador consists in its fisheries, which employ over 30,000 people every summer, and for the prosecution of which its shores, indented at every few miles with coves, bays, and harbors, and fringed with countless islands, are peculiarly adapted. The western portion, extending from Blanc Sablon to the River St. John, belongs to the government of Canada; the eastern and northern portions, to Newfoundland.

The total number of permanent inhabitants on the Newfoundland portion was, in 1856 (when Dr. Mullock wrote), 1,553, of whom 315 were Catholics. But by the census of 1884 we find the population has increased to 4,211; Catholics, 566. The large increase of population of Labrador over that of 1874, ten years previous (nearly double; it was then 2,416), is owing to the cipher that the Moravians are placed at 1,349. Their principal stations are Hopedale, population, 170; Nain, 235; Zoar, 139; Hebron, 207; Okak, 311; Ramah, 69. These figures would seem to be largely above the reality, but as they are supplied by the Brethren themselves, there is no means of testing them. The Rev. Père la Casse, O.M.J., a priest of the diocese

of Riamouski, who makes a yearly visitation to the extreme
northern portion of Labrador, is of the opinion that the
Moravians cannot exceed three or four hundred. " More of
a trading than a missionary establishment, the Brothers have
collected around them some Esquimaux, dignified with the
name of Christian, but, if report speaks true, totally ignorant of any religion, and principally employed in the furring
trade for the missionaries" (Dr. Mullock, MS.).

Whatever truth there may be in Dr. Mullock's remarks
as to the state of morality or religion among the Esquimaux
Moravians, it is certain, and no secret is made of it, that the
principal object of the Brothers is trade. Each "Mission"
consists of three men; namely, a "trader," or business
manager, a carpenter, and a "reader," who looks after the
Spirituals. The different offices or situations are filled
alternately every year by the three men, each taking his
triennial turn at keeping the accounts, keeping the buildings
in order, or looking after the souls, as the case may be. As
the whole concern, however, is carried on as a religious
institution, they enjoy many privileges, such as receiving all
articles free of duty, on account of which they are able to
undersell the Hudson Bay and other furring companies.
This burdensome handicapping has been the cause of a good
deal of ill-feeling and remonstrance.

In the mouth of the St. Lawrence lies a large island, called
"Anticosti," a corruption of the Indian name "Nachitoches."
It was discovered by Jacques Cartier on the 15th August,
1535, who called it "Isle de l'Assomption;" but the Indian
name survived. The barrenness of the soil and the want of
ports have hitherto prevented its colonization. A few families
of light-house keepers and assistants, towards saving shipwrecked mariners, constitute its whole population. In the
year 1820 these two places, viz., Labrador and Anticosti,
were united to the Vicariate Apostolic of Newfoundland.
Joseph Octavius Plessis was Bishop of Quebec, and though he
was opposed to the division of his extensive diocese, still, these
places being so remote and inaccessible, he recommended to

the Pope (Pius VII.) the dismemberment of them from Quebec and their annexation to Newfoundland. Dr. Scallan was consulted on the matter, and consented to the arrangement, though having no means for providing missionaries, even for the part of Newfoundland near his own residence. Perhaps he thought that at some future period he might provide for it, and considered the charge at the time as a mere nominal one.

A Brief was accordingly expedited on the 1st of February, 1820, countersigned by Cardinal Consalvi, dismembering the Quebec diocese, and giving the island of Anticosti, and that part of the land of Labrador bounded by the northern bank of the River St. John, to the Vicariate Apostolic of Newfoundland; that the Bishop should afford to the Catholics living in those regions all the spiritual assistance they required, and endeavor, as far as was in his power, to bring the savages and heretics of that region into the fold of Christ.

Whatever may have been Dr. Scallan's intention, he never had it in his power to send missioners to these places. Sometime after Canada again obtained jurisdiction over all these coasts as far as Blanc Sablon (or L'Anse à Sablon), and when some Canadians began to settle there as sealcatchers, they always looked to Quebec for spiritual assistance. Now and then a Canadian priest, with leave of the Vicar-Apostolic of Newfoundland, visited the scattered settlers, and administered the sacraments of baptism and matrimony. Latterly, since the Canadian Government has erected light-houses and signal-stations on these coasts, the visits of clergy are more frequent, as the priests, by permission of Government, avail themselves of the semiannual trips of the supplying steamers to the different stations. The Newfoundland portion of Labrador was, as mentioned, attended regularly by a clergyman from St. John's until it was made a parochial district, the priest residing at Fortune Harbor, Notre Dame Bay. "The whole arrangement," writes Dr. Mullock, "between Bishop Plessis and Bishop Scallan was faulty, but it has now been rescinded. . . . Anticosti as yet *nominally* depends on Newfoundland."

In the latter part of Dr. Scallan's life, and at his death, the Vicariate was divided into five districts or parishes; viz., St. John's, Harbor Grace, Placentia, Ferryland, and King's Cove. This latter district comprised all the northern bays, viz., Trinity, Bonavista, Fogo, Notre Dame, and the northern shores to Quirpon. There were also many Catholic schools in the principal places, and Catholics had every reason to congratulate themselves on their increase in numbers, wealth, and social standing; on the spread of religion and education, and the near approach of the political influence which they were soon to wield in the destinies of the country.

CHAPTER XXI.

RT. REV. DR. FLEMING, FOURTH BISHOP. — [1829-1833.]

Commencement of Dr. Fleming's Episcopate — State of the Colony — Catholic Emancipation — Its Effects on Irishmen Abroad — Intolerance in St. John's — Degrading Taxes — Funeral and Marriage Fees Imposed on Catholics — Dr. Fleming Refuses to Pay them — Redivision of Parishes — Arrival of Nine New Missionaries — Fathers Troy, Nowlan, Berney, P. Cleary — Dr. Fleming Presents Memorial in Favor of Emancipation — Forwards Subscription to the O'Connell Fund — His Liberality towards Dissenters — Obtains for them Religious Liberty.

THE Rt. Rev. Dr. M. A. Fleming, being Coadjutor Bishop during the last year of Dr. Scallan's life, succeeded to the Vicariate at his demise, and governed it for a period of twenty years, amidst many troubles and contradictions, with great success.

He was born near Carrick-on-Suir, County of Tipperary, Ireland, in the year 1792. His uncle, Father Martin Fleming, a venerable priest, was guardian of the Franciscans in the convent of Carrick, and the nephew desired, after his example, to consecrate himself to God in the Order of St. Francis. Accordingly, in 1808, at the early age of sixteen, he received the habit of St. Francis, in the convent of Wexford, from the hands of Dr. Scallan, then Superior of that House. "The foreign establishments of the Irish Franciscan Province had fallen in the continental revolutions, and St. Isidore's in Rome, the only remaining one, was under sequestration by the French" (Dr. Mullock).

The instructors of the young novice in Wexford were the Rev. Richard Hayes, a well-known controversialist, and, subsequently, delegate to Rome from the Catholics of Ireland to oppose the concession of a veto on the election of the Irish Catholic Bishops to the British Government, and Dr. Henry Hughes, the learned and Apostolic Bishop of Gibraltar. Under these two excellent masters he pursued his studies, and on the 15th October, 1815, he was ordained priest by the Bishop of Ferns. Soon after, he was appointed to the convent at Carrick, under his uncle, and commenced the usual missionary duties of an Irish friar. The old conventual chapel was built just at the cessation of the persecution, and was, as might be expected, a poor and tottering edifice. With the permission of his uncle, Father Fleming threw it down and commenced the new church, which is so great an ornament to the town at present. Before he had time to complete the building, he left Ireland, in 1823, at the pressing invitation of Dr. Scallan, for Newfoundland. A year or two after he was recalled by his provincial; but Dr. Scallan represented to the Propaganda the great dearth of missioners in Newfoundland, and accordingly, by a rescript, his obedience was transferred from the Irish province to the Vicar Apostolic of Newfoundland. He therefore remained in St. John's till his appointment to the mitre, exercising the duties of curate.

For a Mission like Newfoundland he was peculiarly qualified: of an active and energetic temperament and a wiry constitution, a great walker and an excellent horseman, he could, in his youth, go through fatigue which would break down many others. He had, in fact, a love of labor as if for labor's sake, and in his latter years he is thought to have shortened his life by unnecessary exertions.

At the request of Dr. Scallan he was nominated Bishop, with the title of *Carpasia in partibus*, and Coadjutor of the Vicar Apostolic of Newfoundland, with the right of succession.

The Bulls for his appointment were expedited on the 10th of July, 1829, and on the 28th of October of the same year he was consecrated by Dr. Scallan in the "Old Chapel," two priests assisting by dispensation, on account of the impossibility of obtaining assistant Bishops.

The assumption of the government of the Church of Newfoundland by Dr. Fleming marks the opening of another great era in our ecclesiastical history; and it would have been impossible to find a man better suited in every respect for the great work before him than the Bishop whom the Holy Spirit had chosen, — a man endowed with all the gifts of mind and body necessary for a grand and onerous duty; of strong physical powers, great austerity of life, indomitable will, and shrewd mental endowments. Though eclipsed by the great intellectual luminary who succeeded him, the colossal-minded Dr. Mullock, yet the educational acquirements of Dr. Fleming were of no mean order. He possessed a wide versatility of talent, as his rare library and collection of works of art plainly show. Yet for literature, as such, he seemed not to care too much, his books generally touching upon the practical and scientific region, such as agriculture, architecture, and mechanics. The period at which he assumed the spiritual reins in Newfoundland was one of great activity all over the world, — intellectually, politically, and religiously. England at this time was convulsed to her heart's core by the great religious movement which has gone on ever since, and has not yet ceased; which has had such a powerful effect upon her inner life as is likely to result in a complete effacement of her religious and social characteristics for the past three centuries. America, like a young giant, was revelling in the enjoyment of her new-found liberty, and was making vast strides in the realms of science, colonization, inter-communication, and all that constitutes civilization. Above all, she was bringing into the domain of the world that new and wondrous power of steam, which was soon to create an empire for itself, more astounding, even, than the art of printing had done some four hundred years before.

Ireland, which ever held such intimate relations with Newfoundland, and every pulse of whose national life awoke a corresponding throb in our colonial heart; whose joys and sorrows were not merely reflected, as in a mirror, in the souls of her transatlantic children, but were really and actually participated in by them, — Ireland, then, in this glorious year of 1829, was just raising her head from beneath the tyrant heel of oppression. The voice of the great Tribune, armed with the powerful battle-axe of Truth, had cleft down the barricades of prejudice and bigotry, and gained for the downtrodden nation the glorious birthright of religious liberty, — Catholic emancipation.

The effect of this great moral victory was not confined to Ireland alone. It had an elevating and ennobling effect on the whole Irish race, now scattered in their millions throughout the vast territories of America and Australia. The long centuries of persecution, though they had never subjugated the will of the Irish people, nor quenched the light of faith; yet, through forced poverty, with all its degrading accompaniments, blotting entirely out of their lives for generations the soothing and civilizing influences of wealth and social intercourse, had, at last, so crushed down their noble natures as to almost obliterate from their souls the feeling of independence, and to superinduce that state of self-abasement which is ever characteristic of a race of slaves. This sordid feeling, which caused them to cringe in humiliation before their fellow-men, whom they knew only as powerful tyrants,[1] they carried across the wide ocean, and even in the free air of America were found men of Know-nothing type ready to take advantage of this weakness.

Emancipation, however, made them feel themselves at last freemen, and they soon began to hold up their heads and look their fellow-men in the face without shame or fear. The foul miasma of slavery could not survive in the Empire of Western Freedom; but strong efforts were made by the domineering party to keep it alive in the British colonies, and nowhere more so than in Newfoundland. Although, according to the highest legal authorities, and, indeed, to the dictates of common-sense, the penal statutes, devised for the extermination of the national religion in Ireland, should not

---

[1] Our readers may recall to mind a description by A. M. Sullivan, in his "New Ireland," of a party of poor peasants standing trembling, hat in hand, by the roadside, amid a drenching rain, while the cruel and vulgar "agent" leisurely rides by, eying them with all the gross brutality of a veritable slave-master of the Le Drew type.

extend beyond the limits of that country; nevertheless, as we have seen, the spirit of these laws practically prevailed even more bitterly among us. The great distance from the mother-country gave confidence to petty tyrants, who arrogated to themselves all the powers of law, — nay, even the "high dominion" of life and death.

An extraordinary example of this occurred at St. John's, after the passing of the Emancipation Act. The commander of the garrison at that time was Colonel Bourke, a Catholic. By the constitution of the Government he should have been President of the Council; but previous to the passing of the act he was declared disqualified, on account of his religion, for taking his place at the council-table, though not for commanding Her Majesty's forces! — a much more important position and more responsible office, and, for a *disloyal* man, a more dangerous one. When the act became law, he presented himself to take his place at the board, but to his surprise he was told he was still disqualified, as the Emancipation Act did not extend to the colonies, the penal laws not having been enacted for these countries. Such was the illogical reasoning of the Newfoundland Bench. If the penal laws did not extend to Newfoundland, surely neither did the disabilities which were created by those laws; yet the Newfoundland authorities persisted in this lopsided logic, and it was only after a protracted appeal to the Imperial Government, supported chiefly by the purse and influence of Dr. Fleming, that the affair was decided according to law and common-sense, and Catholics were declared to be on a perfect equality with Protestants in the colony. Yet it was long after this, and after they had fought their way, step by step, that the Catholics received anything like justice or fair play. At this period, also, was set on foot in Newfoundland the agitation for *Home Rule*, or Responsible Government, which was at length granted in 1854. This great boon was achieved principally through the efforts of leading Catholics, among whom the names of Kent, Morris, Doyle, Nugent, and others, live ever embalmed in the memories of the people.

About this time also the country was blessed with a generous and noble-minded governor, Sir Thomas Cochrane, the first non-naval governor, and entirely free from that narrow-minded spirit of the fishing admirals, a good deal of which was inherited by the naval governors. He built Government House, opened up roads and streets, inaugurated the Supreme Court, and encouraged in every possible way the advancement of the colony.

Although the mild and conciliating disposition of Dr. Scallan had had an apparent mollifying effect, yet, as Dr. Mullock writes, "it is to be feared that conciliation, carried too far, is, in the end, injurious to religion." While, on the one hand, it induces indifference among Catholics to the essential distinction between the true and the false worship, it does not, on the other, induce any true spirit of tolerance or respect from the persecutors. "A mawkish liberality," continues Dr. Mullock, "induced these Catholics who had pretensions to gentility to despise the prohibition of the Church against going to heretical worship. It was, in fact, quite usual at that day to go to Mass in the morning, and to Church, as it was called, in the evening, to compliment their Protestant friends."

Such was the state of the Church in Newfoundland when that great and holy man, Dr. Fleming, was called, like another Sylvester, to bring her forth from the catacombs of persecution into the glorious light of freedom's sun. With what spirit he entered upon his noble work he tells us with a frank earnestness, devoid of all pretended humility, in his report to the Cardinal Prefect of Propaganda and in his letters to Dr. Spratt : " Before my consecration . . . I passed six years in the Island as a curate, during which time, in the discharge of my duty, I had visited every port and creek in the district of St. John's, and also of Conception Bay, and I felt a peculiar interest in studying the manners of the people, and entering into their wishes, with a view to discover the best mode of supplying their wants and improving their condition" (Letter to Dr. Spratt). "I knew their wants, and I felt myself animated by a vivid desire to satisfy them" ("*Relazione*," p. 41). Before his consecration as Bishop, as we have already seen, he took the matter of education of youth into his hands, and succeeded, in spite of grave difficulties, in placing Catholic education on a firm basis. From what we have also seen of his action in the matter of the Communion festival of the young girls, immediately after his consecration, and during Dr. Scallan's lifetime, it will be seen that he had grasped the reins with a firm and masterly hand, and that the conciliatory, if not almost vacillating, *régime* of Dr. Scallan was at an end. Another difficulty which he had to contend with immediately after his consecration was the matter of marriage and burial fees. When visiting Ireland in the year 1836, a public dinner was given to him by the "Catholic Society of Ireland," at the Royal Hotel, College Green, Dublin. In the course of an eloquent and glowing speech, Dr. Fleming alluded as follows to this subject: "One of the marks of degradation they imposed on the people was forcing the Bishop to pay fourteen pence for each marriage that was performed. I remonstrated with His Excellency on the unjustness of the demand, but in vain. When nothing else was left me to do I peremptorily refused to pay it, and the unjust and degrading impost fell to the ground. . . . Another infamous tax that was imposed upon Catholics was the payment of twelve shillings for every Catholic that was buried, and the most degrading of all was that the Bishops were forced to collect it. I refused to do so, and it no longer exists." In his letter to Dr. Spratt he says: "The Protestant rector required a return of the burials of Catholics, and the sum of twelve and sixpence as burial fees for every individual, even of those buried in the Catholic burial-ground. This was scrupulously exacted during the administration of Dr. O'Donel, the first Bishop of the Island, down to the last hour of Dr. Scallan; and, as even poverty could not claim an exemption from the rector's fee, scarce a week passed without witnessing the heart-sickening exhibition of a party (friends of the deceased) collecting pence from door to door to meet this cruel impost. By a single act of firmness I broke it down. I laughed at the claim, and it sunk to the dust." Fortunately for the historian of these times, Dr. Fleming was a most voluminous writer, and still more so, he always drew a rough draft of every letter, even upon the most trivial subject. A large packet of these original letters has been kindly presented to the writer by the Hon. Mr. Justice J. J. Little, from which a very succinct history of Dr. Fleming's episcopacy can be drawn. Among these letters is one to the Protestant rector (name not given) on this subject. The date, April, 1829, shows that, even before his consecration, Father Fleming had tackled this knotty question with a vigorous hand. Some extracts from it will not, I deem it, be considered out of place, and will serve to show his trenchant style : —

"In reply to your letter of the 31st complaining of the non-payment of fees demanded by you for Catholic interments, . . . and requesting me to give instructions to my sexton to receive for the future the stipend demanded, I beg to inform you that I have nothing whatever to do in the regulations or concerns of that churchyard, unless to perform my duties as a clergyman whenever called there; and as to the grave-digger, he never received any instructions from me, except to point out a vacant spot for the interment of a pauper, and then I felt bound to pay him for digging the grave, or to get some of the neighbors or friends of the deceased to perform the charitable act.

"Although I would regret sincerely that any failure should take place in your fees, and as sincerely deplore that any unhandsome or unjustifiable infringement should be made on the just emoluments of any minister of religion for whom I entertain so high a regard, I must now candidly acknowledge to you what I have never had the opportunity of doing before, that I consider it the most penal act of injustice that could be imposed upon any denomination of Christians to compel them to pay to a clergyman of a different persuasion a fee for the interment of their dead. . . . I am sure you are satisfied to acknowledge that were the Catholic the established religion of this country, you would deem it the most galling act to compel your flock to pay a fee for services which would not, and could not, be performed by her ministers. . . . Should you establish your claim by a legal process, it would be the bounden duty of the Catholic priest, in the first place, to recommend patience and forbearance to his people, and next, by every legal means, to raise his voice, with that of his flock, in petitioning a repeal of so obnoxious a burthen. . . . And however the scale may turn, it shall never, I hope, break one link of that chain of affection and regard which always bound us together."

Soon after his consecration he commenced his episcopal duties by visiting Conception Bay, and while there engaged he was summoned, in May, 1830, to attend the death-bed of his predecessor, and to assume the complete government of the Vicariate.

The first work he turned his mind to was the augmentation of the number of priests and the subdivision of the five districts which then existed in the country. The number of priests in the diocese at this time was only seven, of whom one (Fr. Yore) was then in his eighty-second year. Fr. Hearn, of Placentia, was afflicted with a mental malady. Fr. Brown, of Ferryland, was not very satisfactory. "The curate of St. John's (Fr. Morrison) was in the last stage of consumption" (he died in 1831). So that there were only three active missionaries to be relied on. These were Fathers Nicholas Devereux, D. Makin, and P. Cleary (afterwards Dean).

Dr. Fleming, therefore, set out in the fall of 1830 for Ireland in search of missionaries. He secured nine, of whom six embarked without delay, and arrived in Newfoundland early in 1831.

These missioners also deserve a brief biographical notice in a work like the present. They were not only pillars of the Catholic Church, but men of name and fame, worthy of a place in the general history of Newfoundland. They were the principal actors on the stage who helped in no small measure to bring about the state of political prosperity and advancement which we now enjoy.

First, then, was the Rev. Edward Troy. He was a prominent figure for many years in our ecclesiastical annals. He was a man, physically and mentally, a giant. He was the confidant and right-hand man of Dr. Fleming during all his troubles and contests for religious liberty and for the rights of Catholics. He was the great crusader in the matter of ensuring the observance of the sanctity of the Sunday; the putting an end to "Sunday work," which was then exacted from Catholics by their tyrannical mercantile masters, a struggle which lasted five years; the toning up of Catholic feeling on the matter of attending Protestant functions; in the affair of the dismissal of Judge Boulton for partiality and religious bias. In all the political elections for many years, the name of Father Troy was respected and feared. He was a veritable *malleus hereticorum*, and yet, withal, he was a man of the gentlest disposition when not aroused by religious zeal, and was beloved even by those who feared him. A man of this uncompromising character was sure, however, to make enemies among those for whose abuses and tepidity he had no mercy. Hence a party among the Catholics of the time formed themselves into a sort of league in opposition to Dr. Fleming and Fr. Troy. These were the representatives of the men who followed the more conciliatory system approved of by Dr. Scallan, but against which Dr. Fleming, from the very outset, waged unrelenting war. These troublous times have now passed away, and not even a vestige of these factions remains, and it would be imprudent to recall them to memory. We shall, therefore, pass them over with this mere mention, as a history of the Church in Newfoundland would be incomplete if it omitted all allusion to an organization which played such an important part in it. Dr. Fleming, in his letter to Propaganda, speaks of Father Troy as "a missionary than whom this country has never seen one more zealous, or more ardently devoted to the duties of his sacred calling." Nevertheless, the party of opposition left no means untried to have him removed from the country. They sent a list of complaints against him and the Bishop to the Secretary of State for the Colonies. They, by false representations, secured the influence of "high ecclesiastical dignitaries" in London, and at length succeeded in gaining the ear of the authorities at Rome, where this venerable clergyman was maligned as "the turbulent priest Troy," and the Bishop was ordered to remove him from the Island.[1] Not willing to disobey so peremptory a command, but, at the same time, knowing that it only required the mere statement of the truth at Rome to have the censure removed, Dr. Fleming, by a prudent subterfuge, removed Father Troy from the Island of Newfoundland by placing him on the Island of *Merachien*, in Placentia Bay. Here he carried on the work of the Mission, and built a church and presbytery. From this he was subsequently removed to Torbay, where he remained till his death, in 1872. If we are to judge of the missioner by the result of his labors, we must look upon Father Troy as a truly apostolic man. He built the churches at Portugal Cove and Torbay, bringing the nails in bags upon his back from St. John's, a distance of eight or ten miles, and at a time when there were no roads. He replaced the old wooden chapel of Torbay by the splendid stone edifice now existing, and in the spiritual life his conquests were

---

[1] It was not merely the removal of Father Troy, but of the Bishop himself, that was sought; and so far did the machinations go, that it is said that the Austrian Minister at Rome was directed or requested by the British Government, at the instance of the Colonial Office in London, to endeavor to procure the removal of the Bishop from Newfoundland. The unceasing diatribes against him appearing daily in the press of Newfoundland he treated with silent contempt, but the charges brought against him in Rome, and injudiciously forwarded by the Vicar Apostolic of London, were most galling to a man who was in reality sacrificing himself in the interests of religion, and he comments bitterly on it in his "*Relazione*."

not less numerous. He converted to the Catholic fold almost the entire district of Torbay. So it might be said of him, as we read of St. Gregory Thaumaturgus, Bishop of Neocæsaræa. This holy Bishop asking, on his death-bed, how many infidels were left in the city, was answered, "Seventeen."—"Only so many," he replied, giving thanks to God, "were there of the faithful when I came first."

Second. Among these missionaries was the Rev. Pelagius Nowlan, who came out in the year 1831. He was placed at Little Placentia, where he remained during his long missionary career of nearly forty years. He died in 1871, aged eighty years. Dr. Fleming, in his account of his visitation of 1832, says: "On Monday, 23d (of August) . . . . we got into Little Placentia, . . . where we had the pleasure of meeting the Rev. Mr. Nowlan, who had been lately appointed to that district, and it afforded me the sincerest satisfaction to find that both here and in Great Placentia his congregation were loud in praise of his exertions to afford them the comforts of religion."

Third. Fr. Charles Dalton, O.S.F. He was placed in Harbor Grace, where he labored for thirty years, till 1861. The old wooden chapel, with a tower one hundred feet high, erected by Fr. Yore, was pulled down, and a new one of stone erected by Fr. Dalton, who also built the presbytery. The present cathedral is formed of this church, with the addition of apse, transepts, and dome, erected under the episcopacy of Dr. Dalton, first Bishop of Harbor Grace, nephew of Fr. Charles Dalton. The work of completion advanced but slowly under the troubled episcopacy of Dr. Carfagnini, but was speedily pushed on by the present energetic Bishop, Dr. McDonald, who had a solemn opening of the building in 1885. Fr. Dalton also erected the church in Carbineers'.

Fourth. Fr. Keilly, who did not remain long on the Mission. He died in Ireland.

Fifth. Fr. Edward Murphy, who died in St. John's the following year, 1832.

Sixth. Fr. Michael Berney, who survived until the pres-

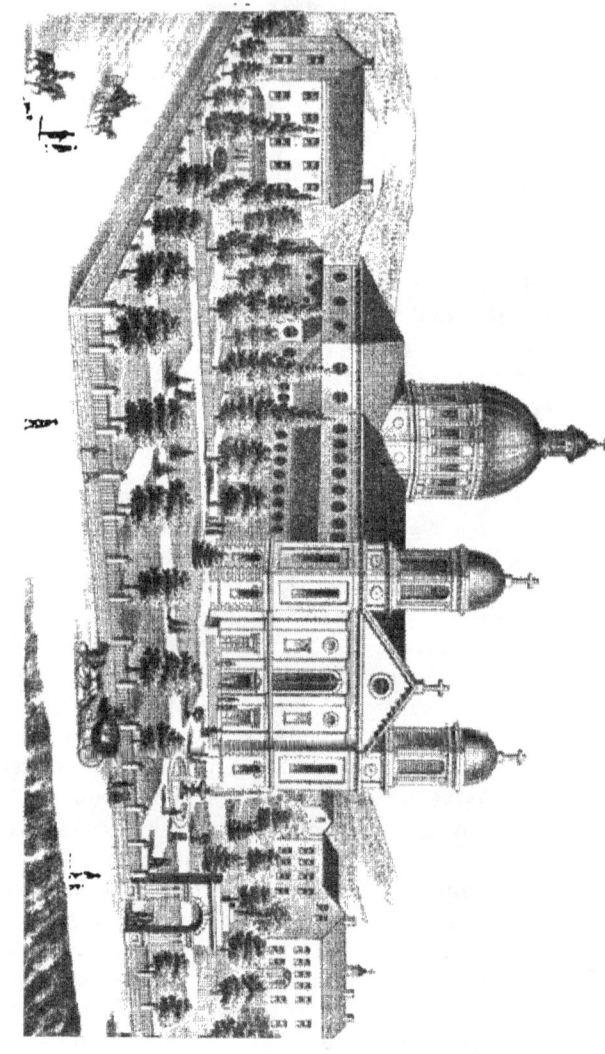

CATHOLIC CATHEDRAL, HARBOR GRACE, CONCEPTION BAY. Page 266.

ent year (1885). He died at Burin. During the past twenty years he had done no active duty, having been paralyzed in the right side, the result of exposure to severe and wet weather during his missionary tours. Lest there might be any dissatisfaction among the clergy at the division of their parishes, he began by showing the good example in his own district. He separated Bay Bulls, and placed there the young priest, Fr. Patrick Cleary, who had come out in 1829, and who had been placed first at King's Cove, as curate to Fr. Devereux.

Fr. Cleary, of late years familiarly known as "The Dean," was another of those noble men who have impressed their names in the memory of more than one generation. To him was vouchsafed that boon, not very usual, of celebrating the "golden jubilee," or fiftieth year of priesthood, and during that half-century, and more, he labored with untiring zeal among his faithful people. Though small of stature, he was a man of iron physique and great strength of mind, and up to a few years before his death he vied in activity and energy with the youngest curate in the country. To his zeal and noble priestly virtues, the parish of Bay Bulls, or Whittles' Bay, owes it that it may be classed as the most thoroughly Catholic district in the Island. To him it owes all that it possesses of advantage, both temporal and spiritual,—not only schools, convents, and churches, but also the finest roads and bridges, wharves, etc., in all Newfoundland. In those days it was not enough that a priest should look to the spiritual advancement of his people, but on him also devolved, in a great measure, the administration of all Government grants, and everything concerning the temporal welfare of the people.[1]

---

[1] One of the parishioners, lamenting the death of the good old Dean, was heard to remark, "And why shouldn't we miss him? Sure, he borned us, an' christened us, an' marrid us, an' berrid us all, fur de last fifty years!"

The Dean died on the 21st October, 1882, in the fifty-third year of his priesthood, and the eighty-seventh of his age, after a noble and virtuous life. He was born in Wexford, in the parish of Bannon, in the year 1796. He made his preparatory studies

Besides thus curtailing the district of St. John's by separating from it the portion which he calls Bay Bulls (and which was afterwards called Whittles' Bay, as the Dean made that harbor his place of residence), Dr. Fleming kept three curates in the palace with himself to do the work of St. John's, which still included Torbay, Pouch Cove, Portugal Cove, Topsail, and Petty Harbor. Harbor Grace was divided, for the present, into two districts, with five priests; and he declares his intention, on his return from Ireland (1837), to further subdivide it into five. Ferryland was also divided; one priest being resident at Fermeuse. This arrangement has continued until the present day, with the exception that the present energetic incumbent, Rev. John Walsh, has removed the residence to Rogneuse, where he has erected an elegant church, convent, parochial house, and schools, all situated on an elevated site above the picturesque village, and forming quite an imposing group of ecclesiastical buildings.

Two additional priests were sent to Placentia, making the whole staff consist of three, which, however, he declares by no means sufficient for so vast a district, embracing more than three hundred miles of coast; but the poverty of the people, "a population of over four thousand, scattered along the shore in coves and harbors," would not permit him to increase the number; and, finally, an additional priest was placed at King's Cove. This gives a total of sixteen priests,

---

in his native country, and completed his theological course at the College of Birchfield. He was ordained in the Cathedral of Enniscorthy by Dr. Keating, Bishop of Ferns, on Easter Sunday, 1829, just six days before the gaining of Emancipation. He came out to Newfoundland the following summer. After serving some time as curate in St. John's, he was sent to King's Cove. He told many amusing and interesting anecdotes, showing the wild state of the northern missions at that time. It was customary for clerks, captains of ships, or any one supposed to be possessed of some *larnin'* to be asked to perform the marriage ceremony. There was a quite notorious functionary of this sort. He had been a hedge school-master in Ireland, and, in consequence of his reputed knowledge of Latin, was in great demand. On being questioned by the Dean as to how he performed the nuptial service, he answered: "Well, yer reverence, I give 'em all the Latin I have, an' that's the *De Profundis* "!

The Dean's faithful successors, Revs. N. Roche and M. O'Driscoll, have erected to his memory, in Whittles' Bay, an elegant monument in the form of a Keltic cross, of Irish granite.

besides the Bishop. But the "*Relazione*" from which these particulars are taken was written in 1837.

Dr. Fleming, on the occasion of his visit to Ireland in 1830, to procure priests, went over to London and presented a memorial to His Majesty's Government on the subject of Catholic emancipation as concerning Newfoundland. We have already mentioned that the authorities in Newfoundland not only presumed that the penal laws of Ireland applied to this colony, but, even with strange perverseness, refused to acknowledge that the effects of the Catholic emancipation, gained the previous year by O'Connell, should be extended to this country.

Dr. Fleming's memorial was graciously received, and he obtained an order by which it was declared that *the penal laws did not affect Newfoundland*. This proof of the growing influence of the Catholic Bishop filled his fanatic opponents with alarm.

That Dr. Fleming took an active interest in the great struggle of the Irish people for religious freedom, under O'Connell, would be only natural to suppose. That he would be able, in any practical way, to help on the movement, we might not, perhaps, expect, considering the poverty of his Mission, and the great works he had undertaken; yet the draft of a letter still extant shows that even out of the richness of his poverty he was able, with the "subscriptions of a few Irishmen, and friends of Irishmen, in this transatlantic colony," to forward to the "O'Connell tribute" the very respectable sum of £117 sterling.

In another letter, without date or address, he speaks of the O'Connell tribute as "a sacred fund, consecrated by Irishmen to national gratitude," and says that every year since its institution he felt increased satisfaction at contributing his mite towards it, "as a small testimony of my estimation of the great advantages won for my country by Mr. O'Connell, and of his extraordinary sacrifices in her cause, and his unremitting exertions to ameliorate the condition of her people." He then goes on to complain that while Ireland enjoys tran-

quillity, in Newfoundland it is quite the reverse, "through
some unaccountable and blighting influence." He asks to
have his name enrolled among "my old and cherished friends,
the excellent people of Carrick-on-Suir, and at the same time
to place thereon the names of several of the clergymen who
desire to participate in the pleasure of thus expressing their
respect and attachment to the father of his country and the
friend of mankind, Mr. O'Connell." They add their subscriptions to his. "Several gentlemen, also, having heard I
was about to send money to the fund, have requested of me to
add their names, — a request it gives me great pleasure to comply with. Amongst them you will find several members of
our Legislature and some of our most respectable citizens."

Thus we see commenced that continued stream of generous
assistance, sent forth almost each succeeding year by the
children of Ireland in the New World, to their fathers and
friends in the old land. In all their times of hardship, trial,
and need, and in their long-continued struggle for national
freedom (which now seems about to dawn on them), Newfoundland, as we shall see, has never been backward in this
noble work. Whenever a call has been made upon her,
whether to relieve distress, to help on the struggle for emancipation and freedom, or for the building of churches and
schools, even down to the latest movement, "the Parnell
fund," her children have ever been ready, with hand and
purse, to help the land of their forefathers, in love and veneration, for which they yield not to any nation that has been
planted by her emigrant sons across the seas.

The uncompromising severity with which Dr. Fleming
treated tepidity or laxness among Catholics, as well as the
determined opposition he showed to their temporizing with
those outside the Church in all religious or sacred services,
might possibly be thought by some to proceed from fanaticism
or sectarian bigotry. But read in the light thrown upon his
character, by his acts of noble generosity, such a judgment
cannot be justly formed. On the contrary, that unflinching
conservatism must be admitted to spring from the highest

sense of honor and religious principle, and cannot but command respect and admiration even from those who differ from him in all religious views. While he despised the Catholic who, through a cringing desire to please his Protestant friends, placed his religious principles underfoot; on the other hand, he had a sincere respect and feeling of friendship for the honest professor of a religious creed different from his own. This was shown in a most remarkable manner by the fact which we here relate. Having gained for his own flock, after a hard fight, the boon of religious liberty, he did not then remain quiet on his oars. His sense of fair play and justice would not permit him to do so while any of his fellow-Christians were suffering under injustice.

Up to this time the Church of England in Newfoundland had assumed to itself, though without any legal authority, all the rights of a domineering establishment. As already remarked, a most unjust tax was extorted from the Roman Catholics on occasions of births, marriages, and funerals. But a tyranny of a still more galling kind was exercised against all *dissenting bodies*, inasmuch as they were altogether deprived (even by paying a tax) of the right to perform their own religious ceremonies.

Dr. Fleming, seeing the very great injustice of this law, drew up a petition on this subject, and had it presented by Mr. John Kent, in the very first session of our newly-acquired local Legislature, on Wednesday, Jan. 30, 1833, which had the desired effect. Hence to this strong-minded Prelate, who was accused by some of bigotry, because he strenuously forbade his own flock attending Protestant worship, the Wesleyan body owe the status and recognition which they to-day enjoy in Newfoundland. It is difficult to get men of the world's way of thinking to see the correctness and truth of the principles of the Catholic Church, which, while she allows and desires perfect liberty for all those *outside* her fold, will suffer no tampering on the part of her own children with the sacred deposit of Faith, of which she is the divinely-appointed guardian.

The petition, though lengthy, I produce here, as it is one of the noblest documents to be found in the annals of our history, and will vindicate for all time to come the character of this great Prelate, and gain for his memory a tribute of respect from all classes and denominations of citizens: —

"A petition from the Right Reverend Michael Anthony Fleming, D.D., prelate of the Catholic communion of Newfoundland, was presented by Mr. Kent, and read, setting forth —

"That the petitioner humbly begs leave to solicit in the most respectful manner the favorable attention of the House to the painful condition to which a large and respectable portion of fellow-Christians, the Dissenters of this country, are subjected by a clause respecting the celebration of marriages, as contained in an act intituled, 'An act to repeal an act to regulate the celebration of marriages in Newfoundland,' which compels the Dissenters of this country to solemnize their marriages according to the ceremonies of another Church, and by a clergyman of a different establishment.

"That the petitioner, while he disclaims any idea of dictating to the House, hopes that it will not be deemed presumptuous in him to express his decided opinion 'that a conciliatory system of policy towards all classes of people is, under Providence, the best and surest support of every government, and that in a free government, like our own, nothing but a necessary regard to the safety of the Constitution can justify the enactment of any laws of a restrictive nature, especially on matters of religion.' Wherefore, when the loyal, peaceable, and pious deportment of the Dissenters of this country is constantly demonstrated, the petitioner relies with confidence on the justice and liberality of the House, that the unmerited stigma which has been impressed on so meritorious a body by so unnecessary a law will be removed.

"Your petitioner humbly submits that, with respect to marriage (unless as a civil contract), the State should have no concern, as each religious sect ought to be left as fully at liberty to regulate the religious ceremonies attendant on marriage as any other part of their ceremonies, as there can be no more reason for compelling a man to be married by a clergyman of an opposite church than for compelling him to participate in the ordinary service of that church every Sunday.

"Wherefore the petitioner considers that the parties, being of Dissenters, or any religionists seeking to be married, and who profess conscientious motives, principles, and rites in objection of those practised and performed in the Episcopal, or any other church, ought not to be forced to violate their conscience; and that to force them, under pains and penalties, to go through a ceremony foreign to their mind is unjust, unchristian, and intolerant, and in direct violation of the fundamental principles of the Constitution.

"The petitioner lays this view of the case before the consideration of the House, and also begs, in the most respectful manner, to say that he would consider it a reflection on the intellect and good feeling by which the present enlightened age is distinguished were such a law suffered longer to exist, — a law which every enlightened man abhors.

"That the petitioner, deeply impressed with these sentiments, and sensible, from experience, of the grievance of being debarred the blessings of civil and religious liberty, should deem himself unworthy of that freedom which, thanks to a wise, paternal government, he now enjoys, could he for a moment be insensible to the hardships of his dissenting brethren, or hesitate to seek, by every constitutional means, the same share of liberty for them. The petitioner, therefore, humbly entreats that it will please the House in the commencement of its important labors to repeal this unchristian and unwise law, and to extend to the Dissenters and Methodists of this Island the privilege of solemnizing marriages in their own church, and by a clergyman of their own establishment,—a measure which will conciliate the affections and gratitude of so extensive and respectable a portion of His Majesty's subjects, and also, by an equal participation of religious as well as civil liberty, effectually consolidate, in one common sentiment of warm, unqualified attachment to the new institution of this country, all classes of Christians."

CHAPTER XXII.

THE PRESENTATION NUNS. — [1833.]

The Presentation Nuns — Mother Magdalen's Narrative — Journey to Dublin — Waterford — Voyage to Newfoundland — Opening of the Schools — The Presentation Convent — "The Fire of '46" — Convent Destroyed — New Convent and Schools Erected — First Religious Reception — Jubilee, 1833-34 — Other Conventual Establishments in America.

HAVING, in the short space of three years, placed the Mission in a state of marked improvement and advancement, having more than doubled the number of clergymen, and provided a pastor for every place where one could be at all supported, so that, although the number was not yet by any means adequate to the fast increasing population, yet there was not left any settlement, however small, which would not have the ardently desired blessing of a visit from the priest at least once in the year. Having accomplished all this great work of organization in such an incredibly short space of time, this zealous Prelate now prepared to set about the accomplishment of what may be considered an equally important object, if not more so, namely, the foundation of a convent and the introduction of a community of Presentation nuns. This undertaking must certainly be looked upon as the greatest work of his glorious episcopate, for though the building of the cathedral was a mighty and noble act, and one which strikes the eye more immediately, still the building up of the moral temple in the souls of his faithful children must rank as a holier and nobler work before the eyes of God, though not so prominent to those of the world. There can be no doubt that Dr. Fleming himself also thought this the crowning work of his episcopacy, and that he had pondered long and seriously upon it even from the very moment of his elevation, and he frequently writes of it in his letters. Thus, in his letters to Dr. O'Connell, P.P., St. Michael's and St. John's, Dublin, after describing the state of education in mixed schools, he continues:—

"Such was the state of things at the period of my accession to the Vicariate, and, impressed with the strong feelings of the importance of summoning to our aid a proper system of religious education for my congregation as far as my means, greatly contracted and overcharged as they were, would allow, I felt the necessity of withdrawing female children from under the tutelage of men, from the dangerous associations which ordinary school intercourse with the other sex naturally exhibited; for whatever care could be applied to the culture of female children in mixed schools, they must lose much of that delicacy of feeling and refinement of sentiment which form the ornament and grace of their sex. Besides, viewing the great influence that females exercise over the moral character of society,—the great and useful and necessary influence that the example and the conversation of the mother has in the formation of the character of her children, as well male as female,—I judged it of essential importance to fix the character of the female portion of our community in virtue and innocence, by training them in particular in the ways of integrity and morality; by affording them the very best opportunities of having their religious principles well fixed; by imparting to them, while their young minds were daily receiving the elements of a general and useful education, a course of religious instruction that should teach them the true value and the proper use of those mental treasures by which they were being enriched; for I felt that which all must feel, namely, that when once the future mothers are impressed with the truths of religion, once they are solidly instructed in the divine precepts of the Gospel, once their young minds are enlarged and enlightened and strengthened by educational knowledge,—the domestic fireside is immediately made the most powerful auxiliary to the school, and instruction and true education, the basis of which is virtue and religion, are instilled into the little ones at their mother's knee, and they go abroad, by and by, into school, or into society, with all the elements that fit them to become virtuous citizens.

"These feelings and opinions were the motives that led me to consider the establishment of a Presentation convent essential to the permanent success of the Mission."

Again, in his "*Relazione*" to Propaganda, he dwells warmly upon this subject, and particularly on the state of society at the time, which rendered it of paramount necessity that a complete separation of the sexes should be observed in the schools. "The boys," he says, "at a very tender age are employed in some way or other about the fishery, in order to earn as much as will support themselves and render them almost altogether independent of their parents. The consequence is, that, free from every domestic restraint, they are much exposed to the temptation *to drink rum, which, according to custom, is served out to them regularly three times a day!*[1] Things being so, and being animated with these sentiments, . . . notwithstanding the subdivision of my district, and the consequent diminution of my income; notwithstanding the difficulty of sustaining three priests in a district so narrowed; notwithstanding the great expense I underwent in bringing out so many priests; notwithstanding, I say, all this, confiding in the benevolence of my people, and still more in the providence of that God who takes care of the welfare of his own little ones, I took my determination of introducing a convent of Presentation nuns, and again, in 1833, I crossed the Atlantic and secured a small community of that Order, to come out to educate our poor little girls."

---

[1] This extraordinary custom — a remnant, no doubt, of the times of the old fishing admirals, who served out the grog according to naval regulations — was in vogue until very late years on most of our large mercantile premises, and is to the present day continued on some of the old English and Jersey houses. Every "hand," boy or man, had his brown jug, with yellow stripe round the middle, called "a yallow-belly," and when the time for the "mornin'," the "eleven o'clocker," and the "evenin'" arrived he approached the rum-puncheon, and, drawing the spile, filled his "yallow-belly."

Dwelling again on this subject, in his letter to Dr. Spratt he says: "You will say, perhaps, that with all these embarrassments there was some degree of imprudence in charging myself with the support of an establishment so weighty. To this I can only reply, that so strongly was I impressed with its necessity, that there is no sacrifice that I would not make for its accomplishment and to ensure its stability. I did lay aside many comforts that I had been accustomed to. I was obliged to reduce the number of my servants, and to content myself with the service of one general servant and a boy, and to retrench at table to such a degree as to subject myself to the charge of parsimony. I had heretofore been able to keep a pair of good horses, and what we here call a 'carriage.' I am now forced to surrender the latter, and limit my *stud* to a single horse."

The history of the establishment of the Presentation nuns in Newfoundland has been very fully reproduced in the excellent " Life of Nano Nagle," by Rev. Dr. Hutch, of Cloyne.[1] The items in Dr. Hutch's account are taken chiefly from an article by the present writer published in one of the local

---

[1] The learned author devotes the greater portion of a chapter to the establishment and spread of the Order in Newfoundland. He will, however, it is to be hoped, forgive an ardent son of Terra-Nova for setting him right in one statement, not biographical, but geographical. The Rev. Dr. Hutch persists in the very common but oft-corrected error of speaking of Newfoundland as a place in the "far north." We can, of course, make some allowance for the poetical license taken in the preface, where the necessities of an elegant antithesis make him speak of the "islands of the southern seas, where the orange groves perfume the air of Australia, and the tropic sun burns up the soil of India, . . . as well as in the far north, where a mantle of almost perpetual snow covers the hills and forests of Newfoundland." The beauty of the picture helps us to condone the inaccuracy of the statement. But, then, in the calmer moments of plain, simple narrative (p. 305) he speaks of Newfoundlanders as "the hardy fishermen of the north." I beg to inform the Rev. Dr. Hutch, Firstly, that Newfoundland is not covered with an "almost perpetual mantle of snow." The snow-mantle generally endures about *four* months out of the twelve. Secondly, instead of being in the "far north," a glance at the map will show him that she is actually about 300 miles nearer to the equator than himself. The latitude of Fermoy, Ireland (whence Dr. Hutch writes), is a little more than 52° N., while St. John's, Newfoundland, is only 47½° N., a difference of more than 4½ degrees, or about 275 miles. In fact, we are situated exactly in the latitude of Versailles, and the most northerly portion of Newfoundland is farther south than the most southerly point of Ireland.

newspapers, on the subject of the Golden Jubilee of Mother Magdalen, which was celebrated in St. John's on the 6th of December, 1873. Since that time another decade of years has been told off on Time's rosary, and the venerable Mother Magdalen still survives, and had the honor of witnessing another jubilee, namely, that of her arrival, fifty years ago, on the shores of Newfoundland.

There are many facts concerning the early history of the Newfoundland foundation which are not given by Mr. Hutch, as they have never appeared in print, but which will most appropriately find a place in this History. They have been taken principally from the *viva voce* testimony of Mother Magdalen. This venerable lady is still in strong and hearty health, and though for some years past deprived of sight, yet is in full possession of all her mental faculties. She is a living example of a holy and virtuous life, full of zeal and burning with the fire of divine love, so strong that the proverbial rigors of our climate, after "fifty years midst the winter's snow and the summer's glow," have not been able to quench those buoyant life-springs.

Mother Magdalen O'Shaughnessy was born in Galway, on the 12th of November, 1793. She is consequently now in her 95th year. She entered the Presentation convent in that city in 1821, and pronounced the solemn vows in 1823, being then in her 29th year. In 1833, the tenth year of her religious profession, she came to Newfoundland. The convent in Galway was, according to her recollection, a fine building, situated a little outside the town. The community consisted of thirty-three sisters. The Superioress, Rev. Mother Mary John, was a most estimable lady, then 90 years old. She belonged to the family of the Powers, of Silverstream, County Waterford. She had a brother in the East Indies who was very wealthy, and who allowed her a handsome annual income.

"I well remember," says Mother Magdalen, "the morning of the 29th of June, 1833. A clergyman appeared at the convent gate carrying a carpet-bag. He said he was an American Bishop, and asked leave to celebrate Mass. This was the Rt. Rev. Dr. Fleming, Bishop of Newfoundland. After Mass he asked to see the schools. I was appointed to show him through. I was young and smart then, you know, like a fly. I explained everything. I suppose I spoke a good deal. He was delighted with everything he saw, and seemed to take a particular fancy to me. He spoke to me in the most fervent tones of the desolation of his diocese. He said, 'You must come out with me to Newfoundland. That is the only way you can save your soul;' and much more to that effect. I told him I thought I could do no good by myself. He then asked me if I would come provided I could get some others to accompany me, and I said I would. When we returned to the community-room he made his request to the Rev. Mother.

"Rev. Mother called all the Sisters, and placed the matter before them, but left it entirely to their own choice. Dr. Fleming said : 'If you do not like the place, I will land you safe back in this parlor again without a penny of expense to the house.' Four Sisters immediately consented to go, namely, Sisters M. Magdalen O'Shaughnessy, Bernard Kirwan, M. Xaverius Lynch, and Xavier Molony.

"Dr. Fleming then went to obtain the consent of Dr. Browne, Bishop of Galway, who was then away at the seaside, at a place named Renville. Dr. Brown immediately consented, and the two Bishops came next morning to the convent. Immediate preparations were made for our departure. The retreat was anticipated, and Dr. Fleming left for Dublin to arrange about our passage out to the New World."

It must not be imagined that Dr. Fleming, in his enthusiasm, was so carried away as to forget the business portion of his project. A letter from Dublin, dated Adam and Eve's Chapel-house (the Franciscan community on Merchants' Quay, Dublin), July 17, 1833, to the Mother Superior shows how anxious he was to provide for the proper maintenance

and comfort of the nuns, and how, amidst a multitude of
business, and almost overwhelming difficulties, even the
smallest detail did not escape his attention. He first excuses
himself for so long a delay on account of the absence of Most
Rev. Dr. Murray from Dublin, then the "press of duties connected with the spiritual retreat and ordination of the young
men who volunteered for the North American mission."[1] He
next states that he had a long conversation with his Grace
on the subject of the foundation in Newfoundland, and that
Dr. Murray "rejoices and thanks God with and for me." He
then enters on the question of means: "£1,500 were lodged
in the funds by my predecessor for the benefit of the Mission;
this sum I intend shall be appropriated to that special purpose." Dr. Murray directed him as to the investment of the
money, and volunteered to become one of its trustees. "I
also stated to his Grace my pledge to you that I would build
a suitable dwelling-house and school without any infringement on this sum, and that I would guarantee £100 per
annum for their support, which annuity should continue till
their own funds would be adequate to all their domestic
wants. But when I speak of £100, I must take leave to
observe that when I consider that these, my dearest sisters,
are to be my coöperators in the works of religion, in promoting the glory of that bountiful Redeemer we are destined to
serve and adore, they may rest satisfied that my most earnest
desire, my most strenuous exertions, will not be wanting to
contribute not only that paltry sum, but all and everything
in my power to promote their happiness." He adds some
glowing words of encouragement to the Sisters, expressing
his confidence in God and in the generosity of the good people of Newfoundland. "I have been greatly disappointed,"
he continues, "in the vessel I had intended to take passage
by. She arrived here on Saturday, and I find, on examining her, that she is rather small to make comfortable accom-

---

[1] These "young men" were five in number, and have since fulfilled their labor and gone to receive the reward of the faithful husbandman. They were the Revs. Bernard and James Duffy, McKenna, Ward, and Waldron.

modation for the ladies. I go this evening to Liverpool to
seek for a good vessel, and I expect to return here by Monday evening. I shall then know more about my movements.
I am all anxiety to return to Galway. My prayers, my
heart, my soul, are all employed in the cause. If these dear
Sisters feel as I do, and unite with me in earnest in promoting the cause of religion, I hope, in the mercy of God, that
our labors will close by an everlasting recompense.

"Soliciting your prayers, and those of your community, I
beg to subscribe myself, with the greatest respect, your
much obliged and devoted humble servant,

+ "MICHAEL ANTHONY FLEMING.

The Rev. Mother replied, giving formal consent that the
Sisters should go, but stipulating that they should be sent
back should such a course become necessary.

The following is a copy of the letter of Rev. Mother: —

"MY DEAR LORD, — I received your letter of the 17th,
which contains everything that my greatest solicitude for the
happiness of my dear Sisters could desire, with the exception of what I now mention, and to which I know your Lordship will not object. It is that this community shall have it
in their power to recall our Sisters at any time after six
years. Should the convent at Newfoundland be then sufficiently established, or should the present flattering prospect
of promoting the great end of our holy Institute, by coöperating in the instruction of the poor female children in St.
John's, *not succeed* to their satisfaction, or should they wish
to return for any other particular cause which they may *deem
necessary*, that, in that case, your Lordship would have them
safely conducted back to their convent in Galway. I would
not have thought it necessary to insert this latter condition
only for the uncertainty of life; for, if the Lord spare you,
as your Lordship has promised it, I feel confident you would
faithfully fulfil that promise. Though we, the Sisters of this
community, deem it necessary to make this stipulation, those

Sisters who, under your Lordship's protection, and with God's assistance, are undertaking this arduous, but gratifying task, unite with us in hoping that it may not be necessary to recur to any such expedient. With sentiments of esteem for and confidence in your Lordship's paternal tenderness and protection, I, with the sanction of our good Bishop, Dr. Browne, resign to your care our dear Sisters for the great work, earnestly soliciting for them a continuation of the kind interest which you now profess to take in their every happiness. I trust those Sisters will not disappoint your most sanguine wishes, but that, faithfully coöperating in your zealous efforts for the welfare of the establishment, and the greater glory of God, your Lordship, with them, shall have the consolation of seeing it perfectly consolidated. To obtain from Heaven this blessing, the prayers of this community shall not cease to be offered. I remain, my dear Lord, with great respect and earnest wishes for your every happiness, and begging a remembrance in your prayers,

"Sr. MARY JOHN POWER,
" *Superioress.*"

"The stipulations contained in the Right Rev. Dr. Fleming's, and in the above letter, are unanimously approved of and accepted by the Chapter of Discreets.

"Sr. M. JOSEPH NOLAN. *Assistant.*
"Sr. M. BERNARD KIRWAN, *Bursar.*
"Sr. M. ALOYSIUS JOYCE, *Mother of Novices.*"

The Rt. Rev. Dr. Browne gave his sanction by a Latin document, of which the following is a translation: —

"I sanction and approve of the stipulation entered into by the Superioress and community of the Presentation convent of this town with the Right Rev. Dr. Fleming, Bishop of St. John's, Newfoundland; and I do, by these presents, authorise and direct the Sisters M. Bernard Kirwan, M. Magdalen O'Shaughnessy, M. Xavier Molowney, and M. Xavier Lynch, to depart from the convent which they now inhabit, and proceed, under the guidance and protecting care of the Right Rev. Dr. Fleming, to the city of St. John's, Newfoundland, there to found and establish a new convent of this excellent Institute, for the instruction of poor female children, and to promote the best interests of religion and society.

+ "GEORGE J. BROWNE,
"*Bishop of Galway.*
"Given in Galway, this 8th day of August, 1833."

To the above document is attached the following: —

"I do hereby appoint Sister Mary Bernard Kirwan Superioress of the intended convent of St. John's, Newfoundland.
+ "MICHAEL ANTHONY FLEMING,
"*Bishop of Newfoundland.*"

All preliminaries having been thus settled to the satisfaction of all parties, the Bishop set about making his arrangements for the safe conduct of the nuns to their new and distant home. It was not so easy a matter in those days to secure a safe and comfortable passage across the Atlantic, especially for ladies unaccustomed to ocean travel, as nowadays, when ocean steamers, like floating palaces, almost annihilating time and space and reducing sea-sickness to a minimum, are leaving, almost daily, all the principal ports of the United Kingdom for America; so that while the Sisters were patiently, but anxiously, awaiting the moment of their departure, Dr. Fleming was expending his energies in endeavoring to procure a suitable vessel for their transport. The following letter will show the worry and annoyance which he experienced: —

"ADAM AND EVE, Monday, 12 o'clock,
"5 August, 1833.
"MY DEAR REV. MOTHER, — I am but just arrived from Liverpool, and although not a little fatigued from a disagree-

able passage, I hasten to reply to your kind letter of the 4th. . . . Since I did myself the favor of writing to you until this moment was a continued round of uneasiness and disappointment. Three or four different engagements I entered into with shipowners, and scarce had two days elapsed with either when these engagements were broken. On Friday evening last I took my departure for Liverpool, for the second time within these ten days, and have, I hope, finally and effectually concluded the matter, as far as a written document between the shipowner (Mr. Brocklebank) and me can bind. By this agreement the vessel is to put into Waterford early next week to take us up. I cannot, of course, withdraw from this contract, as by doing so I should not only be bound to pay the contract money, but be liable for any consequences attending the vessel on the passage to Waterford. I cannot, therefore, think of any other vessel, unless Brocklebank would be satisfied in rescinding the contract. At all events, I strongly suspect that the vessel in your port, to which you allude, is one employed in the timber trade, and in such a vessel I should not like to make passage. And though many persons may take passage in these ships, and be fortunate enough to arrive safe at their destination, in general, thanks is due to the weather, and not to the vessel. They are principally ships that are fit for no other work, being old and infirm. But, whether old or new, they get so strained by the very first cargo of timber that they are never after sufficiently staunch to make them seaworthy for my choice.

"When I take a day or two's rest, for indeed I require it, I shall go direct to Galway. On Thursday morning I intend leaving this. I hope then to have the pleasure of seeing you. Will you tell my own dear Sisters how distressed I have been that the many unforeseen difficulties which I had to meet should for a moment give them any uneasiness, which they necessarily must. But now that a better prospect is opening, and every hope of our being in St. John's before the middle of September is displayed before us, I feel a load of care and trouble fall from my shoulders, and inspired by the most lively confidence that God will grant me now that favor which I humbly and fervently pray for, *every opportunity of contributing to the spiritual and temporal happiness of these my dear Sisters, for His greater honor and glory.*

"With the hope that you will excuse the many blunders of this letter, which could not be avoided from the state of my head and hand after the severe passage of last night, I shall close this with many thanks to you for your kindness, and most affectionate regards to all the Sisters of your community. Your much obliged and very grateful, humble servant,

"+ MICHAEL ANTHONY FLEMING.
"THE REV. MOTHER SUPERIOR,
  "*Presentation Convent, Galway.*"

Now to resume Mother Magdalen's narrative: "Dr. Fleming arrived a second time in Galway, on the 11th August, and we left next morning, the feast of St. Clare. We were all astir at an early hour. We had Mass at 4 o'clock, and all received Holy Communion.

"The mail-coach, by special request of the Bishop, was sent over from Kilroy's Hotel to the convent, and we all got in. There was, of course, great weeping and lamentation among the Sisters, as they knew they should never see us again in this world.

"There were no other passengers in the coach. Dr. Fleming sat on the box by the driver, and used to come now and then to the window to encourage us. Our first halting-place was Ballinasloe. At Athlone we changed horses, and arrived at Dublin in the evening, after dark. We were brought to Ormond Quay, to the house of a lady from Galway named Hughes, owner of a large paper-mill and factory. She knew me, and had a hearty welcome for us all, and set a portion of her large house apart all to ourselves. We had Mass celebrated every morning in the house. A priest from the neighboring Convent of Adam and Eve was sent over to act as chaplain for us."[1]

After some stay in Dublin, by the same antiquated means of conveyance they travelled to Waterford. Here they were received with enthusiasm. There had long been a bond of sympathy between the *Urbs Intacta* and the *Talav an Eask*, the *Land of Fish*, as Newfoundland is graphically called in the Celtic tongue. For many years previous to this time Waterford had been the starting-point for emigrants to the "Wild Plantation," and many of our principal Catholic families had come by that route. The Morrises and Kents had carried on a regular passenger traffic for over sixty years. (See Note 4.) It was only natural, then, that any one leaving for Newfoundland would be welcomed with a *cead mile failte*, and overwhelmed with messages and salutations to friends and relations far away across the ocean. We can easily imagine, then, the enthusiasm with which those holy ladies were received, who were looked upon as noble heroines (for such, indeed, they were), going to offer up their lives and labors for the children of the Far West.

They were taken in charge by a gentleman named Sherlock, and brought to his place (a fine house with large gardens), outside the city. Mrs. Sherlock had a sister, a professed religious in the Galway house, who had written announcing the coming of the nuns. Here they were received with royal honors, "just as if we were princesses," says Mother Magdalen. "The priests and people from the town came out continually to see us. The Bishop, Dr.

---

[1] An amusing incident occurred in connection with this matter, which Mother Magdalen relates with her peculiar *naiveté*. It happened that one morning a very young friar was told off to celebrate Mass for the nuns. On the same morning a venerable father came over from the convent, not knowing that one had already been sent. When he saw the young priest he said, "Well, my boy, what do you know about nuns? You had better go back to your convent." This young friar was no other than Father John Mullock, who was then in his twenty-sixth year, and had been only lately ordained. Little it was thought at that time that he was afterwards to become the Bishop of Newfoundland, and spiritual superior for many years of Mother Magdalen and her little community. And many a time, in after years, did he good-naturedly rally her on this event, saying, "Ha, ha! You thought me too young once to act as your chaplain, and you turned me away. Now I can have satisfaction."

Barron,[1] was most kind; he gave us books and relics, and came out every day to celebrate Mass for us. Sherlock's was a splendid place, with a grand mansion and beautiful gardens. We used to walk in the gardens every day; there was also a very fine library." Mother Magdalen humorously describes the consternation of the young religious on their being attended at dinner by servants in full livery, and presented to ladies and gentlemen in full dress. In fact, so bewildered were the poor Sisters, after their long retirement of cloister life, that they did not at all enjoy the grandeur prepared for them, but begged themselves off on the next occasion, and had a cosey little place for themselves in the library.

Mother Magdalen promised this fine old Irish family that God would reward them for their great kindness, and the reward was not long delayed, for very shortly after three of the Misses Sherlock received the grace of religious vocations, and joined the Ursuline Order.

As soon as Dr. Fleming had all prepared, the vessel appeared in the stream, and the nuns took their final departure from Waterford on the 28th August, the feast of St. Augustin. They were accompanied by Dr. Fleming and his "boy Phil."

As the ship gently floated down with the tide, and put out to sea, the long-pent-up feelings of the brave Sisters at length found vent, and they began vividly, for the first time, to realize the greatness of the act which they had undertaken.[2]

---

[1] Dr. Barron was not Bishop of Waterford, but an American Bishop, who was travelling for his health's sake at the time.

[2] The scene and the circumstances bring forcibly to our memory the lines of Seneca's Medæa (Act ii., Scene 3):—

> Audax nimium qui freta primus
> Rate tam fragili perfida rupit;
> Terrasque suas post terga videns,
> Animam levibus credidit auris;
> Dubioque secans æquæa cursu,
> Potuit tenui fidere ligno;
> Inter vitæ mortisque vias,
> Nimium gracili limite ducto.

The sailors were most respectful during the voyage. Not a loud or unbecoming word was spoken. "George," the cook, an English boy, was most attentive. His usual salutation was, "What will the ladies take to-day?"—though, if the truth must be told, his larder did not give him a very extensive choice, and the question of the *ménu* was generally decided by putting the *kittle* to boil and giving them a cup of tea. Dr. Fleming had secured the cabin entirely for the nuns. He read a spiritual lecture for them every day while they worked. The good ship "Ariel" made a very fair average passage of twenty-five days. The weather was fine; there was one storm. The nuns, of course, thought the passage long and dangerous, and, we may be sure, prayed very fervently. No account of their arrival was received at the convent in Galway for four months, the letter containing the news having been mislaid in Liverpool. The community gave them up for lost. Solemn requiem offices were celebrated for them, copies of their vows burned, and a general mourning took place in the convent. "We arrived," says Mother Magdalen, "on the 21st of September,

---

The following may be offered as a translation:—

> Brave-hearted he who first in fragile bark
> Launched o'er the deep to plough the unknown dark;
> His native shore behind him swiftly flees,
> His soul confiding to the gentle breeze.
> He with a doubtful course divides the flood,
> And trusts himself unto the slender wood;
> Led onward ever in a graceful path,
> But all too dangerous; — 'twixt life and death."

It is in this same chorus that occurs the well-known prophecy of the discovery of Newfoundland:—

> . . . "venient annis,
> Sæcula seris; — quibus Oceanus,
> Vincula rerum laxet et ingens
> Pateat tellus Tiphysque *Novos*
> Detegat *Orbes*. Nec sit Terris,
> Ultima Thule."

> In latter years shall come a wondrous age,
> When ocean shall the chains of things unbind,
> And show the mighty world that lies behind.
> And Tiphys shall a NEWFOUNDLAND explore,
> Nor Thule shall longer be the last known shore!

(See Note 5.)

the feast of St. Matthew. All the population of the town flocked down to the wharves, and climbed up the masts of the vessels to see us and welcome us; and some of the principal inhabitants came on board, vying with each other for the honor of rowing us ashore. We were not allowed to disembark until they had made a new landing-stair. The best carriage in the town (Dr. Carson's) was sent to fetch us."[1]

They were driven to the Bishop's residence, "the Old Palace," cheered all the way by the crowd. By a remarkable coincidence, the vessel bringing out the new priests arrived in the "Narrows" of St. John's at exactly the same moment as the "Ariel." They had left Ireland on the same day, but had not been sighted during the voyage. The nuns remained exactly one month at the "Old Palace." In the meantime Dr. Fleming had procured a house for them; it had formerly been a tavern, with the sign of "The Rising Sun,"—a name considered as a propitious omen, symbolizing the light of faith and education which they came to diffuse throughout the country.

The day of the opening of the schools was one of great joy to the good people of Newfoundland. It is described in glowing terms in one of the local papers of the day ("The Patriot," October, 1833): "On Monday, 21st inst., this infant institution was opened for the reception of poor female children. Seldom has it been our lot to witness a scene of such deep interest, . . . whether we regard the community of ladies of family and fortune, surrendering all the joys of life . . . for the advancement of the glory of Him to whom they have consecrated their lives, or the little applicant for admission, while she tries to read her fate, . . . or multitudinous feelings of the estimable Prelate to whose exertions we owe this blessing. There he stood,

---

[1] An amusing anecdote is told concerning this carriage. It had formerly belonged to Dr. Fleming, and had been sold by him in order to raise funds to carry out some of his great spiritual works. The good old Dr. Carson drove round in it for many years on his morning calls, quite indifferent to the fact that a large gilded mitre was emblazoned on the panels.

witnessing the completion of his dearest wishes." But, notwithstanding that the nuns gave up to the use of the schools all the house except the very small parlor and two bed-rooms, which served them at once for community-room, sitting-room, refectory, and chapel, yet after all they could not receive more than four hundred and fifty children. Again we repeat, never was there witnessed in St. John's a scene of deeper interest than the opening of the Presentation schools.

This house was situated at the foot of Pilots' Hill, and, though it was the best which could be procured at the time, it was still but a sorry makeshift. The school had formerly been a slaughter-house. There was a forge in the immediate neighborhood and a stable in the rear, the only approach to which was through the hall of the house, through which the horse was led daily. Dr. Fleming, one day, visiting the nuns, met this privileged quadruped, and was obliged to yield place to his equine majesty. He had had no idea that the nuns had to suffer such inconvenience; and, though he had hired the place for a year, he determined to remove the nuns at once. The fitting up of this house and school, such as it was, cost about £500, as Dr. Fleming states in a letter to Earl Grey (24th Feb., 1847); it was also subject to an exorbitant rent. So in very little more than one month (viz., 8th December), a more suitable site offering, they removed to a more comfortable and commodious dwelling. This was a house which had been occupied by Archdeacon Wix, near the King's Road. Here the nuns remained for eight years, giving the locality the name of "Nunnery Hill," which it bears to the present day. Here a new school was erected, at a cost of upwards of £600. It was of fine proportions, and Dr. Fleming speaks of it in his letter to Archdeacon O'Connell, of Dublin, 1844, as "large and commodious." It gave accommodations to twelve hundred children. "When you take into account," he continues, "that for nearly eleven years more than one thousand children have been in daily attendance at these schools, you can well estimate what a world of good these pious ladies accomplished."

But still the zeal of this energetic Prelate was not exhausted. He determined to possess a building which would surpass in elegance all that had hitherto been erected in St. John's. The house which he described as commodious at first was now no longer so, the number of the community being doubled. Besides, he found it hard to be obliged to pay such a heavy rent (£80 per annum) for a house old and decaying. He had already paid, between rent and repairs, considerably over £1,000. So he determined, though the new convent was not complete, that he would not renew the lease of Archdeacon Wix's house. The poor nuns, therefore, had to move their camp again. They remained over nine years at Nunnery Hill, viz., from December 31, 1833, to August 31, 1843. This time they were accommodated in a house which had been a ball-alley, situated a little outside the town. Here, again, repairs and a temporary school were necessary, and some three or four hundred pounds expended. The nuns remained at the ball-alley until December 14, 1844, when they were conducted to their magnificent new convent at the head of Long's Hill, on a site which he purchased in November, 1842, and which he describes "as a charming situation above the town, sufficiently near and central. It commands, and is well seen from, almost every part of the town and harbor to Narrows." The building itself was "worthy of the ladies and the glorious cause they were embarked in." He then goes on, with pardonable enthusiasm and great minuteness, to describe this magnificent structure. " It presents a handsomely finished front, flanked at the angles by hexagonal castellated towers; a spacious portico, extending twelve feet, and rising eight feet above the whole building, marking the grand entrance, with two square towers upon the angles, showing between them a splendid gilt Grecian cross." It cost about £4,000.

But, alas! the poor nuns had not reached the end of their pilgrimage. They had, like Moses, got a glimpse of the Promised land, but they had not yet safely crossed the Jordan. This noble building was doomed, within two years, to be crumbled into a heap of ruins. The charity of the good nuns frustrated the prudential cares of the zealous Bishop. It was sufficiently distant from surrounding buildings to be safe from conflagrations from without, but on the occasion of the great fire of the 9th of June, 1846, which laid the whole town in ashes, this very isolation, to which Dr. Fleming trusted for security, was the cause of its destruction. The good nuns opened their spacious halls for the reception of clothes, furniture, etc., of the people who were obliged to flee before the terrible element. Among some of these articles were brought a few smouldering sparks, which soon burst into an uncontrollable flame, and all was lost. The nuns barely escaped with their lives, Mother Magdalen, who remained to gather up what letters and small cash there were on hand, having her habit singed. The community at this time consisted of six Sisters, two having joined the original four.[1]

Dr. Fleming was in Europe at the time of the conflagration, having gone home to secure some additional Sisters. The nuns were conducted first to the Mercy Convent (recently built near the cathedral grounds) and thence to a cottage belonging to the Bishop, and situated about a mile in the country. His Lordship had given to this little farm the name of "Carpasia," that being the title of his diocese *in partibus*. The nuns remained there for five months, sleeping upon the floor of the barn, teaching the children (who still flocked to them) on fine days in the open fields, and in rough weather in the stables and outhouses.

The news of the terrible catastrophe reached the Bishop at Liverpool, where he was *en route* for St. John's with two religious.[2] His consternation may be more easily imagined than described. He immediately offered to release these Sisters from their promise and to restore them to Galway; but

---

[1] These were Catherine Phelan (Sister Ignatius Aloysius) and Amelia Shanley (Sister Antonia), who arrived in 1842, and made their profession on the feast of the Presentation, 21st November, 1846.

[2] These were Catherine Ffrench (Sister Josephine) and Miss Lovelock (Sister F. de Sales).

they nobly chose to come on to their sisters in misfortune in Newfoundland. When Dr. Fleming arrived in St. John's and beheld the ruin and misery on all sides,— the complete destruction of the city, and, above all, the now vacant and unsightly spot where so short a time before he had looked with pride as he went out through the "Narrows," and saw the noble convent, the darling object of so many years of anxiety and labor,— his heart sank within him. When he saw the place where the nuns' beds were laid on the floor of the barn he shed copious tears. He never wholly recovered from the shock which he then received; from that moment, worn out by fatigue and anxiety, his health began to decline. His pen, erst so prolific and so swift, begins to show signs of wavering. He likens himself to the dove cast upon the waters and not able to find rest for his weary wings. He felt that his course was nearly run. Writing in the following year (18th of November, 1847) to the Archbishop of Quebec he says: "After labouring in this portion of the great vineyard for nearly thirty years, I find my health so weakened and my constitution so broken that it is impossible I could ever hope, during the remnant of my earthly career, to enjoy the happiness of meeting your Grace."

Early in the year 1847 Dr. Fleming, feeling his strength failing, applied for a coadjutor, and his choice was fixed upon Father John T. Mullock, the brilliant priest of his own Seraphic Order, whom he had known for the past fourteen years. Dr. Mullock arrived in St. John's in May, 1848. He immediately set to work with that wondrous vigor and strength of mind and will which were his distinguishing characteristics to carry to completion all the great undertakings which he found in an unfinished state. The losses which Dr. Fleming sustained by the great fire were almost overwhelming. In a letter to Earl Grey, 22d of February, 1847, he details the sums he had expended in connection with the convent and other ecclesiastical buildings, amounting to upwards of £10,000. He applied for a portion of the money subscribed in England for the sufferers by the fire. "Surely,

then, my Lord," he says, " it is not unreasonable that I, with the deepest respect, and in all the humility of sad suffering, pray your Lordship to extend here a kind and helping hand to enable me to once more open a school to which no fewer than three thousand children are in vain looking for instruction." This touching appeal, however, proved unavailing. Nevertheless, Dr. Mullock at once set about the construction of the new schools and convents on a still grander scale than before. The foundations of the convent were laid by the Rt. Rev. Dr. Mullock on the 23d of August, 1850.

The present erection is of cut stone, and, with the school-house attached, cost the sum of £7,000. The site is at the eastward side of the cathedral, commanding a magnificent ocean view, and overlooking for many miles the surrounding country. The style corresponds with that of the cathedral, and the spacious grounds in the rear afford ample space for gardens and ornamental grounds. With the foundation-stone was deposited a vase containing several medals, current coins, the seal of Dr. Fleming, the names of the clergy of the colony, of the Bishops of Ireland, of His Holiness the Pope, the journals of the day, and some wheat, the produce of the Island in 1848, etc., together with a scroll bearing the following inscription:—

> The foundation-stone of this Convent of the Nuns of the Presentation Order (first established in this City of St. John's in MDCCCXXXIII, by the Right Rev. M. A. FLEMING, O.S.F, Bishop of Newfoundland) was laid by the Right Rev. JOHN THOMAS MULLOCK, O.S F., Bishop of Newfoundland, on the XXIII day of August, MDCCCL, in the fifth year of the Pontificate of His Holiness Pius IX., and the fifteenth year of the reign of Her Most Gracious Majesty Victoria, Queen of Great Britain and Ireland, Sir John Gaspard le Marchant being Governor of Newfoundland.
>
> Directing Superintendent, PAT'K KOUGH.
> Builder, JAMES PURCELL.

"The local Legislature has voted the sum of £2,000 sterling towards the erection of those buildings. Dr. Fleming left money (£300) in his will, and the congregation present on the above occasion contributed £300. In one year from the present time the whole will be completed, and by the end of this season the schools will be in operation."

In the course of three years this splendid suite of buildings was completed, bidding defiance to the elements, for they are no longer constructed of frail wood, but of imperishable granite. And here, at last, after so many vicissitudes, the good nuns found themselves in a peaceful and permanent home. They had not been, however, idle during the interval between the fire of '46 and the taking possession of the new convent. "Wherever we went," says Mother Magdalen, "and amidst all our trials, we had one consolation, — the children never left us. If we had not the poor little ones to work for we could never have lived through it."

In the month of November following "The Fire" Dr. Fleming brought them to the Mercy Convent, a portion of which was partitioned off for them, and "where [say the annals of the convent] they received all possible kindness and attention from the Superioress, Mrs. Creedon." They remained there five years. A temporary school (the fifth) was erected in the rear of the convent. On the 21st of October, 1851 (the anniversary of the first opening of their school eighteen years previously), not wishing to encumber the Mercy nuns any further, they took up their abode in a portion of their new stone schools, which were not yet completed, and for some time their only roof at night was a sail, kindly lent by one of the merchants. Finally, however, on the 2d of July, 1853, they took possession of the splendid convent built for them by the Rt. Rev. Dr. Mullock. No expense had been spared by him to make it both convenient and conventual. The Sisters now enjoy everything requisite for their happiness, and have the consolation of seeing their institute firmly established in the Island. This is the eighth house they occupied since they left their convent in Galway, during which time they had many trials and privations, but had at all times their schools well attended, which amply recompensed them for all inconveniences.

From this time we begin to see the Order flourish and put forth offshoots into every part of the country. In July, 1851, the first branch house was established in Harbor Grace; in 1852 at Carbineers'; 1853 at Harbor Maine, and also in 1853 at Fermeuse, and at other places. At present there are thirteen branch houses in the Island, and about one hundred and twenty religious, who teach an average of two thousand children annually. After half-a-century of labor and zealous teaching, how much more truth and force are in these words of Dr. Fleming than when he wrote them: "And so the good work goes on. Hundreds of children, nay thousands, are annually sent forth from their schools, trained in the highest principles of virtue and honesty, conferring on our country a blessing incomparably rich, and producing a race of mothers of families such as Newfoundland may be proud of, as having no superior in any part of the world."

The first religious reception ever performed in Newfoundland took place on the 5th of August following the year of the nuns' arrival, viz., 1834. The ceremony, always interesting, was rendered doubly so on account of its novelty, and was witnessed by a large number of people. It had at first been intended to have the ceremony performed in the nuns' private chapel. However, the permission of the Bishop was obtained to have the large upper school-room converted into a temporary chapel for the purpose, for the gratification of those who desired to be present. The proceedings on the occasion are minutely described in a local newspaper, "The Patriot," 12th of August, 1834, at great length. We give here a short account of this beautiful ceremony, besides the symbolic meaning of the mystic right which is always interesting and touching. It must be looked upon in Newfoundland as an event of great importance in our religious annals. The young lady received was Miss Maria Nugent,

sister of John V. Nugent, Esq. The Bishop was assisted
by the Revs. P. Ward, as deacon, T. Waldron, as sub-
deacon, and E. Troy, as master of ceremonies. The Rev.
B. Duffy was also present. The Bishop awaited at the
altar the procession of nuns, who soon appeared, " preceded
by three very young children, nieces of the lady, simply at-
tired in white, one in advance bearing a crucifix and the two
others bearing lighted wax candles in one hand while with
the other they carried between them a beautiful silver basket
containing the habit, the cloak, and the veil. After these
followed two nuns, and then Miss Nugent, fashionably
dressed, and supported by the Rev. Mother on the right
and Mother Assistant on the left. At the conclusion of the
ceremony the Bishop addressed to the newly-received novice
a short and affecting discourse, taking for his text the words
of Luke iv. 18 : 'The spirit of the Lord is upon me ; wherefore he hath anointed me to preach the gospel to the
poor.' "

Here we see the first fruits of the good seed sown by the
faithful children of Nano Nagle, which since that time has
produced such abundant harvests that it is now no longer a
novelty to see the announcement of a religious reception or
profession in our newspapers. This lady, Miss Nugent, not
finding her vocation adapted to the Presentation Order, afterwards joined the Mercy Order, and became a most exemplary *religeuse*, as we shall see farther on.

On November 5th Dr. Fleming published for the first time
in the history of this country a jubilee. On his arrival
with the nuns he found awaiting him an encyclical of Pope
Gregory XVI., addressed to the whole hierarchy, of which
Dr. Fleming, in this his first pastoral, gives a summary :
"It is usual that a Pope on his accession to the pontificate
should address a letter to the Bishops of the Christian world
on the subject of the condition of the Church. . . . The
encyclical letter of his present Holiness will maintain a distinguished place among the monuments of pontifical zeal.
His Holiness appears earnestly afflicted by the news of the

afflictions of the Church; the attacks directed against her; the disordered state of society; the infidelity, insubordination, and vice which had long raged against the Church of Christ, its chief pastors, its prelates, and all its sacred law.

. . . He condemns in the most forcible terms those opinions and maxims which tend to weaken the submission due to princes and to encourage revolt. To these opinions His Holiness opposes the doctrine of St. Paul, who declares that 'all power is from God;' and as the teachers of these opinions have alleged that the first Christians did not revolt because they were not the stronger party, he denounces in the most unqualified terms a doctrine so injurious to religion, so inconsistent with the testimony of history, and so formally opposed to the conduct of the early heroes of Christianity. He quotes the words of St. Eucharius on the subject of the martyrdom of St. Mauritius and his companions, in which the holy martyr says expressly 'that the danger of losing their lives did not induce them to revolt;' and another passage from Tertullian, which states 'that the Christians were very numerous, and that if they suffered themselves to be put to death it was not because they were weak, but because they knew that revolt was never lawful.'"

These observations of the Pontiff were probably called forth by the disturbed and revolutionary state of France at the time. The Holy Father then complains of "indifference in religious matters, bad books, which have been so industriously circulated," and calls on the whole Church to pour forth prayers. The Jubilee in this Island and its Vicariate was proclaimed for two months, viz., from 1st December to the first Sunday in February; the other conditions being the ordinary ones; the visits required being three separate visits of one-half hour to any Catholic church.

This being the first Jubilee of which we have any record in our Church history, I have thought it interesting to dwell in a manner somewhat lengthy upon it.

From this we judge that the Church in Newfoundland was fairly launched upon the career of future greatness. She was beginning to emerge from the antiquated state in which she had hitherto existed, and to bloom with all the beauty of hierarchial development, which fast ripened during the last years of the episcopacy of Dr. Fleming, and came to a grand degree of perfection in the glorious reign of his successor, the Rt. Rev. Dr. Mullock.

CHAPTER XXIII.

DR. FLEMING'S VISITATIONS. — [1834-1836.]

Establishment of a Protestant Bishopric — Dr. Fleming's Visitation Northwards, 1834 — Fogo, Tilting Harbor, Herring Neck, Green Bay, Morton's Harbor, King's Cove — Visitation Southwards, 1835 — Petty Harbor, Ferryland, Fermeuse, Reneuse, Burin — Discomforts of Missionary Life — St. Pierre, Bay d'Espoir, Galtois, Conn River, Indian Settlement — Simplicity and Piety of the Indians — Great Placentia — St. Mary's — Small-pox in St. John's and Petty Harbor.

A PROTESTANT bishopric was established in the Island in 1839, under the title, not of St. John's, but of "Newfoundland." The first Bishop was Dr. Spenser, and on his translation to Jamaica Dr. Feild was appointed his successor. The appointment was, of course, purely a State matter. The words of the instrument of establishment are as follows: "Whereas by letters-patent under the Great Seal of the United Kingdom of Great Britain and Ireland, bearing date at Westminster, the 17th day of July, 1839, in the 3d year of Our reign, We did erect, found, and ordain, make and constitute the Island of Newfoundland to be a Bishop's See, and to be called henceforth the Bishopric of Newfoundland."

During the years 1834 and 1835 Dr. Fleming, notwithstanding all his multifarious business, and the difficulties and obstacles placed in his way, not only in those politico-religious matters, but also in the matter of procuring a site for the cathedral, in which he was then engaged, and which caused him, as we shall see, to cross the ocean three or four times, — notwithstanding all this he found time to make extensive visitations of his Vicariate, both north and west. He has left complete descriptions of these visitations among his numerous writings, particularly in his "*Relazione*" to Propaganda, in his letters to the Annals of the *Propaga-*

tion de la Foi at Lyons, and in his letters to Dr. Spratt, of Dublin. These accounts possess all the interest which generally attaches to voyages and travels, and at the same time give us a vivid picture of the state of Newfoundland at this period. Although some of them have been already published in pamphlet form, yet the others, as far as I know, only exist in the Italian and French, and the latter are now rare and out of print; hence it will be interesting to reproduce them here, so as to preserve them in a more permanent form. I shall, however, strive to curtail them, so as to avoid unnecessary repetitions : —

" When I formed my resolution to visit my poor people in the northern district, I was obliged to accept the kind offer made me by the master, of a gratuitous passage on board a small return fishing-schooner bound for Tilting Harbour, in the island of Fogo. We sailed from St. John's on the 20th of last June, 1834, laden gunwale deep with necessary supplies for the summer's fishers, and I was obliged to go accompanied by only one clergyman, Rev. Mr. Dalton, and without a single domestic, while the vessel was literally crowded with men and women, who were hired for the prosecution of the fishery. Our course being partly along shore, and the wind pretty favourable, we reached our destined port in forty-eight hours.

" The island of Fogo is a barren rock of about one hundred miles in circumference, at the entrance of Green Bay, and only inhabited because the sea around was considered good fishing-ground, having for its capital the Harbour of Fogo. Tilting Harbour, on the south-eastern extremity, is the second principal town, and contains about five hundred inhabitants, and, besides this, there are many little villages containing from twenty to fifty, or one hundred inhabitants each, of which the principal are Jobat's Arm, and another, the entrance to which is called Herring Neck ; and the island gives name to a district returning a member to our Newfoundland House of Assembly. But it is not my intention to give you a geographical description of the country, and therefore, pursuing my tour, I must inform you that at Tilting Harbour I remained four days to recruit after the disagreement of my very uncomfortable voyage, and during my stay I confirmed no fewer than three hundred and four persons, being nearly the entire population.

"From Tilting Harbour I sailed on board a small fishing-boat for Fortune Harbour, situated at the north extremity of Green Bay, intending there to begin, as it is the most remote inhabited part of the British portion of Newfoundland, and next to the French Shore. But the bay is exceedingly open, and generally tempestuous, and as the passage across is not less than from fifty to sixty miles, we could not have much confidence in our little craft, and were obliged, after beating about for a day, to put into Jobat's Arm in distress, where we continued until the next day; and having been obliged to send back the boat that conveyed us so far, we were kindly accommodated with a boat and crew by Mr. Henry Stark, and sailed next morning, but not until I had offered the Holy Sacrifice and administered Confirmation to ninety-eight individuals; but finding, after a day and a night, that a rough sea and contrary winds and threatening weather promised us a longer passage than we anticipated, and seeing that it was only by this boat, and the exertions of the two men who worked her under him, that poor Stark supported his helpless family, I was most anxious to get into some port where I might have an opportunity of releasing them, and procuring a fresh crew; but the worthy fellows felt hurt at the proposition, and when, in the course of the morning after, we were put into the Harbour of Fogo in distress, they exulted at my disappointment when they found I could not procure another boat.

"We sailed from Fogo in a few hours, determined to struggle on, but again, towards the next evening (the eve of the festival of SS. Peter and Paul), were driven into Herring Neck, where we enjoyed the humble, though cordial, hospitality of Mr. and Mrs. Kent, and where, for the first time since we left the comfortable residence of Mr. Burke, of Tilting Harbour, we indulged in the luxury of a bed; and thus were we for four days beaten about at every side of the Island of Fogo, and it was not until the evening of the fifth we entered Fortune Harbour.

"Here were we, then, in an open boat, without the least shelter from the inclemency of the weather, — a boat, taken at once from the fishery, covered with the slime of fish, now rendered putrid from the action of the sun, — after inhaling that putrescence for five days, and being in distress for provisions, at length permitted to land in our destined port; and here we released our poor men and their boat, after so long an abscence from those avocations to which their families were to look for support; and as it happened to have proved, I believe, the only good week of the fishery in that quarter, their sacrifice for our accommodation must have been great indeed, and is to me, even now, a cause of heartfelt regret.

"And now, who can define my feelings on entering this wild district, there to commence the toils of my visitation, at a distance, in the most direct way, of near four hundred miles from my residence, but increased, in my devious and perilous course, upwards of six hundred; or who portray my gratitude to God for inspiring me with fortitude, as He had blessed me with health and spirits, to embark in an undertaking so hazardous?

"I found about forty families, comprising the entire population of this harbour, principally Irish, or the descendants of Irish settlers, and never shall I forget the burst of affection, of exultation, with which we were received among them.

"It was evening on the first of July when we slowly approached the high and commanding shores on the northwest side of Green Bay, and weary as we were, our limbs crippled from constant sitting, our heavy eyelids closing from want of sleep, our spirits depressed, and our crew at length exhausted with exertion; yet, subdued as we were, we could not refrain from admiring the sublimity of the prospect before us: the majesty of the mountains, crowned by eternal forests, as the setting sun poured its 'liquid light' through the foliage. We were becalmed as we stood before the narrow inlet, and our crew were unable to row our craft in. We were perceived from the shore, and curiosity to ascertain who were the strangers brought out a boat to see us. Upon learning who we were they returned, and in a little time after skiffs (for there is not a single sail-boat in the entire harbour) came out to tow us in, and we entered amid the acclamations of all, men, women, and children; all had left their employments, and the evening was devoted to festivity, and closed with thanksgiving to Heaven for imparting to them — who, in the memory of man, had been only twice visited by a clergyman — so great a blessing.

"I remained here three days, during which time there was a total cessation from business, so anxious were the poor people to show us every attention; and the unaffected pain we felt at parting was considerably enhanced by the honest effusion of unsophisticated sorrow that burst from all, and the tear that trembled on the eyelid, or rolled along the furrowed cheek of the weather-beaten fisherman.

"In the entire Island I have not met a people so well instructed in their religion, or among whom reigns so much virtue, or a place where vice is so little known, — and all this good, under God, to be attributed to the virtues of three families. The fathers of these excellent families assemble the entire population alternately at their houses on Sundays and holydays, where public prayer is offered and a spiritual lecture read, and in the evenings of Lent and Advent the Rosary and a lecture; while the mid hours of the Sabbath thoughout the year are devoted by Mrs. Power, that truly Christian matron, in instructing the children of her neighbours to walk in the paths of religion and morality, — in training their infant lips to lisp the praises of Him who thus raises, even in 'the desert,' lights to guide to happiness eternal. This excellent woman is a German, and received her education from a community of nuns in her native country.

"Oh, how did my bosom throb with emotion upon witnessing the fruits, the extraordinary fruits, resulting from the pious example and religious instruction of one good woman, when I reflected that, in a few years, by the instrumentality of my little convent of St. John's, in every harbour, and every creek, and every cove in the Island, would be found mothers diffusing around them, like Mrs. Power, the blessings that Heaven had so abundantly imparted to them! and how it did confirm the confidence I entertained that that invaluable institution, poor as it now is, must flourish, destined, as it is, by God for the regeneration of a people! I met these good people in joy, and parted with them in pain. I said before, that in the entire harbour there is not one sailboat, and, therefore, I must of necessity commence my wanderings home in a small skiff, which they call here a 'punt.' It is something like your jolly-boats, or rather whale-boats, but not as seaworthy; and in this giddy bark, built to contain from two to three quintals, or hundred-weight, of fish, and now sunk to the gunwale by the addition to the crew, consisting of four persons, of us two men, — in this confined thing, where, when crippled with long sitting, we could not extend our limbs, nor dare to stand erect for fear of upsetting the skiff, we pulled off to cross the extensive and turbulent waters of Green Bay.

"This magnificent bay comprehends several smaller bays, each of which in itself would be considered too large to cross in a tolerably-sized sail fishing-boat. We could not, of course, be expected to feel quite secure in our little craft. However, as it was my intention to visit the harbours and creeks along the shore, we continued to coast along until the evening of the first day, when we put into a place called Ship Run, inhabited by only two families, where I exchanged a couple of hands for a younger and fresher pair, and, having passed the night there, sailed in the morning for Morton's Harbour.[1] Here, on our arrival, I first began to feel fatigued,

---

[1] Dr. Fleming met in this harbour one of the native American Indians, and promised to return next June to meet the several Indian tribes of that coast at the River Exploits.

and when I at first essayed to use my limbs, they refused to sustain my body; but, as I could not procure a fresh crew, I was forced to press forward to Fogo, because between these two harbours there was no place in which I could hope to get a boat or crew. But I cannot pass here without adverting to the warm hospitality exhibited toward us by Mr. Taylor, an honest Protestant settler. He lives a little outside of Morton's Harbour, and, upon hearing of our arrival, he at once came down to press us to refresh ourselves at his house. He said we looked fatigued, and that he had comfortable beds, and abundant means of recruiting us amid our hardships, and offered us that strongest of all inducements, a 'hearty welcome,' urging expressly, and with marked kindness, that if he had a palace at his disposal he should feel happy at offering it for our use; and our only regret in leaving the harbour was at our inability to gratify his wishes; but I shall ever retain the memory of his kindness, and if it ever again be my fate to visit that coast I shall not pass without testifying to him the sense I entertain of his sterling worth.

"We sailed now once more for Fogo, and, with excessive exertion, reached that port after a passage of four-and-twenty hours (the wind heading us the entire way); but night coming on I implored the crew to get ashore, that we might renew the circulation of the blood in our long-contracted limbs; and we accordingly did go ashore, and lighting a fire, we lay alongside of it on the rocks and slept till morning,— the soundest and most refreshing sleep we ever in our lives enjoyed.

"But I have exhausted your patience and my paper. Suffice it to say, that, in the course of our short summer, I accomplished a journey of at least more than twelve hundred miles, visiting forty-six harbours in my circuit through Green Bay, Bonavista Bay, Trinity Bay, and Conception Bay; that I administered the Sacrament of Confirmation to upwards of three thousand persons; of Penance and Eucharist to more than that number. For the greater part of the time I knew

not the luxury of a bed, while for days and nights together
I had not an opportunity of reclining even on the thwart of
the boat; I had not been able for days to take off my clothes;
I seldom met with better fare than a hard sea-biscuit and a
little fish, sometimes a bit of fat pork out of the pickle,
while I had not an opportunity of indulging myself in my
exhaustion with a single glass of wine; no variety of food
whatever, except when the men would land on some desolate
rocky island, and, robbing the sea-fowl of their eggs, strike
a fire and roast them on the rocks; while at the same time
the stench of the boat from bilge-water, mixed with putrid
fish, so affected my stomach as to induce a severe bilious
attack, which developed itself upon my return. Add to this,
that I have only painted our hardships by sea; but if I
described our wanderings by land, crossing pathless promon-
tories, and winding round bays, through forests and morasses,
frequently when bathed in perspiration, and fainting with
exhaustion under a burning sun; obliged to plunge into a
river to wade across, and then unable to change till our
clothes had dried on our backs; our shoes worn from our
feet, and our clothes in tatters, torn by the thick underwood,
— you may form some idea of the difficulties of our Mission.

"But why should I close this without acknowledging the
warmth of feeling exhibited to us in King's Cove by Mr.
Mullowney, of Cork, a gentleman truly worthy of representing John Macbraire, Esq., of Tweedhill, in Berwickshire, son
of the late warm-hearted James Macbraire, Esq., the most
opulent merchant of this country, and one of the most benevolent founders of the 'Benevolent Irish Society,' always
remarkable for the munificence of his donations to the poor
and his kindness to the Catholic clergy.

"Mr. Mullowney, Mr. Macbraire's agent, received us with
all that cordiality which marks his character, and tried every
means in his power, and, indeed, with considerable success,
to alleviate our sufferings. Here we enjoyed comforts that
those only can appreciate who have passed days and nights
together ever sitting in one spot and in one posture without

daring to move, and even then only varying by snatching a hasty repose stretched at the bottom of a fishing-boat, or upon the bare surface of the hard rock. We did enjoy the kindness of Mr. Mullowney, but yet not alone in his hospitality, but when we were forced to move for another harbour, he had a boat prepared for our reception, the master and crew of which were directed not to leave us until we had finished our tour; and, in compliance with his injunctions, they brought us to the several harbours in Trinity Bay we intended to visit, and at length returned to King's Cove, after bringing us to Bay-de-Verds, in Conception Bay, where, after having made a visitation of the different harbours, we closed our wearisome wanderings for the season. While speaking of Mr. Mullowney, I must not omit to acknowledge the polite attentions of Mr. Drawbridge, of Greenspond, the respectable agent of Mr. Garland, of the house of George R. Robinson, Brooking, Garland, & Co., who received us with the warmest hospitality."

"Having suffered severely during this visitation from being obliged to make long passages across the bays in small oar-boats, where it was impossible for hours to change posture, one must of necessity keep sitting, for to stand upright would be to endanger the lives of all by overturning the boat. Then to be obliged to pass whole days and nights in this miserable plight was more than my constitution could bear, and for some months after my return I found myself in a very delicate state of health." He determined, therefore, to have a small schooner of about thirty tons built for himself. "The thought of so great an enterprise," he says in his '*Relazione*,' "at first frightened me; but I undertook it, confiding in Heaven, which, as it had helped me hitherto, would not, I felt, abandon me now.

"I gave directions to have a small vessel built of about thirty tons burden, and this vessel was not ready to sail until the middle of July, for which reason I was compelled to abandon my first intention of visiting the northward, and consequently was obliged most reluctantly to disappoint the Indians; but as I was already aware that they were a people exceedingly jealous of the least attempt to deceive them, lest they should happen to be subjected to any inconvenience, or to feel any annoyance at not finding me at the time and place of meeting, I sought and found an opportunity of acquainting them of the circumstance of my detention and consequent change of route, and told them I would certainly meet them in the Bay of Despair about the close of that month.

"The noon of Friday, July 17, 1835, found me weighing anchor on board the little schooner 'Madonna,' with a crew consisting of three hands and the skipper, accompanied by the Rev. C. Dalton, pastor of Harbour Grace, who had been the zealous and unflinching companion of my toils the year before, and the Rev. M. Berney, pastor of Bruin; and although our deck was encumbered with a thousand feet of board, or, as we call it here, *lumber*, we sailed out of the harbour in gallant style, and in a few minutes cleared the southward point, and in an hour cast anchor in the harbour of Petty Harbour, and discharged our lumber for the chapel.

"This little town is within the district or parish of St. John's, and about eight miles distant, and separated from it by a road, or rather path, that is hardly passable but in winter. The entrance to the harbour is esteemed dangerous, but the harbour still affords good anchorage and shelter from every wind. Like almost all other towns, there are no streets, but the houses stand irregularly scattered about; but there is here this peculiarity, which, indeed, occurs in one or two other places in the Island also, that the site of the town is so very rocky as not to afford sufficient earth for the raising of one month's supply of vegetables for the inhabitants. But as I may again advert to this place, I shall proceed with my narrative.

"The wind that served to bring us into Petty Harbour would not answer to take us out again. We were compelled to tarry there for the remainder of that day and the entire

of Saturday, and on Sunday, after having offered the Divine
Sacrifice, we again set sail for the southward; but the wind
again heading us, we were obliged to put into Ferryland,
which place we were not able to make until about noon on
Monday, although distant from Petty Harbour only about
nine leagues.

"This harbour affords quite a contrast to Petty Harbour:
in the latter, to the very water's edge, where the hills do not
come down precipitously to the shore, the land is covered
with immense masses of stone imbedded upon a foundation
of solid rock, so that you would be inclined to think that it
was almost necessary to exercise ingenuity in order to discover a site for a house; and as for gardens, I believe the
largest in Petty Harbour would hardly measure ten yards
square, and even to these the only means of conveying
manure is on men's backs up steep, craggy precipices; while
in Ferryland you find yourself in the midst of a smiling
country, the immediate neighbourhood of the town flat and
fertile, but surrounded by high and sterile hills.

"The harbour itself is rather capacious, being about three-
quarters of a mile wide when you pass an island that stands
at the entrance, called Isle du Bois. It is well sheltered,
except to the north-east, and affords good anchorage; but
the winds from the north-east produce a heavy and dangerous swell within. The houses here are generally more comfortable, and here several large concerns are falling to decay,
owing to the declension of the fishery, which had been
formerly carried on with great spirit on this coast.

"I had not intended to put into Ferryland, at least until I
should be returning, because, as the summer was rather
advanced, I preferred pushing on as quickly as possible, to
give an opportunity to those in squestered situations, who
had never had the gratification of seeing their Bishops, of
approaching the Holy Sacrament of Confirmation, and as I
had a few years before administered Confirmation in that
harbour, I was not so anxious on their account; and for these
reasons, when I did land, I found the people not prepared,

and the clergyman, the Rev. Timothy Brown, absent, and therefore I took a boat and proceeded to Fermeuse, about four miles west, and having chanced to meet the Rev. J. Duffy, the curate of this district, as I was stepping on board, that reverend gentleman accompanied us.

"He had been prepared to receive us at Fermeuse; and when, upon my arrival there, I proceeded to examine those whom he had instructed upon the importance of the Sacrament, and the dispositions necessary to receive it worthily, I was gratified to find that, among one hundred and twenty individuals, there was not one who did not give abundant proofs that a zealous and indefatigable teacher had found a docile and susceptible congregation, and that the seeds which the Rev. J. Duffy scattered had not fallen by the 'roadside' or 'among thorns,' but had been laid in a fruitful soil, and promised an abundant harvest.

"On the next day, Tuesday, the 21st, after having offered the Divine Sacrifice of the Mass at the chapel, and exhorted a densely crowded congregation, I administered Confirmation to that number, and immediately after sent forward a messenger to acquaint the people of Renews that I should visit that harbour next morning.

"On the morning of Wednesday, 22d, having made our matin offering of the Holy Sacrifice, we again took boat for Renews, about four miles distant, and entered the harbour about noon. This is a poor fishing harbour, but inhabited by a very intelligent people; and here, as well as in Fermeuse, the Rev. J. Duffy's zeal in the promotion of religion is manifested in the construction of a commodious church, attached to which will be a comfortable residence for the clergyman. The people here, too, I found exceedingly well instructed, and all the children well acquainted with their Catechism, owing to the unaided exertions of the same reverend gentleman; and on the following morning, Thursday, 23d, I administered Confirmation to one hundred and forty persons, a large proportion of whom were converts to our holy religion.

"From this place we returned the same day to Fermeuse,

where, having again enjoyed the hospitality of Mr. Neill, we joined our little vessel, and on the next day we proceeded on our voyage; but having arrived at Trepassey Bay, we got completely becalmed and enveloped in a dense fog, and therefore found it necessary to come to anchor under Cape Pine, the western entrance of the bay. This being a most dangerous shore, we took advantage of a light breeze that sprung up during the night and got under weigh once more; but after a short time the wind died away, and we again got becalmed at the entrance of this bay, where the tide runs eight knots an hour.

"The night was intensely dark, and we continued drifting for a considerable time, when we were alarmed by the cry of the seamen, 'Breakers astern!' and immediately we could distinctly hear the sullen roar of the surge as it rushed against the rocks, and, breaking, dashed its foam into the face of heaven, as if in anger at the interruption; and inevitable death seemed to threaten. We let go our kedge anchor, but the force of the tide and the violence of the swelling waves rendered it of little avail; yet was it not altogether useless, for by pulling upon the hawser we brought her head a little around, and then cutting away our anchor, a slight air of wind springing up at the same moment, our vessel's side all but touched as she drifted along a ridge against which we had been running; and in this manner, at the expense of our anchor and cable, were we, by the interposition of Divine Mercy, saved from a fearful and instantaneous death.

"We now sailed with a fair wind for our destination; but again in a few hours it altered; and after a fatiguing passage of nearly three days, we arrived on the morning of the 27th July at Burin, into which place I next put, and where I remained an entire week.

"At Burin we enjoyed the comfortable fireside and cordial welcome of the companion of our voyage, the Rev. Mr. Berney; and as the entire population of that portion of the district which lies along the western shore of Placentia Bay is scattered over an immense number of islands, we were.

obliged to defer the time of administering Confirmation there to the following Sunday, the entire week being requisite to advertise the people and bring them together.

"Burin is an island about three miles in length, and lying north and south, nearly a mile from the mainland, and about it you find a large number of islands, some of which are covered with wood; and the population upon these is so thin and scattered that one friend cannot visit another but by boat. The Island of Burin is for the most part a solid rock, scarcely affording anything like pasture; and, in some instances, those who wish to enjoy the comfort of a garden at their house must bring soil from other places, and we used while there vegetables raised by our respected host in a garden so created.

"Upon coming ashore, I was most agreeably surprised to find that all my anticipations of the state of the Church and the parochial residence of the clergyman, etc., were surpassed. The bold position of the church — its site being upon a very commanding height, rising almost precipitously from the shore; its neatly finished Gothic windows; the tasteful manner in which it is painted; the simple and chaste style of the altar; the neatness around you at all sides; the handsome and light galleries; and, then, the sacred habiliments of the clergyman, — all gratified me in the extreme, and found the most pleasing commentary upon the piety and zeal of that reverend gentleman.

"The house is also a very neat and comfortable edifice, adjoining the church, and with a handsome and well-laid-out garden, which runs in front the full length of the house and church, forms an *ensemble* truly creditable to the taste and industry of the Rev. Mr. Berney, and present to the contemplative observer the most convincing proof that the virtues of the pastor are well estimated by the congregation.

"On Sunday, August the 2d, the festival of the dedication of St. Mary of Angels, a large congregation assembled, and after having celebrated Mass, at which an excellent choir assisted, exhorted those who were to be confirmed on the importance of the act they were about to perform, and the happy results that must follow to those who receive so holy a sacrament with the proper dispositions, I administered Confirmation to ninety-four persons, who had been previously well prepared and instructed, and amongst whom were no fewer than thirty-six heads of families, converts to the Roman Catholic faith; and on the next day, Monday, I again administered that sacrament to twenty persons, who came from a great distance, and had not been able to reach in time to be confirmed the day before, making the entire number at Burin one hundred and fifteen.

"Burin is the last ecclesiastical district to the westward; it commences from Little Paradise, in Placentia Bay, and runs down southward to Cape Chapeau Rouge, which, with Cape St. Mary's to the east, forms the entrance to Placentia Bay, being there sixteen leagues and a half wide. From Cape Chapeau Rouge it strikes to the westward as far as Cape Ray, and from Cape Ray runs again north even to Belle Isle in the Straits.

"But what facility do we find in thus defining the limits of a district in Newfoundland? How easy to tell you that the northern district extends from the Grates to Cape John! But when you are told that it includes the vast bays of Trinity, Bonavista, Gander Bay, Bay of Exploits, White Bay, and Bay of Notre Dame, comprehending a coast of probably twelve hundred miles in length, you may have some idea of the manner in which the duties are to be performed by the clergyman; particularly when you learn that in many harbours you will find no more than two families, in some only one, and a large number containing less than ten; and, then, the vast multitude of islands similarly inhabited, for which the coast of Newfoundland is remarkable, — you will perceive clearly that many, very many, indeed, in those remote and isolated places must of necessity appear before the eternal throne of the Most High God unaided by the saving graces communicated in the holy sacraments.

"In that very northern district, if I had it in my power to

have two additional clergymen, one to place in Trinity Bay, and another in Fortune Harbour. These with the clergymen at present in Tilting Harbour, and the Rev. N. Devereux, in King's Cove, in Bonavista Bay, I would hope that the poor people in that quarter would be attended to; but, then, a vast majority of the people of Trinity Bay are Protestants, and the few Catholics are far apart, and poor, so that the clergyman allocated there, as also in Fortune Harbour, should be supported by a stipend raised elsewhere.

"An annoying circumstance, but one which will enable you to estimate the comfort of a lodging in such a dwelling better than any description I could give, occurred to me on my former visitation to the northward. You are aware that I was, on all my little voyages, confined to boats, sometimes small and sometimes large. When I would get into the large class of boats, I could enjoy the luxury of leaning; for, with my back naturally weak, it was my greatest comfort when freed from the stiffness of my position in the smaller boats. Indeed, I could seldom sit upright, but kept constantly leaning forward on that part of the false deck where the people laid the board for our meals; and even while partaking of their rude fare, as it was flung out of the pot upon the board, — for it usually consisted of pork and fish boiled together, which they call 'fish and vang,'—I could not refrain from such indulgence, even though at the expense of my coat.

"At length, one morning when I arose, after having enjoyed the comfort of being able to sleep upon a bed, I dressed, and, on putting on my coat, fancy my surprise at finding one of the sleeves literally taken away; but, upon investigating, I found that the reason was that, my bed having been upon the floor of the house, although what might be called a comfortable one, I had stuffed my clothes along in the spaces to keep out the musquitoes and galleynippers, and that the sleeve of my coat had passed through the interstices, and having been considerably impregnated with the juice of the fishermen's food, imbibed from the 'vang-board,' the entire sleeve, from the elbow, was eaten away by the dogs or the rats.

"On the morning of Tuesday, August 4, at an early hour, our bunting was hoisted, and the Cross floated gallantly at our fore, and the principal people of Burin raised the Union and their several house-flags, to compliment us on our departure. When we got under way we were gratified by a salute with cannon from the battery of St. Patrick, and again from that of St. George; and when the establishment of Mr. Page, a highly respectable English gentleman, opened upon us, we were paid a similar mark of respect, and in a few moments afterwards cleared the harbour of Burin, and bore away for Cape Chapeau Rouge; but having made the Cape, and stretched a few leagues along the shore, the wind proving unfavourable, we were compelled to steer our course for St. Peter's.

"This island is not within the jurisdiction of the Vicar Apostolic of Newfoundland. It is a small French island, about a dozen leagues from Cape Chapeau Rouge, and the curé has jurisdiction immediately from the Holy See. Here we arrived the same evening, and having paid our respects to the Very Rev. Dr. Olivier and his *vicaire*, M. Lamie, we departed on Wednesday morning, with a fair wind, for Bay Despair, and on the evening of the same day anchored in Hermitage Bay, where we notified to the few inhabitants, and among them the old man of the name of Long of whom I spoke before, that on the day after the morrow the Bishop would celebrate Mass and administer the Sacrament of Confirmation at Galtaus, the principal harbour of Long Island, at the entrance of Bay Despair.

"Nothing could equal the delight of these poor people at hearing the comforting intelligence. At first they could scarce give it credence; but as the rumour of our intended visit had already reached them, they were easily led to believe, and shed tears of joy and gratitude. In the morning we sailed over to Galtaus, and on my arrival I was politely accommodated by Mr. Gallop, the highly respectable agent of the house of Newman & Co., with a whale-boat and crew, and in this way proceeded myself to advertise the people in the adjacent coves and harbours of my arrival; and short as was the notice, I, on the following morning, August 7th, administered Confirmation to fifty-four persons, and received two converts into the Church. Next day I left Galtaus for Bay Despair, and our course for that bay was through the narrow defile or strait called Long Island Passage.

"On the 8th of August we entered this passage. It was a delightful day, and we ran along before a light breeze, at the rate of five knots an hour, through what I may call a beautiful marine avenue, running due north about twenty-five miles, and bounded on both sides by most magnificent forests. The sun had already ascended pretty high in his course, and as we brushed along rapidly, nearly touching both shores at the same time, I thought Nature had exhausted all her powers to render the scene enchanting.

"The shore on the right and on the left rose precipitously, and the forests literally hung over the summit, while the sun poured through the foliage its liquid light, giving an ever-varying lustre, shedding an eternally changing charm upon the landscape. We felt as if we were touching an unexplored country, where all that can beautify or embellish, all that can cheer or animate the face of nature is ever bright and ever verdant, and where darkness and sterility are unknown; such was the aspect of the country all along these uninhabited coasts.

"When you pass Long Island you are in the centre of Bay Despair, which here spreads east and west, and throws its vast arms in these directions far into the land; one arm as if anxious to meet with Gander Bay, and the other rushing to embrace the Bay of Exploits, leaving only a few miles of land separating the extremities, so that the Indians, passing from the northern settlement to that of Bay Despair, have little more than one day's journey to travel by land.

"The eastward branch was our course, and we passed along the coast of the charming Isle du Bois; and sailing by the mouth of Little River, at length came in sight of the Indian wigwams at the entrance of Conne River early in the day. These present a singular appearance to the stranger. Imagine to yourself a large collection of tents irregularly disposed, constructed of long straight poles stuck in the ground and coming together at the top, tied with birch fastenings, and the whole kept in a circular form by means of hoops within, and covered with the bark of trees. At the entrance of the river a high sand-bank runs across, leaving barely room for a vessel to enter the pond or basin within, and upon this peninsular bank are those conical tents or wigwams disposed.

"Upon our approach the inhabitants fled, but the instant we hoisted the flag, on which a cross was displayed, to the masthead, confidence seemed restored, and they returned from the woods; and what was my annoyance to learn that, although these poor people had been two months expecting me in this place, for they had heard of my intended route to the westward even before they received my message, some evil-disposed person acquainted them, as if from authority, that no clergyman would visit them this year.

"A few men and women, however, could not be dissuaded from waiting, so that in place of meeting at this rendezvous from two to three hundred Indians, I only found twenty-eight persons, whose joy in seeing us was testified by a thousand little innocent extravagancies. We remained with them till the following Wednesday, instructed them through an interpreter, said Mass every day in their wigwams, heard their confessions, and finally confirmed twenty-seven of their number, the others having been confirmed fifty years ago in Canada.

"The simplicity of the manners of these people is truly interesting; and their piety, the air of recollection they exhibit at their devotions, their attachment to their religion, and their veneration for its ministers, are edifying in the extreme. In rearing their children they are particularly careful to instil into their tender minds a love of purity and attachment to every virtue. Wherever they settle for a season, for they lead a wandering life, the first thing they do is to unite, and by their joint labour erect a large wigwam, which they use as a house of prayer; and should any of their tribe offend against public morals, he is invariably excluded from this church, and, in some cases, is never again permitted to enter until his offence is wiped away in the Sacrament of Penance; and they invariably observe the Sabbath with the most scrupulous exactness.

"On Sundays and holydays of the year they invariably assemble together in the morning, and after singing the *Kyrie Eleison*, the *Gloria*, and *Credo*, they offer the Rosary, and some other prayers, usually occupying an hour; and in the afternoon they again meet and sing Vespers, for they have not only books of devotion written in their own language, but also the principal hymns and psalms set to the Gregorian chant. But the curiosity of some may probably be excited at learning that I heard their confessions, although I did not understand their language. The mode I adopted was simple; and as it deviated from the manner in which they made their former confessions — being through an interpreter — I shall relate it. In the great wigwam or church I caused a partition to be raised of deer-skin, and having seated myself with my interpreter at one side close to the skin or partition, and in such a way as that neither could see the penitent, who knelt at the other side of the skin, I reached my hand behind the partition, where I held that of the penitent. I now put such interrogatories as I judged necessary through the interpreter; and, as I had previously carefully instructed them in the manner in which they were to conduct themselves, the replies were given, not orally, but the affirmatives by a gentle pressure of my hand, and the negatives by a withdrawal of theirs. In this manner I heard the confessions of the whole.

"And now came the period of departure, and nothing could exceed the grief of the entire number, which vented itself alternately, amid sighs and tears, in entreaties to prolong our stay, and complaints of the shortness of our visit; but on the morning of Wednesday, when our colours were hoisted, and they saw us determined to sail, they all turned out armed with long strand guns, and saluted us with several volleys, fired with the most unerring exactness, and several *feus de joie*, that seemed to betray long practice. The dexterity of the women in loading and firing these heavy pieces, seven or eight feet long, was particularly amusing to us; and as long as we continued in sight, these warlike compliments were continued quicker in succession than it is possible for you to conceive.

"On Wednesday, the 12th, we sailed from this interesting tribe for Great Jervis Harbour, at the extremity of the bay, where only four families reside, and having hoisted our flag as a signal to those at a distance, — for we had here no means of communicating with the neighbouring harbours, — we collected about thirty next day, of whom I confirmed twenty-four.

"On Friday we steered for St. Peter's once more, on our return, and on the same evening cast anchor in the harbour, where we experienced the politest attentions from the Rev. Dr. Olivier and the local authorities, and having been pressed to remain for the Sunday, I celebrated a Pontifical High Mass; and on the Sunday following, August 18th, set sail for Cape Chapeau Rouge, and entered the harbour of Great St. Lawrence the same evening, and as a practicable pathway runs from Great St. Lawrence to Little St. Lawrence, the people of the latter place were soon advertised of our coming; but as I was given to understand that a messenger was despatched to Lawn, about seven or eight miles distant overland, where one or two families reside, I waited until Thursday, when, having discovered that the messenger had not gone, I was under the necessity of proceeding without them; and on Thursday, the 24th, I had the satisfaction of administering Confirmation to sixty-five persons, a majority of whom were converts and the children of converts to the faith. Immediately after we set sail for Burin, in order to leave the Rev. Mr. Berney at home, and reached that harbour on that evening.

"On Friday, 1st of August, we sailed from Burin for Great Placentia, at the opposite side of the bay, but much higher up; and having reached the latter rather late, we stood off during the night, and in the morning, the wind proving rather baffling, Mr. Murphy, the worthy agent of my friend Mr. Sweetman, who had received instructions from that excellent gentleman to make our stay in Placentia as comfortable as possible, sent out boats to tow us in, and early on Saturday we cast anchor in Placentia Harbour.

"On Sunday, the 23d, I administered the Sacrament of Confirmation to eighty persons, amongst whom were many, and particularly several of the most respectable inhabitants, who had been converted to the faith; and on Monday I again conferred Confirmation upon twenty-nine persons, who came up from near the extremity of the bay, and had arrived too late the day before, making the number one hundred and nine in all.

"On Monday, the 23d, we sailed from this harbour, having, during our stay, received the kindest attentions in the house of Mr. Sweetman, whose absence in Ireland deprived us then of the pleasure of personally expressing our acknowledgments. In a couple of hours we got into Little Placentia, being only about three leagues to the northward, where we had the pleasure of meeting the Rev. Mr. Nowlan, who had been lately appointed to that district; and it afforded me the sincerest satisfaction to find, both here and in Great Placentia, his congregation loud in praise of his exertions to afford them the comforts of religion.

"Here we remained till Sunday, the 30th. These five days we passed hearing confessions and instructing the congregation, whom we found well prepared by that reverend gentleman; and never did I meet a people more attached to their religion, or more devoted to its ministers, than the people of this entire district, and on Sunday I had no fewer than ninety-four to whom to administer Confirmation.

"On Monday, August 31st, we steered our course for Barren Island, near the head of the bay, on the western shore, where we arrived that evening, and on the next day I confirmed sixty-two persons; and as the day was considerably advanced, and I at length began to feel weary, I deferred our departure till the day following, when we sailed for Meracheen, in the island of that name, which lies a short distance, about a league, to the southward of Barren Island; but that part to which we were bound being seven leagues distant, we reached there on Wednesday evening, where we remained till the Sunday following.

"On Sunday, September the 6th, I confirmed eighty-six persons in this harbour, among whom were twenty-six who had been converted to the Catholic faith; and immediately after the ceremony of the morning I was waited upon by two men who stated that they were Protestants, that they were induced to accompany their Catholic neighbours out of a frolic and through curiosity, and had attended that morning in the place where we had celebrated with a propensity to turn everything into ridicule, but that the instructions there given, both before and after Confirmation, dissipated their errors, and convinced them that ours was the true faith.

"To the instruction of these sincere children of grace I devoted this day, deferring my intended departure till the next. In the course of the same day a third individual was added, and in the evening I admitted them publicly into the Church. In the morning I administered Confirmation to twelve persons, including these three converts, whom God has so signally rescued from the ways of error. Thus was the total number of persons confirmed at Meracheen ninety-eight. Immediately after the close of the ceremonies we departed, bearing away for St. Mary's Bay, and anchored on Tuesday evening in St. Mary's Harbour.

"Here we again met the Rev. James Duffy, against whom there had been a rumor circulated that proceedings at law were instituted for the alleged offence of, with a party of rioters, tearing down and destroying a fish-flake on the premises of

Messrs. Slade, Elson, & Co., at St Mary's, who have a large concern here, over which an agent of the name of Martin presides, who seems exceedingly obnoxious to the people.

"The flake had really been destroyed; but, then, it had occurred in the January before, and we were now come to September, and it appeared to me that this charge was merely kept hanging over the reverend gentleman and the poor people of St. Mary's for vile party purposes; and what tended to confirm this opinion of mine was, that now the Circuit Judge was about to close his labours, after having held his court in all the adjoining harbours, as well as in the harbour of St. Mary's, and yet there were no informations lodged or evidence taken upon the subject; and therefore, under such circumstances, I thought it the duty of his Bishop, where the character of a clergyman was for many months made the butt at which to level every foul and envenomed shaft of the traducer, and yet deny him the privilege of a legal investigation, — I thought it my duty to institute a rigid inquiry into the circumstances, the result of which was that I was compelled to acquit both the priest and people of even the substance of criminality.

"I am quite sure you will acquit me of any intention of impugning your knowledge of any of the liberal arts and sciences if I at once conclude that you know nothing at all of a fish-flake. This is an erection raised for the purpose of drying fish. In this country sea-beaches are very few, so that necessity, the parent of invention, has taught the people, as it were, a mode of creating beaches, even amongst the rudest rocks. A number of shores or uprights are fixed in the ground, and upon these are nailed a sufficient quantity of beams, by which the whole frame is firmly connected. On these beams a floor of wattles, or, as we call them, 'longures,' probably from the Latin *longurius*, is laid. The extremity of this floor generally rests on the ground, or on very low stakes, while the height of the uprights increases as they run into the sea or to the water's edge, so that the floor presents a perfect level, sometimes of several hundred square feet, and then it is covered with the light tops of boughs tied down with birch fastenings, upon which the fish is spread, and in this manner is there, where the beach is insufficient, a valuable substitute provided.

"In St. Mary's Harbour, the house I have alluded to have very extensive premises; and their agent, Mr. Martin, got into the House of Assembly, and although petitioned against by two thousand people as not legally qualified, — not being a householder, — *his own vote was allowed to negative the motion for inquiry into that qualification;* and shortly after he was invested with the commission of the peace, — the only magistrate in St. Mary's Bay.

"I found the harbour of St. Mary's like almost every other harbour in Newfoundland, a collection of houses built at irregular distances, not forming anywhere a street or a lane, and commanding a good beach, backed by rising ground rather clear, which proved useful to the people for all public purposes; and from the oldest inhabitants of the bay, men more than seventy years of age, I learned that, as long as they and their fathers remembered, this beach, and the mound behind, were regarded as public property; nor had any one during that immense lapse of time ever laid claim to a right of proprietary. On the mound, many years ago, had been erected a Catholic church by the people; but, owing to the exposure of the situation, it was blown down. A second was erected on a different site, but this was literally blown over the hill; and now the people, under the direction of the Rev. James Duffy, who has much distinguished himself by his activity in urging on the erection of churches throughout that district, determined to come down nearer the beach, and excavate a site for the church, and thus place it beyond a possibility of meeting a similar fate.

"As this beach was the only place that was not occupied privately, of course it was the only place of landing, not only for the people of St. Mary's, but for the inhabitants of the other parts of the bay, who, as the mound was appropriated as a public cemetery, required the use of the beach as a public passage; and, again, this beach and this mound were the only places on which the people could claim a right to spread out their nets, etc., for drying, or on which they could draw up their boats to remain for the winter, or to repair in the spring.

"In the winter of 1834-5 it seems a poor man named Fewer erected a flake on a part of this beach; but scarcely was it up when Mr. Martin, the magistrate, before day in the morning, brought a party to cut it down; and so far, I apprehend, he acted very properly; but in place of stopping here, he commenced at once to run a new flake for his house *the full length* of the beach, thus at once cutting off the public from a possibility of conveniently using their church ground or their cemetery, and depriving all the inhabitants of the only place on which they could haul up their boats and craft in the winter; and the natural result was, that as the magistrate had clearly shown them, in the instance of Fewer's flake, that a public nuisance, and obstructing the highway, may be legally removed and destroyed by any person, they proceeded with the erection of their church, occasionally giving Martin notice to remove the flake.

"At length the church was finished; and now they cut the flake across at Martin's boundary, and again noticed him that they would destroy the entire of the new flake as it extended from this cut if he did not remove it; and, seeing that after the lapse of several weeks their notices were unheeded, the entire population united, and in the most orderly manner, exceedingly unlike riot or confusion, deliberately took down the flake, as Mr. Martin had done, with this difference, that Mr. Martin, the magistrate, attacked Fewer's flake by night, and they acted in the middle of the noonday; Martin tore down, without any previous notification; the people having given ample notice, and having taken down the affair, they destroyed the materials.

"This, I really feel convinced, is a true statement of this case, which has been made use of in the most unhandsome manner as a pretext for insulting and maligning the people of Newfoundland, — a people proverbial for their obedience to the laws of their country. But, although this case had completely died away, — although months had elapsed and no informations were lodged, — although the Southern Circuit passed over, and the Court had actually held a session in St. Mary's Harbour itself, and on the very spot in dispute, without a single question having arisen upon the subject, no sooner did the honourable the Chief Justice (Mr. Boulton) land in St. John's, on his return from England, than he himself issued a warrant against the people of St. Mary's, and the Rev. James Duffy was arrested by two common catchpoles, and dragged a distance of many miles through a country where a people, though attached enthusiastically to their clergy, gave on this occasion the strongest proof that they are taught to reverence the laws even, if possible, more.

"These constables brought the reverend gentleman before the district magistrates of Ferryland, who, upon his appearance before them, could not restrain themselves from giving expression to their satisfaction at having 'caught' a priest. He gave bail for his appearance at the next session of the Supreme Court, and as this court is held at St. John's, he at once saw there was some object to be gained by omitting to have him tried before the Circuit Judge, and reserving him for the Hon. Judge Boulton, because such was the facility to get witnesses, etc., when the trial was to be had on the circuit, that there was every security for having justice done; and he anticipated the utmost difficulty in getting a parcel of very poor men to volunteer, or, indeed, to consent to come in anyway to St. John's, a distance of a hundred miles, in the depth of winter, and at a time when small-pox, a disease at the bare mention of which the people of Newfoundland shudder, was raging there with fatal violence.

"Upon the opening of the court, the Rev. James Duffy appeared, and another prisoner with him; but although he stated his readiness to meet his accusers, unsupported as he was by a single witness, the Crown, — for it was made matter of prosecution by the Attorney-General, — the Crown drew back and adjourned the case till the next term, upon the plea of not having all the parties accused together; so that here was the priest again sent away, obliged again to walk back to St. Mary's, one hundred miles, having only four days before accomplished the same journey, and with this slur upon his character not to be removed before next November. But such, unhappily, is the administration of justice in Newfoundland, where the character or liberty of a priest is in question.

"The importance of this subject, and more particularly its connection with the objects of my visitation, one of which, and perhaps the most important, is to ascertain the character of the ministers who have the charge of souls, and the manner in which they fulfil their high trust, must be my apology for obtruding this relation upon you; but it will also give you practical illustration of my former observation, that the missionary who zealously discharges his duty in Newfoundland must expect to be replenished with opprobrium.

"The day after my arrival I devoted principally to the investigation of the circumstances connected with the flake, and on Thursday morning I confirmed eighty-five persons; and as this was the last place at which I intended to stop, we set sail, after Confirmation, for St. John's, where we arrived on Saturday, the 12th of September.

"And thus we closed a visitation, in which we had undergone the greatest labours, the greatest hardships, and had more than once incurred the greatest dangers; but, nevertheless, Heaven permitted us to land in safety, and with comparatively unimpaired health. And now I shall close this long letter, reserving for a final one the particulars of the difficulties that awaited us at home, where we found small-pox raging violently, while the people were suffering from extreme poverty.

"I am, my dear Sir, with great respect,
"Your most obliged and very humble servant,
"✠ MICHAEL ANTHONY FLEMING,
"*Catholic Bishop of Newfoundland, etc.*"

"I found my poor people, upon my landing in St. John's, sunk in the greatest misery, owing to the ravages making among them by small-pox; and as upon the breaking out of every epidemic it is the humbler classes whose poverty first invites disease, the poor of St. John's were sufferers indeed.

"At this time, too, the utmost anxiety pervaded the public mind, because now approached the period at which the labours of the fishery came to a close, and when those who had toiled through a long summer naturally expected to meet a recompense in the same manner as they had been accustomed at all times before; that is, from the merchants, for whose advantage they had been toiling. And here observe that the fishing-servants form the most numerous class of the population in St. John's, numbering over four thousand.

"The person who hires the fishing-servants is called *a planter*, and although not *really* the steward of the merchant, yet has always been regarded as acting in that capacity, and therefore the fish and oil procured during the season, through the labour of the servant, has ever been made liable in the merchant's hands for the servant's wages, or where the amount of fish, etc., taken was insufficient, then for a ratable proportion of the proceeds; because the planter is most commonly a man destitute of means to defray the expense; as the steward of a nobleman could not be imagined to be a sufficient security for the wages of the servants he engaged. This has been always the mercantile usage on the subject of servants' wages, and it has been strengthened by repeated acts of Parliament, and confirmed by numberless decisions of the Court of Sessions, and of the Supreme Court, under the administration of Chief Justices Reeves, Forbes, and Tucker; but on the coming in of Judge Boulton he reversed the principle, and exonerated the merchant from a claim which relieved several of them of many hundred pounds wages, and involved the wretched people in a proportionate degree of misery and destitution.

"At the time to which I allude the Hon. Chief Judge was in London, and the utmost anxiety pervaded the poor people to ascertain whether the next Circuit Court would relieve them; but upon the courts opening, it began to be rumoured that the Chief Judge was returning, and, therefore, Judge Brenton actually refused to entertain a single civil case lest this question should be called up; for he had often and often decided it the other way before Judge Boulton's time; and, therefore, it lay over till Judge Boulton landed, and in a few days a final decision dashed the cup of hope from the lps of many thousands who, with their families, were looking to his fiat for means of support, while they saw their little ones dying around them of a loathsome disease.

"Here was a trying occasion for the clergyman who possessed humanity to calm the feelings of a father who saw his offspring perishing with want, after passing the summer in toil and hardship, many hundred miles from home, to enrich an individual who now took an advantage of his situation. In justice, however, to the commercial body in St. John's, I ought to mention that the greater portion of them scorned to take advantage of that adjudication, and have paid with cheerfulness their servants' full demand, — an act of benevolence which will be long and gratefully remembered by the poor people.

"But to make such an individual as the one above described respect the laws of his country, to convince him that he ought to respect the constituted authorities, under whom he had suffered such wrong, could only be effected by mitigating the affliction and soothing the wounded spirit of the individual; and the priest succeeded in restraining them from the commission of acts of violence or outrage so far that never in the history of Newfoundland has there been known less crime to have been committed in St. John's than during the past winter.

"To add to the difficulties of this period, so very many persons who had previously been vaccinated, and some more than once, had fallen victims, upon this occasion, to smallpox, that all confidence in the efficacy of the vaccine matter as a preventive was destroyed; and at all sides they began to inoculate with the natural virus. The number of cases, as stated upon the evidence of the practising medical men before the Grand Jury, amounted to upwards of six thousand in St. John's.

"About the first week in November the disease broke out in Petty Harbour, one of the villages of the district of St. John's, which place I mentioned before as having been the first port I put into on setting out for the southward; and as this place is entirely occupied by people engaged in the fishery, and probably ninety-nine hundredths of them fishing-servants, I at once saw that their extreme poverty would preclude the possibility of procuring medical assistance, and that, for the same reason, I knew they could not provide either the necessary medicines or needful nutriment.

"In such an emergency what was to be done? The Executive had attempted nothing to check the disease or to soften its visitation upon the poor. There were six or seven thousand pounds in colonial coffers, excess over the year's expenditure and debt, and yet not one single farthing was given to relieve the sufferings of the afflicted. There was no hospital opened; no dispensary instituted or recommended; no soup-house founded; not a subscription opened, even though some five or six and twenty thousand pounds sterling of salaries are paid annually out of the public taxes to persons resident principally in St. John's; but the work of death was progressing, and the terrors of pestilence blanched every cheek.

"Nay, there seemed to be arts used, I will not say to spread the contagion, but to add to the apprehensions of the public, and to increase their fears. The Chief Justice on the bench declared it the duty of the Grand Jury to indict any one who came out of a house where persons lay ill of small-pox, and actually in open court reproved Mr. Harding, a respectable citizen living at the Beach, whose amiable and highly accomplished daughter was lying ill of this disease, for having come out of his house, even though he had done so in obedience to a summons of the Court to attend upon the jury;

and such a doctrine, at a moment when hundreds were going
from door to door begging old linens for their children, their
parents, their wives, or their husbands, or food or clothing,
or other comforts necessary to the sick or the convalescent, was
calculated to produce much discontent. In a few weeks,
however, the disease visited the honourable Judge's family,
and he appeared abroad, breaking through the rules he himself had made.

"But I have said that nothing was done to check the disease. I was wrong in saying so, for as soon as ever it began
to attack the families of the *respectable* inhabitants the phy-
sicians were invited by the Executive to attend *gratuitously*
at a house formerly occupied by the St. John's Charity
School, and for which no rent is payable, for the purpose of
vaccinating the poor. At this time there were upwards of
two or three thousand persons after having undergone inocu-
lation with the *natural* matter, and when the disease exhibited
itself as on the decline. However, on the opening of the
House of Assembly, the Governor, in his speech, asked for a
grant of money to stem the progress of small-pox; and a sum
of five hundred pounds was granted some time in March or
April, when not one case existed in St. John's.

"Upon its breaking out in Petty Harbour, I went to that
little place, as I was unwilling to subject the excellent family
of Mr. Keilly, where I usually lodged (and where for the last
forty years bishops and priests have always received a warm,
welcome, comfortable, and hospitable home), to the danger
of infection through me. I resisted their kind entreaties to
reside with them, and begged the use of a waste house near
our church; and here I planted my medicine-chest, and set
it up as the village dispensary; and here I stayed for the remainder of the winter.

"I now applied myself sedulously to the improvement of
this interesting little harbour. I was engaged, as I remarked
before, erecting a beautiful little church here, for here there
is a congregation of about seven hundred persons; and as the
cemetery was in the very centre of the little town, I was solic-

itous to remove it to some place where sufficient soil to cover the bodies might be had; for as three persons who died of that dreadful disease had been interred before I came, I was apprehensive that danger might arise from leaving them, and allowing others to be buried in some instances within three or four yards of the doors of the houses.

"The vicinity having been explored, a place perfectly suitable, and at about half-a-mile distant, was discovered, and to it I had all the bodies forthwith removed.

"At my own expense I purchased a piece of ground adjoining the old cemetery, in order to make it a useful square for the public around our church, and at great expense, by blasting the rocks, reduced it to a level, so that it forms quite an embellishment in a little place where there is not a single level spot of six yards square in any other part of the harbour.

"In fact, what with the building of the church, the purchasing ground, the clearing and levelling, etc., I had expended upon that little town upwards of eight hundred pounds; yet did it tend to bring more annoyance upon me. What was my surprise to learn one day from the Governor, upon the occasion of my waiting on him, that some of the Protestants of Petty Harbour had just petitioned against me! I then found that they had been worked upon — for they and I had always been upon terms of friendship, nor did I own any difference between Protestant and Catholic in my attentions to the sick, or in the gratuitous diffusion of medicine and nourishing food.

"The Protestants, then, I had just found, had been worked upon to get this petition up to prevent my finishing the chapel-yard, or square, for its professed object was to forbid my removing or interrupting the repose of the mortal remains of some of their deceased friends. Even Governor Prescott himself must have seen through this, and considered it got up for party motives, for in his reply to my official explanation on the subject, he recommended my waiting until those prejudices should be removed by remonstrances; and I am sure it is to His Excellency I owe it that they were almost immediately removed, and one of their clergymen, I understand, was pleased to applaud my motives, and admit that what I had done was for the improvement of the condition of the people."

Dr. Fleming spent the winter of 1835–6 at Petty Harbor, assisting in a most heroic manner those who suffered from the small-pox. He returned to St. John's in April, and on the 20th of that month confirmed "1,390 persons, principally children." On the 1st of May he confirmed 602 in Torbay, and on the 8th, 449 in Portugal Cove, and on the 15th, 413 in Petty Harbor, — "thus making a total of 2,854, amongst whom were 304 converts to the faith."

"On Friday, May 27th (this was Ember week), I set out from St. John's, at seven o'clock A.M., for Portugal Cove, in order to consecrate the Church of St. Patrick, at Brigus, at the other side of Conception Bay; and as it was so early, the Rev. Edward Troy and I, with two or three lay gentlemen who accompanied us, forbore to take our collation before we left town; and when we arrived at the Cove, the wind was so inviting, that, promising as it did a passage of only two or three hours, we preferred starting immediately, and stepped on board, having just barely broken our fast.

"This may give you some idea of the uncertainty of communication in this country. There was not on board the packet either meat or drink, for what need of either where you could see the landing-place before you; but having been becalmed, and headed by the wind afterwards, we were tossed about the bay that entire day, the entire of the night following, and arrived at our destination not till eleven o'clock A.M. next day, when we landed in a complete state of exhaustion from want of food.

"I shall not tarry to describe the true Irish welcome we met from the people of Brigus, or their truly good pastor, the Rev. Denis Mackin. Suffice it, that we continued wind-bound here for several days after the consecration, and that on the occasion of that ceremony there assembled people of all creeds, from the most distant parts of the bay, so that so great a multitude of people had never before assembled in that part of the country.

"On the following Sunday, June the 5th, I had arranged to consecrate the beautiful Church of Corpus Christi, at Torbay, erected almost solely at the expense of the Rev. Edward Troy, a missionary than whom this country has never seen one more zealous or more ardently devoted to the duties of his sacred calling. We, therefore, sailed the very first favourable moment, and on Sunday consecrated this church for a truly good congregation.

"And now one duty more remained to be fulfilled before my departure, for I had long promised the people of Harbour Grace to take the earliest opportunity of administering Confirmation to them; and in order to comply, I sailed on Tuesday, the 7th, again accompanied by the Rev. Edward Troy, for Carbonear; and here I arrived in a few hours, and on Wednesday confirmed upwards of six hundred persons in Harbour Grace, amongst whom were many converts; but as the next day was wet, I thought that children could not well be brought on that morning from a distance, I put off the Confirmation of Carbonear till Friday, when seven hundred persons were admitted to participate in that sacrament, immediately after which we set sail for the Cove, and arrived in St. John's on the same evening; and as upon my arrival I found that several persons who had been disappointed on the former occasion were now well prepared here, on Whit-Sunday I confirmed four hundred individuals, making the total in the district of St. John's 3,254.

"And thus have I brought this narrative down to the period of my departure; and I pray ardently and earnestly before my God that these details may tend to induce attention to the spiritual wants of an interesting but long-neglected people, and awaken the good and the wealthy to the spiritual distress of thousands of souls who are wandering without a shepherd around the snows of the Labrador and on the bleak coasts of Newfoundland.

"Believe me, with sentiments of esteem, your devoted and humble servant in Christ,

"✠ MICHAEL ANTHONY FLEMING.

"The Very Rev. John Spratt."

CHAPTER XXIV.

THE CATHEDRAL. — [1836-1849.]

Commencement of the Cathedral — Difficulty of Obtaining Ground — Reception of Dr. Fleming on his Return from Rome — Further Difficulties placed in his Way — He returns to England in Winter, 1838 — Correspondence relating to Cathedral Ground — Assistance Rendered by the Irish Paliamentary Party, O'Connell, Lynch, Moore O'Farrell — Father Troy Appointed Vicar-General — Letter from Dr. Fleming to him — The Ground for Cathedral secured — Enthusiasm of the People — Mullins' Ghost — Mickle's "Crooked Furrough." — Fencing in the Ground — Preparation of Material for the Cathedral — Laying the Foundation Stone, 1841 — Completion of the Cathedral.

HAVING, by the introduction of the nuns and the establishment of their schools, provided, as we have said, for the *moral temple*, — the building up, that is, in the hearts of the children of his flock that spiritual edifice whose foundations are laid deep and firm in a sound religious education, — Dr. Fleming immediately turned his mind to the great and absorbing work of erecting the material church; that is, the great cathedral, which stands to-day a glorious monument of his zeal and faith. From the first moment of his episcopacy he had held steadily in view this noble project. His motives and sentiments on this subject are described in his letters to the Rev. Dr. A. O'Connell, "On the State of Religion in Newfoundland:" —

"I am engaged in the construction of a cathedral on a scale of unusual elegance, extent, and beauty. But as it has been said by some that it is an undertaking upon my part somewhat approaching presumption to think of the erection of an ecclesiastical building such as I have undertaken, and a building of stone in a country where there never was raised a single temple save of the most perishable material, — a building of such an extent and such a plan, exhibiting the beauties of such architectural design as necessarily to involve a considerable outlay of money, and in a mere fishing colony, — I may be permitted to say thus far, that it is of very little consequence to me in what sort of dwelling I offer up my unworthy prayers during my brief sojourn in this life; it matters not to me whether I bend my knee in a temple or a hovel; but when I consider that if in the old law God himself deemed it requisite to instruct his people to erect a temple to his worship of the most gorgeous magnificence and the most costly materials, how much more should it not be deemed of consequence in the Christian dispensation that the blood of the Lamb be offered in a church suitable to so august a mystery? How can I think, then, as a minister of the Most High God, without pain and mortification, upon being every day obliged to offer up the Holy of holies — to offer up the Body and Blood of Christ Jesus — within a building that is unworthy of being used as an asylum for the beasts of the field?

"The Catholic Church of the capital has hitherto been the *meanest* house devoted to public worship in St. John's. It is a rude, ill-shaped wooden building, falling to ruin, nearly out of lease, and held at an enormous yearly rent; add to which that it is so far from being adequate to the accommodation of our rapidly-increasing congregation, that in the midst of winter, on every Sunday, you may behold several hundreds of the poor people assisting at the Holy Sacrifice exposed to the piercing winds, to the pelting of the bitter snow-drift, and kneeling imbedded in snow; and this building being incapable from want of space of any increase or addition, I thought it my duty to God, to the people committed to my care, to give them, if possible, a temple superior to any other in the Island, — a temple at once beautiful and spacious, suitable to the worship of the Most High God, and that may be regarded in after times as a memorial of the piety of the faithful, a pledge of the permanency of our holy religion, and an object of holy pride to the fervent Catholic.

"I looked around me and I could neither see a favourable

site on which to erect a new one, nor had I the means of purchasing it was there one in view, nor a shilling in my pocket to commence the building. I was penniless, and I might almost say friendless; and yet in proportion as my poverty appeared great, in proportion as the prospect appeared gloomy, and as difficulty crowded upon difficulty had almost assumed the garb of impossibility, He who delights in proving himself the friend of the destitute, the strength of the feeble, who loves to make the humble and lowly the instruments of His greatest works, inspired me to extend my views, to enlarge my conceptions, and to see only the great object to be accomplished, and to shut my eyes to the barriers that presented themselves to its completion, reflecting only that the work was for God's glory and the comfort of my poor people, and that in the warm hearts and pious dispositions of the faithful I had a mine of wealth calculated to sustain and support me throughout the great undertaking.

"Inspirited by these reflections I began literally without a penny my arduous struggle, in 1834, by memorializing the Government for a piece of ground; it certainly is a valuable spot, beautifully situated, almost in the centre of the town, and containing about eight acres. To give a detailed account of all the circumstances connected with this application would fill a volume. I shall merely content myself by saying, that before I succeeded in obtaining the object of my prayer to the Crown, it cost me nearly five years of vexation and annoyance, without pause or intermission. How much of tribulation did I not endure during that period! Every effort that malice the most ingenious could devise has been resorted to to thwart my views; calumny, insult, and opprobrium were heaped upon me to impede the accomplishment of my wishes, to blight the prospect of my success; but, conscious of the integrity of my intentions, I persevered; and after having travelled 20,000 miles of the Atlantic Ocean solely upon this business, amid storms, tempests, danger, and death, and undergoing all the hardships and privations that human nature could endure, God ultimately crowned my hopes with the completest success. That high-minded nobleman, Lord Glenelg, then in the colonial administration, having at length acceded to the prayer of my petition, I was put in possession of the present valuable piece of ground that forms the site of our cathedral."

"As usual," writes Dr. Mullock (MS., p. 72), "in all his undertakings he had to encounter the most determined opposition." That Dr. Fleming should have had opponents in the troubled arena of politics, and even in the matter of schools, is not altogether to be wondered at, but it seems strange that in such a purely religious matter as this any should be found to oppose him. One reason for this opposition we may find in the fact that the site on which the cathedral stands, and which is now the centre of what may be called the "upper town," was some forty years ago a *barren wilderness*, and was considered by the easy-going folk who lived in the lower town as "out in the woods;" hence they condemned Dr. Fleming's idea of building the cathedral "on the barrens," and predicted that no one would ever go up there to attend Mass or religious services. Time, however, has shown that Dr. Fleming saw farther into the future than these would-be wiseacres.

The cathedral site is now the central point of a new and beautiful city which has grown up around it, — a city which may be truly called an *urbs in rure*, for though within two minutes' walk of the central business parts, it is, by its great elevation, entirely removed from the noise, bustle, and dust of trade, and surrounded by quiet terraces and gardens; and yet the immense congregations of from five to seven and eight thousand which throng its ample aisles at each of the five Masses celebrated every Sunday, and which pour their living streams like a mighty flood from its many portals in all directions after Vespers, — all this gives the lie to the predictions of the grumblers of Dr. Fleming's time.

It would be unnecessary to trace minutely the intricacies of the struggle which this great Prelate went through to procure this site of land; but some brief account of it will be interesting to those of the present generation. As we have already seen, he travelled twenty thousand miles of ocean, that is to say, he crossed the Atlantic back and forth five times before he succeeded in his great enterprise. In a letter to the Central Council of the Society for the Propagation of the Faith, dated 20th May, 1838, he describes some of his trials and difficulties in this matter: —

"In 1834 I had addressed a memorial to the British Government, to obtain a large piece of land at St. John's to build a cathedral, a convent, schools, and episcopal residence thereon. I also desired a suitable place for a cemetery. . . . The following year I renewed my application, and in 1836 I went to London for the purpose of following up my request. I was in Rome in the month of June, 1837, when I received a reply from the Secretary of State. It informed me that instructions had been sent to the Governor of the Island to comply with my demand. Immediately on the receipt of this news I returned to Newfoundland, anxious to take possession of the land granted by the Government, and to commence the buildings so long looked for by the people. . . . On the morning of my arrival the news spread on all sides. All the people, leaving their work, came to the shore. Before leaving the vessel I received a deputation of the young men of the Island, who presented me with an address, and begged permission to row me ashore in a boat which they had elegantly prepared for the occasion, and which displayed the banner of the Cross, — that Cross by which and for which I had surmounted so many dangers. On setting foot on land I was saluted with cries and tears of joy. . . . The Assembly, which was in session at the moment, adjourned, and all the members came to the wharf to compliment me.

"After having saluted my priests, who came to meet me,

I gave the signal, and we went in procession towards the
church, following the principal streets of the city. We had
not proceeded far when a ceremony occurred which I had
not in the least expected, and which awaked in me the most
sweet emotions. The two ranks of the procession opening
suddenly, I saw advancing a swarm of young girls, dressed
in white and carrying a banner of white satin, on which was
embroidered a gilt cross crowned with flowers. This banner,
which was the work of their own hands, was at the same
time an emblem of the purity of these young souls, and a
souvenir of the Mission of Newfoundland. They knelt down
in the street to receive my blessing, and I could not restrain
the tears which escaped from my eyes at this new testimony
of the affection of my dear diocese. These children, of
whom the oldest was not more than twelve years of age,
belonged to the schools of the Presentation convent, which
I had established only three years ago. They then took
the head of the procession, and when the entire *cortege* had
entered the church, they came to the foot of the altar to
present their banner to me.

"After having rendered thanks to the Sovereign Dispenser
of all these benefits, I addressed a few words to those
assembled, and informed them of the success of my efforts.
. . . I recounted to them the numberless proofs of good-
will and the special favours which were showered upon me in
Rome by His Holiness and by the Cardinal Prefect of Propaganda ; the gifts which they were about to send for the
Mission ; the lively interest which was shown at Lyons in
the bosom of your Council ; the generous donations which
your noble Society had destined for us.

"My first care was to demand from the Governor the concession of the lands granted by the Imperial Government.
But I found my enemies had been at work. . . .
Although I had in my hands the order of the Colonial Minister
for the concession of the site, the Governor refused,' and
pressed me to choose either of two other sites, each equally
unfavourable. . . .

"The affairs of the diocese did not permit me to undertake at once another voyage to England, yet it was absolutely necessary. I did not set sail till the month of January, that is to say, in the most unfavourable time of the year. We passed the first four hundred miles in the midst of ice. The weather was most tempestuous, and it was with great difficulty that we arrived at Falmouth. I went immediately to London, to make my report on the opposition offered to me. My protest was favourably received. I obtained a formal order defining particularly the spot to be given, precisely as I pointed out. It is a magnificent site. It commands the city, the harbour, the ocean, and a vast expanse of country. The Cross elevated on these heights will be a consoling sight for the poor inhabitants of these countries. . . . And so my hopes were realized. . . . May the heavenly Protector, who has deigned so far to bless my feeble efforts, enable me to find the means to conduct the enterprise to a happy conclusion!"

The correspondence concerning this matter consists of an immense mass of letters, memorials, petitions, etc., stretching over a period of nearly three years. It will be found complete in the Appendix to this volume. (See Note 5.)

To forward his project, Dr. Fleming engaged the services of O'Connell, Moore O'Farrell, one of the high officials of His Majesty, Mr. Anthony Lynch, the learned Representative for Galway, and several others of the Catholic leaders. The enthusiasm which animated the venerable Prelate seemed contagious, and all who met him were inspired by his zeal, as may be seen from the following extracts. Mr. Anthony Lynch, member for Galway, writes from London, 24th of March, 1837: —

"I made many efforts to find your Lordship in London, and at length learned you were in Rome. . . . I hasten to communicate to you a piece of information, which will be most grateful, and it is that I have succeeded in securing the grant of land for your church."

Moore O'Farrell writes as follows. I have not the date, and only a Latin translation of his letter, made for the use of the authorities in Rome. I restore it to the original: —

"I congratulate you on the obtaining of your object. I have received a letter from Lord Glenelg granting the piece of land described as follows." Then follows the description as laid down in the report of Engineer Walker. "At length you are rewarded for all your labors." He then speaks of the accusations made against Dr. Fleming and his priests, and says he will have an opportunity of defending him. "You will be glad to hear that a society has been instituted to take particular cognizance of all affairs of maladministration in the colonies, and to bring them before Parliament. If the ministry be not changed before next session, I will invite them to a discussion relative to the affairs of Newfoundland, and if you should have leisure, I would wish you to supply me with particulars."

On leaving St. John's, July 4, 1836, Dr. Fleming appointed the Rev. Father Troy Vicar-General, giving him full charge of the spiritual administration of the diocese. He writes to Father Troy, from Liverpool, on July 17, "after a passage unprecedented, . . . both as respects expedition (13 days) and the fineness of the weather."

It was Sunday morning, and as soon as they anchored off the King's dock he went ashore to hear Mass. Having learnt that a vessel was about to sail "on return tide" for St. John's, though not having the use of his fingers, he cannot refrain from scribbling a line to announce his safe arrival, and to ask the people to give thanks. He would start for London at once, as Parliament is not yet prorogued, but he cannot get his trunks ashore before "12 o'clock to-morrow;" he expects to be in London on Tuesday evening. He desires to be remembered to the priests, the Sisters, and the dear people; he will not particularize names, but cannot refrain from mentioning "Messrs. Nugent, Kent, Doyle, S.

Morris, Dillon, and O'Mara." He enjoins on him to write by "every vessel sailing for England or Ireland."

On Sept. 10th, 1836, he writes Father Troy from No. 7 Ayr Street, London. He complains of not having yet had one line from any person in Newfoundland. "I have been rather unfortunate," he continues, "as yet in my application to Government. In fact, I came here at the wrong time, when the ministers, harassed by a long session, and every member of the House of Commons from whom I could expect any assistance or sympathy, had gone to their respective country homes. I think, however, I shall eventually succeed, but not, I believe, before October.

"I have not had a moment's respite since my arrival here, writing letters by night, and endeavouring to press their consideration by day on the heartless few about the seat of Government, that I am heartily tired of them. But in order to guard against the worst, I expect you will immediately wait on my friend Mr. Wakeham, and tell him, in the event of Williams's Plantation being put up for auction, to make the purchase for me; and should the chapel funds in hand be insufficient to cover the amount of purchase, let money be raised by mortgaging my farm or any other property I have, if necessary. . . . You may rely on the integrity of Mr. Wakeham; but let no person be aware of your negotiating with him on the subject of that purchase, lest it should go abroad, and we should be thereby deprived of that only spot that can be rendered available for all our purposes. . . . You can mention the circumstance in confidence to John Casey and James Treacy; get them to attend the sale and make an offer for it, in order to throw the enemy off his guard." He states that he is pressed on all sides to remain in Europe the winter, but had not made up his mind. As a matter of fact, he did, and visited Rome, of which we shall treat more fully hereafter.

While at Rome, in June, 1837, as we have seen, Dr. Fleming received the favorable news that his petition concerning the land was granted. He immediately set out for

Newfoundland, and arrived some time before October 3d; for there exists a letter written by him on that date at St. John's to the Colonial Secretary, the Hon. James Crowdy, asking for " the allowance made by the British Government to the Catholic Bishop of this Island, which was due since the early part of the year." Dr. Mullock (MS., p. 74) states that " in the month of December, a week after his arrival, he was once more on the Atlantic on his way to London." This is not, however, quite exact, as we have seen that he himself states (letter to the *Propagation de la Foi*) that he could not leave till January. On the 30th of January, 1838, he writes from 32 Craven street, London, Strand, to Father Troy, and states that " after a tolerable passage I landed in Falmouth on the 19th of January. The captain was truly kind to me, and never did I feel in better health." He then speaks of his interview with Mr. Nugent and Dr. Carson, who were at that time in London as a delegation from Newfoundland, of which some notice will be given in a future chapter; at present we are concerned only with that part which relates to the struggle for the plot of land. " I am sure," he says, " of getting the ground, notwithstanding the obstacles thrown in my way in the most influential quarters. . . . I am at a loss to determine whether or not I shall purchase Williams's property. I cannot take my heart off that spot, — the site the place presents, and the accommodation it affords for all the purposes I contemplate; still the idea of laying out all my disposable fund alarms me. May God direct me! The papers are signed, and I can purchase whenever I please. Write me at once, and tell me what you think. How much have you offered to Monier Hutchings? I find Arthur Carter's claim is out of the question."

On March 7, 1838, he wrote the final appeal to Government (No. 14 of the correspondence already alluded to[1]) which secured his object. It is a masterly letter, full of strength and force. He speaks with the strong feeling

---

[1] See Appendix.

of truth and honesty, refutes in a crushing manner all the
machinations planned against him, and carries conviction to
even the most biassed mind. There was no further question :
the land was granted at once. On April 7 he writes a
letter of thanks to Sir George Grey, from No. 8 Surry
Street, Strand : —

"Sir, — I have the honour to acknowledge the receipt of
your letter of to-day, . . . wherein you acquaint me, by
direction of Lord Glenelg, that His Lordship has ascertained
from the Master-General and Board of Ordnance that there
is no objection in a military point of view to the grant to me,
for the erection of a school-house and chapel, on the land to
the eastward of Fort Townshend, formerly occupied as the
garrison wood-yard, and which was the land originally applied for by me; and further, that as it appears that the
other portions of land which had been offered to me do not
possess the same advantages, His Lordship has directed
Captain Prescott, if no insuperable objection should exist, to
put me at once in possession of the land to the eastward of Fort
Townshend. Allow me, Sir, through you, to express to His
Lordship my sincere thanks, . . . and to assure him
of my gratitude to Her Majesty's Government for the consideration they have testified for the comfort and convenience
of so large and so loyal a portion of Her Majesty's subjects,
affording to the infant population a means of acquiring education ; to the adult an opportunity of offering up their orisons
for their Sovereign ; and a place of lasting repose for the dead ;
and to me the happiness of laying the foundation of a suite
of erections which, I trust, will long remain a monument
to the liberality and beneficence of our glorious and good
Queen."

This was the last of that circumlocutory correspondence
continuing over a period of nearly four years, and involving
the crossing of the Atlantic five times by the indefatigable
Bishop. But he was well rewarded for his great struggle.

The announcement to the people by Father Troy that the ground had been obtained was the signal for great rejoicing; but on the arrival of Dr. Fleming himself, in the month of October, their enthusiasm burst all bounds. The reason why Dr. Fleming did not return immediately to St. John's is explained in a letter of June, 1848, to the Propagation of the Faith. "It was in the spring of 1838 I had thus succeeded" namely, in securing the ground, "but before I returned to St. John's I thought it important to communicate with some of the first architects of the day, in order to be furnished with the necessary designs for the cathedral. I had communication with several, but our climate is so peculiar, our frost so intense, and the quantities of snow falling every winter so heavy, I at length judged it better to proceed to the north of Europe, and at Altona, on the Elbe, obtained from the architect employed by the Danish Government, M. Schmidt, in that city, all I desired, so that it was not till the end of October I was enabled to arrive in Newfoundland."

M. Schmidt's designs are still preserved in the Episcopal Library in St. John's, from which it will be seen, that though the general style of his plan has been preserved, yet it has been greatly modified, particularly by the abolition of a portico and the addition of the transepts. The final plan, which was the one actually worked upon, is drawn by Murphy, of Dublin.

Dr. Fleming describes his arrival as follows:—

"It would be impossible to describe the enthusiastic fervour that has been evinced by the people of St. John's upon the occasion of the accedence of that grant, so deeply interested were their feelings; and so thrilling was the announcement of that success, that the whole population turned out and assembled simultaneously upon the ground, some bearing longuers, some conveying posts, and even children bringing nails and implements; and in the incredible space of ten minutes the whole space, containing upwards of eight acres, was enclosed with a substantial fence five feet high.

"The next demonstration occurred upon my requesting

timber for scaffolding for the building. Notwithstanding that the woods where such stuff was to be obtained were not less than twelve miles distant, yet in one day, and before one o'clock in the afternoon, I had placed on the ground more than £500 worth of timber and spars.

. . . .

"At the north side of St. John's stands a rocky hill, called Signal Hill. Upon this hill, many years ago, a vast quantity of huge rocks of red granite had been raised from their beds for the purpose of opening a road to the barracks which stands on this hill; they lay there in confusion. Upon these, in my solicitude for procuring a suitable foundation for my building, I cast my eyes. Their removal would be a benefit to public improvement. The Government were scared from it, because the expense necessarily incident upon it would far outbalance any immediate benefit to be derived by them from it. I applied for them to the Colonel of Engineers, who at once granted me permission to take them. I gave notice on the Sunday that on the Wednesday following we should commence this undertaking at nine o'clock in the morning; and at that hour upwards of six thousand persons were on the spot prepared for the undertaking. I recommended them to form themselves into large parties; and never was there exhibited a greater degree of emulation than was testified by those bodies, — each vying with the other either in bringing the heaviest stones or the greatest number of loads in the course of the day. The season gave us a beautiful snow-path, particularly adapted for the slide-hauling; and before the close of the evening there had been deposited on the ground above 1,200 tons of stone for the foundations.

"Much of this stone had to be drawn over an extensive and dangerous lake; yet no sentiment of fear daunted the minds of any of the men, while I stood by filled with anxious solicitude lest the slightest accident might occur to damp their ardour. I observed a few of our hardiest class, the pilots, at work disengaging an enormous mass of rock from its bed in the side of the hill, immediately over the lake,

and terrified at the danger, in the first place, lest some of
them should be crushed, I induced them to desist. They
pretended to comply, but watched the opportunity of my
withdrawal to renew their efforts. I had not gone far when
I heard a wild shout. I turned, and saw about a hundred
men hauling with ropes the identical rock which they had dislodged, in spite of my prohibition, and dragged it with great
swiftness across the lake, otherwise its great weight would
have doubtless sunk through the ice, and buried it, and, perhaps, many persons also, in the bosom of the lake. This
stone was estimated to contain upwards of seven tons.

"Again, when I notified my desire to have the foundations
excavated, the appearance of the people was truly edifying and
affecting. There you might behold all classes of the population join without distinction in this laborious undertaking;
even women, bending under the weight of years, assisting to
convey away the clay or gravel in their aprons; so that in less
than two days the whole foundations were excavated, containing 79,200 cubic feet, or 8,800 cubic yards.

"But nothing could more strongly manifest the feelings of
the people than the zeal exhibited in conveying the building-
stone for the erection of this edifice. Every Catholic owner
of a schooner or boat, and even some Protestants, volunteered
to send their vessels gratuitously to Kelly's Island, a distance
to many of them of more than two hundred miles by water,
for a cargo of stones, which were there quarried for the purpose, and the fishermen offered themselves to form the crews;
and no sooner are these cargoes landed than the farmers of
St. John's send their carts, although this work necessarily
occurs at their busiest season; and the mechanics in the town,
— smiths, tailors, victuallers, coopers, carpenters, shoe-
makers, and the pilots, as good and virtuous a body of men
as live, and even shopkeepers and merchants, — all take a
day, each department alternately, to load and unload those
carts; even the female portion of the congregation insisted
upon devoting one day in each week to those works; and you
might behold hundreds of females, young and old, married

and single, rich and poor, assembled every Monday morning, furnished with barrows, acting the part of labourers by bringing stone from the most distant part of the ground, where it had been placed, to the foot of the scaffolding; and this manifestation of zeal and devotion (continued as it has been from the first week until the close of the building season) is without parallel in the history of the Church in any country."[1]

---

[1] The fathers and mothers of the present generation glory in recounting to their children how they took part in these works, and many an anecdote, amusing or interesting, is rehearsed thereanent. The people, having learned by experience how necessary it was to obtain secure and undoubted possession of the land, were not satisfied with fencing it in. They thought that if they could but have one corpse buried in the ground it would be a double security, as they did not believe that even their bitterest enemies would attempt to move the dead. But to get the *corpus delicti*, that was the rub. Who would be accommodating enough to die? Or whose faith was strong enough to allow himself to be buried alive, or made a victim of? Behold! "the ram is found sticking fast among the briers." A certain notorious character in the town of the name of Mullins took occasion most opportunely to die (at least so it was said), and he was buried with great pomp in a back part of the new ground, not far from where now stands the ball-alley. Some said it was a clever trick of old Mullins to die at that time, as otherwise he never would have got a *decent burial*, much less a grand funeral. But not long after this the veritable Mullins appeared again in the flesh, though many averred (and will aver to this day) that it was his ghost. The fact was that poor Mullins " is not dead, but sleepeth," having been induced by " the boys" to take an over-draught of a certain somniferous decoction to which he was rather partial; and it was but a coffin full of stones that was buried with honors!

I am tempted to relate one other anecdote on this subject. A few years ago it might have been noticed that there was a rather singular curve on the western boundary of the plot of land in question. It cannot now be noticed, as, since that time, under the Bennett Government, an additional piece of the Ordnance ground was obtained, and the road was moved farther westward; but at the time the road passed underneath the Palace windows, and immediately in front of St. Bonaventure's College. The line of road, instead of running in a straight line, curved suddenly westwards at the corner of the Palace. On remarking this fact one day, and wondering what caused it, an old man who was working about a drain looked up and said, " Well, yer Rev'r'ns, I can tell ye all about it, for it was I done it meself. Yes, God forgi' me, 'twas the first *crooked furrough* I ever opened in me life, and the last, too. But sure only for the case was in it I'd never disgrace meself be lavin' sich sod as that afther me, as crooked as a shovel handle!" — " Why, how was that, Mickle?" — " Well, ye see, yer Rev'r'ns, when Bishop Flemin' (God be good to his sowl!) got the bit o' land afther thrav'lin' meny a thousan' mile o' the salt ocean, the boundharies was laid out wud stakes, and I was axed to come wud me horses an' plough to run a sod, so they could see where to put the fince. Well, I come jes' before dawnin' o' day in the mornin', an' I yoked-to and started. I see at wanste the way thim fellas o' the Garrison laid off the line. Av I folly'd it sthraight it 'ud run down a'most to nothing there beyant be the front road, jes' where the Bishop wanted to have the Catathedral facin' on. So, ses I, in the name o' God, though it goes agi'n me heart to make a crooked sod, for this wanste I'll do it! So I gev a little chuck o' the rein, an' I turned 'em out towards the Garrison gate. An' sure, yer Rev'r'ns, ye can see yerself av I went sthraight I'd cut right

With such an enthusiastic people we may be sure the work of construction was not permitted to flag. But even allowing for all this zeal and energy, it still remains a wonder and a proof that such a building, equal in size and architecture to many of those which, in the Old World, have taken centuries to build, could be erected in Newfoundland and that, too, in such an incredibly short space as nine years; for the foundation-stone was not laid till 1841, and Dr. Fleming had the crowning happiness of celebrating the first Mass in it in 1850, a few months only before his death.

For nearly three years after the securing of the ground the time was employed in gathering in material from all sides. Like Solomon of old, he sent bands of men into the forests to "hew the fir and the cedars," and to "hew stones in the mountains; and to bring great stones, costly stones, for the foundations of the temple, and to square them." The remainder of his life was principally taken up with this great work, and he made many voyages to England to procure materials and further the work. While the stones were being quarried in Kelly's Island, in Conception Bay, he lived there in a hut, used the pick and crowbar, and assisted to carry the stones to the water's edge, whence they were generously conveyed to St. John's by the owners and captains of our vessels. "He might, however," writes Dr. Mullock, "have avoided this unnecessary fatigue, and the affair would as well be carried on under his direction; but such was his disposition and anxiety to do everything himself."

The material of which the cathedral is built, with the exception of the ambulatory walls, which are of Kelly-Island stone, was principally imported from Ireland. The main walls are faced with cut limestone from Galway, and the

---

through the agency of St. John in the arch below." And sure enough, though St. John would have erected the cathedral, and having been dead there many years also, yet the one which remains just was in a sort a matter as to have deserved the great name of the reformer. It is indeed amusing to see that after all the prayers and invocations to military and civil authorities contrary to the new times years, the work of after-ages should at the end be rounded by Mullock having overcome his scruples about making "a cruder form of it."

CATHOLIC CATHEDRAL OF ST. JOHN THE BAPTIST, ST. JOHN'S. Page 352.

With such an enthusiastic people we may be sure the work of construction was not permitted to flag. But even allowing for all this zeal and energy, it still remains a wonder and a prodigy that such a building, equal in size and architecture to many of those which, in the Old World, have taken centuries to build, should be erected in Newfoundland, and that, too, in such an incredibly short space as nine years; for the foundation-stone was not laid till 1841, and Dr. Fleming had the consoling happiness of celebrating the first Mass in it in 1850, a few months only before his death.

For nearly three years after the securing of the ground the time was employed in gathering in material from all sides. Like Solomon of old, he sent levies of men into the forests to "hew the fir and the cedars," and to "hew stones in the mountains; and to bring great stones, costly stones, for the foundations of the temple, and to square them." The remainder of his life was principally taken up with this great work, and he made many voyages to England to procure materials and further the work. While the stones were being quarried in Kelly's Island, in Conception Bay, he lived there in a hut, used the pick and crowbar, and assisted to carry the stones to the water's edge, whence they were gratuitously conveyed to St. John's by the owners and captains of our vessels. "He might, however," writes Dr. Mullock, "have avoided this unnecessary fatigue, and the affair could as well be carried on under his direction; but such was his disposition and anxiety to do everything himself."

The material of which the cathedral is built (with the exception of the ambulatory walls, which are of Kelly-Island stone) was principally imported from Ireland. The main walls are faced with cut limestone from Galway, and the

---

through the *statute* o' St. John on the arch below!" And, sure enough, though St. John would have escaped the dissection, not having been placed there till many years after, yet the line would certainly have run in such a manner as to have destroyed the grand piazza of the cathedral. It is, indeed, amusing to think that, after all the reports and investigations of military and civil authorities, continuing for over three years, the whole affair should in the end be decided by Mickle's having overcome his scruples about making "*a crooked furrow*"!

CATHOLIC CATHEDRAL OF ST. JOHN THE BAPTIST, ST. JOHN'S. Page 352.

quoins, mouldings, belting, and base courses, window-frames, heads, sills, and mullions, are of Dublin granite. Dr. Fleming sought, at first, for cut stone from the neighboring colonies. On the 29th of June, 1839, he wrote Michael Tobin, Esq., of Halifax, inquiring about freestone, which he hears can be had on very reasonable terms in Nova Scotia. He had seen some which had been lately imported from there for the new Custom-House which appeared very good. This effort failed evidently, as there is no freestone in the cathedral. These two years of preparation were a period of continued bustle and excitement in St. John's. Day after day schooners and vessels were arriving with stone from Kelly's Island and Europe, and gangs of citizens were told off to unload them at the "Bishop's Wharf" and the Ordnance Wharf, which had been kindly loaned. All classes of the people — tradesmen, shopkeepers, laborers, farmers — attended in turn, vying with each other in their enthusiasm.

"Never," says Dr. Mullock, "even in the Ages of Faith, did a people exhibit greater enthusiasm than did the Newfoundlanders in the erection of this temple. Hundreds and thousands of tons of stone, landed at the Bishop's Wharf by the gratuitous labor of the people, were by them gratuitously carted to the cathedral grounds three hundred feet over the level of the water. One day a thousand tons of cut granite, for quoins, window mouldings, and string courses, would arrive from Dublin; in a few days the whole would be landed and deposited on the cathedral ground without a shilling's expense for labor or cart-hire. Again, cargoes of stone from Kelly's Island would continually arrive, gratuitously conveyed in ships belonging to St. John's and the outports; and again the people, day after day, month after month, year after year, discharged them, and conveyed them to the building, untiringly laboring for the glory of God."

As to Dr. Fleming himself, he seemed endowed with supernatural strength. He crossed the Atlantic again in 1840.

And we may form some idea of his labors from the following extract from a letter written to the Cardinal Prefect of Propaganda, on the 23d September, 1841. His Eminence had written to Dr. Fleming in November, 1840, inviting him to visit Rome, and, having received no response, wrote again in January, 1841. This letter also remaining unanswered, the Cardinal writes in a rather severe tone in July, 1841, enclosing copies of the former letters, and complaining that, though he (Dr. Fleming) had visited Europe subsequently, he had not come to Rome. Having explained that he did not receive the letters, they having been unaccountably mislaid, Dr. Fleming continues: " In good truth, had I really received the letters, notwithstanding the profound respect and veneration which I entertain towards the Sacred Congregation, it would have been impossible for me to comply with the request. . . . My whole stay (in Europe) only amounted to the short space of six weeks, and during that time I had no opportunity of enjoying one day's repose. I had to visit Ireland, whence to procure three additional priests; I had to make arrangements for their passages; I had to superintend the making of models for the ornamental stone necessary for our new cathedral; I had to look to the cutting of that stone in Dublin; I had to procure an engraving, to be cut, of the new edifice in a state of completion, that the sale of the plates might increase the resources for the building; I had to fly to Birmingham to procure medals commemorative of the laying of the foundation-stone, which I intended should take place early in the ensuing spring, in order by their sale to still further augment my funds; I had to hurry to Liverpool to contract for vessels to bring out the so-cut stone at the opening of the new year; and ever and anon to adopt every offer of a vessel departing for Newfoundland to expedite my works there in progress. My days were one unbroken round of toil; my nights given more to thought, and the transmission of those thoughts to paper, than to repose, until at last I had, in that short space, matured all my business. I once more returned to Liverpool to take shipping for Newfoundland, where, now exhausted and subdued, my health failed me, and my shattered and harassed frame sank upon the bed, whence for the first time I arose only to step on board the vessel and brave the hardships of a voyage of two thousand miles."

On his arrival on this occasion he was greeted with more than the ordinary expressions of joy and welcome. In October, shortly after his arrival, he addressed the people from the altar in a most fervent expression of thankfulness to them and gratitude to God for the great success which had thus far attended their glorious efforts, and he gives a graphic account of the state of the works.

There were many who had directly opposed the great work, and others who looked on indifferently, who, not enlightened and sustained by the burning faith with which animated his own breast, looked upon his efforts with a sneer of contempt as the vain attempt of an enthusiastic dreamer. "It is impossible," they said, "to complete such a work in Newfoundland!" Dr. Fleming had said that he would have the whole plot of land fenced in in half an hour. "Impossible!" said his opponents; and they calculated the immense number of posts and shores, the stupendous quantity of longures, the masses of nails. "It could not be done in a fortnight." "So it had been with the croakers, even from the very dawn of the faith. 'There is a lad here,' said one of old to Jesus, 'who has five barley loaves and two little fishes; but what are they among so many?' You know the sequel. Jesus blessed them, and they fed the multitude of five thousand, and there were twelve baskets of scraps left. We had given *half an hour* for the work of the fencing; but God blessed it, and you accomplished it in *ten minutes;* and there remained as much material as would fence it over again."

In his letter to the Society of the Propagation of the Faith he describes more minutely the scene of the fencing of the ground: "The refusal of the Governor to give the land brought me a fourth time across the ocean. Nor did I leave

London until I learnt that the grant had actually been placed in the hands of my curate, and the ground taken possession of. The concession was announced on Sunday to the congregation, and they were asked to help to fence the land. . . . The morning proved auspicious. At an early hour every part of the town was filled with joyous groups making preparation for the event. At 10 o'clock the church bell rang out, and immediately all assembled at the ground. The old and the young, the healthy and the infirm, even the women and children; . . . and so had they, as if by common impulse, disposed themselves that where there were persons too young or too feeble to assist in the erection of the fence, some of them brought a few pickets, some a few nails, some a saw, some a hammer, or some such implement. All then took up their positions around the space to be enclosed, supplied with the necessary posts and shores and longures, and *in less than twenty minutes* these nine acres of ground were enclosed with a substantial fence six feet high."

To continue Dr. Fleming's discourse in the "Old Chapel":—

"It was impossible, said my opponents, to bring the stone from Kelly's Island; but God inspired his people, and the work was accomplished. Finally, it was *impossible* to move it to the cathedral ground. Yet it is now laid there ready for the hammer of the mason. . . . What shall I say to you who have worked so well and so faithfully in the sacred cause? How can I thank the fishermen of Newfoundland? How shall I repay the farmers and the laborers the deep debt of gratitude I owe them? What return shall I make to the mechanics and shopkeepers? Oh! a life of service could not be regarded as an equivalent. It is God only, that God, for the promotion of whose divine worship they have labored, that can reward them. . . . You will be gratified, my dear people, to learn that at this moment there are upwards of sixty stone-cutters employed in preparing cut stone in Dublin, which I shall have ready for exportation by the first vessels in spring, a season when freights from Ireland are always lowest, and it is no harm for us to save some five or six hundred pounds in freight. I have also ordered 400,000 of brick from Hamburg. . . . Thus will I be provided with such a quantity of material as will enable me to commence the work without further delay.

"I have also come provided with a model of the work, — not a picture or a painting, — but a *cathedral church* in miniature. The whole edifice complete: its aisles, porticos, towers, ambulatories, altars, sanctuary, and all, constructed in the most exact symmetry and proportion, whereby we shall effect a still further saving in the construction, and greatly facilitate the progress of the work." He then calls upon the schooner-owners to bring more stone in the spring, "for, great as is the mass of stone upon the ground, I assure you we are far from having a sufficiency."

The preparations were now so far advanced that there was no doubt that all would be ready for the great event early in the ensuing spring. And at length, on the 20th of May, 1841, the foundation-stone was solemnly blessed and laid by Dr. Fleming with all the imposing ceremonies of the Catholic Church, and the work really commenced.

The following description is from a local newspaper, "The Newfoundlander," of Thursday, May 20, 1841:—

LAYING OF THE FOUNDATION-STONE OF THE CATHOLIC CATHEDRAL.

"On Thursday last, the day appointed for the purpose, this interesting ceremony took place. At 12 o'clock the procession commenced forming at the Roman Catholic chapel, and soon after moved slowly onwards, proceeding down Queen's Street, through Water Street, and to the cathedral ground by Cochrane Street. The day was not particularly favorable, but the weather continued sufficiently fine to admit of the proceedings of the day being terminated without much inconvenience. Competent judges, who viewed the multitude on the ground, estimated the number assembled at ten to twelve thousand; and we think it did not fall short of it, for, as the procession proceeded, it seemed as though it would never end. After the ceremony of laying the stone had been gone through a short but impressive address was delivered by the Right Rev. Dr. Fleming, pointing out the importance of the great work he had now commenced, of the difficulties that stood in the way of its accomplishment, but which he confidently expected to surmount. A collection was then opened on the ground, and the handsome sum of £2,600 ($10,400) raised on the spot. The proposed edifice is to be on a scale of magnitude unequalled in any of the North American colonies. It will be a stupendous work; but the energy, perseverance, and zeal of Dr. Fleming will, we think, be sufficient eventually to accomplish it, for in the furtherance of the interests of the Church over which he presides he allows no obstacle to arrest his efforts, no difficulties to stand in the way of what he conceives calculated to promote her advancement. It is because of all this that we look to the successful progress of this herculean undertaking, which we should otherwise deem to be wholly impracticable.

PROGRAMME

OF THE

ORDER OF PROCESSION

IN MOVING, THIS DAY,

For the Purpose of laying the Foundation-stone of the New Cathedral.

At 12 o'clock persons who are disposed to unite in this solemn ceremony will assemble in the vicinity of the Catholic Church, whence the procession will move by Queen's Street, down the Lower Street, up the Beach, and by Cochrane Street towards the Cathedral ground, in the following order:—

CROSS-BEARER,

In purple tunic, and on each side of the Cross two acolytes in white, carrying waxen torches.

OF NEWFOUNDLAND. 359

THE BAND, three and three.

A Banner with a painting of the present Pontiff, Gregory XVI., borne by a person dressed in scarlet.

A CARPENTER,
carrying the Plans, supported on the right and left by two Masons, one bearing, on a cushion, a square and mallet, and the other, on a similar cushion, a square and trowel.

A MASON,
carrying, on a cushion, Plans of the Altar.

THE MODEL OF THE CATHEDRAL,
supported by four persons with sashes.

Masons, two and two, with aprons; Tradesmen in general, two and two.
A Painting of the Redeemer, carried by a person in white.

Female Children, three and three; Christian Doctrine Society, two and two; Boys, three and three.

A Painting of St. John, supported by two persons wearing white sashes on each shoulder.

Fishermen, three and three; Mechanics' Society, with their own banners.
Benevolent Irish Society, with their own banners, and preceded by two persons carrying the embroidered figure of St. Patrick.

Farmers, three and three, preceded by one bearing a figure of Daniel O'Connell.

Gentlemen, three and three.

A BAND.

A Banner with a figure of the Queen.

Society of the Blessed Virgin Mary, three and three, preceded by two persons bearing a painting of the Blessed Virgin.

A PRIEST,
carrying in his hands a copper box containing the parchment with the inscriptions, coins, latest periodicals, etc., and supported on the right and left by two Clergymen, one bearing in his hands a vase filled with Holy Water, and the other an Asperges.

PRIESTS,
two and two.

THE BISHOP,
supported by two Priests.

The foundation-stone was a huge mass of granite about two tons in weight. It was placed under the corner of the western tower. In the cavity was placed a parchment roll with the following inscription: —

To the Great Honor and Glory of God.

THIS FIRST STONE OF THE CATHOLIC CATHEDRAL OF ST. JOHN'S, NEWFOUNDLAND,

DEDICATED TO THE MOST HIGH GOD, UNDER THE PATRONAGE OF

THE BLESSED ST. JOHN THE BAPTIST, WAS LAID BY THE RIGHT REV. DR. FLEMING,

IN THE PRESENCE OF THE PRIESTS WHOSE NAMES ARE HEREUNTO SUBSCRIBED,

AND SEVERAL THOUSANDS OF OTHER PERSONS, ON THURSDAY 20TH DAY OF MAY,

IN THE YEAR OF OUR REDEMPTION 1841, IN THE 4TH YEAR OF THE REIGN OF HER MOST GRACIOUS MAJESTY QUEEN VICTORIA,

AND THE ELEVENTH OF THE PONTIFICATE OF HIS HOLINESS POPE GREGORY XVI.

The following are the names of the priests who signed the document, all of whom have gone to their reward: —

Very Rev. C. Dalton,	Rev. P. K. Ward,
Very Rev. Denis Mackin,	Rev. Jno. Foristal,
Rev. Thomas Waldron,	Rev. Jno. Cummings,
Rev. James Murphy,	Rev. Kyran Walsh,
Rev. P. K. Cleary,	Rev. Ed. O'Keefe,
Rev. Pelagius Nowlan,	Rev. John Ryan.

The foundation of the cathedral of St. John's marks the commencement of a remarkable era in the history of Newfoundland. "One generation after another," writes Dr. Mullock, "of adventurers retired with wealth, but still Newfoundland remained a pathless wilderness, without roads, without postal communication, even, with the mother-country; without any improvement since the days the red Indians roamed through the land, unless a few wooden stores, some wooden villages scattered along the sea-coast, and a miserable wooden town for its capital. The erection of the largest church in North America, on the most commanding position in St. John's, was a grand protest that Newfoundland was no longer to be merely the home of a migratory fishing population; but that henceforth she should take a place among the infant nations of the New World, destined, from her position, her resources, and her maritime population, to be hereafter the Queen of the Northern Ocean!"

The work of the cathedral progressed rapidly, so that Dr. Fleming, writing in 1843, was able to say: —

"The main walls of this noble edifice are now raised about thirty feet, and the extern walls are finished; yet I am obliged to pause until I shall have obtained from Ireland a sufficient quantity of cut stone for its completion. But it has often been a subject of remark how it happens that I, who can command such assistance from my people, should come to Ireland for cut stone? Simply because the difference of wages paid in colonies and in Ireland more than meets the amount of freight to Newfoundland, as vessels engaged in the North American timber trade, being obliged generally to go out in ballast, are ready to take freight at what will barely pay the expenses of the voyage. As it is necessary that new contracts be now entered into for the remainder of the building, I therefore found it requisite to revisit Ireland once more for this purpose; for it is only in winter I could think of absenting myself from Newfoundland, even for the shortest period, without materially interfering with the progress of this structure; and although I am quite sensible of the difficulties before me, yet my reliance is upon the benevolence of the faithful; and when I reflect that in all my undertakings hitherto, however great the expense, and however limited my humble means of meeting it, Heaven was always ready to open a way to their accomplishment. I must say that I have never entertained a doubt that He who planned the great temple of antiquity and endowed it with the wealth of the nations of the world; and He who, upon the base of the humble fishermen of Galilee, reared a church conspicuous for its grandeur, and magnificence, and extent, will not withhold His assistance when there is a question of raising up in the midst of the wilderness a temple to His worship, intended to attract the wanderers to the fold, and to last for ages as a monument of our fidelity to that creed to which we are devoted. When there is a question of the establishment of an edifice where the little ones of His promise shall be brought up in the ways of peace, and schooled in the paths of virtue and religion, He will open the hearts of the faithful followers of His sacred cross to lend their cordial and zealous assistance."

Nevertheless, some mistakes were committed in the furtherance of the work. He unfortunately endeavored to carry out the building without the superintendence of a qualified architect, and, in consequence, met many grievous disappointments; portions of the work had to be taken down before it was completed, and the roof had to be renewed immediately after his death. He was also frequently deceived in the purchase of materials. He labored under one great difficulty, the want of good workmen. Very few stone buildings then existed in the city. The churches, courthouse, and public offices were all of wood. Architectural beauty or durability were not thought of, and, consequently, skilled workmen, especially masons and stone-cutters, were with difficulty procured. It was, then, a herculean task to undertake such a building, and while his whole energies were given to the work, a constant fire of complaints was kept up against him at the Colonial Office and the Propaganda.

In 1846 occurred the ever-memorable fire. Dr. Fleming was in England at the time, as has already been stated. He lost by the fire £4,000 ($16,000), and on his return to St. John's he applied for a portion of the money collected in England (£31,516 stg.) for the restoration of the city of St. John's, but was refused.

Notwithstanding the great blow received from "The Fire of '46," which also laid in ashes his beautiful new convent, the energetic Prelate still pushed on the great work of the cathedral. In June, 1848, he describes, in a communication to the Society for the Propagation of the Faith, the state of the building: "It is now, in the seventh year after the laying of the first stone, brought so near to completion that the oldest man who looked upon its commencement may not unreasonably hope to be spared to see it opened for divine worship." And notwithstanding the series of misfortunes which the country met with during those years from fire, tempests, etc. (for the "Year of the fire" is known also as the "Year of the gale"), yet the church is clear of all debt. "Nor shall we owe a shilling until the completion of the altars, which will be about the middle of next summer."

During the year 1848 and 1849 Dr. Fleming was in correspondence with Messrs. Tobin, of Halifax, Gilmore and Rankin and others, of New Brunswick, in relation to the timber required for the cathedral. In a letter to Dr. Dollard, Bishop of New Brunswick, 31st January, 1848, he speaks of the cathedral as follows: —

"I have now completed the structure of this beautiful edifice as to the externals. The walls, the roof, and the towers are all finished, and I have only the interior now to struggle through." "But this," he says, "considering the size of the building and the state of the poor people, stricken by fire, by tempest, and by famine, is a matter of no mean magnitude."

This is the last letter extant concerning the great work of Dr. Fleming's episcopate. At the risk of becoming tedious I have thought it well to dwell at length on these touching pictures drawn by the holy Bishop at the very time that he was occupied, mind, and soul, and heart, with his stupendous enterprise. It is true they are more matters of biography than history; but as these pages are written chiefly for Newfoundlanders, who cherish with fond affection the remembrance of those glorious days, I would deem this work imperfect were I to omit any portion of these descriptions. The finishing and adorning of the cathedral, the erection of the grand altars, the placing of all the splendid works of art, painting, statuary, mosaic, etc., belong rather to the life of Dr. Mullock than Dr. Fleming, and shall be treated of at length in a future volume. For the present I conclude this chapter by repeating, that Dr. Fleming lived to see this crowning labor of his life and love so far completed that he was able to celebrate the first Mass in it on Easter Sunday, 1850, though he was so weak in health that he was obliged to have a chair placed at the altar, on which he rested several times during the sacred function.

CHAPTER XXV.

THE MERCY NUNS. — [1837-1850.]

Persecution of Dr. Fleming — The "Secret Affidavits" — His Visit to Rome — Honor Conferred on him by the Pope — Appointed Domestic Prelate to His Holiness and Assistant at the Pontifical Throne — Introduction of the Sisters of Mercy (1842) — Arrival of the Nuns — Enthusiastic Reception — Sister Frances Creedon — Sister Joseph Nugent — Mother Mary Vincent — The "Famine Fever" (1848) — The Cholera (1856) — The Orphanage — Mother Xavier — The New Orphanage — St. Bride's Academy.

FROM what has been written in the last chapter, showing the almost herculean labors of Dr. Fleming in the pushing on of the great and gigantic work, the building of the cathedral, it might well be thought that it would have absorbed every faculty of his mind, every energy of his body, every moment of his time; yet it was not so; for during this period, notwithstanding his frequent voyages across the ocean, his flying from one city to another, consulting with architects and modellers; making contracts with workmen and superintending their operations; arranging for the transshipment of material to Newfoundland, and the thousand other details connected with his undertaking, he contrived to pay his official visit to Rome (*ad limina*), and there to draw up and publish in Italian his "*Relazione*," a most exhaustive treatise on the state of the Mission. He also undertook, during the most active years of the cathedral progress, the introduction of the Sisters of Mercy, a work which alone would have been sufficient to monopolize all the attention of an ordinary man. But, besides all these matters appertaining more immediately to his spiritual charge, he took a most active part in the new political life of the colony, just then developing itself. But what is most wonderful is, that all this time he was the subject of a constant attack, and a species of persecution, which would have prevented one of a different disposition from giving attention to any serious matter; in fact, would have driven him to despair. All this, however, only seemed to nerve Dr. Fleming on to greater deeds, and to add new determination to his will, new force to his physical powers.

This systematic and relentless opposition Dr. Fleming had to contend with throughout the whole of his episcopate; and what made it more painful was that it came, as it were, from "his own household;" that is to say, a certain party of his own flock, who seemed disposed to condemn and criticise all his actions. It was amazing to what lengths this cabal proceeded, leaving no stone unturned to procure the dismissal or withdrawal from the country of this noble Prelate. First, the civil arm was tried: complaints were made to the Colonial Office accusing him of disloyal conduct. The prejudices of the local governor (Captain Prescott) were enlisted against him, and a series of affidavits, *secretly* taken by him, were sent to London; but all to no purpose. Then the spiritual power was enlisted: Bishops and Prelates in high authority in London and in Rome were, by false representations, persuaded to raise the cry against him; and, finally, Lord John Russell, then Prime Minister, ordered the Foreign Secretary to communicate with the Austrian Minister, Prince Metternich, to have the complaints against Dr. Fleming laid before the court of Rome. As long as the accusations were confined within local and colonial limits, Dr. Fleming could afford to despise them, and, as it were, trample them down by the great moral strength of his character and that almost heroic confidence which he felt from the inward conviction of being right. But when efforts were made to damage his character in Rome, then, at last, a sensitive point was touched, and he felt himself moved to action to vindicate his doings. In the year 1837 he went to Rome. He was received with the most marked courtesy, and triumphantly vindicated his action against his accusers, so as to gain the highest approval from the Vatican. The statement of his case, already alluded to, and largely quoted from in this volume, the "*Relazione*," was so interesting and important that the Holy Father ordered it to be printed at the Propaganda printing-office.

It was in the year 1837 that, being in England on one of his journeys about securing the plot of land for the cathedral, "with no prospect of returning to the home of my heart," as he writes to Father Troy, "for some months to come," he made up his mind to go and receive the Pontifical Benediction at Rome, as well as to rebut once for all the calumnies insinuated against him. The first difficulty to be encountered was the shortness of funds. But he found a kind friend in a Mr. Wright, a banker in London, who gave him a letter of credit for twice as much as he would require to spend. He travelled by easy stages, "loitering his time along the Continent," as he modestly says; but we may rest assured that his active mind and observant eye and indefatigable energy were all at work to profit to the utmost by this journey,—to acquire useful hints in architecture, or add to his store of ecclesiastical knowledge; to pick up rare and interesting books, paintings, and works of art. He consequently did not arrive in Rome till the 12th of March, and, to his great regret, he found that it was too late to be able to make the preliminary arrangements to enable him to take part in the ceremonies of Holy Week. In the first place, he had not the robes necessary to wear on being presented at the Papal court. "Mere accident, however, put in my way the robes of a Franciscan Archbishop," which had been left at St. Isidore's. "But still I could not attend the ceremonies without being first presented, and it was too late for that now. Thus was I situated on the evening of the 18th of March, deploring in silence my misfortune, when I perceived a dragoon galloping towards the convent of St. Isidore's, and I immediately was presented with a letter from the Master of the Apostolic Palace informing me that the Holy Father, having learnt of my arrival and disappointment, had been pleased to dispense with the ceremony of presentation, and signifying the desire of the Pontiff that I should attend the

functions, and take my place among the Bishops next day
(Palm Sunday), and that the Holy Father would give me an
audience afterwards.

"This was a very special favour, particularly as it was
granted without memorial or solicitation, either direct or
indirect. On the third day of my attending the *Cappella
Sistina*, while all were sitting, the Pope on his throne, the
Cardinals in choir, during the singing of the *Credo*, . . .
I was conducted from where I sat, among Bishops of every
nation, and placed as one of the assistant Prelates to the
throne, and constituted Chaplain to His Holiness."

He felt overwhelmed by this honor paid to one so
insignificant as himself, in the presence of Cardinals,
Bishops, Princes, and Prelates of all ranks. He made,
while in Rome, a collection of splendid paintings, with other
substantial gifts, for the benefit of Newfoundland. "I must
remark," he writes, "that the greatest enemies are often
destined by Heaven to accomplish the greatest amount of
good for those against whom their hostility is directed. I
would hardly ever receive those marked attentions had not
my name attracted the notice of the court of Rome through
the medium of my enemies." He alludes to a report set
afloat that he had been appointed to Waterford, as Bishop;
again, that he should not leave Rome. "But," he says,
"solemnly before Heaven I declare there is not a situation in
the Catholic Church I would accept this moment if it were
to keep me from Newfoundland." He closes this very interesting
letter, of which only a small portion has been extracted,
by asking Father Troy to send on whatever money
he can possibly spare. "The expenses of a Bishop here are
enormous. My dress, as assistant at the throne, cost 200
scudi ($200) ; and then every Bishop must keep a servant in
livery with an enormous cocked hat."

For many years Dr. Fleming had meditated the introduction
of a religious Order for the instruction of children of the
more wealthy classes, who were both able and anxious to pay
for their education. The institution of the Presentation

Convent was intended for the education of the female poor, not only of St. John's, but of the whole Island. "But so attractive had it proved," writes Dr. Fleming to Archdeacon O'Connell," that very many children of the wealthier classes have attended their schools; some even have been sent from the most remote parts of the Island to obtain their education there, and not a few from the neighbouring colonies.

"Still did I feel that more was needed. I certainly was every day more and more gratified at beholding the happy progress of this invaluable institution, although for several years the whole burthen of the school fell upon the four foundresses of the establishment; but at length their great usefulness attracted the attention of others, and four more have since been added, whose assistance is most valuable. Yet I saw that so far I had only provided for the religious instruction of a portion of my people, and I sighed over the wants of the more respectable, the more wealthy, and comfortable classes, because the want of good female schools even for these was deplorable.

"Anspach, in his 'History of Newfoundland,' written in 1815, tells us such was the character of the intellectual portion 'of the inhabitants of the capital that Paine's "Age of Reason" and "Rights of Man" had more authority among the inhabitants of St. John's than the sacred Scriptures. Infidelity had taken fast hold of the public mind, and the most detestable opinions upon these momentous subjects were unblushingly espoused and advocated by individuals holding some of the most important situations in society.' This picture, to be sure, is drawn by a Protestant clergyman; but we must admit that there was much truth in it; and to this may be added the great laxity that at that time, and, indeed, until recently, prevailed amongst Catholics, some of the most respectable of whom would go to the Protestant church or to the Methodist meeting-house openly to a mid-day or evening service, to exhibit their *liberality*. These things greatly embarrassed the morning of my Mission; but although they have, thank God! nearly faded away, yet from the aping after gentility (because good care is taken by our rulers to keep Protestantism the 'genteel religion,' for the amount paid in salaries to public officers is upwards of £20,800, annually, and out of which there is only £820 paid to Catholics, and even this small sum was kept from them until within the last five years, since when three Catholic appointments have been made) — from the aping after gentility, particularly amongst those who wish to be considered as respectable Catholic young ladies, you would be astonished to behold their eagerness to show themselves off at a Protestant ceremony, or to marry any little Protestant that may present himself.

"Thus was it incumbent on me, by every exertion in my power, to apply a remedy to this evil; to raise the character of Catholicity; to give it a position in public estimation that it had not before; and, therefore, as no school had ever been established in Newfoundland where respectable Catholic ladies could receive a good and religious education, I determined, as the means best calculated to accomplish this end, to introduce a community of nuns of the Order of Mercy, whose rule would permit them to keep a pension school; and in compliance with this determination I sent to their parent institution, at Baggott Street, under the care of the sainted foundress, the late Mrs. McAuley, a young lady who had resided several years in Newfoundland, and who was intimately acquainted with the circumstances of the country, and the peculiar wants that I particularly needed to supply, to pass there her novitiate, in order that she should return to me after her profession, together with such other ladies as should be inspired to accompany her, in order to found a Convent of Mercy at St. John's and open a school, — a day-school for such as could pay for their education, — a school where children may be taught the elegant and fashionable accomplishments of the day, and at the same time may have their young minds properly imbued with the principles of religion. Two ladies of that Order accordingly did come. In May, 1842, they sailed from Dublin, accompanied by three ladies, postulants for the Presentation convent, and five priests for the Mission, and arrived all in good health at St. John's after a passage of twenty-eight days. The ladies for the Presentation Order were at once conveyed to their convent. The priests were soon placed in their respective Missions, — the Sisters of Mercy taking up their abode at my residence, which I had given up to them *pro tempore*, until I should have prepared for them a more suitable and comfortable dwelling."

These pioneers of the Mercy Order in the New World arrived in St. John's on the feast of the Sacred Heart, the 10th day of June, 1842, about six months after the death of the saintly foundress, Mother McAuley.[1] This was the first house of the Order founded in America, and there is a tradition of the Order that Mother McAuley herself had intended to come to Newfoundland to found the house here had not death taken her away. The young lady alluded to by Dr. Fleming in the extract was Miss Creedon, who was appointed first Rev. Mother of the new establishment, and to her in a great measure is due the existence of the Order in Newfoundland to-day.

The arrival of the first Sisters in St. John's is thus described by Dr. Fleming: —

"The signal of the approach of the 'Sir Walter Scott' on the morning of the 10th inst. produced among our population the most gratifying excitement, and as the wind was off-

---

[1] The Order of the Sisters of Mercy was founded by Catherine McAuley, in Dublin, in 1827. This saintly woman was born on the feast of St. Michael (Sept. 29), 1787, at Stormantown House, County Dublin. She was endowed with a most affectionate and charitable disposition. She felt a peculiar desire to console sorrow and affliction wherever she encountered it. She lost her parents when young, and on coming into possession of her property she at once set about the erection of her institute, which was destined to occupy such an important place in the Church. She purchased a piece of ground in Baggott Street, Dublin, and on the feast of Our Lady of Mercy (24th Sept.), 1827, the new building was solemnly blessed by Dr. Blake (her sincere friend and spiritual director, afterwards Bishop of Dromore), when she at once opened her schools for poor children, and obtained permission to visit the sick in the hospitals. In June, 1830, the new institute was confirmed by Rescript of Pope Pius VIII. The Order soon began to spread. Applications came from all parts for the establishment of colonies of the Sisters. She died, in the odor of sanctity, on the 11th November, 1841.

shore, and she could not make the harbour early in the day, towards the afternoon I took a pilot-boat and proceeded to sea to greet our pious friends upon their arrival, and, if necessary, to bring them ashore, lest they should be compelled to add another night to their weary voyage.

"I reached the vessel about four miles from the shore, and was happy to find all on board in excellent health. I was, indeed, almost surprised to see our reverend Sisters so very well after a transatlantic voyage of thirty days, unused as they were to the sea, and that their spirits were not in the slightest degree subdued.

"The captain, Mr. Byars, whose kindness and attention throughout were subjects of much praise, now informed us that he could not expect to enter the harbour that evening, in consequence of which we made immediate preparations to get the nuns and six clergymen ashore. For this purpose we used the boat which I had brought, together with that belonging to the pilot on board, and which had remained with the vessel, and in a short time got all on board the boats, although, from the great height of the vessel and the heaving of the sea, it was attended with some difficulty to get the ladies safely and comfortably placed there." He then gives a graphic description of the "Narrows," the town, the fish-flakes and stages, and speaks of the surprise and interest taken in all these things by the Sisters. "On approaching the wharf of the Hon. James Tobin, we found it and those adjoining thronged with multitudes who were eager to extend a welcome to those who had made so many and such great sacrifices for the promotion of the spiritual interests of the people of Newfoundland, and, as they neared the landing-place, cheers, loud and long, testified the delight of the expectant multitudes.

"On landing, the ladies were conducted by the Hon. Mrs. Tobin to her residence, where they remained until my carriage arrived to remove them, upon which they repaired to the Presentation convent, where, having left the two postulants, they proceeded to the church to offer thanksgiving, and to invoke a blessing on their Mission, prior to entering my house, which had been hastily fitted up for them, their own convent not being yet finished, notwithstanding the activity with which the work progressed.

"They are now actively engaged in their sacred employ, daily visiting the sick. Indeed, so pressing were they to be permitted to enter upon their labours immediately on their arrival, that I was obliged to consent to it on the subsequent Monday. . . . And such has been the industry of their attendance, and the efficacy of their instructions, rendered still more efficacious by the suavity of their manners, that they are looked up to with the greatest reverence and affection by all classes of the community. In the meantime I proceeded actively with their convent, and in a few months, with an expenditure of more than two thousand pounds, I was enabled to conduct them into a commodious and comfortable edifice adjoining the cathedral, in a commanding position, presenting from the town and harbour an extremely interesting object. They are now joined by a fourth lady, of high literary attainments, who, as she had previously completed her novitiate in another house, has been already professed.

"On the 1st of May of the past year (1843) they opened their school, and in a very brief space of time they had a considerable number of pupils, whose progress even now, from the exceedingly judicious system, gives great satisfaction; but the community is now so small, and as they are engaged in teaching between the hours of ten and three, without a moment's relaxation, the necessary result of this is, that during that time the sick must be entirely neglected.

"Would to God that the Spirit of the Holy Ghost would inspire some three or four daughters of the Island of Saints, gifted with an education and accomplishments suited to the fulfilment of the varied and important duties of such an institution, to embark upon a mission that promises so rich a harvest! How happy should I feel at receiving upon our shores a treasure so valuable! How gratified to be able to add to those pious Sisters a sufficient number to render the performance of the school duties facile, and at the same time to save the sick *poor* particularly from the privation of which, since May, they have been thus to a great extent necessarily subjected!"

The convent spoken of by Dr. Fleming was of wood. It has been replaced by one of stone, of superior style and accommodation, erected by Dr. Mullock, on the same site, in 1856. It was solemnly opened on the feast of St. Michael, 1857. The two ladies who accompanied Miss Creedon to found the convent were Miss Lynch (Sister Mary Rose) and Miss Freney (Sister M. Ursula). These latter returned to Ireland, in November, 1843,[1] leaving the sole charge of the institution on the shoulders of Sister M. Francis. For nine months, during a period of great trial, did she alone maintain the existence of the Order, when, owing to some untoward circumstances, the Bishop was all the time undecided as to whether the convent should be preserved or suppressed. The indomitable perseverance of Miss Creedon triumphed. Day after day, week after week, month after month, she went regularly through all the routine of convent discipline, — rang herself to prayer, to meditation, to refectory, to choir; performed by herself the Office, the spiritual lecture, the visit; attended the sick, taught the school. In a word, continued every practice just as if there were a whole community under her charge. At length she was joined by Miss Maria Nugent, who took, in religion, the name of Sister M. Joseph. This was a lady of remarkable character and talents. She is the same who, in a former chapter, is mentioned as having been the first postulant received in Newfoundland. She was received for the Presentation Order, but finding she had not a vocation for that institute, she retired to the house of her brother, John V.

---

[1] Sister M. Rose retired from the Order, and is still living at Toulouse, in France. Sister Ursula went to Australia and founded a branch of the Order there. She died, full of merits and good works, this present year, 1886.

Nugent, Esq., where she lived the life of a recluse, never appearing in public except at church, and never casting aside the religious habit. She was a lady of refined taste and cultivation, a classical scholar, and mistress of the modern languages. She occupied her time in the education of her brother's children. As soon as the Sisters of Mercy came she felt revive within her the strong religious vocation, which only wanted the proper channel to develop itself. She was joyfully received by Sister Francis, who was a sister of Mrs. Nugent. She fulfilled with exemplary zeal all the duties of a true Sister of Mercy for the period of four years, when she fell a victim to her holy calling. The year 1848 is ever memorable in the history not only of Ireland, but also in Newfoundland and Canada, as "the year of the famine." Thousands of poor, starving immigrants, striving to escape the dreadful death from hunger at home, endeavored to crowd themselves aboard the ships bound to America. Then ensued all the miseries of squalor, disease, and fever, ending in wretched death and promiscuous burial on the first point of land reached for those who had not already been thrown by hundreds into the ocean. This terrible "famine fever" found its way to St. John's, and the victims were placed in the hospital, and were attended by the Sisters of Mercy.

Among those unfortunates was one who turned a deaf ear and hardened heart to the exhortations of the priest. Sister Joseph undertook the task of reconciling him to God. All day long she watched, and prayed, and exhorted, and instructed by his bedside, till God heard her prayer, and the poor wretch opened his heart to the inpouring of divine grace. The priest was at hand, the poor soul was shriven, the body anointed, and death soon came.

Sister Joseph returned to her convent, her heart full of thanksgiving; but, alas! the germs of the fatal malady had taken deep hold of her. A few days and she too was laid in the grave of the fever-stricken,—a martyr to the spirit of her sacred vocation.

Immediately after Sister Joseph's death Mrs. Creedon was

joined by Miss Agnes, eldest daughter of John V. Nugent, Esq., and niece of both ladies, so well known afterwards as Mother Mary Vincent. Mother Vincent, besides inheriting the bright gifts of a learned race, had had also the advantage of a training of the first order, and a classical education, with all its accompanying refinements, under her aunt. She at an early age manifested a strong and fixed desire to enter religion. She was received into the Order by Dr. Fleming. This was the last act of the kind performed by that venerable Prelate, and he rose from a sick-bed to pay this honor to a family for whom he had so great a respect. Her profession, on the 8th December, 1850, was made in presence of Dr. Mullock, so that her career forms, as it were, a connecting link between the two episcopates.

In 1850 the orphanage in connection with the convent was erected by Dr. Mullock, the funds for the purpose having been left by Dr. Fleming. Mother Vincent was appointed Superior, and removed with the orphans to the old Monastery of Belvidere in 1859, when a young ladies' boarding-school, under the title of "St. Clare's," was opened in the orphanage building.

From this time forward the Order flourished vigorously in the Island, and constant new instalments of novices and postulants arrived from Ireland to fill its ranks. On the occasion of the profession of Mother Vincent, the white veil was taken by Miss Theresa Bernard, a young lady just then arrived from Limerick, and who has lived among us for the past half a century as Mother Xavier. Both have now gone to receive the reward of long lives of labor and love.

In the year 1856 the cholera broke out in St. John's, and raged with great violence. Then were seen the Sisters of Mercy in their true element. From daylight till dark, and often through the night, they worked indefatigably. No part of the city slums was too dark or too filthy for them. They entered the houses of the plague-stricken when all others had abandoned them, lighting the fires and preparing some humble food; scrubbing and cleaning up the little tenements;

dressing and washing the sick; and, finally, carrying the dead bodies to the coffins, which were placed at the doors on the streets by fearful officials. But it is unnecessary, as it would be impossible, to recount all that was done by them in those dreary days. It is enough to say they were true to the spirit of their holy Order.

In the course of time the Order spread throughout various parts of the Island, so that there are now seven communities and over fifty Sisters in the country. Of late years a great impetus has been given to the Order in both the charitable and the teaching branches. A magnificent new orphanage, in brick and stone, has been erected at a cost of about $20,000 at Belvidere, furnished with all the latest improvements and modern appliances, for the accommodation of from eighty to one hundred orphans. At the Mother House, the school of the Guardian Angels, for infant boys and girls, has been opened, to be conducted on the kindergarten system; and a new young ladies' academy, opened at the beautiful grounds of St. Bride's, Waterford Bridge, which, though yet only in its infancy, has given already great promise of future success.

CHAPTER XXVI.

POLITICS — [1832-1838.]

General Review — State Politics — Petition for Home Rule — Local Legislature Granted (1832) — First Elections — Judge Boulton — Affair of Drs. Carson and Keilly — Patrick Morris, Esq., Attacks the Judge in the Assembly — Messrs. Nugent, Kent, and Carson Appointed a Delegation to London on the Boulton Case — Dr. Fleming's Views on the Subject — His Great Influence at Home, and in Local Politics — Judge Boulton Condemned and Removed.

FREQUENT allusion has been made in these pages to the political state of the Island during Dr. Fleming's time; and, though this work claims to be but a history of the ecclesiastical affairs of the country, yet, so intimately are they connected with its political life, that a biography of Dr. Fleming would be incomplete without a more particular mention of them.

The period at which Dr. Fleming obtained the reins of spiritual jurisdiction in Newfoundland was one of great political activity in Ireland, and, in fact, throughout the world. The spirit of autonomy and independence awakened by the French Revolution had spread like a fire among all peoples. The old-time sentiment of feudalism and conservatism was shaken from its throne, and the people, under the high-sounding title of the *Democracy*, began to claim a voice and a right in the management of the affairs of their nation which they had never before thought of.

It is not my intention here to pass any judgment on this modern innovation; possibly it may have its advantages as well as its drawbacks. One of its effects undoubtedly was the relaxation of religious, or rather denominational, conservatism, which also is a doubtful advantage, but which, at all events in England, paved the way toward the concession of religious liberty to British subjects belonging to the

hitherto "abominable" Church of Rome. The immediate
fruit of this sentiment of toleration, dexterously and deter-
minedly manipulated by O'Connell, was the undeniable boon
of Catholic Emancipation. This boon once gained, the
Irish people, having thus secured, at least in some measure,
though not completely, their rights as Christians, immediately
set about considering how they should secure their rights as
citizens, — those civil privileges and recognitions which had
been so long denied them. Then arose in the national breast
those aspirations which in our own day have culminated in
the Home Rule movement, now at last on the eve of being
crowned with success.

It is but natural that all these agitations and movements
of political life in the mother-country should immediately
react upon the colonies, and that the same scenes should be
there repeated on a smaller scale. Particularly was this the
case in Newfoundland. Firstly, because she is the nearest
transatlantic colony to the mother-country; and, secondly,
because the majority of her population were composed of
immigrants fresh from the scenes of political and religious
strife "at home;" and the tales of Vinegar Hill and The
Bridge of Ross were rehearsed of winter nights by actual
participants in these encounters. It is no wonder, then, that
the spirit was kept alive. During the years 1831 and 1832
petitions were sent Home from the people demanding a local
Legislature. The prayer of the petitions was granted
at length, and in 1832 the first elections took place. As
might be expected in a country hitherto unaccustomed to
the exercise of the political franchise, considerable excitement and denominational discord was created. Hitherto all
the public offices in the country had been filled to the
exclusion of the Roman Catholics. These latter, having the
majority among the voting population, elected members of
their own Church; and deeming that the time had at length
arrived when they should obtain justice, probably became
somewhat arrogant, and allowed their feelings of injured
right to verge very closely on the borders of vengeance, if

not to outstep them. The dominant party, on the other
hand, seeing their long-possessed power and influence about
to be wrenched from their grasp, no doubt made desperate
efforts to retain their hold. Hence we can easily see that
feeling must have run high on both sides.

In November, 1833, the year of the first local parliament,
Judge Boulton arrived in Newfoundland. He had been
removed from the position of Attorney-General of Canada
owing to some political trouble. He was a man of great
legal knowledge, but of most domineering and passionate
character. No sooner had he arrived in the country than
he began to make sweeping innovations in the laws and
established customs, especially those regarding the empanelling of juries and the relations between the merchant and
the fisherman. The other two judges of the Supreme Court,
Messrs. Des Barres and Brenton, awed by his superior
forensic acumen, became pliant tools in his hands, and
acquiesced in all his judgments. The people, however,
soon began to resent these encroachments on their rights.
He altered the law as regards the empanelling of juries in
such a manner as to enable the merchants to select special
juries entirely of their own class. He abrogated the law
which gave the fisherman a first lien for wages on the voyage
and preference in payment for current supplies. But these
were not the worst of his faults. A suit was instituted by
Dr. Carson against Dr. Keilly for defamation of character
in the matter of the case of a certain Mrs. Antle. Dr.
Keilly was physician to the judge's family, and the judge
showed a marked prejudice against Dr. Carson. He went
so far as to say from the bench that if the case had resulted
in the death of the woman he would have Dr. Carson indicted
for murder, and he would make the Grand Jury bring in a
true bill; and he wound up by saying, "I would certainly
hang you! Yes, I would hang you!" So far did he at
length compromise himself in these matters that the case
was brought before the Imperial authorities, and in 1838
Patrick Morris, Esq., made a most powerful attack upon the

judge from his place in the Assembly. He was joined by Messrs. Nugent and Kent, and so serious were their accusations that the judge took out an action for libel against them. The words of Patrick Morris on this occasion have a ring about them worthy of O'Connell, his great prototype. The following extract from the speech of this great champion of liberty in Newfoundland deserve to be embalmed in the pages of a history such as this: " The Chief Justice has exhibited on various occasions great partiality on the bench. His adjudications have been biassed by strong party prejudices; his judgments have been unjust, arbitrary, and illegal, opposed to the mild and merciful principles of British law; opposed to public liberty, to *Magna Charta*, which proclaims that 'freemen shall not be amerced for small faults or above measure for great transgressions.' . . . Judge Boulton has totally subverted the ancient laws and customs of the country; has set aside the decisions of all former courts and judges. This is a statement I have frequently made for the last three years, . . . at public meetings and in published letters, when I could not claim the privileges of a member of this House. . . . I was determined to abide the consequences. No punishment could be too severe for me if I had, without foundation, made these charges. The proof of their truth, I think, I might rest altogether on the fact of their never having been denied. The judges did not deny them, the bar did not deny them; the lawyers who owed Judge Boulton so much for giving them a monopoly did not stand forth in his defence. No man has been found publicly, either through the courts or the press, to defend him. The facts are notorious and undisputed. . . . He has trampled on the rights and privileges and immunities of the British subject."

To cap the climax of all his illegal proceedings he laid aside the ermine, descended from the bench, and pleaded his own cause. Finally, an address to the Imperial authorities was drawn up by the House of Assembly; but he, in his capacity of President of the Council, had it rejected. A deputation was then appointed, consisting of Messrs. Carson, Nugent, and Morris, who proceeded to London and succeeded in having the matter tried before the Privy Council and obtaining the removal of the obnoxious judge. The Privy Council, in sentencing the judge, though endeavoring to screen him from the more serious charges, yet recommended his removal for having indiscreetly allowed himself to so much participate in the strong feelings which appeared unfortunately to have influenced the different parties in the colony.

It was but natural that the Catholic Bishop and clergy should take an active interest in this matter. They were fully convinced that the judge was prejudiced against their flock, and that they could not expect justice from him. Dr. Fleming being in London, 1838, during this trial, thus writes to Father Troy: "On the second day of my arrival here I found out the address of Dr. Carson and Mr. Nugent, and finding them so comfortably housed, I joined them, and now here we are a trio. I did this to show that with them, and with the people of Newfoundland, I wished to be identified, and that with them I should prosper or perish." He then states that from the tone of persons in authority at the Colonial Office it appears pretty certain that "Mr. Boulton is disposed of. I expect soon to hear of the appointment of one to succeed him whose conduct, wisdom, and judgment will, I trust, make reparation for the injuries and heart-burnings inflicted on Newfoundland by that man. . . . The reception of the delegates at the Colonial Office was truly flattering. I am very confident that everything will be done to meet the wishes of the people. . . . Tell the people to be of good heart. Newfoundland will, and must, flourish!" He then states that Lord Durham had been appointed to settle the affairs of Canada, and that he was informed by a gentleman conversant with these matters that he (Lord Durham) was also authorized to take under his care the business of Newfoundland. "You may take this as a fact, that Lord Durham is and will be uncontrolled. His own judgment . . . will be his sole and only guide; . . . and be assured that there is no nobleman within Her Majesty's dominions more capable of forming a correct estimate of affairs or more willing and determined to support the liberties of the people. . . . Dr. Carson feels, as he always did, interested in the happiness of the country and in following up the object of his mission. Poor Nugent is indefatigable. Newfoundland can never sufficiently repay him for his services."

There is a postscript to this letter marked "Private." It may be published now with impunity. It will show the great influence possessed by Dr. Fleming over the political destinies of the country, and will give some ground for the opposition raised against him, which culminated in his being accused before the Home Office, as we have seen. The postscript is to this effect: "It would be most important that the members of the House of Assembly should *peremptorily* refuse to meet until the return of their delegates."

The great political influence acquired by Dr. Fleming, and enjoyed ever since in the colony by his successors, though it was thought a dangerous implement by many, even among his own flock, was never used by him except in the true interests of the country and the people whom he loved so well, and whose temporal welfare, advancement, and comfort ranked in his mind as second only to the salvation of their souls.

CHAPTER XXVII.

"AFTER THE FIRE." — [1847-1850.]

After "The Fire" — Sufferings of the People — "The Camps" — Generosity of the People in Subscribing to the Relief of the Famine-Stricken in Ireland — Dr. Fleming Applies for a Coadjutor — Father J. T. Mullock, O.S.F., Appointed — Arrives in Newfoundland, May, 1848 — Newfoundland Erected into a Diocese, to be Annexed to the Province of Quebec — Dr. Fleming Objects to this Arrangement, also Dr. Mullock — Arrangement Rescinded by Rome — Project of a Colonial Ecclesiastical Seminary — It is Opposed by Dr. Fleming — He Gives his Reasons — His Prejudice against a Colonial Priesthood — Noble Views of Dr. Mullock on this Subject — Establishment of St. Bonaventure's College — Distinguished Newfoundland Priests Abroad — Revs. T. Brown, S.J., Ryan, S.J., Kavanagh, S.J., and Bennett, C.S.S.R. — "First Native Priest" — Father Meagher, S.J. — Rev. Messrs. Greene, Mulloy, Hogan — Sister M. Baptist, First "Native Nun" — Rev. James Brown, First Actual Missionary Born in the Country — Last Days of Dr. Fleming — He Celebrates the First Mass in the Cathedral — His Death and Funeral.

IN the year 1847 St. John's began to rise like the phœnix from its ashes. The tale of her sufferings had been sounded abroad through the world, and generous relief had poured in from all sides in the shape of money, provisions, and clothing. Vessels laden with goods came from England and America. An energetic committee was appointed and organized under Colonel Law, acting governor, and afterwards directed by that most excellent of all our governors, Sir Gaspard Le Marchant, whom a benign Providence had sent at this crisis to mitigate the severity of the great blow inflicted on the country. Through the well-managed agency of this committee the wants of all were supplied, complaints and grievances examined and adjudicated upon, and a *pro rata* money compensation made to all for their losses by the fire. The Benevolent Irish Society, always at the front in cases of emergency, handed over to the use of the committee their building, the Orphan Asylum; and daily were seen crowds awaiting their turn at its doors to receive their dole, forming *queues*, after the manner of the famished inhabitants of Paris at the time of the Revolution. Tents, camps, and sheds were improvised to shelter the people, all the vessels in the harbor being laid under contribution; and though many suffered extremely from the severity of the winter, yet such was the good management and zeal of the Relief Committee that not one could be said to have died of actual exposure, though no doubt the hardships undergone may have hastened the deaths of many. Several camps or sheds had been erected on the cathedral ground, where many families passed the winter. In the ensuing August (1847) there were still some fifteen families, comprising some forty souls, as yet unhoused; and foreseeing the probability of being obliged to pass another such winter, they memorialized the Relief Committee, through the Rev. John Forristal, imploring him to lay before them (the committee) their apprehension of encountering the rigors of another winter, exposed to the same unspeakable miseries. "No one," they say, "knows better than your reverence the hardships, the diseases, and the deaths entailed on the unhappy inmates by such utter exposure to the severities of this inclement climate." They were all well housed before the following winter; the sheds were converted into snug and comfortable cottages, and though they still retained the name of "The camps," they did duty for the housing of the poor for many years, until the erection of the Poor Asylum in 1864.

An example of the buoyancy of trade in Newfoundland, and also of the wondrous generosity of the people, is found in the fact that, in this very year of 1847, as they were yet only recovering from the effects of the great fire, they were able to send a most munificent donation to the poor people of Ireland, then suffering from the effects of bad harvests. The following letters are found in the archives of the Secretary's office: —

"SECRETARY'S OFFICE, 22 June, 1847.

"SIR, — By direction of the Governor I transmit to you, for the information of the subscribers to the fund for the relief of the distress prevailing in Ireland, the accompanying copy of a despatch which H.E. the Governor has received from the Right Hon'ble the Sec't'y of State for the Colonies.

"I have the honor to be, Sir,
"Your obed't serv't,
"(Signed) CHRISTOPHER AYRE,
"*pro Sec'l'y.*

"To B. G. GARRETT, Esq., *High Sheriff.*"

"DOWNING STREET, 20th May, '47.

"SIR, — I have to acknowledge the recpt of Colonel Law's despatches, numbered and dated, No. 53 of the 1st and No. 58 of the 27th March, transmitting two Bills for the respective sums of £500 and £350 stg. (being amt collected at a public meeting in St. John's for the relief of the distress prevailing in Ireland), and accompanied by a letter addressed to me by the Sheriff.

. . . .

"(Signed) GREY.
"To SIR G. LE MARCHANT, *Govr. &c.*"

Dr. Fleming, seeing at length the noble edifice, the object of his constant cares and labors for the past ten years, now nearing completion, and feeling his own energies fast succumbing to his many toils and labors, at length besought the authorities in Rome to grant him a coadjutor. His prayer was acceded to, and towards the close of the year 1847 Father John Thomas Mullock, of the same Seraphic Order of St. Francis, was appointed, with the title of Bishop of Thyatira *in partibus*, and with the right of succession. And never did the mantle of a noble Bishop fall on the shoulders of a worthier successor. He was consecrated in Rome on the 27th December, 1847, by His Eminence Cardinal Franzoni, and arrived in St. John's in May, 1848.

At the same time that this appointment was made the Vicariate Apostolic of Newfoundland was canonically erected into an episcopate, Dr. Fleming being thus translated from the nominal See of Carpasia *in partibus infidelium* to the actual See of Newfoundland. The Church of Newfoundland was now considered thoroughly well established and in a flourishing condition, endowed with a cathedral, various churches, convents, etc., so that the authorities in Rome judged it seasonable to thus establish its hierarchy on a permanent basis.

The Bull of the Pope making this canonical erection of the diocese of Newfoundland was forwarded to the Archbishop of Quebec, Monseigneur Joseph Signay, and through His Grace was communicated to Dr. Fleming. The reason of this was that another change was contemplated, namely, the placing of the new diocese as a Suffragan See under the archiepiscopal province of Quebec. To this arrangement, however, Dr. Fleming strenuously objected, and he gives his reasons in full in a letter addressed to the Archbishop on the 18th November, 1847 : —

"I would not," he says, "be discharging my duty to your Grace, to myself, and successors, or to the Church of which I am the humblest Prelate, were I to neglect expressing my opinion of an act the consequences of which can hardly fail to prove injurious to the best interests of religion. . . . One of the principal objects proposed to be attained is the facility of access of the Suffragan to the Metropolitan, and the meeting in Diocesan Synod periodically. But Newfoundland is distant from Quebec no fewer than twenty degrees (about 1,200 miles). There is between that country and this no commercial intercourse. The navigation of the Gulf of St. Lawrence, from its entrance at Cape Ray and the Magdalen Islands, and between the wilds of Anticosti and the dreary shores of Cape Gaspé, to the mouth of the river, is regarded by our most experienced mariners as pregnant with perils while the wrecks of hundreds of Canadian traders that strew the southern coasts of our Island, and the thousands of bones that bleach upon its shores, testify to the dangers that must be surmounted before that gulf or great river can be reached; while, if the more devious route of Halifax be chosen, although the dangers be scarcely mitigated, the distance is nearly doubled.

"When the discharge of an imperative duty, however, is in question, he would be unworthy the name of priest of the living God who would suffer himself to be scared by the terrors of travel, be it by land or sea. But, then, Newfoundland, for six months of the year frequently, at least its eastern shore, is bound by an impassable barrier of ice from 50 to 100 miles wide, which would render it impossible to calculate on leaving this for the westward before July, . . . as the summer is the only season during which we can have access to the various settlements of the country. The temporary withdrawal of the Bishop from his people at that season of the year would be attended with the worst consequences." He hopes that when His Holiness is made acquainted with the circumstances he will revoke the decision. For himself, personally, he says it would be a matter of indifference, for " after labouring in this portion of the great vineyard for nearly thirty years, I find my health so weakened, and my constitution so broken, that it is impossible I could ever hope, during the remnant of my earthly career, to avail myself of the happiness of meeting your Grace, although, from the facilities afforded of communicating with Europe, it is only recently I arrived here from England. Indeed, under any circumstances, it would be far less inconvenient, and attended with far less hazard to the Bishop of Newfoundland at any future time, were his diocese made Suffragan of the Midland District of England, of the diocese of Dublin, or of any of the dioceses of northern France."

No doubt the difficulties are stated in a very exaggerated manner, even for that time, and whatever portion of them did really exist has been greatly diminished since then by the introduction of steamers and railways, and also by a notable change in our climate. Yet, the arguments of the Bishop prevailed, and in his opposition to this arrangement he was strongly seconded by his coadjutor, Dr. Mullock, so that the matter being reconsidered, it was rescinded. Dr. Mullock founded his opposition on the grounds that at some future time the Church of Newfoundland should itself be erected into a Province, and a clause to that effect, *quam primum*, was inserted in the Bulls of his successors.

In the above-quoted letter Dr. Fleming thanks the Archbishop of Quebec for sending a priest to Labrador, and remarks that it would be far more convenient if that place were attached to the Archdiocese of Quebec. That the annexation of this coast to St. John's diocese was made, not by the Bishops of Newfoundland, but by recommendation of a predecessor of His Grace in Quebec.

One other matter of importance occupied the attention of Dr. Fleming before his death, namely, the project of forming an ecclesiastical seminary in Nova Scotia for the education of students for the service of the Mission in all the dioceses of Canada, or at least of the Maritime Provinces. This idea had been conceived by the Rt. Rev. Dr. Walsh, then lately appointed Bishop of Halifax, and was first broached to Dr. Fleming by Lord Stanley, Secretary for the Colonies. In a letter to the Cardinal Secretary of Propaganda, Dr. Fleming expresses his disapproval of this project. He is surprised that the first knowledge of the scheme should have come to him from such a source. He thinks that the colonial Bishops should have been consulted in a matter of such a nature before it had been laid before the Government. He objects strongly to that portion of the scheme in which the Government is asked to subsidize this college, on account of the influence and patronage it would acquire over such a college and the nomination of its staff. He points to the example of Ireland, where the Bishops almost unanimously opposed the establishment by Government even of lay schools. How much more so ought we to object "to the instructors of colonial Catholic ecclesiastics being selected by a British Minister." Again, he says that his experience of the Mission taught him that the missioners best suited to this country are those who have hitherto served it, namely, "young men drafted from Irish colleges." He thinks that to educate young men belonging to the colonies would be fraught with consequences dangerous to peace and concord; that the communities are very small generally, and the people who have acquired wealth are "men of very limited education," consequently inclined to be arrogant; that their children are greatly inclined to a spirit of party and a tendency to combination, which they could hardly escape imbibing at their own firesides. Finally, he thinks that while there are so many colleges in Ireland, France, and Rome, "we ought not to think of creating an institution calculated to foment divisions between natives and colonists."

Until very late years a strong impression existed in the minds of the immigrants from the Old World that there never could be what they called a "*native* priest." It would seem as if Dr. Fleming, too, was tainted with this prejudice. The wider and nobler views, however, of his colossal-minded successor, Dr. Mullock, soon dispelled this false notion. One of his first works was the erection of the diocesan seminary of St. Bonaventure's, and it was soon seen that all that was wanted was a channel for the development of vocations to the priesthood among the children of Newfoundland, and that transportation across the Atlantic had not dried or frozen up the fruitful sources of that grace with which St. Patrick had endowed his faithful people in the Old Land; on the contrary, like the grafting of a new branch upon the old stock, it had but served to make it shoot forth with renewed vigor and fecundity. Dr. Mullock soon saw himself surrounded by a noble staff of "native priests," who, instead of realizing the fears of Dr. Fleming, and "fomenting divisions," worked hand to hand and shoulder to shoulder with the veteran pioneers from Ireland in the missionary field.

This prejudice against a colonial priesthood, amounting almost to a superstition, was not peculiar to Newfoundland, but, it seems, was a general impression brought across the ocean from the Old World to all parts of America. It arose, probably, from the fact of there being no means in the New World of educating youth for so high a calling. But in the course of a few years this absurd notion was dissipated by the march of events and the growth of ecclesiastical seminaries in the infant Church of America. No sooner was an opportunity opened up than it was immediately availed of. In Newfoundland, hardly had the diocesan seminary of St. Bonaventure's been thrown open to the rising generation, than vocations for the sacred ministry manifested themselves more numerously than the needs of the Church required. Hence, at the present time, many of the children of Newfoundland have chosen foreign missions, and, joining the Jesuits, the Redemptorists, or some other of the religious Orders, have now places of distinction and honor. Among these may be mentioned the Very Rev. Thomas Brown, S.J., lately elected to the high and responsible position of Provincial of the Irish Province of the Jesuits. He is a native of the Harbor of Carbineers'. Also the Rev. F. Ryan, S.J., and Rev. L. Kavanagh, S.J., both distinguished members of the Order, — the former a native of Baccalieu; the latter, of St. John's; the Very Rev. Father Bennett, C.S.S.R., a distinguished preacher of the Redemptorist Order, and lately nominated to the Bishopric of Dunkeld, in Scotland.

During the twelve years of Dr. Mullock's episcopate in which the college of St. Bonaventure was in existence it sent forth about thirty students who were elevated to the ranks of the priesthood. But even before that time some of the sons of Terra Nova had become enrolled in the sacred ministry. The question as to who was the first native priest is one of considerable interest, and is shrouded in some obscurity. I have made a very close investigation into this matter, and the result of the inquiry will not be here out of place. It has been stated that the Rt. Rev. Dr. Kinsella, formerly Bishop of Kilkenny, was a native of Bonavista, Newfoundland. The Rev. Patrick Meagher, S.J., was born in St. John's, somewhere about 1780. His father, Thomas Meagher, came out about that time from his native

place, Clonmel, and was in humble circumstances, as many
others who had been plundered of their ancestral estates at
home. He married a wealthy widow, a Mrs. Crotty. Two
of his children, Thomas and Patrick, were born in Newfoundland. He afterwards returned to Waterford. Thomas was
the father of Thomas Francis Meagher, the Young Irelander.
Patrick became a priest and joined the Jesuit Order. In Bat-
tersby's Irish Directory for 1836 a description of St. Francis
Xavier's Church, Upper Gardner Street, Dublin, is given,
after which follows a list of the priests attached to it, among
whom appears the name of " P. Mehar," " under which spelling," says the " Irish Monthly " (Nov., 1881), " is disguised
the uncle of Thomas Francis Meagher, the *Verginaud* of
the Young Ireland of '48."

A young man of the name of Greene, a native of Carbineers', and brother of the late Randal Greene, Esq., of the
Union Bank, was sent to college in Ireland, about the year
1830, by Father Yore. He was ordained deacon by Dr.
Fleming in Ireland, but for some reason was never raised
to the priesthood. He took this so much to heart that in
the course of a year he died. Thus, no doubt, giving new
strength to the popular belief.

Old Father Cleary, of Placentia, sent to college to Quebec
a young man named Mulloy, a native of Burin; but he
turned up in Carbineers' as a *medical doctor*, and practised
there some time. A brother of his was also sent to college
to France. He was in Paris at the time of the three days'
émeute (1830), and was obliged, with the other students,
to fly. He came home to Newfoundland. Dr. Fleming
refused to ordain him, on the ground that, having carried
arms in the defence of the college, he had incurred an irregularity. He went to Canada or the United States, where he
was received and ordained without difficulty, and officiated for
many years. It would appear that Dr. Fleming's scruples
on this point extended also to the other sex, as he refused
to receive a lady (Miss Tarahan) into the Order of the
Sisters of Mercy on account solely of the *bar sinister* on

her escutcheon of having the misfortune of being *native born*. She was, however, afterwards received and professed as Sister M. Baptist, being the first "native" nun, and became, notwithstanding, an excellent *religeuse*. She died in 1867 at the early age of thirty-six.

There was also a young man of the name of Hogan ordained. He was a native of St. John's, but never officiated in the Island after his ordination.

The first priest, then, who actually remained and officiated in his native country as one of her established clergy was the Very Rev. James Brown, P.P., of Harbor Main. He was born in Carbineers' in 1825, and is a brother of Very Rev. Thomas Brown, Provincial of the Irish Jesuits. He studied in the college of Waterford, and was ordained by Dr. Mullock about the year 1850. For the past thirty-six or seven years he has worked with all the zeal of a Xavier, having charge of the whole north-eastern portion of the coast, from the southernmost point of Green or Notre Dame Bay round by the north to Kirpon and the Straits of Labrador, extending over a distance of a thousand miles of coast. Yearly, without fail, he made the visitation of this vast district, travelling always in small, open boats, rarely seeing a fellow-priest except on his annual visit to St. John's. He has lately been appointed to the more compact and less laborious parish of Harbor Main, in which he may enjoy a moderate share of that repose so well merited by well-nigh half a century of apostolic labors.

At length the career of the saintly Prelate drew near its close. He retired to the monastery at Belvidere for the last few months of his life. He had erected this building with the design of introducing a convent of Franciscans, and of passing the latter years of his life in the strict observance of that Seraphic Rule, the spirit of which he had never lost, even during the thousand distractions of his busy life. But the years which he may have counted on were reduced to months. As soon as the stimulus of activity was withdrawn the physical energies began rapidly to decline, and it was soon easily observed that his days were numbered. Like another Moses, however, he was permitted to see the Promised Land; nay, more, to taste of its first-fruits, by being spared to celebrate the first Mass in the new cathedral. It is true it was not then completed, and its beauteous proportions were concealed by masses of *débris* and unsightly scaffolding; yet could he by imagination picture to himself the grand scene to be presented therein some five years after, when adorned with its nine beautiful altars, its rare paintings and costly statuary; when aglow with brilliant lights and sweet flowers, and its massive walls vibrating to the tones of the majestic organ, its sanctuary adorned by a galaxy of distinguished prelates in their rich robes, it was to be consecrated by the great Prelate of the American Church, the Most Rev. Dr. Hughes, Archbishop of New York. All this gorgeous scene no doubt passed before the mind's eye of the dying Prelate as he sat there, weak and exhausted, at the rude temporary altar. He had made a last great effort to go through the ceremony of that day. He arose from his bed of sickness, and when the ceremony was finished, he retired, never again to appear in public. Well, indeed, could he repeat the ever-beautiful words of the Apostle, "The time of my dissolution is at hand. I have fought a good fight. I have kept the faith;" and with great confidence could he hope for the imperishable crown which is prepared for the good and faithful servant.

He died on the 28th of May, 1850, supported by all the consolations of Holy Church, and was laid to rest beneath the confessional of the new cathedral.[1]

---

[1] His funeral was one of the greatest demonstrations of universal respect and sympathy ever witnessed in Newfoundland. All classes joined in the *cortege*. The coffin, covered with a purple pall, was borne on the shoulders of six men through the streets of the town. This procession forms one of the earliest recollections of the present writer. The faithful people vied with each other in striving to be permitted to carry the bier for a short distance, and to the present day it is one of their proudest boasts that they had "*a spell* out of him."

APPENDIX.

ERRATA.

Page 69, seven lines from bottom, for "20th April" read "30th April."
Page 364, three lines from bottom, for "Easter Sunday" read "Feast of the Epiphany."
Page 894, ten lines from bottom, for "28th of May" read "14th of July."

APPENDIX.

NOTE 1. (*Page* 76.)

Mosquito. I am inclined to believe that the original name of this harbor or cove was *Musketto*, from the *musket*, a form of firearm just then introduced, as the neighboring harbor was called *Carbineers' Harbor* (now corrupted into *Carbonear*), from *Caribineer*, that branch of the military service being probably stationed or employed there. It is not likely that the name *Mosquito* would have been given to any particular settlement, as that troublesome little creature was equally to be found in all parts of the country. Whitbourne (1619) thus speaks of them: "Neither are there any snakes, toads, serpents, or any other venemous wormes, that euer were knowne, but only a very little nimble fly (the least of all other flyes) which is called *muskeito*. These flyes seeme to haue a greate power and authority upon all loytering and idle people, for they have this property, that when they find any such lying lazily or sleeping in the woods, they will presently be more nimble to sieze them than any sargeant will be to arrest a man for debt, neither will they leave stynging or sucking out the blood of such sluggards, untill like a Beadle they bring him to his master, where he should labor, in which tyme of loytering those flyes will so brande such idle persons in their faces that they may be knowne from others as the Turkes doe their slaves." The word *mosquito* is Spanish, and it is stated by Don Fernando Columbus that his brother Christopher was called "the Admiral of Mosquito Land." The land skirting the Isthmus of Panama is called *Mosquito;* but I am still inclined to believe our Musquito is derived from *musketto*. This particular instrument of warfare was much in use in those days. Whitbourne (page 4) describes how the Indians of Heart's Content "were frightened by the shooting off of a muskett." In a map of Conception Bay, by Capt. Taverner, of 1747, this harbor is distinctly given as "Musketto or *Musket's Cove*." But I must also acknowledge that the mosquito was sometimes so called.

Thus, Sir David Kirke, writing to Charles I. (1629), asking leave to fortify Quebec, says: "A besieging army cannot stay above three months (in summer) all in which time the *musketts* will soe tormente him that noe man is able to be abroade in centry or trenches, day or night, without loosing their sights at least eight days." In a list of the articles found at Quebec when captured by Kirke from Champlain we find mention of "thirteen whole and one broken muskett." The word is derived from the name of a young hawk, much in vogue at the time of the invention of firearms; the new weapon which took down its prey so swiftly was hence called a *muskett*.

NOTE 2. (*Page* 129.)

Copy of Brevet of Concession of Point Verde to M. de Costebelle, Governor of Placentia, before the Treaty of Utrecht, 1709:—

"BREVET DE CONCESSION FAITE AU S^R DE COSTEBELLE DE LA PRESQUISLE DE LA POINTE VERTE.

"Aujourdhuy Unzieme du mois d'aust mil sept cent neuf Le Roy estant a Versailles. Le Sr de Costebelle gouverneur du fort Louis de Plaisance dans l'isle de Terre Neuve a fait remontrer a Sa Ma^{te} qu'il a fait construire sur le terrain de la presquisle de la Pointe Verte Esloignée d'une petite lieue du fort Louis de Plaisance dans l'isle de Terre Neuve des logemens avec une depense considerable pour y placer une famille de laboureurs qui y est actuellem^t avec une nombre de toute sortes de bestieaux; et qu'il en fait depuis deux ans defricher les bois dans l'esperance que la d. terre pourra produire des grains. Et en même tems il a fait supplier Sa Ma^{te} de luy conceder le d'terrain a titre de fief et Seigneurie, haute moyenne et basse justice a quoy Sa Ma^{te} ayant egard en consideraõn des services du d'Sr de Costebelle et des depenses cy dessus. Sa Ma^{te} luy a accordé la presqu'isle de la Pointe Verte Eloignée d'une petite lieue du fort de Plaisance, Nord et sud de l'entrée de la rade, bornée au sud par une langue de grave appelée le Birgeron. Separée par un grand estang des graves des habitants, regardant a l'est l'entrée du goulit et l'ouest du coste de la grande mer. Pour en jouir par luy, ses heritiers, et ayant cause a pérpétuité comme de leur propre a la charge de foy et hommage au fort Louis de Plaisance et aux droits et redevances ordinaires sans que põ co il soit tenu ny ses heritiers et ayant cause, de payer a Sa Ma^{te} ny a ses successeurs Roys, aucune finance ny indemnité de la quelle a quelq^e somme qu'elle puisse monter Sa Ma^{te} leur a fait don et remise par le p͠nt Brevet. Et en cas que dans la suite Sa Ma^{te} eut besoin de quelq^e partie du d'Terrain p͠o y faire construire des forts, batteries, places d'armes, magazins Eglises ou autres ouvrages publics Sa Ma^{te} pourra la prendre aussy bien que les arbres qui seront necess^{res} p͠o lesd. ouvrages publics sans estre tenue d'aucune dom̃agem'.

"Et pour temoinage de sa Volonté Sa Ma^{te} luy a accordé le d'Brevet quelle a voulu signer de Sa Main et estre contresigné par moi con^{al} Secretaire d'estat et de ses commandemens et finances.

[TRANSLATION.]

BREVET OF GRANT MADE TO MR. COSTEBELLE, OF THE PENINSULA OF POINT VERTE.

To-day, eleventh of the month of August, one thousand seven hundred and nine, the King being at Versailles, Mr. Costebelle, Governor of the Fort Louis of Placentia, in the Island of Newfoundland, has represented to His Majesty that he has caused to be constructed upon the land of the Peninsula of Point Verte, distant of a small league from the Fort Louis of Placentia, in the Island of Newfoundland, certain lodgments, at a considerable expense, in order to place there a family of laborers, which is actually there with a number of all sorts of cattle; and that for the past two years he has caused the woods there to be cleared, in the hope that the said land might produce some grain crops, and at the same time he has caused His Majesty to be supplicated to grant to him the aforesaid land, in title of fee and lordship, high, mean, and low jurisdiction. To which having regard His Majesty, in consideration of the services of the said Mr. Costebelle, and of the expenses aforesaid, His Majesty has granted to him the Peninsula of Point Verte, distance of a small league from the Fort of Placentia, north and south of the entrance of the roadstead, bounded on the south by a tongue of beach called the *Birgeron*, separated by a large pond from the beaches of the inhabitants, looking on the east towards the entrance of the Gut, and the west on the side of the Great Sea. To enjoy the same by him, his heirs and assigns, forever as their own, on the condition of fealty and homage to the Fort Louis of Placentia, and to the ordinary dues and rents, without being on that account held, nor his heirs nor assigns, to pay to His Majesty nor to his Successors Kings any fine or indemnity, of which to whatever sum it might amount. His Majesty has made to them gift and remission by the present Brevet, and in case that hereafter His Majesty might have need of some portion of the said land, to construct thereon any forts, batteries, parade grounds, magazines, churches, or other public works, without being held for any damages.

And in testimony of his will His Majesty has granted to him the said Brevet, which he has deigned to sign by his hand, and to be countersigned by me counseller (?) Secretary of State and of his ordinances and finances.

LOUIS.

PHELYPEAUX.

The document has two indorsations in English, as follows: —

Whereas the within-mentioned Plantation and ground were formerly bounded by a gutt of water, which by a late storm is now entirely filled up, I do hereby forbid any person or persons to cutt grass therefrom, or by feeding of Beasts of any sort on the said ground where the water formerly flowed, to damage the af^d plantation or grounds, or in any other manner to molest the same, finding that the aforesaid Gutt was the property to the af^d premises. Given under my hand at Placentia, Septr. ye 6th, 1748.

Edwd Jekyll

PLACENTIA, May 20th, 1803.

We do hereby transfer and make over our sole right and title of the within Brevet to Mr. Ml Greene, only reserving the right of drawing Netts & Seynes on the said fort, and the privilege of a flagstaff for the purpose of making or repeating signals thereon, as specified by a deed of sales bearing date as above.

NOTE 3. (*Page* 215.)

ELEGY ON THE RIGHT REV. DR. O'DONEL.

Now, closed his course of labor and of years,
    The goodly, great O'Donel rests in peace;
He asks not now our wailing nor our tears,—
    But shall his praise with Death's procession cease?

Forbid it, Poesy! Thy sister mourns,
    Thy sister, Eloquence! Religion, see!
Holds high his roll of service. Erin turns
    With pensive look, with heaven-toned harp to thee.

Poor Erin! 'twas no wonder that each strain
    Flowed plaintive from her harp, attuned in grief;
Ah! many an "Auburn" wept, for o'er the main,
    Year after year, her children sought relief.

Beyond the western world of waters still
    The curse of penal code, attendant found
In youth, forbade the lore that tames the will;
    They grew as wild as desert woods around.

With pain O'Donel saw the darkness spread;
    Religion's sigh he heard; and, strong with zeal,
Left friends and country distant shores to tread,
    Where heart of man was hardening into steel.

With words of fire incessant as he preached,
    And all the woes of savage life deplored,
His voice the inmost breast's recesses reached,
    And awe-struck sinners tremblingly adored.

His life alone would win to virtue's side;
  His social charms would happiness impart;
His manners, plain and free, yet dignified,
  Were not too high for laughter of the heart.

In him the gospel charities were seen;
  True to his own, indulgent unto all,
The cordial welcome of the Isle of Green
  Was ever felt within his lowly hall.

Their cheerful offerings proved how fond his flock;
  Nor Britain could withhold her grateful mite;
But think not hence she ever dared to mock,
  With aught like "*veto-pay*," his work so bright.

His day of parting for dear Erin's shade
  Was, through St. John's, a sorrowing day, indeed;
Their splendid gift and warm address displayed
  How loved, revered, by all of every creed!

There may the writing of these lines renew
  Heart-felt emotion for his cherished name;
And there, while Heaven has paid the homage due,
  May Christians bless his labors and his name!

J. E.

BALLYVALLOCK, CO. KILKENNY.

NOTE 4. *(Page 287.)*

In the year 1776-9, an English traveller named Arthur Young made a tour in Ireland, and in his journal has some interesting items touching on the early intercourse between Newfoundland and Ireland. "The staple trade of Waterford," he says, "is the Newfoundland trade. . . . The number of people who go as passengers in the Newfoundland ships is simply amazing, from sixty to eighty ships and from three to five thousand persons annually. They come from most parts of Ireland, from Cork, Kerry, etc. Experienced men will get eighteen to twenty-five pounds for the season, from March to November. A man who never went will have from five to seven pounds, and others rise to twenty pounds; the passage out they get, but pay home two pounds. An industrious man, in a year, will bring home from twelve to sixteen pounds with him, and some more. A great point for them is to be able to carry out all their slops, for everything there is exceedingly dear, one or two hundred per cent. dearer than they get at home. They are not allowed to take out any woollen goods but for their own use. The ships go loaded with pork, beef, butter, and some salt; and bring home passengers, or get freights where they can — sometimes rum. The Waterford pork comes principally from the barony of Iverk, in Kilkenny, where they fatten great numbers of large hogs; for many weeks together they kill here three to four thousand a week; the price, fifty shillings to four pounds each; goes chiefly to Newfoundland. One was killed in Mr. Penrose's cellar that weighed five hundred and a quarter, and measured, from the nose to the end of the tail, nine feet four inches."

The "Annual Register and Chronicle" of 1815 contains the following interesting extract: "Some idea of the extent of emigration from Ireland may be formed from the following extract of a private letter dated at St. John's, Newfoundland, 23d of this month (June): 'The arrivals from Ireland, which have exceeded any in the Custom-house book, exclusive of these vessels which have made no return, are three thousand and twenty-six men and three hundred and seventy-three women to this harbor alone, but the numbers far exceed the returns. The captains have brought out so many that they are ashamed to return them. The wretched creatures are most dreadfully treated on the passage. One man declared to me he was but three nights below decks the whole of the voyage, nor could he get down. Strange complaints have been made by a set of wretches who came yesterday of the very nearly starving condition they were in. Indeed, Government must put a stop to such proceedings, or really a contagion will be bred in our streets; and what will become of them in winter God only knows.'"

NOTE 5. *(Page 289.)*

The first convents established in the New World were of French origin. As early as 1639 we learn from the History of Abbé Brasseur de Bourbourg the first French convent was established in Canada. The Duchess of Aiguillon, niece of Cardinal Richelieu, founded the *Hotel Dieu* at Quebec. The Augustiniennes of the Hospital of Dieppe, of the Congregation of the Mercy of Jesus, accepted with joy the offer to take charge of it. Three of them were sent out. Madame de la Peltrie, a young widow of Alençon, at the same time secured the services of the Ursulines, for the education of the young. She went to Tours, and there obtained consent to have sent out the celebrated Mère Marie de l'Incarnation (Marie Guyert) and Mère de St. Joseph. She gave up all her wealth to the project and came out herself with them, and arrived at Quebec on the 1st of August, 1639, after a long and boisterous passage, having set sail the 4th of May.

Other French establishments were founded in America. In 1697 the Ursulines at Quebec, the mother-house subsequently of the Boston community; in 1727 the Ursulines were established in New Orleans, which then formed part of New France, and which did not become a portion of the United States till 1803.

In 1790 the Rev. Father Neale, a descendant of one of the Catholic families brought out by Lord Baltimore, procured from Ireland, with the consent of Bishop Carroll, a colony of Carmelite nuns. These were the first English-speaking community that crossed the water, and were four in number, and were settled at Fort Tobacco, Maryland.

In 1812 Father Anthony Kohlman, S.J., V.G. of New York, introduced three Ursulines into that city from Black Rock, Cork, but not receiving any subjects, they returned in 1815.

In 1817, at the earnest request of Father Thayer, three young ladies (Misses Ryan) of Limerick came out to found a convent in Boston. They went to the convent of Ursulines, of Three Rivers, Canada, to complete their novitiate, and founded the convent at Mt. St. Benedict, Charlestown, near Boston. This convent was wrecked and burnt by an infuriated mob in 1834, who were excited by the lying and sensational stories told by a Miss Reed, whom the nuns had admitted out of charity. (See Bishop England's works, Vol. IV.) Next in order of time came our nuns of Newfoundland. They were the first of the Presentation Order who crossed the ocean. The outrage on the convent at Charlestown was but the bursting of over-wrought fanaticism, and must not be looked upon as the normal state of American feeling. In the following year, 1835, we have an account of the arrival of another colony of Ursulines under Miss Mary Hughes. They were received at Philadelphia in a most affectionate manner by the people of every persuasion. They were escorted on their way to Charlestown by Bishop England, and in passing through Washington were presented to President Jackson, who received them warmly, and rendered them every assistance and protection in their pious undertakings.

NOTE 6. *(Page 343.)*

The following correspondence has never been printed *in extenso*. It has been lithographed, but copies are now rare, if, indeed, any exist at all besides the one in my possession; and even that, as will be seen, is slightly imperfect, letter No. 8 being wanting. Notwithstanding the great length of the correspondence, I deem it worthy of preservation; but as it would make too great a break in the historical narrative, I here place it among the notes.

[No. 1.]

SECRETARY'S OFFICE, 19th August, 1835.

SIR, — I am directed by the Governor to inform you that your petition, addressed to His Majesty, praying that a certain portion of the land named " The Barrens," in the immediate vicinity of the town of St. John's, may be granted to the Catholic inhabitants of the Island for ecclesiastical purposes, and also that an annual allowance may be made to you for the support of a small vessel, to enable you to communicate with your flock, has been received and laid at the foot of the throne by the Principal Secretary of State for the Colonies, who had His Majesty's commands to return to it an answer, of which the following is the substance:—

In regard to the first part of the memorial, viz., the prayer for a grant of the portion of the land called " The Barrens," at present in the possession of the Ordnance Department, His Excellency has to inform you that until the arrangements at present in progress with the above department, in regard to the delimitation of military works, shall have been finally settled it is impossible to entertain an application for a grant of land reserved for military purposes; nor could such an application be, under any circumstances, decided upon without a previous reference to the Master General and Board of Ordnance. The consideration of this part of your memorial is therefore unavoidably deferred. Should you, however, wish hereafter to renew it, your representation must be transmitted through the Governor, in order that His Majesty's Government may be furnished with His Excellency's report upon it.

Upon the second point, viz., the allowance of an annual sum for the support of a vessel, His Excellency is desired to acquaint you that Lord Glenelg regrets that it is not possible to accede to your wishes. Considering that an application is now pending before the Imperial Parliament for a grant of a large sum in aid of the funds of this Colony, it would be hopeless to propose that a further sum should be granted for the service indicated by you. The sum for which application is made to Parliament will, if voted, be so entirely consumed in defraying the indispensable charges of Government, that no portion of it will remain applicable to such a purpose; and there is no fund within the Island at the disposal of His Majesty's Government from which the desired assistance could be afforded. His Lordship is therefore under the necessity of referring you to the Colonial Assembly, who, moreover, will be more competent than His Majesty's Government to decide upon the urgency of the demand for assistance, and the extent to which it should be allowed.

Finally, His Excellency, by his Lordship's order, desires me to observe to you that by the course you adopted in transmitting your memorial, not through the Governor (according to the established rules of official correspondence), but direct to the Secretary of State, His Majesty's Government have been deprived, in the consideration of it, of the advantage of that practical information which they could otherwise have received.

I have the honor to be, Sir,
Your obedient humble servant,
(Signed) JAS. CROWDY.

[No. 2.]

SIR,—I have the honor to lay before you, for transmission to His Majesty's principal Secretary of State for the Colonies, an Address, a copy of which I enclose, praying his Lordship to present to His Majesty a memorial which I had had the honor to enclose to the Right Honorable Thomas Spring Rice, two or three days before your Excellency entered the port of St. John's; as in this Address the principal features of the memorial are portrayed, I would fain request that your Excellency would have the goodness to support my prayer.

Your Excellency perceives that the Catholic clergy of Newfoundland stand foremost in the improvement of the country; your Excellency has observed the handsome and spacious parochial dwelling-house and Catholic church of Harbor Grace, erected by the late Rev. Mr. Ewer, which form the principal embellishment of that town, and also the church of Carboneer, raised by that lamented gentleman's successor, the Rev. C. Dalton.

In Brigus, your Excellency has probably observed the residence of the Catholic rector, the Rev. D. Mackin, raised at his own expense, and the church of that town, erected by the same rev. gentleman. In the northern district, under the Rev. N. Devereux, several harbors are embellished with parochial houses and churches, even as far as the distant and sequestered harbor of Tilting Harbor, in the island of Fogo. In the district of the Bay of Bulls, and of Ferryland, the same spirit is evinced there as far as St. Mary's Bay. In Placentia district, five churches are rising through the activity of the clergymen in the district of Burin, and the zeal of the Rev. Mr. Birnie is equally conspicuous in the erection of handsome edifices for the convenience of His Majesty's subjects to assemble in worshipping their Creator.

The churches of Petty Harbor, Portugal Cove, and Torbay, your Excellency has also seen; and I am convinced you will say that each in a marked degree improves the little town in which it has been raised; and not only have they brought an improvement in the locale, but as each has cost several hundred pounds, the introduction of so much money, the principal part of which has been expended in these places, has diffused considerable comfort amongst the poor.

Your Excellency is, I believe, aware that the principal part of the expense of these erections was defrayed out of my own pocket. In fact, the three have cost me nearly two thousand pounds. There were one hundred pounds collected in St. John's and Conception Bay towards the church of Portugal Cove, but the people of that cove were not able to subscribe one shilling. For the church of Petty Harbor, the people of that little town subscribed about £60; and the people of Torbay raised amongst themselves about the same amount for the church of Torbay, and about £63 were collected from the strangers who attended at the consecration.

In these harbors I have removed the dead from the doors of the poor people, and given them ample cemeteries, in some instances by purchasing the ground out of my own pocket, and in Petty Harbor by the kindness and bounty of your Excellency in giving a grant of an excellent site for that purpose.

Your Excellency is probably aware that the Catholic cemetery of this town is filled to an extent calculated to endanger the public health, and there is no ground suitable for the purpose within the precincts of the town, save the ground mentioned in the accompanying address, and which forms the subject of my memorial to His Majesty; that is, the vacant ground on "The Barrens," near Fort Townshend, on which the old wood-yard stands.

It is under these circumstances that I beg again to request your Excellency will be pleased to support the prayer of my petition to His Majesty for a grant of that vacant patch of ground, bounded on the south by the road from Fort Townshend to Fort William, on the west by another road, and on the north and east by fenced grounds, which piece of ground I understand is at present in the occupancy of the Honorable the Board of Ordnance, an accedance to which will enable me immediately to commence a suite of buildings of stone, which will prove, I trust, a real and substantial improvement to St. John's, and will considerably promote the extension of the town to that healthful though bleak situation.

I have the honor to remain, Sir,
Your Excellency's, etc.,
(Signed)   + MICHAEL ANTHONY FLEMING.
To H. E. Gov. PRESCOTT.
June 21, 1836.

[No. 3.]

TO THE RIGHT HONORABLE HIS MAJESTY'S SECRETARY OF STATE FOR THE COLONIES: —

MY LORD, — A few days before the arrival in this country of His Excellency Governor Prescott, and while Sir Thomas Cochrane was making preparations for his departure for England, I had the honor to address a memorial to His Majesty, through His Majesty's then Secretary of State for the Colonies, the Honorable Thomas Spring Rice, setting forth the claims of the Catholic population of Newfoundland upon His Majesty, superadding those of the Catholic clergy, and praying for a grant of waste ground called "The Barrens," near Fort Townshend, now in the occupancy of the Honorable the Board of Ordnance, for the erection of a church, a dwelling-house for the clergyman, a school-house, and convenient, also, for a public cemetery.

In that memorial I took care, my Lord, to urge that the Catholics of Newfoundland had never had from His Majesty's Government, directly or indirectly, a single mark of favor, notwithstanding that they had exhibited the most marked loyalty in seasons of the greatest difficulty, and had always distinguished themselves as useful citizens and good subjects; while the Protestant portion of the population have had, either directly or through The Society for the Propagation of the Gospel in Foreign Parts, the most substantial proofs of the royal protection.

I have shown the Protestant population in the enjoyment of an ample church, with a spacious cemetery adjoining, a handsome residence, with a garden, etc., for the rector, besides glebe grounds to contribute to his support; and the Catholics obliged to pay an enormous rent for the bare site of their church, in a situation so circumscribed as not to admit of increase, although the present edifice is so small that frequently several hundreds of the congregation are compelled to abide the pelting of the pitiless storm, in all seasons, while assisting in the worship of their Creator, in the capital of the Colony of Newfoundland.

I have shown that, all-insufficient as this building is in extent for the congregation, it is in a considerably dilapidated state, and that it would not be judicious to erect a new one on the same site, particularly as none but a terminable lease can be had of the ground.

I have shown that the Protestant rector, the Archdeacon, and I now might add, I believe, another clergyman of the Church of England, in St. John's, and all the Protestant clergy in the rest of the Island, received large salaries from Government, either directly or through the same medium, and adverted to the princely pension of the Bishop of Nova Scotia; while the duties of chaplains to the jails and the garrisons, and the hospitals, etc., both military and colonial, in addition to the routine duties of the Mission, have been cheerfully discharged by Catholic clergymen during the last fifty years all over the Island, without the least prospect of remuneration, save the small pittance of £75 annually doled out to the Bishop; and that in addition to all those favors before alluded to bestowed upon the Protestant population, even in the year 1834 a grant was given by Sir Thomas Cochrane of the site of a second Protestant church in St. John's.

My Lord, in enumerating some of the good things enjoyed by the Protestants of Newfoundland, believe me, I am not actuated by any selfish feelings of envy; nor do I think His Majesty's Government have, in the slightest degree, exceeded the rigid bounds of duty in according these favors. No, I have the honor to enjoy the friendship of many of that communion, and particularly the Rev. Rector of St. John's; and I will say, that they are highly deserving the countenance bestowed upon them, and that that amiable and reverend gentleman is truly worthy the enjoyment of the comforts of his rectory. But while I make this admission, I do think that the Catholic population are equally, in the abstract, entitled to the consideration of His Majesty's Government; and that that claim comes more strengthened in proportion as their number is greater than the others, and the number of Catholic clerics, as compared with Protestants, in this Island, is fully as three to one.

I attempted, My Lord, to prove that inequality of protection is calculated to induce distrust and dissatisfaction; but that a diffusion of religion to all awaken allegiance, which an equal participation in the favors of the Crown can perhaps best render durable.

My Lord, in my present prayer to His Majesty I cannot have a self-interested motive; my holding is only for life; and when I reflect that in the mere discharge of the ordinary duties of my care, I have wasted my strength and impaired my constitution, I feel that tenure cannot be expected to be long. It is not, then, for myself I pray,—it is to be enabled to advance the best interests of His Majesty's subjects, and to promote the glory of God.

My Lord, your Lordship has been pleased to communicate that my memorial, not having been transmitted through His Excellency the Governor, has been regarded as informal; but that informality arose principally from the circumstance of Sir Thomas Cochrane being about to depart from this country, and my having no idea as to whether it was likely a successor would be appointed speedily; and as your Lordship has been pleased to say that I might at a future time renew that petition, permit me, my Lord, to request, as I have the honor to transmit this address to your Lordship, through His Excellency Governor Prescott, reciting as it does the principal arguments or facts of that petition, and a copy of which I have had the honor to lay before His Excellency, that your Lordship, regarding my memorial now as " transmitted through the Governor," will graciously please to lay it at the foot of His Majesty's august throne, and by advocating its humble prayer, enable me forthwith to commence the erection of a suite of stone buildings that will, I trust, prove a credit to the colony, and will stand forever a monument of the liberality and munificence of our King.

I have the honor, My Lord, to subscribe myself,

Your Lordship's most obedient, humble servant,

(Signed)   MICHAEL ANTHONY FLEMING.

June 21st, 1836.

[No. 4.]

To the Right Honorable Sir George Grey, Bart. :—

Sir,— It will be in your recollection that I took the liberty of troubling you with an address, dated the 21st of June, containing the principal arguments and facts of a petition which I had the honor of laying before His Majesty's Secretary of State for the Colonies, the Hon. Spring Rice, two years ago, praying for a piece of waste ground, called "The Barrens," outside the town of St. John's, for the erection of a church, a school, a residence for the clergymen, and also for a public cemetery.

In that address I took leave to state the claims of the Catholic priests and Catholic people of Newfoundland upon His Majesty's Government, but I omitted to urge on your consideration the entertainment of my own individual claims, and now beg most respectfully to submit, that for the last twelve years I have made many most severe sacrifices for that country.

My visitations in that Island are made amid every privation that can render life uncomfortable, obliged to beg a passage in a fishing-schooner to an out-harbor, and then to cross extensive and turbulent bays in open boats, to pass night after night sleeping in the woods upon a few boughs or among rocks, for weeks without lying upon a bed or changing a single raiment, to convey the soothings of religion to His Majesty's Catholic subjects. At my own expense I have established an institution for the education of the poor, and from my own pocket maintain that establishment, at which a thousand children are daily receiving a gratuitous education. I pay sixty pounds per annum, with board and lodging, for an extra clergyman to attend the garrisons, the jail, and military and colonial hospitals. For all these sacrifices which I have made and am daily making for the benefit and improvement of His Majesty's subjects, unmixed with any other motive whatsoever, I must beg to say that I feel I have strong claims on His Majesty's Government; and all these claims I willingly add to the claim of the people, praying you, in all humility, to take that address into your kind consideration.

The piece of ground I pray for is that part of "The Barrens" on which the garrison wood-yard stood, containing about ten acres, perhaps eleven, as described on a map, which I should feel anxious to lay before you, if you allow me the honor of an interview.

Sir, in acceding to the Catholics of Newfoundland, either by a grant or for a small purchasable rent,— because it is the only spot unoccupied by buildings, or, in fact, the only spot within the precints of the town that can be held in fee, — would go far to convince the people of the paternal solicitude of His Majesty for their general interests. It is a favor that could not fail to be ever alive in their memory; it is a boon that we have reason to think ought to be granted, for we are a Catholic people, who having maintained, amid occasions of much difficulty, and danger, and temptation, a loyalty and attachment to our King and Constitution (witness, my Lord, the Newfoundland Volunteers, principally Catholic, in the days of trouble), yet never have we received a single mark of Royal favor, — not a single acre of ground for any public purpose whatsoever.

The receipt of a note from Mr. Sheil informing me of the kind manner in which you have been pleased to express yourself to him and to Mr. Ball, on the subject of my application, awakens in me an ardent hope that you will advocate our cause, and plead in the proper quarter for the long-neglected, though loyal, people of Newfoundland; and if, in presuming to call your attention now to a subject so interesting to the poor Catholics of that country, I have trespassed too far on your time and patience, I beg to offer as an apology that my limited circumstances would be much affected in this expensive place by a lengthened delay, and also the danger to which my life would be exposed by approaching that coast after the middle of September, are the reasons which induce me humbly to beseech you to give it your earliest consideration, and you will lay me, and the 70,000 Catholics of that Island, under a deep and lasting obligation to you.

I have the honor, Sir, to subscribe myself,

Your most obedient, humble servant,

(Signed)   MICHAEL ANTHONY FLEMING,
Catholic Bishop.

No. 7 AIR STREET, August 15th, 1836.

[No. 5.]

DOWNING STREET, 17th August, 1836.

SIR, — I have received and have laid before Lord Glenelg your letter of the 15th inst., on the subject of your application for the grant of a piece of land in Newfoundland for the purpose of erecting upon it a place of worship, a school-house, and a residence for a Catholic clergyman. In reply, I am to inform you that a former communication from you on this subject having been received from Captain Prescott, it was immediately referred for the consideration of the Master General and Board of Ordnance, in whose possession the land at present is. Lord Genelg has directed a further communication to be addressed to that department, requesting them to favor him with an early answer on the question.

With respect to your wish for an interview with me at this Office, I must express my regret that during the session of Parliament the multiplicity of my duties will hardly admit of my naming a time at which it would be possible for me to receive you.

I have the honor to be, Sir,
Your most obedient serv't,
(Signed) GEO. GREY.

Rev. Dr. FLEMING, Air Street, Piccadilly.

[No. 6.]

DOWNING STREET, 31st August, 1836.

SIR,— With reference to my letter of the 17th inst., I am directed by Lord Glenelg to acquaint you that the Master General and Board of Ordnance have informed his Lordship that without further information from their officers in Newfoundland they are unable to decide whether the land for which you have applied could without detriment to the public service be appropriated to the purposes contemplated by you. The Governor of the Colony and the Ordnance officers on the station will therefore be directed immediately to transmit the necessary information for the guidance of the Master General and Board, and when that shall have been received no time will be lost in deciding on the application which you have preferred.

I have the honor to be, Sir,
Your most obedient serv't,
(Signed) JAS. STEPHEN.

Rev. Dr. FLEMING.

[No. 7.]

DOWNING STREET, 27th January, 1837.

SIR,— In answer to your note of the 24th inst., I am directed by Lord Glenelg to inform you that the Master General and Board of

Ordnance have reported to his Lordship that before deciding on your application for a piece of land on which to erect a church and school-house it will be necessary to obtain from the Governor of Newfoundland a comprehensive report on all the public buildings which it is proposed to erect on Ordnance lands, in order that some general plan may be adopted with respect to them. Captain Prescott has accordingly been directed to furnish such a report, on the receipt of which no time will be lost in coming to a decision on your application.

            I have the honor to be, Sir,
                  Your most obedient servant,
                        (Signed)   GEO. GREY.
The Rev. Dr. FLEMING, 5 Conduit Street.

[No. 8, missing, is from Sir George Grey to Dr. Fleming. It is alluded to by Dr. Fleming in No. 12. It stated that if the concession of the land would not interfere with Fort Townshend as a military station, the land would be granted. It was dated Feb. 9, 1837.]

                     [No. 9.]
                DOWNING STREET, 25th March, 1837.

SIR, — With reference to my letter of the 9th ult., I am directed by Lord Glenelg to enclose herewith for your information the copy of a letter from the Secretary to the Ordnance conveying the decision of the Master General and Board on your application for certain land in the vicinity of Fort Townshend in Newfoundland. I also enclose, in explanation of Mr. Byham's letter, a copy of the report from Captain Walker, of the Engineers, to which allusion is therein made.

Lord Glenelg desires me to state, that in conformity with the decision of the Master General and Board of Ordnance, the Governor of Newfoundland will be instructed to grant to you so much of the land in question as may be necessary for the ecclesiastical buildings which it is your intention to erect.

            I have the honor to be, Sir,
                  Your most obedient servant,
                        (Signed)   GEO. GREY.
Rev. Dr. FLEMING, 5 Conduit Street.

[No. 10.]

OFFICE OF ORDNANCE, 8th March, 1837.

SIR, — Referring to the communication, which by command of the Master General and Board of Ordnance I had the honor to make to the Secretary of State for the Colonies, in my letter to you under date the 12th Dec., 1836, on the subject of the requested appropriation of a part of the Ordnance ground near Fort Townshend, Newfoundland, as a site for the erection of a Roman Catholic chapel and schools, —

I have the honor to acquaint you, for the information of Lord Glenelg, that in consequence of a further explanation from the applicants, by which it appears that all they desire is a grant of the ground on which to erect their chapel and schools, without any protection in a military point of view, the Master General and Board have resumed the consideration of the subject, whether the ground in question, on that understanding, could be given up without injury to the public service, and have decided (as it is not in contemplation to restore Fort Townshend as a work of defence, and that as soon as the new barracks are constructed on Signal Hill the troops will be removed from the former post) to grant such portion of the ground, referred to in Capt. Walker's report to the Colonial Secretary of the 13th October last, as may be sufficient for erecting the proposed chapel and schools, — the plots of ground being marked yellow and blue on the sketch to which Captain Walker's letter refers, — but the precise quantity the Master General and Board submit should be fixed by the local Government, and the result reported for their information; and I am to request that you will move the Secretary of State to give the necessary directions for this purpose, corresponding instructions having been given to the commanding Royal Engineer at the station.

I have, &c.

(Signed)   R. BYHAM.

[No. 11.]

ENGINEER'S OFFICE, Oct. 13, 1836.

SIR, — Referring to your letter of the 11th inst., I have the honor to state for the information of the Governor that the ground on the western side of Fort Townshend is crossed by a road leading from the fort, and that part of that ground has, at much labor and expense, been fenced and brought into cultivation as gardens by the men of the Royal Veteran Companies. The want of these gardens would be felt by the men as a very serious privation, besides the loss of the interest and occupation which the cultivation of the ground affords and which tends so greatly to their good conduct. In the accompanying sketch the ground to which I have generally referred is tinted red; any location of three or four acres on this ground, reserving the road and gardens, would be of an inconvenient figure for the intended erections, and would, besides, approach much too close to the fort.

The Governor will, perhaps, permit me to direct his attention to two fields to the north and south of this ground respectively, and separated from it by the public roads, affording to them a ready access, either of which possibly may meet Dr. Fleming's views; the first, tinted yellow, containing two acres and thirty-six perches, has been fenced and cultivated by the successive commandants of the garrison; the last, tinted blue, containing about four and one-half acres, is uncultivated, and, if I may be allowed to offer an opinion, is well adapted for the site of the church, etc., which Dr. Fleming proposes to erect.

      I have, etc.,
       (Signed) A. WALKER,
              Capt. R. E.

[No. 12. Plan of Ordnance ground which accompanied Colonel Walker's report.]

[No. 13. Plan of the ground applied for by Dr. Fleming.]

      [No. 14.]
    32 CRAVEN STREET, March 7th, 1838.

MY LORD,—Having been absent from England, I had not the honor to receive your Lordship's letters of Feb. 9th and March 25th until the month of June. You were good enough to enclose a letter, dated March 8th, from the Secretary of the Ordnance, "conveying the decision of the Master General and Board of Ordnance on my application for certain lands in the vicinity of Fort Townshend, in Newfoundland, together with Lieut.-Col. Walker's report." Permit me, in reply to these communications, respectfully to observe:—

First. That I had had the honor to transmit to Government in the autumn of 1834 a memorial praying for a grant of a certain piece of land to the eastward of Fort Townshend, being that portion of ground then occupied by the Board of Ordnance which lay nearest to the town of St. John's, and being the only portion thereof which presented a frontage suitable to the purposes for which it was asked, viz., the erection of a Catholic church for a congregation of upwards of twelve thousand people, a residence for the clergy, and sufficient parochial charity schools, the rear to be laid out as a burial-ground.

To this memorial the substance of your Lordship's reply, dated 19th August, 1835, was communicated to me by His Excellency the Governor, whereby I learned that until " the delimitation of military works should be finally settled, it was impossible to entertain an application for a grant of land reserved for military purposes."

Secondly. A short time after the receipt of this intimation, I learned that the arrangements regarding "military works" had been completed (see Appendix No. 1). I addressed a letter through the Governor (No. 2) to your Lordship, dated June 21st, 1836 (No. 3), renewing my memorial, because I then understood that Fort Townshend had been condemned as a military post, and on my arrival in London in August following, by letter to Sir George Grey, of date 15th August (No. 4), repeated that renewal again, distinctly specifying the particular piece of land I was seeking.

The ground laid down for deferring the consideration of my memorial, viz., the necessity of first satisfying the Board of Ordnance that the grant of that piece of land would not interfere with the arrangements rendered necessary for the military works of that country, formed the subject of Sir George Grey's reply of the 17th of the same month (No. 5), and on the 31st Mr. Stephen's letter (No. 6) reiterates it, if possible, more strongly, stating that the Board of Ordnance, until they had *further* information from Newfoundland, were "unable to decide whether *the land for which you* have *applied* could, without detriment to the public service, be appropriated to the purposes contemplated by you."

In this manner, my Lord, during the years 1835 and 1836, all the communications from your Lordship, Sir George Grey, Mr. Stephen, and Capt. Prescott, led me to consider that the only obstacle standing in the way of the Catholic people of Newfoundland on this occasion was founded on the contingency whether or not Fort Townshend should continue a military station. Such was the only ground of objection adverted to by your Lordship in your despatch to Governor Prescott in 1835 ; such was the only objection mooted by Sir George Grey and Mr. Stephen, and I naturally expected that if the Board should at any time decide that this piece of land was not wanted for " military purposes," no new ground of objection could arise.

Thirdly. My Lord, the letter last alluded to of Sir George Grey (Aug. 31st, 1836) could leave no doubt on my mind that my application must be successful, founded as it was upon strict justice. I was aware that Fort Townshend had been condemned as a military station, and as this letter acquainted me that the Colonial Office needed more information than they had had in the original report of the Ordnance officers, of which report I have not been honored with a copy, and that the Governor had been communicated with on the subject, notwithstanding that the delay subjected me to great personal inconvenience, notwithstanding that it must necessarily induce the abandonment of my poor but numerous congregation for the entire winter, I determined to await the result in patience.

Fourthly. In January, 1837, at length I once more respectfully called your Lordship's attention to my claim, convinced that, after a lapse of five months since the date of your Lordship's last communication, the requisite information must have been had; but I own my astonishment was great to find by Sir George Grey's reply, Jan. 27, 1837 (No. 7), nearly three years from the date of my first application, that before the Board of Ordnance could now report, a new reference must be made to the authorities in Newfoundland for a comprehensive report on all the public buildings which it was proposed to erect on the Ordnance lands.

Fifthly. Thus, my Lord, a new and most unexpected delay was created to any decision in favor of accommodation for religious worship and for the education of at least three-fourths of Her Majesty's faithful subjects, the inhabitants of the town of St. John's. These most important and interesting objects were to be postponed until the discretion of the local authorities should be satisfied upon matters of certainly trivial comparative value, — local authorities, too, of whom I may be permitted to say, I had reason to know I could not expect from them the same impartial consideration which I was sure I should meet from your Lordship. It was therefore that I felt the greatest satisfaction at the honor of receiving the communications of the 9th February and 25th of March, 1837 (Nos. 8 and 9).

Sixthly. The letter of the 9th February closes in these words: "Lord Glenelg did not feel at liberty to come to a decision on your application without the further information required by the Master General and Board of Ordnance respecting the effect which the building to be erected near Fort Townshend would have on that post *as a military station.*"

The perusal of this letter, my Lord, I confess proved to me a source of great gratification, because it convinced me that, in the consideration of my claim upon the Government, and of the Catholic inhabitants of Newfoundland, the bickerings of party in that country, and the veiled slanders of the enemies of everything liberal and charitable, the stumbling-blocks in the way of the improvement of the country, would be totally disregarded; and your Lordship's letter of March 25th (No. 9) served still further to convince me that you had determined that your administration of the Colonial Department should be distinguished by the first act of kindness, the first favor, ever bestowed upon the Catholics of Newfoundland by the British Government.

It was impossible I could entertain any doubt on the subject when I found that the letter of the 25th of March concluded with these emphatic words, which I respectfully beg leave to copy: "Lord Glenelg desires me to state that, in conformity with the decision of the Master General and Board of Ordnance, the Governor of Newfoundland will be instructed to grant to you so much *of the land in question* as may be necessary for the ecclesiastical buildings which it is your intention to erect."

I, of course, communicated the gratifying intelligence to my flock, of the paternal protection they were sure to experience from Her Majesty's Government, as evinced by this most consolatory though somewhat tardy concession, and I immediately hastened to Newfoundland to make the necessary arrangements for erecting, as rapidly as possible, buildings so all-important to the Catholics of Newfoundland.

I waited on the Governor shortly after my arrival. I called his attention to this subject, or rather, indeed, His Excellency even anticipated me. He observed that I must choose either a piece of ground denominated the "Commandant's field," or an unenclosed piece to the north of the fort. I remonstrated, I explained, I pointed out that the Commandant's field was at a great distance from the town, that it was cut off townward, by private property, from every possible approach, and that if in other respects desirable, it was quite insufficient in point of extent, inaccessible in winter, and inconvenient from its shape, being an irregular quadrangle, having two of its angles extremely acute. He then pointed to the piece of unenclosed land before mentioned; but I made His Excellency admit that this place was unfit, from its remoteness and its marshy character, and that otherwise, both in its distance from the town, its backwardness, and utter ineligibility, as a site for public buildings.

I showed him that when I undertook to build churches I made these churches in every harbor arise in such beauty as to attract the eye of every visitor, and even to invite His Excellency himself minutely to examine their structure; and that as the contemplated edifices were to be constructed of durable materials, I was determined they should not derogate from that character, for the promotion of the improvement and embellishment of the country acquired by the Catholic priesthood of the Island through the means of personal sacrifices unexampled.

My Lord, the Secretary of the Colony was present during this conversation, and both he and the Governor at length concurred with me that both places mentioned were perfectly unfit for the purpose of raising edifices that ought to be accessible to the public at all times and seasons, as well to the child as to the grandsire. In fact, that they were two places upon which no private gentleman would engage to expend in building the sum of one hundred pounds. And finally, my Lord, before I withdrew, so far did the Governor appear to coincide with me that he assured me if I put my objections to these places in writing he would transmit them to your Lordship with his recommendation to accede to my prayer for the only piece of Ordnance ground available for my purpose, viz., that which I originally solicited.

My Lord, I was not a little surprised, on the next day, to find the Governor's orderly come to my house to request I would again call upon the Governor. I, however, instantly complied, when, what was my astonishment, upon Captain Prescott's opening the conversation, at his telling me that he sent for me to say that, *on reflection*, he could not recommend the Government to grant me the ground I asked for; that I must take one or other of the pieces he had before offered, and make an immediate election.

Under these circumstances, my Lord, it occurred to met o see the matter out, and I said that in that case I should make a choice, when His Excellency at once asked me would I build on the piece I should so choose? I replied that I would not deceive him, that I certainly would not build on either, but that I would take it that instant, and try to turn it to advantage for the promotion of my undertaking; but His Excellency closed by insisting, that if he gave a grant of the ground it should contain *a proviso* (although he admitted it was perfectly inadequate to the purposes intended, and every way unfit) — *a proviso* that I should expend thereon such a sum annually on buildings as, in a given number of years, should amount to the sum of twenty thousand pounds!

I need not tell your Lordship that I declined the acceptance of His Excellency's terms; I need not say I withdrew upon this declaration, nor need I mention that here closed all communication with Captain Prescott on the subject; but, my Lord, these singular circumstances induced me again to refer to your Lordship's letters of Feb. 9, and particularly again to that of March 25, and I feel that this latter could only be construed as having reference to the ground mentioned in my memorial, again mentioned in my renewal thereof, and all along kept clearly in view in all my communications to your Lordship, and never departed from in a single instance by your Lordship in your replies.

However, I naturally referred to the letter of the Secretary to the Ordnance before mentioned, conveying the decision of the Board on the subject of my application, and here for the first time I saw that in reality your Lordship may possibly have intended, in your letter of March 25, to refer to the "*land in question*" in this single letter of the Secretary to the Ordnance, and not at all to bear reference to the "*only land*" which had ever been "*in question*" between your Lordship and me to that hour.

In this letter of the Secretary (see No. 10), my Lord, there is a reference to Colonel Walker's report; and, certainly, a more extraordinary document I never before perused as coming from a Government officer, approved of by a body so high and so intelligent as the Board of Ordnance, and appearing to bear the sanction of the Colonial Office, as this report of the head of the Engineer Department in Newfoundland. (See No. 11.)

I am to suppose, my Lord, for I have not been favored with a copy of it, that the instruction communicated by Captain Prescott to Col. Walker, in the first instance, must have been not to seek to discover lands the least valuable to the Government, the most worthless to the people; not to look out for lands the least suitable for the uses intended, the most unfit for the erections required. I am to suppose that his instructions were *bonâ fide* to report, as it is mentioned in Mr. Stephen's letter of August 31, 1836, "*whether the land for which you have applied could*, without detriment to the public service, be appropriated to the purposes contemplated by you," — to report whether, as it is described in Sir George Grey's letter of Feb. 9, 1837, "the ground near Fort Townshend, *for which you have applied*, could be conveniently parted with."

Now if, in reality, the instruction of the Governor to Lieut.-Col. Walker were to make his report on the utility for Government purposes of the ground I solicited, surely then his report is most extraordinary. I asked for *a certain* patch of perfectly waste land *to the east* of the fort. He reports upon all the lands to the north, to the south, and to the west, but not one word of the land to the eastward. I asked for particular ground, and it appears that it is the only land in the hands of Government on that side of the town that would answer for the purpose, and he reports of all other lands except *that*, — and reports especially of the two patches which are, of the whole lot, the most unfit for the purposes for which it is required. In fact, there is not the most distant allusion to the ground he is asked to report on, while he says everything about lands of which no question was offered, but modestly closes by constituting himself the very best judge of what would be most suitable for the Catholic congregation of St. John's as a site for the erection of a church, schools, etc., and selects ground for the purpose of the accommodation of infant children to which their fathers could scarce reach during seven months of the year, and these, too, in the only season at which the schools are full.

True, my Lord, I also spoke in my memorial of the cultivated lands to the south-east of the fort, that is, between the fort and the town, which were formerly cultivated by the military, and left it optional with the Government to choose that or the waste piece adverted to so often before; and Captain, now Col. Walker does not omit to make mention of a portion of the cultivated ground in his report, but it appears to be mentioned only because there appear some plausible pretexts connected with it, on which to ground a recommendation to refuse it to the people. His report states that this ground was, " at much labor and expense, fenced and brought into cultivation, as gardens, by the men of the Royal Veteran Companies. The want of these gardens would be felt by the men as a very serious privation, besides the loss of the interest and occupation which the cultivation of the ground affords, and which tends so greatly to their good conduct."

These latter observations, my Lord, would appear to throw upon me an imputation of being actuated by feelings of exceeding hostility to the gratification and comfort of the men of the Royal Veteran Companies; that I must strongly repudiate, for I was always of opinion that agricultural or horticultural pursuits ought to be strenuously promoted amongst the military, particularly at Newfoundland, where they have but one station on the whole Island, and where, in that one, the duties are so exceedingly light as to leave much leisure to the soldiers, which I think of the utmost importance, in a moral point of view, to fill up by some recreative occupation; and I assure you, that I never saw the soldiers engaged in their gardens without being filled with sentiments truly pleasing.

But my memorial, your Lordship will remember, was preferred in 1834, renewed in 1835, and at that time the Veterans had been deprived of these gardens by order of the then head of the Engineer Department, and it was during the time they were so unoccupied that I looked for their appropriation to the purposes of the Catholics of St. John's, for a church, poor schools, a residence for the clergy, as also for a cemetery. Nay, I have every reason to believe that, even at the period at which Col. Walker's report bears date, that even then these grounds were not appropriated to the uses of the Veterans, and I even doubt if they have been up to this hour, whereas the withdrawal of the troops to Signal Hill, a great distance from the fort, must, of course, show that the gallant Colonel's objection is given on mere speculation.

My Lord, I have now undertaken a perilous wintry voyage across the Atlantic, being my second voyage to London for the purpose of urging the claims of the Catholics of that ill-used country, —and for what? for a patch of ground that by the report, the tardy, long-delayed, and reluctant report, of the Board of Ordnance, is declared unnecessary for not only the "military," but for *all purposes* of the Government.

This report, my Lord, must be so construed, for it is consequent not only upon the "military" report of the Officer of Engineers at St. John's, but also on the civil report of the Governor; and yet this piece of ground, thus proved of so little value as not to be esteemed by Col. Walker as worthy of notice in his report, even though he is asked especially to report upon it, is still withheld from Her Majesty's faithful Catholic subjects.

There is one circumstance, however, connected with this part of the subject, which, though trivial in itself, I must not omit to notice to your Lordship, and I only do so because it has excited great astonishment among the people of St. John's, and because it appears to me as extremely difficult, from its coincidence with other concurrent circumstances, to admit of a satisfactory explanation.

If your Lordship would take the trouble to refer to my memorial, or to my letter of renewal, you would at once perceive that I not only mention that the ground I ask for is situated to the east of the fort, but that also I described it as that piece of ground on which the "old wood-yard" of the garrison stood. No sooner had the report of Col. Walker been transmitted, referring, as I before had remarked, only to the land lying west, north, and south of the fort, than orders were given, and quickly executed too, to transfer the wooden walls of the "old wood-yard," which, for time immemorial, stood on the eastern side of the road which leads into the country north-eastward of the fort, to the side opposite, so that now the "site of the wood-yard" would be as objectionable a place as any.

I have already mentioned the conversations I had had on two consecutive days last autumn with Governor Prescott on this subject, his agreeing with me on one day and promising to use his influence with your Lordship in favor of my application for that particular spot which formed the subject of my memorial; his, on the next day, withdrawing from his promised support, and insisting on my taking land that would not answer the purpose for which I wanted ground, and which unfitness he at the same moment admitted; but I regret much that, instead of the ordinary courtesy of a written answer, he gave no other than a verbal reply.

My Lord, I had already been compelled to spend upon this subject more money than would three times purchase the fee-simple of the entire place, and I entered upon that expenditure well knowing that the ground I asked for was intrinsically valueless as compared with the expenditure I must incur; but, my

Lord, I have been actuated by higher than pecuniary motives, — I have ever been solicitous that the Catholics of that country should at length be led to consider themselves as not under a political ban; that they should not regard themselves as political parias, cut off from all connection with the Government of their country, excluded from the participation of the protective powers of that Government; that they should cease to esteem themselves only in the relation of sufferers under severe task-masters, and not subjects of a beneficent monarch; in fine, that, excluded as they have been, and still studiously are, from every office of honor or emolument in that country, excluded as they *universally* are from the slightest countenance or consideration from the local Government, they should at length be made to feel, by the extension to them of some mark of favor or kindness, that in the Government of England there were individuals ruling over their destinies who, scorning to be swayed by motives of bigotry or prejudice, entertained for them those feelings which become the great and enlightened statesman.

My Lord, I have proved the sincerity of my profession by the great sacrifices I have made of my own personal comforts, of my health and my income to promote the interests and *happiness* of that class of Her Majesty's subjects in Newfoundland. I have purchased many sites for public churches in other harbors; I have purchased sites for public charity schools; and in the town of St. John's alone I have expended upwards of fifteen hundred pounds towards the support of one school within the last five years for the children of the poor of Newfoundland, without distinction of creed or country, on which the Government never expended a single shilling, and I ask, Under such circumstances would it, or could it, be for a moment expected that I could be induced to run the hazard and subject myself to the annoyance of voyages across the Atlantic which, by the time of my return to Newfoundland now, will amount to nearly twelve thousand miles, merely to save the amount of the purchase of this piece of ground?

I now freely leave the matter in your Lordship's hands. You have all the information before your Lordship which the Engineer and the Ordnance Department and the Governor of Newfoundland can convey, and surely your Lordship may then estimate the propriety of granting or withholding, not grounds I have never asked for, but the lands I have been five years soliciting. I trust, therefore, that your Lordship will please take these circumstances under your Lordship's consideration, and that, if your Lordship can, consistently with your duty to your Sovereign and the true interests of the Government, you will bestow upon the Catholics of that country the piece of ground I have prayed for, or allow them to purchase it at its full value, which, under the circumstances, will be considered as great a favor as a gift.

I, however, beg to mention to your Lordship before I close that I have been given to understand that as the barracks on Signal Hill are now nearly completed Fort William is about to be abandoned, the soldiers being to be withdrawn to the Hill, and the ground, etc., sold. I mention this, my Lord, to show that here is more ground coming into the hands of Government than which a better sight could not offer for the purposes for which the Governor desires the part I sought.

Earnestly requesting your Lordship will favor me with as early a reply as shall be consistent with your Lordship's convenience,

I have the honor to remain,
Your Lordship's most obedient, humble servant,
(Signed) MICHL. ANTHONY FLEMING.
Right Hon. LORD GLENELG.

P.S. — Your Lordship will find annexed to this a copy of the plan of the Ordnance ground which accompanied Col. Walker's report (No. 12), together with a plan of the same ground (No. 13), exhibiting somewhat more clearly the ground I prayed for; annexed to which I also send your Lordship a third plan, exhibiting the elevation, whereby your Lordship may yourself be able to form a tolerable conception of the utter ineligibility of the grounds offered by Mr. Prescott.

MICHL. ANTHONY FLEMING.

www.ingramcontent.com/pod-product-compliance
Lightning Source LLC
Chambersburg PA
CBHW022140300426
44115CB00006B/274